JEWISH
RENEWAL

ALSO BY MICHAEL LERNER

Surplus Powerlessness: The Psychodynamics of Everyday Life and the Psychology of Individual and Social Transformation

The Socialism of Fools: Anti-Semitism on the Left

Tikkun Anthology (editor)

JEWISH RENEWAL

A Path to Healing and Transformation

MICHAEL LERNER

A GROSSET/PUTNAM BOOK
PUBLISHED BY G. P. PUTNAM'S SONS
NEW YORK

A Grosset/Putnam Book
Published by G. P. Putnam's Sons
Publishers Since 1838
200 Madison Avenue
New York, NY 10016

Library of Congress Cataloging-in-Publication Data

Lerner, Michael, date.
    Jewish renewal : a path to healing and transformation/Michael
Lerner.
        p.   cm.
    "A Grosset/Putnam book."
    Includes index.
    ISBN 0-399-13980-X
    1. Judaism—Essence, genius, nature.   2. Judaism—20th century.
3. Judaism and social problems.   4. Spiritual life—Judaism.
I. Title.
BM565.L36   1994   94-10596 CIP
296.3—dc20

Book design and composition by The Sarabande Press
Printed in the United States of America
1 2 3 4 5 6 7 8 9 10

This book is printed on acid-free paper.

To my father, Joseph H. Lerner,
and in loving memory of my teachers
Abraham Joshua Heschel and Marshall Meyer

God's dream is to be not alone,
but to have humanity as a partner
in the drama of continuous
creation. By whatever we do, by
every act we carry out, we either
advance or obstruct the drama of
redemption.

—*Abraham Joshua Heschel*

Contents

PREFACE

This book is written for several different audiences and hence attempts to operate on several different levels. It is meant for people who have no previous background in Judaism, for those whose background included going to after-school Hebrew school for a few hours a week and stopping at the age of thirteen, and also for people who took courses in Jewish studies or even have dedicated serious portions of their lives to thinking about Jewish issues; for people who were turned off to Judaism and who remain skeptical that there's anything in it for them personally, and also for those who have been living committed Jewish lives. It is for people whose previous encounters with liberal and progressive politics have turned them off, either because the actions of the political groups seemed too one-dimensional, or because of the totalitarian quality of some of their tendencies toward "political correctness," or because of the insensitivity in these communities to the legitimate interests and concerns of the Jewish people; for people who feel that their Jewishness consists solely in their being liberal and caring, and that their Jewishness is manifest in their political or aesthetic sensibilities, thus they don't need all the rest of the religious and ritual framework; for people who say that they are culturally Jewish but don't find themselves drawn to Jewish texts or to Jewish issues; and for those who are deeply learned in those texts.

I've been able to gear this book to these different kinds of Jews by writing at a level that does not presuppose previous background, but does address many issues that will have resonance to those who do have a previous background or even considerable familiarity with current debates in the literature.

At times I say things that will seem very new for one of the constituencies for this book, and yet very "standard" or even ho-hum for another constituency. So, for example, one group of readers may wonder why I frequently repeat words like "cruelty," "repetition compulsion," "compassion," "healing, repair, and transformation (*tikkun*)," or "the possibility of transformation and healing" almost as mantras. For those who are familiar with these concepts, there are moments when this book is going to seem repetitive. (I'm reminded of the story of a patient of Freud's who responded to a given interpretation by saying, "No, no, no, Dr. Freud, that couldn't possibly be right. In fact it's quite mistaken," to which Freud responded, "One 'no' would have been sufficient." For some of the readers, one time around on the ways that we get stuck in the patterns of the past would have been enough.) Yet for many others, even many who intuitively understand what I mean, the application of some of these categories to the Judaism that they knew (and rejected, for some, and observe, for others) is going to involve a process in which they must be shown how these concepts actually get worked out in detail, and so I've tried to do some of that in the book, even at the expense of some repetition.

My attempt to make this book inclusive in audience also precludes filling the book with footnotes or fully explaining some debates to which I sometimes allude. Some of those engaged in these issues professionally may be rightly angry or hurt that I have not acknowledged their specific contributions to which I allude or from whose works I have drawn in the process of formulating my own thinking. One of my goals is to help people enter into a conversation that has been going on for thousands of years, and any serious attempt to cite all those from whose interpretations and contributions this book is derivative would have made the book so cumbersome that it would fail at the goal of bringing people in. If it does succeed, far more people will be interested in moving beyond this work and into the further discussions that abound in Jewish thought, soon enough encountering the worthy and sophisticated discussions that characterize much of contemporary Jewish scholarship.

I do not attempt here to prove my points but only to present an interpretation of Judaism, to show how the world might look viewed from the perspective I call Jewish renewal. I'm well aware that there are many texts that could be read in different ways. Parts of the Torah and the subsequent Jewish corpus stand at variance with my reading. In fact, I argue that within both the texts and the people who read and interpreted them there have always been two contending tendencies, one which I call the voice of God and one which I call the voice of accumulated pain and distortion. It's no surprise to me that our texts or tradition do not embody only the former. I'm well aware of the Books of Joshua and Samuel, of certain passages within Deuteronomy, and certain other places in our tradition that are chauvinistic, triumphalist, and sometimes cruel in their ways of dealing with others, and that underrepresent the God of compassion. I'm aware that in my own citations of Midrash and in my interpretations I select parts that fit my approach.

In my view, every attempt to present Judaism must necessarily be a selection that highlights some aspects of the tradition and dismisses or downplays others. The prophets were among the first to utilize this process of selective readings of the tradition when they emphasized similar themes, and I identify with their selective methodology. The entire project of creating Rabbinic Judaism through Mishnah and then later selecting certain mishnaic portions and writing extensive debate about what they "really" mean (in the Gemara) was a selective process, often leading them to obvious violations of the plain meaning of some of the texts.

Similarly, those halakhists (developers of Jewish law) who took the Torah injunction "You shall love the stranger" (an injunction which, if it were taken seriously, would today make it difficult to justify the behavior of some Israeli West Bank settlers), and transformed its meaning by rereading the word "stranger" as "convert" or "resident who abides by Jewish laws," were engaged in a similar process of reinterpretation. Though I don't agree with their particular reinterpretation, the fact of transforming the obvious meaning of texts in order to facilitate a particular reading of Judaism is not illegitimate but part of the tradition itself. In fact, this process is inevitable, given the fact that different parts of the texts or different strands and sensibilities in the tradition are sometimes openly contradictory and reflect ways in any given era in which different views subtly contend for what Judaism should or could be. Those who have found textual support for notions of an afterlife in Judaism, for example, must certainly know of the psalmist who declares "the dead shall not praise God, neither those who go down into silence."

Similarly, those who argue that the real truth must depend on retaining all the contradictory strands and not privileging any particular one are themselves making an interpretation and a particular possible reading. I understand that others believe that everything in the Torah or even in later Jewish works and halakhic decisions is the voice of God, or that everything in the Torah and Jewish tradition is just the voice of human beings, and I'm contending against each of these by claiming that sometimes we have the voice of God and sometimes we have the voice of pain. Yet where I draw the line is only one possible way of doing so, one possible reading in a world of contending readings.

The criterion for my selection is based on values that I learned from the Torah itself. It was from the Torah that I learned a profound radicalism and a commitment to revolutionary transformation. It was from the Torah's story of Abraham critiquing God about the threatened destruction of Sodom that I learned that not everything one hears in the name of God is truly God being God.

Yet it would be foolish to contend that my reading isn't also influenced by my own background, the historical assumptions of this period, and the particular reading and interpretive communities of which I have been part. The categories that I bring to my reading derive in part from my own training in Torah, Talmud, Hebrew literature, Jewish philosophy and history, in part from my training as an academic philosopher, in part from my training and experience as a clinical psychologist. In proposing a conception of Jewish renewal that is an intricate weave of ideas, some of which derive from the Torah's revelation of the deepest truths of the universe, some of which derive from the unconscious or dream material of the Jewish people at a particular period in its development, some of which derive from the application of some streams in contemporary psychoanalytic and sociological theory, and some of which derive from my own humble attempts to grapple with issues that have perpelexed minds far more sophisticated and adequate to the task than mine, I recognize that I read the texts of Judaism and Jewish history as only a modern can, and perhaps only as someone whose life experience in an affluent society in the post-Holocaust period may permit. Yet with all these limitations, I still believe that I am accessing truths that are not merely partial but universal, and which may have universal validity.

My goal is to provide an approach to Judaism's texts and to the history and contemporary reality of the Jewish people that enhances the readers' ability to live lives filled with awe, wonder, and radical amazement at the grandeur of the universe, alive to bringing God's presence into every interaction and every aspect of daily life, sensitive to the needs of others, respectful of non-Jews as well Jews, dedicated to ending hunger and homelessness, involved in efforts to promote idealism and to decrease selfishness and cynicism.

This is not the only possible goal one might have in reading texts or studying history or interpreting contemporary reality. One might read the texts and the subsequent history, for example, with the goal of enhancing the degree to which one will live a life according to Jewish law, or to highlight textual complexities and subtleties, or to mine literary values, or to discover historical data, or to present the most complex account of existing data and its relationship to "grand theory." Yet from my standpoint, the book is a success if it promotes the ethical and spiritual goal cited in the previous paragraph.

Many of the ideas presented here are derivative of the contributions made by those who call themselves the "Jewish Renewal movement," based in Philadelphia around the organization Aleph, and inspired by Rabbi Zalman Schachter-Shalomi. Rabbi Schachter-Shalomi has ordained and inspired many brilliant rabbis, teachers, and healers, and their ideas and his are central to this book. Moreover, these people are at the cutting edge of much of the creative Jewish spiritual teaching in contemporary America, and when I refer in this book to Jewish-renewal communities who are already doing something, I'm often referring to their work.

And yet, in some important ways, when I talk about Jewish renewal I'm not really referring to the Jewish Renewal movement from which I continue to learn so much, for at least two reasons: first, because that actual movement does far more splitting of "political" from "spiritual" and privileging the latter than I think is appropriate or consistent with what I am calling Jewish renewal in this book; and second, because the Jewish renewal that I see taking place includes that movement but also includes activity, thinkers, theorists, and activists that I see already at work in the Orthodox, Conservative, Reform, and Reconstructionist movements, as well as those involved in organizations like Peace Now, New Israel Fund, New Jewish Agenda, Israel Peace Lobby, Mazon, Netivot Shalom, Jewish Fund for Justice, Jewish feminist collectives, *Tikkun* magazine, Shomrey Adamah, Jewish Funders Network, gay and lesbian synagogues, the social action committees of many synagogues, *Bridges*, *Lilith*, some branches of the American Jewish Congress, and much more. This larger constituency does not always recognize itself as a movement, but many of those involved are redefining the meaning of Jewish life in this period in a way that is in germ the beginning of what I am discussing in this book.

Nevertheless, I need to stress that when I talk about Jewish renewal, I am *not* attempting to make high-level generalizations about existing trends in the Jewish world, but to define an attitude and an approach to Judaism. At some points my definition corresponds with what already exists, at some points it suggests what ought to exist or what I see slowly coming into existence over the course of the *next several generations*. In the final analysis, this is *not* an empirical but a conceptual work, aimed as much at creating as describing a reality, and aimed at forging a way of thinking and acting.

I wish to give special recognition not only to the creative and talented people in many social-change movements whose insights helped shape this book, but also to the millions of secular Jewish humanists, Communists, and Socialists who embodied in their striving for economic and political transformation a Jewish sensibility whose Jewish roots they often failed to acknowledge. In *The Socialism of Fools: Anti-Semitism on the Left*, I wrote about the distortions and anti-Semitism in these movements, and yet they deserve tribute as well. I have also learned from the examples of many Zionists who rejected a stultifying version of Judaism in order to find the social and intellectual space to create an empowering project of social transformation, and from the inspired and courageous work of people that I saw in Breyra and the New Jewish Agenda, in *Jewish Currents* and *New Outlook*, in other branches of the Jewish Left, and in the local activities of thousands of individuals who generation after generation sustained a discourse of critique and mobilized demonstrations against injustice under very difficult and often personally risky circumstances.

Many of the ideas and approaches in this book derive from the transformations in thought that arose from feminism and the women's movement. I believe feminism is the most significant revolutionary movement of the twentieth century, and its insights were the precondition for my being able to move from the sterile world of academic philosophy to a much deeper understanding of human reality.

I have been inspired as well by the civil rights movement, ecology activists, peace and antinuclear activists, and the many Christians of all denominations who turned the teaching of love into lives committed to social justice. Most of all, it has been the experience of the Jewish people in all its complexity that has inspired me: the experience of Orthodox Jews who *daven*ed with a passion that excited me, and whose little acts of kindness and compassion gave me hope that the love and caring embedded in Jewish teaching actually means something real; the experience of family members who had survived the Holocaust and who managed to maintain a degree of humanity and gentleness that was healing to others; the experience of a people that could be murdered but could not be morally and spiritually defeated; the experience of a people that kept its sense of humanity and its commitment to *tikkun* so alive that it pulsated through every pore of its communal being; the experience of my mother, may her memory be a blessing, whose passion and determination made the seemingly impossible possible, and who showed me that Jewish ideas could be embodied in an individual's life; and the experience of my father, whose humor and Zionist idealism permeated my childhood and whose example as a young man in his eighties full of life, energy, vitality, and hope embodies much of what is best in Jewish tradition.

This work continually draws on the intellectual contributions of Peter Gabel, a respected writer on social theory, who was one of the founders of Critical Legal Studies, has been the associate editor of *Tikkun* magazine for many years, is president of New College of California, and whose theory of recognition and the denial of desire permeates this book more than is possible to cite at each moment it appears. To his brilliance I am deeply indebted. My interpretation of the tradition also draws from midrashic literature, psychoanalytic object-relations theory, the writings of Eugene Borowitz, David Hartman, Mordecai Kaplan, and Joseph Soloveitchik, but also from Spinoza, Sartre, and de Beauvoir; Wilhelm Reich, critical theory, and Marxism as taught to me by Richard Lichtman and Herbert Marcuse.

One of the many blessings showered on me was the opportunity to learn from many inspired teachers. From the moment that I first met Abraham Joshua Heschel, my life was transformed, and in the subsequent years when I studied with him I was graced by a unique encounter with one of the great reflectors of divine energy and thought. My *rebbe* and the originator of much contemporary Jewish-renewal theology, Zalman Schachter-Shalomi, remains one of the inspired conveyors of a new revelation that will shape generations to come. If only the organized Jewish community could understand what a priceless gem they have in this man and give him the support that he deserves! If you have an opportunity to study with him, grab it! I do not belittle the tremendous wisdom and inspiration (and sometimes very specific ideas in this book) derived from others about whom I'm not going to talk in detail, though each also gave the world and me guidance: Rachel Adler, Jessica Benjamin, Rabbi Arthur Green, Rabbi Burt Jacobson, Immanuel Levinas, Arthur Waskow, and Rabbi David Wolfe-Blanke. I apologize to them for all the times their ideas are incorporated without specific acknowledgment.

This book is also derivative from the wisdom and insights of my son Akiba Jeremiah Lerner, who assisted me in doing research and with whom I engaged in endless discussions on these topics throughout the past decade, learning from him and rejoicing in his insights (many of which are incorporated in this book). It draws upon the courageous example of the life of Rabbi Marshall Meyer (z"l), whose opposition to the military dictatorship in Argentina and to the conservatism and conformism in the organized Jewish community in North America became a beacon of hope for thousands of young Jews.

I would also like to thank the following colleagues who gave useful feedback to me in the drafting of this work: Rebecca Adams, Rabbi Arik Asherman, Amy Bachrach, Michael Bader, David Biale, Rabbi Tzvi Blanchard, Daniel Boyarin, Laurie Zoloth Dorfman, Estelle Frankel, Heather Fulsom, Colin Greer, Joshua Halberstam, Rabbi Moshe Halbertal, Rabbi Rolando Matalon, Rabbi Tzvi Marx, Deborah Meyers, Debra Osnowitz, Rabbi Michael Paley, Rabbi Einat Ramon, Rabbi Chaim Seidler-Feller, Rabbi Michael Strassfeld, and Michael Zweig. I also wish to thank Jane Isay, my editor at Putnam and the publisher of Grosset Books, whose many editorial comments and questions helped focus my writing, and whose enthusiasm and wisdom helped sustain me throughout the long process of writing and editing this book.

INTRODUCTION

J udaism presents the world with a challenge: that the world can and
should be fundamentally changed; that the central task facing the
human race is *tikkun olam*, the healing and transformation of the
world. And Judaism has deep insight into how that can be accomplished. Yet in every generation, this insight has been muted, avoided,
abandoned, or outright denied by many, including those who claim to
be the official priests, spokespeople, leaders, rabbis, teachers, or
orthodox embodiments of Judaism.

Jewish renewal is the process, repeated throughout Jewish history,
in which Judaism is "changed" back to its origins as the practice of
healing, repair, and transformation.

We are at the beginning of such an era today. A new generation of
teachers, rabbis, community activists, and thinkers has begun to
reclaim the central insights of Judaism. It is no wonder that after
having faced massive and staggering destruction and dislocations,
many Jews feel spiritually and emotionally dead. We sought refuge
from pogroms and genocide in societies that were themselves spiritually and emotionally dead, and we did our best to assimilate our
Judaism to these societies because we hoped that inconspicuousness
would keep us from becoming targets. It has taken many decades for
Jews to feel secure enough to begin to renew the spiritual tradition.

We are witnessing today the miraculous regeneration of the primary ideals of Judaism that have been part of our tradition since Abraham and Moses. This process of Jewish renewal sometimes appears as a rejection of Judaism, but it is in fact a vigorous affirmation of and reconnection to it.

The historical project of the Jewish people is to be witnesses to the possibility of healing, repair, and transformation of the world, and the rejection of all forms of cynicism and pessimism that lead people to reconcile themselves with systems of oppression. Many people who think of themselves as atheists or agnostics may nevertheless find themselves comfortable with the God of Israel: the Force in the world that makes possible the transformation of that which is to that which ought to be. Though historically some Jews have envisioned God as a father or as a powerful heavenly being, and though these and other pictures have tended to enter into Jewish theology or prayer (which often mimics current trends in the larger society of the historical period in which the prayer is constructed or the theology developed), Judaism's second commandment, which prohibits the creation of all images, should give pause to those agnostics and atheists who think that they know exactly who the Jewish God is, namely the patriarchal authority who rules in heaven and in whom they don't believe! Many religious Jews are leaving behind these antiquated notions of God and returning their attention to God as the Force that makes possible healing and transformation.

To the extent that Judaism is the metaphysics of healing and transformation (the Hebrew word is *tikkun*), the community built around it often generates ideas and understandings that can be useful to all of humanity, not just Jews. Yet it is precisely these universal principles that have caused some to challenge the value of Jewish particularism. Why can't we state our universally applicable and important insights in a form that abstracts from the Jewish context? After all, isn't that what Jesus, Marx, Freud, Einstein, and others did?

I had that idea in mind when, after years of study at the Jewish Theological Seminary as a disciple of the Jewish theologian Abraham Joshua Heschel, I went to Berkeley and became involved in the social-change movements of the sixties. I believed that it would be possible to take what was best about Judaism and express it in a secular language for the larger socially transformative movements.

But after twenty years, I concluded that the universal truths I had learned in Judaism could not be conveyed without referring specifically to the Jewish experience, and without using the language and the categories that have emerged from that experience.

In this book, I show you some of what I discovered in my own grappling with Judaism, in the hopes that it will intrigue you to go far beyond this book, to study Jewish texts and Jewish history, and to immerse yourself in the process of Jewish renewal. As Rabbi Hillel is said to have responded when asked to teach the Torah while standing on one foot: "Do not do to others that which is hateful to yourself. All the rest is commentary. Now, *go and study*."

Go and study, but also go and create. Jewish renewal is not merely a process of "discovering" truths that were already there, but also a process through which the Jewish people in our own day are re-creating Judaism, taking Judaism out of the hands of its official representatives precisely so that it can get back to its transformative message and mission. Tens of thousands of American Jews are involved in this process, and they are living Judaism more authentically than those who have passively absorbed a religious tradition that does not deeply move or challenge them. In every historical period, there has been a re-creation of the tradition through commentary, Midrash, and creative reinterpretation. In every period, those who have been engaged in such re-creation have faced the scorn of others who have seen them as engaged in a subversive enterprise, one that would destroy the true Judaism.

The Judaism built by Ezra the Scribe in the fifth century B.C.E. was almost certainly radically different from the Judaism practiced by King Solomon, and the Judaism forged by the talmudic rabbis in the wake of destruction of the Temple and the consequent elimination of sacrifice was a radical step away from Ezra. The innovations of one age become the orthodoxy of the next, but at the moment of innovation, the innovators are seen as "trendy" or "inauthentic."

In this book you will not find "the true reading of Judaism" but only one possible reading of the tradition and of Jewish history and of Jewish renewal. Attempting to prove that one particular approach is the "true" reading of the tradition is always bound to fail, particularly in Judaism, where there has not been one central religious authority, and contradictory elements abound. For any claim of the form "Judaism believes X" one can almost certainly find a set of quotes in the Bible or Talmud that provides alternative readings. So what I offer is a plausibility argument for the notion of a revolutionary conception of God within Judaism, a God of transcendence and compassion, rooted in Torah and providing us with a compelling way to understand why we ought to remain Jewish; why Jews have often tried to hide themselves from this God; what struggles are necessary to reclaim the revolutionary voice in Judaism; and why the revolutionary conception of God forms a basis for the healing and repair of the world. Yet I am always aware, and want you to be aware, that after each thought in this book there should be the following added caveat: ". . . according to this particular reading of Judaism."

A major premise of this book is that human beings become more fully themselves through a process of mutual recognition, and when that process is stymied it provokes angry and sometimes oppressive behavior. God is the Force in the universe that makes possible this process of recognition, and part of *what* is recognized is the God within each of us (namely, the way that we are created in the image of God and hence equally worthy of respect and love). The fears, the accumulated angers and pains, the legacy of cruelty that combine to make it difficult for human beings to recognize one another have been a major source of evil throughout history. Much of twentieth-century psychoanalytic thought has been dedicated to understanding the unconscious forces that sustain this tendency to pass on the pain and cruelty from generation to generation. It is only recently that psychoanalytic theory is beginning to discover what Judaism has asserted all along: that there is also a tendency toward transcendence and health in the universe. The Power that makes this transcendence possible is what we Jews call God.

Understanding God in this way, it is particularly moving for me to be able to write these words at a historical moment when the Jewish people are beginning to overcome some of their defensiveness and tendency to do unto others what was done to them (what Freud calls the repetition compulsion), and to engage in an act of mutual recognition with the Palestinian people. However tentative the steps, however many partial retreats may take place along the way, the process of mutual recognition is itself a manifestation of God's presence as a force of healing and transformation in the world. I am proud of the courage of many Israelis who are moving their society in this direction toward peace and reconciliation.

A second contention in this book is that much of what has turned people away from Judaism have been aspects of Judaism that are themselves the product of a process of Jews having run away from God's message and having become "realists," more attuned to the logic of power and self-interest of a world dominated by materialism and selfishness than committed to challenging and transforming this world.

From the renewalist perspective, many people who call themselves Orthodox or who are superobservant or supernationalistic can actually be highly assimilated or highly Hellenized Jews. They may wear religious garb, be strictly kosher, and go to synagogue to pray every day, root their every action in quotes from the Talmud or the various codes of Jewish law, but when they go into the economic marketplace or into politics, they think and act in accord with the logic of a system that encourages unlimited accumulation of power and money without regard to human consequences. Talk about what kinds of changes it would take to turn "love your neighbor as yourself" or "justice, justice shalt thou pursue" into operative principles in the economy and politics, or in their thinking about dealing with the vast economic inequalities in this society, and they become superrealists whose consciousness is determined more by Wall Street than by Sinai. At the deepest level, these people have accepted the "realism" of the Hellenists, giving up on the commitment to social and this-worldly transformation that is central to Torah's worldview, and made peace with existing social arrangements and systems of power and oppression.

Unfortunately, many of the people one meets in the synagogues and in Jewish institutional life are assimilators in this sense, though they maintain Jewish ethnic, religious, or nationalistic ties. They become the public face of Judaism. When younger Jews see this accommodation dressed up in religious garb, and find themselves unmoved or even repulsed by it, they think they are rejecting Judaism. They are not— they are rejecting Hellenized Judaism in religious drag. They are sickened by a Judaism that speaks the language of *tikkun* but wallows in the materialism and conformism of the well-to-do.

In the late twentieth century the powerful are so well ensconced and so well protected that they merely laugh at those who take Judaism seriously and still hope for a different kind of world. For the powerful, ironic detachment and cynicism have replaced inquisitions and anti-Communist crusades. The common sense of the age tells us that nothing can be fundamentally different, that earnestness and commitment to repair are delusions, and that anyone who persists in believing in the possibility of a more ethically and spiritually centered world is either a charlatan or a fool. *Commentary* magazine's editor Norman Podhoretz called one of his autobiographies *Making It*, thereby capturing the spirit, vocation, and mission of the assimilated intellectual in contemporary America. Having achieved literary, economic, intellectual, or political respectability and power, they now imagine themselves so secure within American society that it is emotionally impossible to identify with the slaves who made it out of Egypt, and hence with the religious tradition that insists that we see the world from the standpoint of those slaves. Having correctly rejected Soviet-style communism, they incorrectly assume that every other movement for fundamental change must be either totalitarian or a cover for self-interest and self-delusion of the participants.

But the celebration of selfishness that forms the core of neoconservative-style Jewish identity leads to a dead end. So vapid are the pleasures that a society based on this principle offers that many people desperately reach out for communities of meaning, even willing to accept communities of meaning based on hierarchy, patriarchy, and subordination of one's critical intellect. Glorification of materialism and the cult of individualism prove so unfulfilling in part because people wish to be valued for who they are, not how well they've "made it." But too many of the communities that claim to offer meaning mix that meaning with xenophobic nationalism, racism, or fundamentalist religion. Eventually people wake up to the dehumanizing and invalidating aspects of these communities, and in outrage at the hoax they charge back toward a liberalism that promises individual freedom and rejects all higher meaning as nothing but illusion. Economic and political life becomes the pursuit of self-interest, which leads to the dog-eat-dog economic marketplace in which selfishness and cynicism become the dominant values. Yet this cynicism cannot sustain itself as a way of life. Nor can a one-dimensional liberalism whose highest goal is to validate the rights of each individual to make any choices that s/he desires. The world created by this kind of liberalism becomes so unfulfilling that people are once again attracted to new versions of community, and once again what they are offered is hierarchical and in the service of inequality and domination. This alternation between periods of ultra-individualism and periods of immersion into xenophobic nationalism or fundamentalism characterizes much of the past century and may continue in the twenty-first. The revival of anti-Semitism as an

explicit force in Russia, Po
elements in the African-America
of this process. At the very mome
celebrating the worldwide victory of s
as "realism," they are actually laying the
much pain that it could easily revert to the
mentalist, and anti-Semitic pseudo-solutions
were permanently defeated.

The only way out of this endless cycle is through a
mation on the personal, social, and communal levels. We
a different model of spiritual community: one whose explic
break down hierarchies and inequalities, and to validate each
ual as essentially precious and deserving of respect. Jewish ren
suggests a politics of meaning that could help the world create th
kinds of communities that would not be subject to the appeals of
selfishness and the unbridled pursuit of self-interest that a market-
dominated liberalism offers, nor to the demeaning of the other that so
often accompanies religious and national communities in today's
world. And a Judaism that embodies Jewish renewal could be a model of what such a community of meaning and purpose might look
like.

One need not adopt a naive optimism in order to combat the culture
of selfishness and cynicism about how easy it will be to build Jewish
renewal. Throughout this book I argue for the possibility of radical
transformation of the world, but I do *not* argue that this transformation
is easy or requires nothing more than individual acts of will. I argue that
cruelty is not destiny, but I do not argue that our legacy of pain and
cruelty can easily be dismantled from our inner selves or social institutions. On the contrary, I am a strong believer in the need for struggle—
to change social institutions—and psychotherapeutic and spiritual
practices—to help change us as individuals. The revolutionary transformation that Judaism proclaims takes generations, so beware of the
person who thinks it is around the corner or who tells you that the
Messiah has already come. The despair facing many who believed in
the Lubavitcher Rabbi Schneerson (z"l) is another indication of how
dangerous messianism sometimes can be.

But beware also of those who are so cynical about fundamental
change that they are unable to see the actual opportunities that *radical
hope* can engender. All too often those who counsel caution are sub-

at exist at the
ssimism.

different from
ny New Agers,
piritual energy
rd an exclusive
nied by a senti-
s and a corre-
pression in the
ry. For Jewish
y connected to
gements. Jew-
e live in luxury
vorld in which
physically and
se" to "look out
Spirituality di-
ange the world

land, Germany, Italy, and among some
n community is a predictable outcome
nt when Jewish conservatives are
lfishness and cynicism parading
groundwork for a world in so
acist, xenophobic, funda-
that we all had hoped

piritual transfor-
must develop
t goal is to
individ-
ewal
e

is necessarily one dimensional, shallow, and *not* what we have in mind when we talk about the holy. Individual or communal acts of charity, fundraising for victims, and even caring for others are important—but *not* enough, unless linked to a more deeply transformative program aimed at changing the underlying economic and political institutions that cause the problems.

The commandments of Torah are about social relations. Jewish spirituality is not just about finding some private truth, but about creating a public world that reflects and embodies the spiritual truths we have learned. While individual healing on the psychological and spiritual level is an *indispensable* part of the process, the real "care of the soul" cannot be accomplished fully by the lone individual. The health of the soul requires involvements in a community that is itself deeply committed to healing and transforming the social and political world even as it provides ways for people to heal one another and develop a deeper inner life. New Age accounts have largely ignored the need for collective action aimed at political and social transformation, and so they become psychologically reductionistic, assuming that individual change is sufficient.

Yet Jewish renewal is equally distant from Marxist accounts of reality that do not acknowledge the spiritual dimension or that believe the focus on psychological change and spiritual growth is a diversion from the *real* work, which is solely aimed at changing economic and political institutions. For far too long, liberals, progressives, and the Left have led themselves into oblivion or into distorted social practice because they fail to understand the ethical and spiritual natures of reality and the ethical and spiritual needs of every human being. This one-dimensionality guarantees that their institution-changing agenda will fail or yield distorted results.

Though Jewish renewal typically finds itself aligned with the progressive social-change movements, we are also very critical of the insensitivity of these movements to legitimate Jewish interests and concerns. I will not deal with this issue in this book, because I've explored it fully in my book *The Socialism of Fools: Anti-Semitism on the Left*. But I do want to restate that book's opposition to those who, while supporting everyone else's liberation struggle, make Jews feel parochial when they insist on the legitimacy of the Jewish liberation struggle—or those who underplay the dangers of anti-Semitism. Jewish liberals and renewalists are deeply aware of the anti-Semitic danger of xenophobic nationalist forces that are reemerging throughout the world, just as we are aware of the danger posed by some tendencies within the African-American community that are irresponsibly channeling black people's legitimate anger at continuing economic oppression in an illegitimate direction (against the Jews). Our commitment to fighting for self-determination and against oppression does not mean that we will be patsies in the face of Jew-hating, however subtle or refined. Nor does our support for the oppressed extend to giving them a blank check for being irresponsible toward Jewish sensitivities and interests. By renewing our own tradition in ways described in this book, and by emphasizing our concern for others, we are in a stronger position to defend Jewish interests. Jewish particularism and universalism are ultimately not counterposed but mutually reinforcing.

Needless to say, Judaism is not only a critique of certain versions of the Left and certain versions of New Age thought, but it is also a critique of post-modernism and every system of moral relativism, de-centered individualism, and ontological despair. Its assertion is clear: the world has a transcendent meaning, and we are part of the process by which that meaning becomes revealed and actualized.

In the first part of this book, I focus on reclaiming the revolutionary conception of Judaism. In the second part, I show how that conception could have profound implications for our understanding of the political and social world. In the third part I focus on reclaiming the religious dimension of Judaism, exploring what a renewal would look like, not just as an idea, but as a way of life.

In Martin Buber's essay "Renewal of Judaism," renewal is seen as "something sudden and immense—by no means a continuation or an improvement, but a return and a transformation." Buber goes on to tell us that just as in the life of the individual "there may occur a moment of elemental reversal, a crisis and a shock, a becoming new that starts down at the roots and branches out into all of existence, so do I believe that it is possible for such an upheaval to take place in the life of Judaism. . . . Precisely this is what I believe will take place in Judaism: not merely a rejuvenation or revival but a genuine and total renewal."[1] Such upheavals have taken place several times in Jewish history, and we are in the midst of just one upheaval today, one that is likely to last through the next several centuries.

This book is in part a celebration of what Judaism is or could be, but it is not meant to negate the strength and beauty and value of lessons from other traditions or religions or from those whose spiritual path avoids theocentric language.

The renewal of all these traditions is part of a move toward the resacralization of the planet that has been moving in fits and starts for the past fifty years. The twentieth century has seen the greatest accumulation of knowledge and the greatest systematic misuse of that knowledge in the service of domination in recorded history. Knowledge divorced from ethical and spiritual guidance has provided human beings with greater abilities to exploit nature, but has not given us wisdom, increased compassion, or enhanced our ability to treat one another lovingly. Through the renewal of religious and spiritual traditions around the world, hundreds of millions of human beings are challenging the disenchantment of a world that has turned everything into a commodity. Sometimes, however, the reenchantment of the world can take dangerous forms, recrediting religious orthodoxies and fundamentalisms that have been experienced as oppressive or spiritually stifling. When I talk about "renewal" within a religious tradition, I am talking about that part of the current religious revival

---

[1]Martin Buber, *On Judaism* (New York: Schocken Books, 1967), pp. 35–36.

that specifically seeks to reclaim those aspects of spirituality that are consistent with a respect for human rights, the dignity and self-determination of the individual, and the tolerance for difference and diversity that were absent in some religious traditions in the past.

The resacralization of the world must finally make a difference in our everyday lives, not just in some split-off part that we define as our "spiritual" time or space. All space is potentially sacred space, all time is potentially sacred time.

During the 1950s and 1960s, Jews in America helped make a book on Jewish theology called *Peace of Mind*, by Joshua Loth Liebman, into a best-seller. For the first generation after the Holocaust it is understandable why "peace of mind" became the central issue. But Jewish renewal is not primarily about comfort and inner peace. The call for healing and transformation (*tikkun*) provides a challenge to the world and a challenge to the Jewish people that is upsetting, destabilizing, and energizing. Judaism's emphasis on *tikkun*, repeated thrice daily in the Aleynu prayer, became central to medieval kabbalistic notions of a world fragmented and badly in need of repair.

That repair requires deep inner work—healing our psychological pain, reawakening our spiritual selves, and allowing time in our daily lives to nurture our souls. Yet the uniqueness of Jewish renewal is its insistence that this indispensable inner work must be intrinsically linked to our participation in a community that is as fully involved in revolutionary transformative, political activity as it is in spiritual growth and in celebration of the grandeur and wonder of God's creation.

This book is an invitation to join with me in shaping and forging the process of Jewish renewal. I hope my words give you some tools to use as you reflect on the texts, on Jewish history and culture, and on your own lives. If parts of this book move you, apply them in your own ways, build a Jewish renewal that makes sense to you, and let me know what you are doing, what has worked and what has not, and what ways we can work together. All my life experience leads me to believe that I have much to learn from you, my readers, and I hope that this book is just a first step in opening up a discussion among us. I do not put myself forward as the embodiment of the ideals articulated here, but only as one other flawed person trying to transmit as best I can what I have learned and what I have heard. Please do not let my own obvious deficiencies and failures deflect you from finding and using what may be helpful in these pages. The task of shaping Jewish renewal is immense, the territory is wide open, and there is plenty of room for you.

This ongoing process of religious transformation *is* the Jewish tradition. After reading the Torah on Shabbat morning, Jews return the Torah to its ark or resting point, and in fervent devotion sing a moving prayer: "It is a tree of life to those who hold fast to it, and its precepts are right. Its paths are paths of pleasantness, and all its paths are peace. Return us to thee, Lord, and we shall return. *Renew our days as of old.*" This prayer does *not* mean, "Let us live *the same* lives as our ancestors," but rather, "Just as our ancestors engaged in the process of renewing, so too we wish to participate in Jewish renewal—let us be part of that great enterprise which in every generation makes this Torah a tree of life."

WHY JEWS LEFT JUDAISM

WHAT TURNED JEWS OFF

I went to Hebrew school in the 1950s. Twice a week after "regular" school, and once a week on Saturday mornings, I would spend two hours trying to learn something about Judaism, Jewish history, and Hebrew. There were 125 of us who graduated Hebrew school the year of my bar mitzvah, but only five of us continued through Hebrew high school and graduated that four-hour-per-week program four years later. Very few of the original 125 felt any particular connection to Jewish tradition by the time they reached their twenties. Most of them looked back on Hebrew school as an ordeal that they went through to please their parents, and once they were free to make choices of their own, they ran from the Jewish world as fast as they could.

The organized Jewish community had an explanation for this flight. That explanation had a common core that ran something like this: "Of course these people left their Jewishness, because being a Jew is very difficult. They live in a society that encourages people to seek their own pleasures and to take the easiest path, the path of assimilation to the mainstream values of American society. Only those who have something special in their souls, a special sensitivity to Judaism, can possibly survive the allures of assimilation. You, who have stayed connected, are very special and different, and morally and spiritually on a higher plane than those who have left. Meanwhile, don't worry, because many of those who have gone away will come back once they see how empty that other world really is."

It was a smug and self-satisfied message. And it was not true.

I knew many of these kids quite well, and I had a different sense of who they were and why they left. So in the 1980s I began to reconnect with several of them, listen to their stories about their lives and their relationships to Judaism. At first this was done haphazardly and by chance encounter; later in formal phone conversations which, with the permission of the participants, were taped. And then I asked friends and colleagues to recommend other people between the ages of twenty and fifty who could speak to me about their experiences. I went to a "young leadership" conference sponsored by the United Jewish Appeal and interviewed people who had remained involved in the Jewish world. And I went to a variety of Jewish community centers, to universities, to professional associations, and even recruited some subjects at polling places in inner-city Jewish neighborhoods. All in all, I spoke to 357 people in every part of the United States, Canada, and England, and asked them about their lives, their values, and their relationships to their Judaism. I found that most Jews who distanced themselves from the Jewish community or from Judaism did so *not* because Judaism was too different from the materialistic and self-indulgent ethos of American society, but because the Jewish community and Judaism were *too similar* to the larger society. The Judaism that they had been offered was stultifying and, like the dominant culture in American society, spiritually deadening—it had never engaged them on a spiritual, intellectual, emotional, or aesthetic level. While many had warm memories of specific holidays and so had adopted some form of observance of these holidays, few felt that the tradition and the teachings had commanded their attention or allegiance. I do not present the interviews as systematic or objective data, but rather am presenting a subjective interpretation of what I heard.

Here are some of the issues that they raised with me:

Materialism

The Jewish world that they encountered seemed to be obsessed with money and power. Some reported watching their parents prepare for going to *shul* on the High Holy Days. There was no spiritual preparation, but instead a major focus on getting fancy new clothes, furs, jewelry.

Many reported witnessing business discussions in *shul*—about what companies to invest in, what properties were available, or gossip about who was making how much. Still others reported feeling one-down because their families didn't have enough money to pay for membership in the synagogues. Inside the synagogues, and even more so in the major communal organizations of Jewish life—like the United Jewish Appeal or Jewish Federation, but also including the American Jewish Committee, Hadassah, B'nai B'rith—the people who had the most power and money had the most influence. Everyone intuitively understood this: that what really counted was how much money you had and how much you could give, or alternatively how well you did at being a fundraiser and getting others to give.

At first when I heard these complaints, I reacted defensively. As much as I had shared these feelings of distaste as a child, I had now come to understand that the fundraisers were often very decent people and that what they were doing with their money was far nobler than what people in other communities were doing. Proportionate to their population or to their wealth, the Jewish community is one of the most charity-minded communities in the United States. Such a generosity of heart ought not to be held against the fundraisers. Moreover, to be realistic, a voluntary community *does* need financial support, so naturally those funders are going to be important.

But my interviewees made some important points in response. Their first point was that while they did not experience materialism in the Jewish world as dramatically worse than the materialism in the larger society, neither was it so clearly better as to justify attachment to a community that made demands on them to be different, to learn Hebrew, to study Jewish texts, to observe special commandments. If being different in Jewish ways helped forge a spiritually deep community, it might have been worth the effort. But, they argued, learning Hebrew and texts had proved to be little more than a way to feel comfortable in a community that embodied the same materialistic ethos that pervades American society. The Jewish community, they felt, gives its real respect and highest honors not to those who are learned or spiritually or ethically developed, but to wealthy people who have no such knowledge or interests.

Not that my respondents *themselves* were claiming to live higher ethical or spiritual lives than those of people inside the organized Jewish community. Their point was that *if* they were going to be attracted to a religious or spiritual community, it would have to be one that tangibly exhibited that spirituality. Part of the reason that some of these respondents now feel perfectly comfortable living a life aimed primarily at material comforts, they told me, is that they have come to believe, based on their experience in the Jewish world, that such a life is what everyone "really" wants, because even in the heart of Jewish culture it is these kinds of wants that seem to be shaping everything. But if this is the bottom line even within the allegedly spiritual community, who needs all the ritual trappings?

American Jews were not worse than anyone else, and my respondents understood that it was one of the traditional canards of anti-Semites to represent Jews as somehow *more* materialistic. They could even see that Jewish giving made the Jewish community a bit less materialistic than others. But the materialism was nevertheless pervasive in Jewish institutional life: They had experienced it deeply as children, and it had failed to excite them and motivate them to want to learn more about their tradition or to make the sacrifices of time and energy required to learn Hebrew and Jewish texts. It wasn't, they assured me, that they had made some complicated calculation. It was just that what they had experienced hadn't gripped their souls enough to turn them on.

I pointed out that their very sensitivity to the issue of materialism came from Jewish values they had unconsciously absorbed as they grew up in the Jewish world. They acknowledged that this was true, but responded by saying that the Jewish world articulated good values but did not embody those values in the ways that synagogues were actually run. For example, many complained bitterly about high costs for synagogue membership, fees for Jewish day schools, and costs for Jewish summer camps. I pointed out that the money to run these institutions had to come from someplace. They countered by mentioning that if instead of sending so much money to Israel the Jewish community used its resources to lower costs, they would not have gotten the impression that Jewish institutions were designed primarily for those who had flourished economically.

Second, they acknowledged that Jews should get credit for being charity-oriented, but that the experience they had was much more contradictory and full of double messages. Yes, they had surely gotten from the Jewish world a sense of obligation about the suffering of others. These messages were clearly in the texts, talked about by rabbis in sermons, and embodied by a few prominent Jewish organizations that had supported the civil rights movement in the early sixties before it took a turn toward Black Power. Yet my interviewees insisted on reminding me that there had been an equally strong (some claimed "stronger") message that Jewish charity must be directed only at Jews, that we had suffered and so we deserved, that the others had let us down and never helped us so why should we help them, and that our help for others could be justified only if it could be shown to be in our own survival interests. In fact, they pointed out, Jewish fundraising had been directed primarily toward Israel—the Jewish State—and to support American Jewish institutions that primarily served Jewish constituencies. In practice, Jewish caring was often limited to caring about Jews. So, as children, they had experienced a community that was giving off two very different messages: one about caring for others; another, often given with greater emotional charge, that we should stop giving to others and worry only about ourselves.

Spiritual Emptiness

Many of my interviewees reported that they didn't even know what spiritual reality meant until they had come in contact with other religious communities or spiritual traditions—it simply had not been there in the Jewish world except on very rare occasions. Far too much energy was given to the mechanics of observing Jewish practice, far too little to the meaning behind the practices, and far, far too little time had been devoted to actually delving deeply into these meanings and letting them have an impact on the experience. Take, for example, the blessing after the meal. Most American Jews do not know that Jewish tradition requires them to spend time after each meal to recite a rather longish prayer thanking God for creating a world with the capacity to feed every living thing. But those who do know it, often because they were exposed to it in Hebrew school or summer camps or at home, reported to me that they cannot recall a single time in their childhood when they experienced themselves as part of a family or religious community that actually was consciously and intentionally thanking God for the food. The blessing was said, true enough, but it was said merely as a song with good spirit or as a prayer that had to be rushed through before going on to the next thing, *not* as a conscious act of gratitude. I could argue with them that singing joyfully and prayerfully is the *intention* of the *mitzvah*, the commandment; it functions precisely to heighten a certain kind of consciousness. But their response was, not only had that not happened, but nobody had ever told them that it was *supposed to* happen.

No wonder, then, that some turned to other spiritual practices or even other religions. Many had discovered within themselves a deep spiritual hunger, but on the basis of their childhood experiences, few of them had suspected that their spiritual needs could be satisfied within the framework of Judaism. Those of us, and I was one, who had happened to stumble onto those areas of the Jewish world where spirituality *was* emphasized, could count ourselves lucky indeed. We were provided with a different understanding of what was potentially available within Judaism. But most American Jews had little such exposure.

Holocaust Trauma and Joylessness

"All I can remember hearing about Jewishness was about how much we suffered. I don't blame anyone who went through that for being trau-matized, but it certainly wasn't something I wanted to pass on to my children. There just wasn't enough joy in Jewish life. If it's all pain, why pass it on?"

Each time I heard this I wanted to argue, "But don't you know about the joy of Shabbat and the joy of doing other *mitzvot*?" But the truth is, they *didn't* know about this joy. In fact, when I once did raise this issue, one of my interviewees simply didn't know what I was talking about. She described her experience in a large suburban synagogue, the formal decorum, the singing of prayers in a set way led by a cantor who seemed unmoved by the words he sang, the Oneg Shabbat afterwards in which people ate small pieces of neatly cut pastry and drank coffee and tea and politely greeted one another, and she could not recall a single moment in her entire experience of Judaism in which she ever noticed somebody actually being joyous, getting into some prayer or some moment in a spontaneous and free way. The only memory she had of any expression of feelings was when people said Yizkor or Kaddish (prayers for the dead).

Others reported that the only two subjects Hebrew school teachers seemed to be excited about were Israel and the Holocaust. Some talked of a morbid fascination that teachers, Hebrew school principals, or rabbis had with the details of suffering. It seemed to my interviewees as if their Jewish teachers seemed moved only when talking about someone else's Judaism (namely, that which might, or might not, be available in another country), or talking about suffering and pain.

Some of this was hard for me to listen to. Parts of my family had perished in the Holocaust, and I wanted their memory kept alive. Yet I couldn't deny what these people were saying. For many of these younger Jews, not only wasn't suffering a good enough reason to remain a Jew, but it was actually a good reason to stop being interested in Jewishness, since suffering wasn't that appealing. "Fine," said one of my respondents after hearing my argument that part of our suffering was a response to the unique role Jews play in history, "teach me about that unique role. If I saw a point in the suffering, if I knew that it was a consequence of a Judaism that was worth holding on to, maybe I wouldn't be so negative about the suffering component. But the way I learned it, what I was supposed to be *proud of* and *identify with* was the suffering itself. There was nothing more to the religion than a focus on the Holocaust and the redemption from that suffering made possible by the creation of the State of Israel—and for me, that wasn't a religious message that could take me very far. I don't want to deny the importance of the Holocaust, but I also don't want to build my life around it."

Exclusivism and Specialness: Only We Count

Many respondents felt that the Jewish world tried to teach them a parochialism of Jewish suffering. Too many Jews acted as though nobody else had ever suffered. The uniqueness of the Holocaust was then used as a way of dismissing all the pain of everyone else. Many of my interviewees told me that they felt that the way the Jewish world used the Holocaust, they were essentially being asked to choose whose suffering was most important. They felt less inclined to be part of a Jewish world that seemed to make this affirmation of the primacy of Jewish suffering the necessary condition for Jewish membership.

Many of them had heard some variant or other of the argument that Jewish liberals cared only about *other* people's suffering, but never about Jewish suffering, whenever they showed interest in the oppression of blacks, Vietnamese, American Indians, or anyone else. A number of the respondents mentioned how, later in life, they had heard these same arguments presented in an updated form: "We did everything for blacks, fought for their civil rights in the sixties, but now they aren't one bit grateful, and that just proves our point that Jews should take care of Jews, because nobody else is going to do it and you're not going to win any loyalty for doing it. So stop playing up to non-Jews or trying to show how universalist you are." They were particularly annoyed by this argument because, when they were younger, the same kinds of people in the Jewish world had *opposed* their involvement. They remembered very few Jewish institutions in the fifties or sixties that had a culture of support for these struggles.

I pointed out that there were some rabbis who had gone down South to participate in civil rights marches, that organizations like the American Jewish Congress had played a good role in the fifties and sixties before taking a rightward turn in the seventies and eighties, and that some parts of the Reform movement had given serious material support. But my respondents were unimpressed. Their *experience* of being in the Jewish world had *not* been one in which there was a culture of support for civil rights or antiwar activism, and this contrasted dramatically with some of their experiences in civil rights–oriented or antiwar-oriented churches. Yes, they had sometimes found specific individuals in the synagogues or Jewish institutions who expressed concern for others and supported those causes, but they also emphasized to me that these kinds of sensitive-to-others individuals within Jewish institutions *perceived themselves to be isolated or having to be courageous in the face of a dominant ethos of self-centeredness.*

Conformism and Intolerance of Dissent, Particularly about Israel

Many of my interviewees talked about feeling stifled in the Jewish world, about having their questions dismissed as irreverent or even as subversive. Some told me of knowing people who had been made to feel uncomfortable because they held liberal political views while they experienced the Jewish community as moving to the Right. But there were others who told me that they suspected that the substance of their views wouldn't have mattered. Having passion and deep commitment to anything seemed out of place.

The most frequent specifics concerned Israel, whose policies we all were taught not to question. From the earliest days of our Hebrew school experiences, we were told that we should care about Israel, be loyal to Israel, and be fearful of the enemies of Israel. So when we asked questions that had a critical edge, we were quickly silenced. If we dared to wonder about the fate of Palestinians living in refugee camps, if we questioned the official rationale for refusing to allow the return of those who had fled what they believed to be a war zone, if we dared to suspect that some of the refugees might have been encouraged in their flight by Jewish terrorists or even by the Israeli army, we were quickly told that we were being disloyal.

Others reported that the Holocaust was always being used as a club. Because others suffered, they were not allowed to have doubts about Israeli policy, or doubts about anything. Because six million died, they had to do X or Y or Z. All too often they reported that this manipulative use of the Holocaust had turned them off.

Sexism and Homophobia

Most had no language to describe their experiences as children, but by the late 1980s my interviewees had learned to describe in vivid detail the ways that they had felt invalidated as women or as gay people. So many of the women I spoke to could now articulate the anger and rage that they had experienced when discovering that their sex was the reason they could not share in the same experiences as the boys. Now, decades later, they still were angered, because even though officially Reform and Conservative Judaism had made a place for them, it still felt like a begrudging place. And the more these women began to grapple with the tradition, the more they found that sexism was deeply intertwined with some of what was best in Judaism.

Even during the past two decades, when sexism had been "officially" banished from the Reform and Conservative movements, my respondents felt that the sexism continued in practice. Not only in regard to who really has power in most institutions of organized Jewish life, but in the allocation of funds. For example, several pointed to the low priority in Jewish institutions given to child care. Because this is traditionally "women's work," Jewish institutions rarely prepare adequate, much less creative child-care arrangements when they hold public events or religious services. For example, if one holds a commemoration of the Holocaust or a celebration for the State of Israel or a talk from a noted speaker, few communities design parallel programs that will hold the attention and interests of children, and still fewer worry about providing quality child care so that parents can attend adult functions without feeling that they are sacrificing the interests of their children.

Only one of my classmates felt safe enough to come out to me as gay. He told a horrific story about recognizing himself as gay at age twelve and being constantly fearful that he might say something that would reveal this identity, knowing that the tradition totally condemned it. He reported being relieved the moment he was bar mitzvahed and would never have to set foot in a synagogue again.

Lack of Democracy

Few of my interviewees raised this issue directly. But when I asked them why they had not stayed in the Jewish world and fought to change it in the ways that they might have wanted, I quickly got responses about the lack of democracy. Most Jewish institutions are run by those who have the most money or those who know how to get those who do have money to give it. Some reported their own later efforts to enter Jewish institutions and attempt to reform them from within. Overwhelmingly, these were stories of failure and frustration. There are few institutional means to challenge those who have power.

Consider the Jewish media. Most Jewish weeklies in the United States are owned by the Jewish federations, and though they purport to be presenting the news, their most pressing responsibility is to ensure that the federations continue to raise money. As a result, they typically slant their news coverage to make Israel and American Jewish leaders look good, and to censor or distort voices of dissent.

Other interviewees wondered why they were always reading about Jewish leadership that they had no voice in selecting. They would read in the *New York Times* that "Jewish leaders" supported Shamir or that "American Jews" felt upset with some development or other, and they would ask themselves how these leaders had gotten chosen and what these organizations were that supposedly spoke for American Jews. They were mystified, sometimes angry, and always felt that this world of American Jews was not *their* world.

Most of my interviewees had not themselves personally engaged in struggles to change the organized Jewish community. They had learned early that such struggles were impossible. Some had learned the first time they raised questions in Hebrew school that challenged some basic assumptions—and had been responded to in disrespectful ways that implied a warning ("don't go farther or you will be in trouble"). Others had learned when their parents had made comments that indicated their own frustration with the way things were organized, and *their* understanding that little could be changed by working from within. But those who had not learned that when they were children had learned it as adults, and that had reinforced some of their other reasons for not wanting to invest too much energy in the Jewish world.

One of my interviewees, for example, told of being estranged from the Jewish world till her mid thirties, when she had become involved with a man with strong Jewish ties. She had been politically active in her union and in various feminist causes, and had decided that she would now become active in her Orthodox *shul*. The *shul* was very responsive to her, and soon she was selected to be the representative to the local Jewish community relations council (J.C.R.C.), an organization that issues political statements in the name of the entire Jewish community. Sensitive to group dynamics, skilled as an articulator of ideas, she found herself quickly accepted and respected. Until the issue of Israel came on the agenda. Then, when she began to raise some questions about Israel's policies during the Intifada (the Arab "holy war"), the rug was pulled from under her. The executive director of the organization stopped phoning her to ask her opinions, and when she asked the organization to vote on various resolutions she proposed that questioned Israeli policy, she was told that the resolutions could not be voted on by the council without first being approved by all the constituent bodies. But this had never been a consideration for any other resolution, and she asked why. The answer she was given was that on the other matters the council knew the will of their own constituents, whereas on this matter they did not. But my interviewee knew just the opposite—that on most matters being discussed by the J.C.R.C., no one in most of the constituent organizations had been consulted or had ever ventured an opinion, and that there was *no way* for the council to know whether or not they were expressing the view of a majority. But on Israel, the community was talking about the issues and hence the representatives were more likely to know what people were thinking. Nevertheless, she decided to wait, to give the constituent organizations time to debate the relevant matter. But to her dismay, she found that in meeting after meeting for the next two and a half years, the discussion was stymied, her resolutions blocked from consideration, and the officials of the council responding as though she were distracting them from important issues, as though discussion of the Intifada were a side issue, as though she had decided to raise the issue of how many angels could dance on the head of a pin. When she ultimately resigned from the council and began to share her story, she found many people with the same kind of story in other Jewish institutions. Those who persisted in these kinds of organizations had already given up on challenging questions.

Most of my interviewees were not spiritual seekers, antimaterialists, or people with a strong critique of Israeli policy. Many were ordinary American Jews, largely indistinguishable from their non-Jewish neighbors except for the fact that most still didn't celebrate Christmas and many gave gifts on Chanukah, and they attended some kind of Passover meal that they dubbed a seder. The possibility of living a life based on principles fundamentally different from those of the mainstream had not been convincingly shown to them. Some would eventually return to synagogue affiliation or participation in Jewish organizations, in large part because they wanted their children to have some exposure to Jewishness, either to please their own parents or because they sensed that there was something in the Jewish experience that transcended what had turned them off as children, and they didn't want to deny their own children the chance of discovering what they personally had not been able to find.

There was a significant minority of the people with whom I spoke who had broken with the mainstream values of American society. These people had consciously devoted some important part of their lives to pursuing some ideals that reflected a deep caring for others, a passion for spiritual or aesthetic truths, or a sustained commitment to living a moral life even when that put them at financial risk. I might want to argue that some of these values were learned subconsciously from their families and even from the influence of Jewish ideas and practices, but what is relevant here is that they did not see it that way. They had come to believe that their Jewishness was largely irrelevant to their values. Some had broken away totally, others had decided to reaffiliate, either because the synagogue provided a good way of forming social connections or because they wanted to give their children bar or bat mitzvahs, but very few because they believed that the Jewish community or Judaism could sustain or deepen their own moral or spiritual quest. And quite a large number of these actually thought that the Judaism that they had encountered in the organized Jewish community stood in direct opposition to the values that they held. Precisely what they wanted to struggle against in the larger society they perceived to be central to the Judaism they had experienced.

JEWISH CONTINUITY

The interviews revealed that Jews had left their Jewishness not because it was too different from American society, but because it was too similar. It was *not* because they sought the easy path, but because the Jewish path neither provided an alternative way to conceptualize their lives nor offered a set of meanings that could help them make their way through the contemporary world.

These would all be very good reasons for not feeling particularly attached to Jewishness. But the Judaism that they abandoned, however, was not Judaism, but only one specific reading of Judaism, based in part on the accommodation that Jews had made to living in contemporary America. Precisely what many Jews found offensive in their Jewishness was a historical product of Judaism's adaptations to a world of spiritual and moral vacuity.

In fact, the values that led many young Jews *away* from the Jewish world were particularly Jewish values, reflecting a moral sensibility that was distinctively Jewish. Conversely, those who owned and controlled the institutions of Jewish life were embodying values many of which were distinctively *not* Jewish, or more precisely, were contemporary manifestations of the Hellenistic tendency within a certain strand of Judaism, a tendency that accommodates to the powerful and diverts Judaism from its revolutionary ethical/spiritual roots. I believe that the process of Jewish renewal—insisting on spiritual aliveness, reintegrating the politically transformational elements into that spirituality, reconnecting with the Power in the universe that makes possible transcendence and compassion—has the capacity to recapture the moral imagination and spiritual yearnings of these alienated, sensitive, and gifted Jews.

Starting in the 1990s, the organized Jewish community woke up to the reality that huge numbers of younger Jews were not affiliating, and that at the present rate American Jewry would shrink dramatically in the next several decades. Millions of dollars suddenly became available for what the Jewish community federations call "Jewish continuity." Their operating assumption is that they need to do a better job of selling Jewish life to the young. But most of my research shows a very different conclusion: that the problem is not in the public relations, but in what is being sold. Unless the Jewish community is willing to rethink some of the fundamentals of the values it projects, it is likely to face severe decline in the next fifty years. Many of those who are now embarking on careers in Jewish life will find the rug pulled out from under them, because the resentments built up in childhood that are leading people away from the Jewish community are not easily reparable and will not be "fixed" by smart P.R., more trips to Israel for teenagers, weekend seminars and encampments, or even more outreach programs to singles or divorcees (though these are good things to do). Jewish life at its center will have to feel more spiritual; moral; God-centered; politically committed to social justice, respect, and caring about the problems of the larger non-Jewish world; pluralistic; democratic; nonsexist; joyful; full of intellectual ferment; and open to dissent if American Jewry is not to shrink dramatically. And it is precisely these elements that a Jewish-renewal perspective seeks to nurture within Judaism.

One final caveat. Though I've highlighted reasons why people have left Judaism that are connected with the failures of the Jewish community to embody Jewish values, this process itself takes place within a larger context of the triumph of secularism and the abandonment of Judaism that cannot be seen entirely as a choice. If you consider not only the fear generated by centuries of persecution culminating in the Holocaust, but also the more subtle anti-Semitism built into the social norms of society that make many Jews subconsciously feel that they are physically unattractive, socially gauche, or in other ways just not right to the extent that they embody Jewish ways of thinking and acting, you begin to recognize that the choice to play down or abandon one's Jewishness has been heavily shaped by external social and psychological processes that have been internalized by many Jews. This "internalized oppression" is always present for Jews, and part of what Jewish renewal can do is to uncover these dynamics and help Jews support one another in affirming that which is best in our Jewishness despite the ways that may violate media-induced notions of beauty, manners, appropriate behavior, or other societal norms that are imposed upon us as though they were descriptions of objective reality. Leaders of the Jewish community who guided the Jewish world in conformist or materialistic directions that have been self-destructive deserve some compassion; their actions often were as much the product of internalized oppression as were those of the Jews who decided to leave their faith altogether.

Unlearning internalized anti-Semitism is part of the process of Jewish renewal. I have organized Jewish-renewal weekends focused on dislodging the unconscious resistance so many Jews have developed that keep them from affirming what is most beautiful and deep in Judaism and in their fellow Jews. In a world in which anti-Semitism can pop up in the strangest places—for example, among people who know no Jews (in Japan), or among people who have been beneficiaries of Jewish support in the past (African-Americans), or among otherwise sophisticated intellectuals and culturally liberated types—don't be surprised if many Jews find it hard to affirm unequivocally their Jewishness (no matter *what* their experiences in the Jewish world). They need *both* the kind of rethinking of Judaism that Jewish renewal makes possible, *and also* a therapeutic process in which they can explore the complex ways that they have come to believe that Jewishness is "less than" or "unattractive" or something which one ought to play down because it will otherwise reasonably offend others. The issues raised in this book are part of the process of rethinking these assumptions, but a full Jewish healing will require that individuals go through an experiential process as well. Just as many women needed small consciousness-raising groups to help them unpack the deep ways that they had internalized sexist assumptions about themselves, many Jews need a similar process in which internalized anti-Semitism can be brought to consciousness and fought against. By reclaiming a Judaism that no longer offends our ethical and spiritual sensibilities, Jewish renewal strips away the "rational defenses" and brings many Jews to the point where they can explore their societally conditioned resistances to Judaism.

NOT EVERYONE WAS ALIENATED FROM THEIR JEWISHNESS

I was fortunate to have discovered in Judaism precisely what might have turned others on: a spiritual understanding of the world that

helped make sense of history and contemporary reality, a method for
encountering God, and a set of directions about how to live a meaningful life. Over the course of the years I met many others who had found
these same insights within the Jewish tradition, and today many of
them are involved in Jewish renewal.

For some, their paths began with a loving exposure to Orthodox
Judaism in their own homes, and a rigorous introduction to Jewish texts
through religious day schools. Eventually they began to grapple with
the issues of how to make sense of the contemporary world, and this led
some to leave orthodoxy, others to remain and struggle within it. There
are Orthodox Jews who are deeply involved in Jewish renewal today, and
there are many formerly Orthodox Jews who have become involved as
well. Of course, I've met a lot of formerly Orthodox Jews who were
deeply angered by their experiences growing up in Orthodox families.
They talk about the authoritarianism, the squashing of intellectual
curiosity, the sexism, the heterosexism, the narrow-mindedness and,
most particularly, the fear and hatred of others (not just non-Jews, but
non-Orthodox Jews).

I came from a very different background, as did almost all of the
people I knew as a child and most of the hundreds of people I interviewed. My parents were Zionists, not primarily because of a religious
commitment, but because they feared Hitler and the continuing legacy
of anti-Semitism. Despite a set of experiences in their youth that had
turned them off to traditional religious observance, they huddled
around the Jewish community for protection, social and economic and
political connections, and a sense of meaning that they could get by
being part of a people. Though my father's father was a rabbi and a
Bratslaver Hasid who traced his familial lineage to the Ba'al Shem Tov,
religious observance had become so joyless for my father as a child that
it generated an ambivalence about Orthodox Judaism even while its
sweeter elements fostered an attachment to Jewishness that would
shape much of his adult life. My mother had bitter stories to tell of the
way that she had been discounted as a girl in the Orthodox world of her
childhood, experiences that left a bitter taste and that might have led
her away from all religious commitment but for her own spiritual needs
as an adult. When they sent me to Camp Ramah (a Hebrew-speaking
religious camp sponsored by the Conservative movement) it was more
to strengthen my national identity as a Jew than to foster in me any
particular religious commitment.

My luck at having been sent to Ramah and to have encountered Abraham Joshua Heschel might be termed divine grace. Certainly it was not because of any internal merit of mine that I found myself suddenly encountering a Judaism that was a different world from the Conservative synagogue which my parents had joined so that I could be bar mitzvahed. Temple B'nai Abraham of Newark, New Jersey, contained some two thousand seats underneath a huge gold-lined dome. Its choir was hidden from sight in the room that also contained the immense organ whose melodies wafted through the building. I once found the hidden staircase leading to the choir room and on one Yom Kippur wandered in as choir members sat eating their ham sandwiches, perfectly appropriate since none of them was Jewish, and their ethereal voices sang words they neither understood nor were involved in. On those High Holy Days, when the synagogue was packed with the finest furs and jewelry available to the dentists, stockbrokers, realtors, liquor merchants, doctors, lawyers, accountants, and their wives who filled the pews, off-duty Newark policemen guarded the doors to ensure that no one who could not afford the very costly tickets (in 1994 dollars, they would have been close to $2,500) would be able to sneak in. (When children were let in to find their parents, they were not allowed to stay unless they had tickets, almost like the line from a Jewish joke: "Okay, you can go in for a second to find them, but don't let me catch you praying!")

Yet what I discovered at Ramah and then through my exposure to Heschel—first through his books and then as my mentor in the years I studied at the Jewish Theological Seminary—was a Judaism that stood as a radical critique of what was claiming to be "official" Judaism.

I discovered that the very tension and conflict I was experiencing was a central theme in Jewish life and in the development of Judaism itself. From the very beginning, there were conflicting interpretations of what the tradition was really about. The prophets had emerged in Judaism precisely to proclaim that priests and kings were, according to their understanding of God's will, distorting the essence of Judaism. The greatness of Judaism was that it eventually embraced these prophets, recognizing that from their critiques, a form of Judaism resulted that was deeper and truer than the established norm.

With one caveat: it was always the Judaism of the past generations that could be seen as having had these errors. The prophets of the past were revered, but those of the present continued to be seen as radicals who were breaking with the "authentic" tradition to fit some private or personal agenda that they were now inflicting on the Jewish community.

So, yes, prophecy was accepted and the prophetic message incorporated, but there was always an attempt to incorporate it in ways that would not too deeply shake up the present. Hence, the prophetic message could be read in synagogues every week, but always kept at an acceptable distance.

Yet, what I discovered also was that there were some religious Jews who understood that the subversive and revolutionary message was not about some other time or place, but about this time and this place.

One such religious Jew was Abraham Joshua Heschel. Heschel was a mystic, a scholar, and a Jewish theologian. The logic of his political involvement—in the civil rights movement, in the demonstrations at Selma, in the March on Washington in 1963, and later as the Jewish cochair of Clergy and Laity Against the War in Vietnam—flowed directly from his involvement in the prophetic Judaism that had been passed down through the generations and which Heschel found ingredient in the entire Jewish tradition.

Heschel was the spiritual founder of Jewish renewal in the contemporary period. As one of his disciples, I found myself deeply moved by his interpretation of Judaism. In private meetings in his office, Heschel introduced me to a way of reading the texts and understanding Jewish history that inflamed my soul and gave words to the spiritual journey that I had begun at age twelve. It was under Heschel's tutelage that I first read Hegel, Heidegger, Buber, Levinas and, most importantly, the prophets. So much of what I say in this book derives from his insights that in some ways I see this whole book as a footnote and update to his thinking.

What Heschel taught was also known in other strands of Judaism. There were Orthodox Jews in Israel who did not know Heschel and who had begun to build a peace-oriented consciousness. There were Hasidim who drew from the same spiritual roots as Heschel and who passed their teachings down from generation to generation (Heschel himself was the scion of one noted Hasidic family). And there were many inspired people in the Reform, Conservative, and Reconstructionist movements who, in their own languages and situations, also understood much of what Heschel so eloquently articulated. Many could resonate to Heschel's teachings.

In subsequent years I was to benefit from learning with many of these people, most importantly Rabbi Zalman Schachter-Shalomi, a Lubavitcher rabbi who had eventually moved outside the confines of the Lubavitch movement in order to shape his own understanding of Jewish renewal; and Rabbi Marshall Meyer, who, as a rabbi in Argentina, became legendary for publicly challenging the ruling military junta in the late 1970s, and who later returned to the United States, where he championed the Israeli peace movement, feminism, and gay rights.

I was one of tens of thousands of Jews who were beginning to reclaim Judaism from the conservatives, the conformists, and the spiritually obtuse. A whole new generation of Jews had begun to break from the old models, the old fears, the Holocaust trauma, the subordination of our Jewish hearts and minds to rigid authoritarian and patriarchal models. We were implicitly deciding that the accommodationist forms of Orthodox, Conservative, Reconstructionist, and Reform Judaism were inadequate alternatives to the secularism and materialism of the larger society. So within each of these movements, Jewish-renewal energy began to take root.

Ironically, just as this renewal energy was taking shape at the end of the twentieth century, a neoconservative Judaism was triumphing in many corners of the Jewish establishment and among many rabbis, Jewish leaders, and bureaucrats. Though many of these could no longer identify with *Commentary* magazine (if only because it had become openly opposed to the official peace-oriented policies of the Israeli government), they nevertheless embraced a pessimistic and paranoid worldview which they attributed to Judaism and to the "lessons" of Jewish history. Harvard professor Ruth Wisse, writing in 1992, embodied the spirit of this neoconservative worldview when she warned that liberalism was undermining Jewish self-interest. Citing polls that show that for many Jews liberalism remains the strongest expression of their Jewish identity, Wisse laments the "new kind of Jewish liberation theology" that has been articulated in *Tikkun* magazine.[1] Her book, aptly subtitled *The Liberal Betrayal of the Jews*, reflects the tension between a large sector of American Jews, still seeking at the end of the

---

[1] Ruth Wisse, *If I Am Not for Myself: The Liberal Betrayal of the Jews* (New York: The Free Press, 1992).

twentieth century to find a way to reconcile their ethical sensibilities and their Jewish identities, and an elite group in the organized Jewish community that sees the world in either/or terms and has come to believe that if Jews are *too* sensitive to the needs of others, they will have no energy left to take care of themselves.

This struggle persists. Neoconservative tendencies have particular resonance in an American society reveling in the alleged "triumph of the market" and loudly proclaiming that "selfishness works." Neocons seem to be expressing the common sense of the society when they insist that Jews stop trusting others and focus on "taking care of number one": themselves! How convenient to find a Jewish sanction for selfishness—and how easy a sell that form of Judaism *is* to many wealthy Jews who fund the institutions of the organized Jewish community.

It is precisely this focus that is most self-destructive to Jewish life (and hence to the very institutions that support these neocons). Jews don't *have to* remain Jews today. Every Jew is to some extent a Jew by choice. If Jews want a society based on self-interest, they can get that in the larger society. Most Jews will remain attached to a Judaism that stands for something that is substantially different from the selfishness and materialism of the larger society. If they don't find it in the Jewish world, most will walk away.

Yet that "something" does not have to be invented—it can be re-claimed in the substantively conservative process that I am calling Jewish renewal. That renewal involves a process of returning to Jewish intellectual and spiritual roots, taking them seriously, and applying them to today's realities. I believe that this process provides the best hope for Jewish continuity. By reclaiming Judaism's message of tran-scendence and compassion, by reaffirming the revolutionary integra-tion of spiritual and ethical truths that are central to Judaism, Jewish renewal provides a direction that could assure Jewish survival with moral and spiritual integrity.

PART I

THE METAPHYSICS OF HEALING AND TRANSFORMATION

The world we inherit is deeply flawed. Yet, according to Judaism, its flaws are *not* part of its essence.

God, according to the creation story in Genesis, looked at the world, "and, behold, it was very good" (Genesis 1:31). The distortions, the evil, the cruelty, the class structures, the imperialism, the murder, the rape, the anger and hatred—these are not built into the fundamental structure of reality, and they are not inevitable.

If not inevitable, though, how can they be changed?

Judaism is one part of the answer to that question. It provides the metaphysical foundation for the healing and repair of the world that we so badly need.

But the healing will be done by flawed human beings. Hence, Judaism's message of the possibility of transcendence of that which *is* must always be coupled with compassion for those who are to bring this message and attempt to be healers and transformers.

Judaism tells this story by focusing not on *all* peoples, but on one people, thereby giving concrete particularity to a message of healing and repair that might seem both too distant and incredible had it been articulated in purely abstract philosophical terms. By telling the story of this one people and its wrestling with this message, it provides all people with an understanding of what it would be like to attempt to embody timeless ethical and spiritual truths in the real world. The errors, the weaknesses, the ways that we sometimes retreat from what we know—all these are parts of the path to healing and transformation. In grappling with the story of this one people, we open ourselves to lessons that are applicable for all peoples.

CHAPTER ONE

CRUELTY IS NOT DESTINY

The Jewish people came to historical consciousness in a world dominated by great imperial powers, first in Mesopotamia, then in Egypt. No wonder, then, that the first issue confronting them was how to understand the nature and meaning of cruelty. One can read the Torah as a first, conflicted, sometimes ambiguous but often enlightening meditation on how to handle the cruelty that the Jewish people were encountering in the world. But this was not only external, something imposed upon pure and noble beings by the outside, but also it was in us as well, and distorted us even as we sought to transcend it.

Abraham, Moses, and later Ezra were themselves products of the world of cruelty. Their perceptions and the ways in which they heard the voice of God were shaped by the ways they had been distorted by the cruelty that reverberated through their own lives. Yet what they heard when they heard the voice of God was a message that was very different from that heard by most of their contemporaries.

The ancient world was full of religious systems that validated the wonder and mystery of the natural order. The cycles of nature were revered and feared. But most of these religions saw the social world as another part of this same natural reality. Existing class systems, unfair distributions of wealth and power, were as much a part of the natural order as the sunset. Throughout much of recorded history the oppressed have been socialized to believe that cruelty and oppression are inevitable, an ontological necessity, part of the structure of reality. Spirituality for them became identified with reconciliation to a world of oppression: either through learning to "flow" with the world as it is or through imagining that the material world in which they lived was a prelude to some higher nonmaterial world, and that the task of the living was to escape material reality into this spiritual realm which embodied the purity and deeper reality that could not be imagined on this earth.

What the Jews heard was a very different message: that this world could be fundamentally transformed. Spirituality and morality were not features of some other reality apart from this world, but were inherently ingredient in this world, because the God who created the universe is *also* the God who brought morality into the world, and *we* embody God's spirit by being made in the divine image. Cruelty was built into social institutions and into the psychological legacy of human beings. It appeared to be an "objective fact" about human reality only because oppressive social arrangements are very hard to change, and psychological legacies are very hard to uproot. But "very hard" is different from "impossible." One need not be overly optimistic about how quickly it is possible to overcome the legacy of cruelty—that might take thousands and thousands of years. But from the standpoint of this Jewish sensibility, what we do, how we live, the kind of society we build, can contribute to the defeat of cruelty.

Recovering this revolutionary message is one of the central tasks of contemporary Jewish renewal.

Not that Torah has some naive notion of how easy that might be. Very early in the childhood of the human race, cruelty and violence emerge, so, as Genesis tells us a few chapters later, *yetzer ha'adam rah mee ne' urav,* which can be roughly translated as: there is some part of human beings that was already distorted from the experiences of our youth. The early experiences of the human race have left a legacy of pain that is passed on from generation to generation, creating a tendency toward malevolence that is *also* part of our situation.

What causes that distortion? Torah does not tell us. What it points to is the pain, anger, and fury that come from nonrecognition. Cain seeks God's acknowledgment that his contribution, his sacrifice, is as valuable as that of his brother Abel, yet he does not get that sense of being recognized as valuable and contributing. In his pain and fury he kills his brother Abel. When confronted by God and asked, "Where is Abel your brother?" Cain responds with what became the classic line of distorted consciousness, as much the line of those who turn their backs on the homeless and the starving of the world today as it was of those who have in every age allowed themselves not to see the pain of others: "Am I my brother's keeper?" Torah's unmistakable implication is that the moment one recognizes one's "other," one must simultaneously recognize the obligation toward caring and mutual concern. But what Torah does not explain is *why* that recognition breaks down. If blame is to be assigned at all, it is to God, who failed to give Cain the recognition that he so badly needed; and it is perhaps out of this understanding of His own culpability that God does not kill Cain but instead only banishes him. Yet in raising the question about responsibility and in recounting Cain's punishment, the Bible makes clear that it does not accept evil as some inevitability that must be accepted, but as a distortion that must be combated. This is *not* part of God's scheme, and it causes God shock and upset to discover this kind of behavior.

We have the germs of what might be called a Biblical theory about the origins of violence. Cruelty is made possible when human beings do not recognize in one another the image of God that is the essence of their own being—and hence turn away from others; do not hear their pain. Once this process begins, it builds upon itself, becomes a powerful force that is transferred from generation to generation. The people living in material abundance, fearful that they will not have enough if they share with everyone who is hungry, protect themselves from knowing others' pain by allowing themselves to believe that these others are really not human beings like themselves. Hence it is okay to turn their backs on others' pain.

Racism of all sorts stems from this moment—the need to deny the other's right to be taken care of by finding some aspect of that other which makes the other not *really* a human being like ourselves. Yet the need to deny the other's similarity or humanity is itself a reminder of the degree to which we do immediately grasp our obligation to the other, our obligation to care for, respect, and even love the other. It is precisely this recognition, difficult to repress, that requires the adoption of systems of psychological defense by making the other *very* other. One can imagine that shutting one's eyes to the other has its rewards—the overcoming of scarcity as you take from others what you need for yourself without regard to the effect it has on them; the elimination of one's own hunger may in part drown out the nagging awareness that the other who is hungry is essentially the same as oneself. But as elaborate cultural systems begin to develop that define one's own group as the only one *really* deserving of consideration, it becomes easier to forget even the lingering doubts and memories of connection.

As generations and centuries pass, the habit of cruelty becomes embodied in social institutions. Objectifying the other in some external group allows shutting one's ears to the pain of others, and facilitates one's ability to treat people even within one's own group in this way. The subordination of women by men, the creation of slavery, the establishment of hierarchical orders of privilege within the society—all these are new forms in which the insensitivity becomes generalized. Eventually people begin to forget that it could ever be another way. The cruel rule the world, and those with the greatest ease in acting cruelly seem to have the greatest power and greatest success.

The important news of Torah, its optimistic message, is that the world is governed neither by malevolence nor by a set of contending forces, in which evil and good have an equal chance of triumphing, but rather by a Force for good that is the Source of the good. That is the claim being made in Genesis when the text says that God shapes people in God's image.

The God of the Bible is the Force that makes possible this transformation of the world: from one characterized by estrangement and lack of mutual recognition, to one in which moral actions and compassion abound, based on an understanding that every single human being is infinitely precious and deserving of respect and love. Not just Jews or some special subset of humans—Torah insists that all human beings derive from a single founding father and mother who were created in the image of the Divine.

This claim, of course, is not a claim that generalizes from some set of knowable facts. Rather, it is a principle that guides us, helps us to organize the facts, and tells us where to place those facts that seem to stand in contradiction to it. The meaning of belief in the God of the Bible is, in my reading, to believe this claim about the world.

Judaism becomes the metaphysics of social transformation: the system of belief about reality that makes possible revolutionary change.

Judaism places transcendence on the agenda of the human race. Human beings need not be stuck in a world of pain or oppression. We can regain contact with a deeper level of being, a level more consonant with who we really are—namely, beings who are created in the image of God, who embody an inherent tendency toward goodness and holiness, toward being "embodied spirituality." Transcendence is not transcending *this* world, but rather our ability to bring more fully into being *in* this world aspects of ourselves and aspects of reality that surround us but to which we have become tone deaf. Every inch of creation, every cell of being, not only contains atoms stored with physical energy, but also contains and reflects the spiritual and moral energy that we call God. Much of the pain and oppression we experience in this world is a reflection of the way we do *not* recognize God in the world, in one another, in ourselves.

Many other religions had the intuition that something was fundamentally missing from human experience, but then they created "spiritual" experience by pointing to some higher reality in a different or spiritual world that was necessarily divorced from the world of daily life. Judaism insists that this split is *not* an ontological necessity, that God's absence from the world can be repaired and that human beings are partners with God in the process of repair (*tikkun*). Bringing God back into the world involves recognizing one another both for that which is unique about each of us but also for the way that each of us shares this common potential to partially embody God's presence in the world. We have the capacity to overcome the many blinders that have, throughout history, kept us from fully recognizing ourselves or recognizing others as vehicles of God's presence. Transcendence, then, is a psychological, political, ethical, and spiritual continuum involving a transformative and healing praxis of *tikkun*, rather than a spiritual escape from a fundamentally flawed world.

We become fully human when we come to know ourselves through a process of recognition by the other, whom we simultaneously recognize as a self-constituting subject capable of reflecting God's goodness and love, and as capable of seeing those same capacities within us. This mutual recognition is recognition not only of that which is unique within each of us, but also and most deeply of what we have in common: the way that the energy of God manifests in each of us, making it possible for us to be free, creative, loving, caring, spiritually sensitive, conscious, and self-transforming beings who both receive and embody God's energy.

Transcendence of our past is in part this breaking through to the understanding that we do not have to do what we have been taught to do, that we do not have to treat one another in the way that we have been treated.

But transcendence is only possible, not inevitable. Each generation has layered into its psychic structure the histories of the past failures of transcendence, the accumulated legacy of the world of oppression. Those failures are embodied in the increasingly textured and powerful structures of domination that shape the social order, just as they are embodied in the individual's psyche and belief system. The system of persecution and oppression does not inhabit only the external world, although it is importantly and centrally there. It also infects our internal worlds of belief and feeling.

The world's cruelty has been internalized as much by the victims of cruelty as by the oppressors. As Peter Gabel points out, each of us, needing recognition and validation from others, has gone through a complicated process of socialization in which our pain at not having received adequate recognition is transformed into anger and cruelty toward others. The nonrecognition is communicated in thousands of ways from the moment the child is born. It is not unusual for children to have fantasies of violence; it is common to discover children engaged in little acts of cruelty—both symptoms of a child's need to control the already existing cruelty that he or she is subconsciously absorbing and reacting to in family life, preschool programs, television, and social institutions.

The amount of cruelty and the way it gets internalized into our sense of self and into the ways we deal with others differs from person to person and from culture to culture. But the cruelty is there. Yet Torah insists that it can be defeated.

True enough, God is depicted as getting frustrated with human beings by the time of Noah's flood. Eventually God switches Her/His focus to a vanguard people, the people of Israel, who are to become the vehicle through which a consciousness of human possibilities may be returned to a world distorted by cruelty and violence. But God's frustration is itself a reminder that what *is* in the world of oppression is not all that *could* be. It is precisely because the world does not have to be dominated by violence that God is angry when it becomes that way.

What a contrast with many religious systems that teach as their highest wisdom that one must learn to accommodate to a world of oppression, that struggles to change that world are fundamentally misguided and represent an attachment to the illusions of the material world, and that our goal is to emotionally, intellectually, and spiritually disinvest.

Because cruelty is rooted in choices made in the childhood of the human race and that recur in our own childhood experiences, the task of liberation is to break the hold of the past over the present, to reconnect ourselves with the possibilities of transcendence that lie within each of us and within all of us acting together as families, communities, peoples, the human race. We can come to recognize one another once again as created in the image of God.

Consistent with this insight, Torah takes a complicated stance toward the transcendence that is needed. On the one hand, transcendence is always possible, always potentially at hand, and rooted not in mere wishful thinking, but rather in the fundamental power that governs the universe; on the other hand, since human beings are in fact rooted in a complicated and flawed set of social relationships which have been internalized in all of our emotional and intellectual lives, we must therefore strive for transcendence in a way that manifests an adequate level of compassion for the ways in which we and others will fail to overcome our own inner and outer legacies of oppression.

Hearing God's voice in this way is the brilliance and power of Torah. The task of Jewish renewal in every generation has been to allow ourselves to hear that voice as clearly as we can. Yet this is not the only way to hear God's voice, nor the only way it was heard by those who put the Torah together. In every generation those who have heard the voice of God have also heard the voice of cruelty, violence, and pain, and have often attributed that voice to God as well. The compilers of the Torah were no exception—they were human beings who struggled to hear the voice of God but who were simultaneously terrified to stay connected to the message of radical freedom that they heard. They retreated at times into hearing the more familiar messages, ones that seemed more congruent with their worlds of pain and oppression.

Whether you hold that the Torah was put together by some committee of editors or central redactor in the days of Ezra following
the restoration of Jewish rule in Judea after the Babylonian exile, or
whether you hold that the Torah was received directly by Moses from
God and recorded by Moses, whoever wrote down the Torah was
hearing or reflecting the accumulated wisdom of more than one take
on God. If we hold to the language of the Orthodox tradition, in
which Moses received the Torah directly from God, we can say that
the human receptor, Moses, was himself a severely limited being
whose record of God's message reflected his inevitable human limitations. Even if we agree with Bible scholars who see the Torah as a
compilation of preexisting sources, we still can see that in the text as
we have it there is more than one voice and one conception of who
God is and what God wants. "Turn it and turn it, because *all* is in it,"
one of the many traditional sayings about Torah, can also mean that
not only is God in it, but so is everything—including the voice of
accumulated pain.

For those who wish to articulate this same insight in the language
of traditional belief, one can say that when God dictated the Torah to
Moses, God included within it systematic ambiguity that would allow
for a variety of different interpretations. Human beings could,
through the process of their own growth, learn to differentiate strategies of reading consistent with their own development at different
moments in history.

But to listen for the voice of God in Torah is simultaneously to
recognize that some of what we hear will reflect the distorted interpretations of those who listened in the past. We do not have the
unmediated voice of God in Torah—for as the tradition itself proclaims, *zot ha'Torah asher sam Moshe lifney b'ney Yisrael, al pee ha'Shem
b'yad Moshe* (this is the Torah which Moses placed in front of the
children of Israel, by the mouth of God by the hand of Moses)—that is,
through the mediation of Moses. So every act of listening is, in part, an
act of interpreting. Some of what Moses heard as the voice of God was,
I shall argue, the voice of cruelty coming from inside Moses and
mistakenly attributed to God.

When interpreting, we start with one aspect of Torah that helps
generate considerable trust: that Torah does not present its heroes,
our ancestors, as though they were wonderful and enlightened
human beings, or as always inspired and acting from the highest of

motives. Rather, it is precisely because we get an account of very flawed human beings that we can trust the story, empathize with their dilemmas, and recognize them as reasonably related to us.

Ultimately, though, there is no escaping our obligation to be the interpreters of what we hear, to separate out what is the voice of God from what is the voice of human distortion in Torah. In the late twentieth century we accept that we are interpreting Torah from our standpoint; in previous generations some of the interpreters were not conscious that they were interpreting, but thought of themselves as conveying what the Torah *really* said.

We who inherit the oldest revolutionary tradition in human history, who have heard the command to heal, repair, and transform the world, are ourselves wounded healers. What makes our Torah so perfect, what the tradition calls *Torah temima*, is that it does not ask us to hide this fact from ourselves.

THE SHADOW

Anyone who has witnessed the violence of the twentieth century will feel uncomfortable with a tradition that denies the reality of cruelty and evil in human life. So the insistence on *tikkun*—healing, repair, and transformation—seems naive if asserted in ways that suggest that this is an easy process that can be achieved through simple acts of will. Torah is well aware of the tendencies within human life toward evil. The Jewish people's formative experience was that of our slavery and the attempted genocide of our firstborn males. Throughout our history Jews have been subjected to extraordinary pain and cruelty. So a progressive Jewish sensibility ought never to deny the shadow side of contemporary human consciousness.

Much of what progressive Jews have been concerned with is developing the psychological and social technologies that might allow us to take steps toward decreasing the pain in the world. Psychoanalytic and Socialist movements face the fact that cruelty and evil are deeply embedded in individual and social structures; they suggest a process of individual and social change that will begin to undo that complex layering. The notion that the past exercises a tyranny over the present, central to the thinking of psychoanalytic theories, suggests that we humans face a long and difficult process of undoing our social and psychological inheritance.

Yet what *is* being denied is this: that the evil is Evil, that the cruelty is Cruelty—that there is anything necessary or ontological or fixed about the shadow. It may take generations to undo the legacy of cruelty, but it is not a fixed and permanent part of what it is to be human. It can be overcome, however slowly and cautiously.

If I say that it can be changed only after hundreds of years, what really is the difference between saying that and saying that it really can't happen? But there is a difference. Even to make it happen over the course of hundreds of years will take enormous leaps of faith, risks, acts of courage, and hopefulness. And those risks and acts of courage are rarely forthcoming from those who say it can't happen, or people who are locked into a fascination with the "shadow" part of our existence.

Of course it is logically possible that one might take risks to advance the struggles for human liberation even while deeply believing that there is a fundamental Evil in human beings that will continually reassert itself regardless of what forward steps we take. But in my own experience I've rarely encountered such people in the movements for social justice or peace that have acted to improve the lot of humanity. Those who ontologize evil often use this belief as an explanation for focusing more attention on their own personal lives. When asked to join the civil rights marchers protesting segregation in the South, or struggles for women's equality, or struggles to end homelessness, they will resort to arguments about not wanting to demonize the other (with which I agree). Since we all have a shadow side within ourselves, the protesters may be using the struggle against some other to avoid dealing with the shadow within themselves (sometimes true, but irrelevant to whether they ought to be protesting or not), while they themselves, they say, are too involved in that inner struggle to have energy for the outer one. This is a position that allows cruelty to flourish in the world.

To be sure, one might be equally discouraged if one expects a steady and progressive moral improvement and then is confronted with backsliding, irrationality, insensitivity, and acts of evil. To assert that cruelty is not destiny is *not* to deny the depth of distortion of our psychological and social inheritance. But it is to say that it can be changed, and that it matters what we do.

But how can one really know this? If I point to the Jewish experience of moving from slavery to freedom, or the recent experience of social movements that succeeded in ending the war in Vietnam, ending apartheid in South Africa, increasing women's power and rights in the

United States, or any other specific historical advance, there will always be some who can point to the ways that these advances have not really brought the fullest liberation expected, and how there have been some negative consequences associated with each advance.

In the final analysis, then, the assertion about the possibility of overcoming cruelty is not an empirical one but a statement of faith in the God of Israel, just as its denial is a statement of faith in the religion of "cynical realism." I see no plausible definitive test case that could establish either the truth or the falsity of the position. That certain leap is part of what is at stake in believing in God: believing that there is a Force in the world that makes possible its transformation from what is to what ought to be, and acting in the world on that belief. Those who do believe this do believe in the God of Israel, even though they might not call it God. And those who do not share this belief, while they may say they believe in the God of Torah, actually don't.

A DIFFERENT CONCEPTION OF GOD

If you think of God as a big and powerful daddy sitting up in heaven and pulling strings to make things happen in this world according to His whim or pleasure, you are going to have trouble understanding some of what I'm saying about God in this book. Conceptions of God in Judaism have changed and evolved along with our understanding of ourselves and our world. The God who takes a stroll in the garden of Eden (Genesis 3:8) made little sense to the rabbis who constructed the Talmud, so they reinterpreted Bible stories in ways that made God into a spiritual entity without a body. As Rabbi Zalman Schachter-Shalomi teaches, there was a time when we imagined God as a Being who could be softened up and put in a good mood by our offering Him the right food and smells, so we roasted Him some lambchops and offered up some incense in the Temple that stood in Jerusalem. Later we thought it was certain words that would put God in the right mood, so we constructed prayers that at once praised God and reminded Him of Biblical promises that He should be living up to.

Today we are moving toward a conception of God that is based more on a conception of a Force that both includes all of Being as we know it, and surpasses all that we ever can know (not because we are puny little nothings, as the older ways would have had it, but because we have limited sensory apparatus that can pick up only small fragments of the dimensions of Being that are part of God). In this emerging conception—based in part on developing kabbalistic notions of God, like Shechinah (the dwelling place) and Eyn Sof (that which is without limit), which tend to emphasize the immanent dimension of God's Being—we are part of God, part of God's process of becoming self-conscious, and part of God's process of healing and transforming the world.

Moreover, the emerging concept of Jewish renewal taught by Rabbi Zalman Schachter-Shalomi imagines a whole different kind of causality—a causality from the future to the present. It is as if God is the voice of what could and ought to be, calling us from the future and moving us toward the fulfillment of our possibilities. To be in tune with that voice is to reject any idolization of that which is, to refuse to bow down to the gods of "reality," always to be moving toward that which we know and feel could and should be, even though it transcends that which seems "realistic," given the ways things have been. To be called by this God is to be in touch with the God of Israel. Though Jews have changed the specific way that they understand this God, the concepts and language that they've used to describe this Ultimate of ultimates, it is my contention that it is *this* God that was encountered by Abraham and by Moses and it is *this* God that has energized the Jewish vision.

I shall return to a fuller discussion of God at the end of this book, but first I shall explore how we encountered this God and how we have been both drawn to and repelled by the implications of this encounter. It is my contention that one of the most powerful implications of this encounter has been our growing awareness as Jews that cruelty is not destiny, and that not only can the amount of evil in the world be decreased, but that it is our task to decrease it.

To talk of God as a Force that makes possible transcendence is to use a language that seems to empty God of the power, the fiery presence, the spirited Being that we have used in our descriptions of Him/Her. I believe that God's energy permeates every ounce of Being and every moment of existence, that God is constantly sending us messages and constantly not only making possible our transcendence but demanding and begging us to join with Her/Him in this process. We are constantly in God's presence, separated by a thin membrane from God's spiritual energies, which we constantly intuit and are both drawn to and of which we are terrified. So to speak of God as the Force that makes for the possibility of transcendence and transformation is not to deny the noumenal reality, the mysterium tremendum, the *yir'ah* and trembling that must take place in God's presence. It is not meant to sanitize or limit the incredible power that is heard above the mighty waters, the voice that is heard in the whirlwind, the voice that transcends all our categories and reduces our language to silence.

But since I've taken upon myself the task of talking about God despite the absolute impossibility of doing so, and the task of talking about God in a world where Her/His pulsating energy and constant messages are not always so obvious, I'm attempting to enter the realm of divine energy through a vantage point made accessible to the Jewish people through Torah—namely, that aspect of God's reality that asserts the possibility of transcendence and transformation. And since that aspect is both what is most distinctive about the Jewish view of God and also what makes the Jewish message most threatening to the world, it makes sense for us to explore God through this entry point.

The Kabbalah suggests that God has different *partzufim*, different ways in which S/He presents Her/Himself to the world, depending in part on the needs of human beings in different historical periods. So I choose to enter God through the appearance of God as healer and transformer of the world, because currently the world has greatest need to embrace this aspect of Her/Him. In so doing, I do not intend to negate other aspects of God's Being or to reduce God to the parts of God's Being to which we seem to have greatest access.

And it is the splitting off of this aspect of God, the willful or unconscious denial of this face of God, that has formed the basis of some of the distortions in the religious and spiritual traditions of the past several thousand years.

Abraham and Moses confronted two of the greatest imperial powers of the ancient world: Mesopotamia and Egypt. Those empires had highly developed religious traditions that acknowledged the glory and grandeur of the universe, and they had no problem singing praises to the gods who were responsible for the creation of the world. They built elaborate and joyous festivals to celebrate the eternal rhythms of nature, seeing in them a spiritual reality that transcended their particularity. But they did all this as adjuncts to a social system that was oppressive, that sanctioned slavery and oppression. Judaism emerged as a challenge to this rupture of the ethical from the spiritual. It affirms a God and a spirituality which insists entirely on the unity of the forces of the creators (*elohim*) and the Force (YHVH) that allows for world repair, based on mutual recognition, love, compassion, and justice.

In my interpretation of the Torah, idolatry consists of taking that which is and treating it as all that could be—worshipping the real without noticing that a key aspect of the real is its ability to be transformed into that which could be. Whenever we look at reality without simultaneously apprehending the voice from the future pulling what is to what could and should be, we are in a potentially idolatrous mode.

And human beings . . . who are we? We are a song sung by the universe, a momentary flash in God's emerging consciousness, a vehicle through which God comes to know and act. Each one of us emerges for a moment in history, has the opportunity to sing briefly God's song with all its contemporary limitations and distortions, rejoice in the beauty, contribute to the healing, and then hopefully transmit to the next generation some of what we have seen. That process of passing along some of what we have learned—not just through books or instruction but also through changes in ordinary language, poetry, prayers, gestures, and humor—is our connection to eternity. Nothing that the universe needs is ever lost to it—it remains alive in the collective unconscious, in the words, inflections, melodies, and sometimes even in the holy texts. For us as Jews that process of summing up and passing on wisdom became most focused when young Abraham smashed the idols in his father's house and went to create a new life in the land of Israel.

CHAPTER TWO

ABRAHAM AND THE
PSYCHODYNAMICS OF
CHILDHOOD

ABRAHAM AS SURVIVOR OF CHILD ABUSE

The rabbis in the era of the Talmud, and those who followed them, have often been deeply critical of much of Abraham's behavior. They were offended by the manipulative and demeaning treatment that Abraham affords to his wife Sarah when he presents her as his sister to the pharaoh of Egypt, who, in turn, assuming Sarah to be single, takes her into his house while Abraham saves his own life and builds up his store of sheep. We have here a picture of an ancient desert sheikh or warlord. Why should this particular man have been chosen to be the founder of our people? Why honor him?

In attempting to answer the question, the rabbis turned to a set of explanations not found directly in the text, but which may be presumed to have accompanied the text for hundreds of years. Some of these stories were collected in what became known as the Midrash, though others were invented by the rabbis themselves as a way of deepening our understanding. Yet many of these stories have roots running deep into the historical memory of our people, and we may presume that at least some have been based on collective wisdom and recollection that was preserved from generation to generation.

It may be a surprise to readers who think that psychological explana-

tions were invented in the contemporary world to know that the midrashic stories immediately draw our attention to Abraham's childhood.
Torah tells us little about Abraham or why God chose him to become
the father of the Jewish people. But a thousand years later, R. Hiyya (in
Midrash Rabbah 28:13) jumps in and recounts the stories of Abraham's
childhood that accompany Abraham's legend. Abraham was the child
not just of an idolater, but of a manufacturer of idols in the Sumerian
city of Ur. Yet Abraham managed to see through the prevalent idol
worship and reject it. In so doing, of course, he also broke radically with
his father.

Consider the words of the Midrash:

Terah was a manufacturer of idols. He once went away somewhere
and left Abraham to sell them in his place. A man came and wished
to buy one. "How old are you?" Abraham asked him.

"Fifty years," was the reply.

"Woe to such a man!" he exclaimed. "You are fifty years old and
would worship a day-old object!" At this the man became ashamed
and departed.

On another occasion a woman came with a plateful of flour and
requested him, "Take this and offer it to them." So he took a stick,
broke them, and put the stick in the hands of the largest.

When his father returned he demanded, "What have you done
to them?"

"I cannot conceal it from you," he rejoined. "A woman came
with a plateful of fine meal and requested me to offer it to them.
One claimed, 'I must eat first,' while another claimed, 'I must eat
first.' Thereupon the largest arose, took the stick, and broke them."

"Why do you make sport of me," he cried out; "have they then
any knowledge?"

"Should not your ears listen to what your mouth is saying?" he
retorted.

Thereupon Terah seized Abraham and delivered him to Nimrod.

Abraham, the son, challenges the worship of idols that is his father's
livelihood. His father has lost control of the rebellious son and now
delivers him for punishment to the ruler, Nimrod. Nimrod, the Midrash
tells us, raises the issue to a higher level of sophistication—if he can't
get Abraham to worship something made from the earth, the idols,

perhaps he will worship one of these other elements: fire, air, or water. But in each case, Abraham recognizes the limits of the fundamental elements. Ancient science is not going to entice him any more than the system of power is going to intimidate him. Nimrod is enraged once he recognizes that Abraham is rejecting the idol worship that is central to the established order of the kingdom, and is accepting instead a god who is the God of the universe who created all things but is not reducible to any particular thing or set of things.

Nimrod, according to the Midrash, acts on his anger at the rebellious child Abraham by throwing him into a fiery furnace. Miraculously, Abraham is saved. According to the Midrash, he emerges from the fire unburnt and unscathed. But is he really saved? Has he not really been burnt and scathed inwardly?

What the Midrash tells us is that Abraham had a traumatic childhood. Unable to accept the political/religious system in which he grew up, he is immediately placed in conflict with his own father, the mediator and representative of the reality principle. What gives Abraham the strength to challenge existing reality? It is the recognition that there is something more in the universe, something that transcends daily reality—and it is this belief that saves him.

Yet at the same time, Abraham is a victim of intense cruelty. If he emerges alive from the fiery furnace, it is not that he has emerged unharmed. On the contrary—Abraham is a man who has been traumatized, to some extent made insensitive to others, a man whose experience of pain in childhood will remain with him in adult life, just as each of us carries into our adult life the pain and oppression of our childhood.

THE REPETITION COMPULSION AND THE BINDING OF ISAAC FOR SACRIFICE

Freud talks of the repetition compulsion—the tendency for human beings to act out on others the fundamental trauma that we experienced as children, in the hopes of thereby mastering situations in which we were powerless and victimized. He might have chosen Abraham as the first historical example. The fundamental failure to be recognized that Abraham experiences—his father's willingness to be more attentive to his idols, and by implication to the political/religious system of the kingdom, than to the reality of his own son—creates a searing pain, and eventually an emotional deadness within Abraham. Abraham will live this out in his relationship with his family.

Abraham's adult life contains a series of emotional betrayals of those who are close to him. Faced with the difficulties of famine, confronted with the realities of a society in which rape and murder are a way of life, he is willing emotionally to abandon Sarah his sister/wife, allowing her to be brought into the house of Pharaoh and/or Abimelech.

But isn't Abraham's behavior what patriarchy is all about—the subordination of women to the power needs of men? Yes, of course. But to use patriarchy here as an explanatory tool doesn't get us very far because we need to know what makes it possible for an individual to participate in a patriarchal reality. And it is my contention that we can't answer this simply in terms of the great benefits of male power that patriarchy provides, because those benefits are great only if they provide what human beings really want. Yet power is *not* what Abraham the child originally wanted—his is not the story of a worshipper of power and control. For power and control his path is clear: cooperate with his father and the political/religious system of his time, inherit his father's idol-manufacturing business, and become the next generation of patriarchy in Ur. But Abraham wants something more. He is troubled by his recognition that something is fundamentally wrong in the universe. And that makes him leave his society and seek something else.

In the Torah when God first addresses Abraham, it is with the injunction to leave behind the world from which he came and to try to find something very new. *Lech lecha me'artzecha, u'mee'moladateecha u'mee beyt avicha el ha'aretz asher ar'eka*—Get thee out of your land and your homeland and your father's house to the land that I will show you. (Genesis 12:1) There is no possibility of reforming the old world, God seems to indicate to Abraham. No set of steps will make it possible for him to live in peace with the place from which he came. He must get out, break with his country, his homeland, his father's house. The demand to leave the old order by going to something that is not only new, but indeterminate—this is the first command faced by the first Jew. If Jews have been "wandering" ever since, they have been wandering toward the reality that we can transcend the cruelty and pain of the places from which we came.

Yet in the deepest sense, Abraham continually fails to live up to this command. Physically he is able to cross the river, to become an *ivri* or "Hebrew." Theologian Rachel Adler points out that to be a crosser of boundaries, to break the normal barriers and to pass beyond the established constraints—this is the root meaning of the word *ivri*. Abraham is the first boundary smasher who does not recognize the constraints of "reality," who rejects what is and seeks what ought to be. To the extent that Jews have internalized this cultural and religious legacy—to be the Hebrews or boundary smashers who go beyond the "is" and fight for the "ought"—we become children of Abraham and he becomes our ancestor.

And yet Abraham, like all of his children throughout the ages, cannot fully live up to the command. He gets out of the corrupt land whence he came, and the painful and oppressive childhood of his father's house. But he can't get the oppression and corruption out of himself. In the deepest sense, he cannot leave his father's house. He remains loyal to the insensitivity and pain that have been inflicted upon him. The failure of recognition that he experiences with his own father, the betrayal of human caring and connection, will now be acted out on others. So Abraham turns his back on Sarah.

Not only are some of Abraham's actions perverse, but so are the actions of those people who told this story and managed to leave out the full story of Sarah. We will never know how many women told the story differently, because the text that we have received gives us only traces of who Sarah was, her power, her sense of mission, her frustration at being with a man who could be so full of contradictions, so full of transcendence and yet so deeply a product of his own social conditioning, so unable to recognize who Sarah, our foremother, was. I mourn the absence of Sarah's story. If Jewish renewal succeeds, Jews will never again leave out the perspective of women.

The Torah story tells how Sarah, unable to give Abraham progeny, encourages him to have relations with the Egyptian slave-woman Hagar, who bears Abraham's son Ishmael. Yet Sarah's jealousy of Hagar leads her to drive Hagar and Ishmael away. Abraham allows it. The emotional deadness within him allows him to distance himself from the whole reality that the woman he has slept with and the son she has borne to him may soon perish in the desert.

How can our people begin its religious history with such a monumental failure? Abraham's first son, Ishmael, is discarded and ignored. The pain resulting from that absence of recognition will reverberate through the ages. According to the tradition, Ishmael is the father of the Arabs. Islam identifies with him. Perhaps partially in reaction to

Abraham's actions, Islam took many of the ideas of the Bible yet managed to demonize the Jews, and sometimes to oppress us in Islamic lands. It is only in the most current period, with the agreement of mutual recognition between Palestinians and Israelis, that the possibility of healing this first misrecognition appears.

But there is more to the story than Abraham's emotional distancing. Just as Abraham managed to transcend the deadness that surrounded him in his idolatrous culture and so could emerge from the furnace into which he had been thrown, in two Torah stories he is able to transcend the logic of the world as constituted.

The first such Torah story about Abraham is widely known. God tells Abraham that S/He will destroy Sodom, the city of the plain that is the living embodiment of evil and insensitivity. When Abraham hears of the level of destruction that is about to come upon the earth, he challenges God to defend His/Her actions. After all, it was precisely the absence of compassion and the prevalence of cruelty that made Abraham rebel in his childhood and leave his homeland. No matter how imperfectly he has managed to stay true to his own ideals, no matter how much the logic of the world and his own childhood have combined to make him lose touch with his original rebellion against cruelty, Abraham now reasserts his deepest vision of what the world ought to be like. In a striking argument Abraham questions whether God has not forgotten the spark of compassion that is central to God's Being. "Will not the judge of all the earth deal justly?"

In this Torah story we have Abraham challenging God, just as he had challenged Terah, insisting upon the possibility of compassion, reminding God that there must be attentiveness to human suffering. We can imagine Abraham having this argument with the voice of God within as he witnesses what must otherwise have been the incomprehensible event of massive earthquake and destruction. After all, the God for whom he left his childhood home cannot be a God who is indifferent to human suffering.

It may have been easier to show some feeling and identification with Sodom than with those closer to home (like Ishmael). Abraham has less invested in Sodom, and its destruction may not raise for him a direct confrontation with the internalized pain of his childhood. So he can challenge the evil in the world without yet having to face the evil within himself. But the Akedah—the binding of Isaac for sacrifice—is quite a different matter.

The Akedah has become one of the central events of Jewish religious history, but I believe that its meaning has been lost over the centuries, replaced with interpretations quite different from those that may have originally indicated Abraham's greatness.

Abraham, the boy who was thrown into the flames, the child who was so deeply abandoned and betrayed by his father, is finally blessed with a son, Isaac, by his elderly wife Sarah. And yet Abraham has never finally broken with the pain of his own childhood, the emotional deadness, and the need to master that reality. The repetition compulsion that shapes all of us suddenly makes its tragic reappearance in Abraham's life. And so, like so many of those in the land that he left, Abraham hears the voices of the gods of his past, now in the voice of God, telling him to do to his own son what was done to him. As he was thrown into the fire, so he will pass on the pain to his own beloved. "Take your son, your only son, the one whom you love, Isaac, and offer him in burnt offering in the place I will show you."

In this moment Abraham must confront the central problem facing every religion and every historical manifestation of God in the world: the difficulty in separating the voice of God from the legacy of pain and cruelty that dominates the world and is embedded in our psyches.

The greatness of Abraham is *not* that he takes his son to Mount Moriah, the Temple mount (the place where today stand both the Western Wall sacred to Jews and the Dome of the Rock sacred to Islam), so that he can sacrifice his son. No. The greatness of Abraham is that he doesn't go through with it. As he looks into the eyes of the son he has bound for slaughter, he can now overcome the emotional deadness that allowed him to cast Ishmael off into the desert. At the very last moment, Abraham hears the true voice of God, the voice that says, "Don't send your hand onto the youth and don't make any blemish." Don't do it, Abraham, says God. You can break the pattern of passing on to the next generation the pain and cruelty that you have suffered. This is the moment of transcendence; the moment in which Abraham finally accepts as real the commandment that started his journey, to leave his father's house. The real God of the universe is not the voice of cruelty that he had experienced and heard in childhood; it is rather a God of compassion and justice who does not command the sacrifice of the innocent.

Startlingly, the text itself points to two different voices that Abraham has heard, not *one* voice that has changed its mind. In Hebrew, when the text talks about the voice that tells Abraham to take his son, it is *ha'elohim* (which could be translated, "the gods"). But the voice that tells Abraham *not* to lay his hand on the young boy is a messenger of YHVH, the four letters that Jewish tradition identifies with the embodiment of God as the Transformer and Liberator from Egypt. It is YHVH who tells Abraham that the chain of pain can be broken—and that makes it possible for Abraham to recognize Isaac as another human being created in the image of God, and hence infinitely precious.

THE DANGER IN BREAKING THE CHAIN OF PAIN

It is this moment of breaking the chain of necessity—transcending the psychological repetition pattern which makes us do unto the next generation that which was done to us—that makes Abraham the father of our people. No wonder that Jews read this story on Rosh Hashanah, the holiday on which Jewish tradition tells us we can wipe our own slates clean and begin again. The liturgy for the Jewish New Year tells us clearly that the past events in our lives do not ultimately and completely have to bind us, limit us, make us less than we could and should be. If Abraham could transcend the voices of his childhood, the tradition is telling us, so can we! Our personal lives and our collective lives can be radically reconstructed. Abraham's choice becomes the paradigm for our choice: just as he managed to transcend his past, so can we. Nor are the social implications hidden: the Rosh Hashanah liturgy explicitly presents us with the utopian possibility as a real possibility—that God will govern the earth, that the kingdoms of arrogance will be utterly destroyed, that righteousness and goodness will triumph. Written at the time when the king of Persia called himself "the King of Kings," the prayer insists that the *King* of the King of Kings actually runs the world. It is a revolutionary message: all systems of oppression can be toppled.

And it was understood as such by the rulers of the world, who found Judaism anathema. By choosing to stay in the Jewish world and to continue its revolutionary message, Jews understood that they were de facto making a choice of putting their children into situations where they would face persecution and possibly even death. The very act of adhering to the Jewish way of life and rearing one's children accordingly becomes a mini binding of our own Isaacs. Wasn't this, then, the ultimate irony: to bring our children into a revolutionary people was to subject them to the very cruelty in the world whose nonnecessity we were proclaiming? We ourselves were making our children vulnerable to oppression, assault, rape, homelessness, expulsion, and murder, and we were doing this in the name of staying true to our God, just as Abraham was sacrificing Isaac in the name of his God. Nor were the Jews always passive victims in this process: we were often a cantankerous force in the ancient world, challenging the power of Rome and other imperial systems, having learned from our own history that oppression was neither necessary nor inevitable.

But when our message provoked the heavy hand of imperial oppression and we were subjected to intense physical persecution, the meaning of the Akedah was transformed in popular Jewish consciousness. Abraham's greatness was remembered for his willingness to sacrifice his son, rather than his ability to transcend what I am calling the voices of pain and cruelty. Abraham became "the knight of faith"—in Kierkegaard's imagery, the man who could defy the rational constraints of the world to loyally obey the command of his God. This construal of Abraham made it possible for many Jews to understand their own religious and political persecution and choose martyrdom or risk of death, seeing in that choice a repetition of Abraham's faith. Generations of Jews, confronted with the choice of giving up their Jewishness or facing death, chose martyrdom—a death that could sanctify the Name of God (*kidushat ha'Shem*)—by their insistence on remaining faithful to God's commandments. These martyrs kept alive the stubborn spirit of defiance to a world of oppression. And their example has encouraged Jews throughout the ages to subject themselves to pain and oppression rather than give up the message of Judaism.

And yet, in the process, some of the message was lost. The original message was that cruelty is not inevitable—it could be overcome. But by the time the Jews faced the overwhelming power of Greece and Rome, many found it hard to remain witnesses to this truth. The world seemed so powerfully to be giving another message: that cruelty is endemic. So instead we get a different kind of reading of Torah, one that sees this cruelty as part of God's will, so that our task is to be faithful to God's cruelty but to disallow human cruelty. This is a compromise position, not one that gave in to Greek or Roman imperialism, but one that rejected their power. In this reading, Abraham's greatness becomes his ability to accept the cruelty that God intends in the world (read: the triumph of various forms of imperialism), but to reject the gods of Greece or Rome and to stay loyal to our one God. To the extent that this reading of the texts becomes authoritative, Jews shift their focus from Judaism as a religion of transformation and begin to construct it as a religion that accepts the evil of the world, and retains faith that there is a God who gives meaning to the evil and will ultimately redeem the world in ways that we cannot understand and in a manner that has little to do with our actions.

My interpretation of the text proclaims that the pain and suffering in the world are not ultimately part of God's plan or God's will. We may have to be prepared to sacrifice ourselves and our children, *not* because God is cruel, but because the flawed human world generates cruelty and leads some people to hurt those who want the world to be different. And no one gets more hurt than those who proclaim to the world that violence and pain are not necessary, that it all can be changed, that what has been done to us need not be passed on to others. The Jews have experienced some of the worst oppression of any group in human history precisely because we proclaimed that suffering and barbarity could be overcome.

For many Jews who are faced with the overwhelming cruelty of the world, it seems more plausible to reject my reading and to believe that it was really God who ordered Abraham to sacrifice Isaac, and that their own sacrifices are somehow sanctioned as part of God's. It may be easier to face pain if one believes that this is what God wants, if the evil is somehow part of God's plan for the world or God's plan for the Jews or God's test for the Jews. So if we have to suffer in order to be true witnesses to God, why not attribute that agony to God rather than see it as a consequence of some stupid and evil people?

Yet I reject this view of God. What kind of a God would order what Abraham heard ordered? It is not a God very different from the gods that Abraham supposedly left behind. Abraham's problem is our problem: to distinguish between the word of God and the unconscious legacy of pain presenting itself as if it were the voice of God. The moment at which Abraham is able to distinguish between these two voices is the moment in which he hears God telling him to not pass on the pain to his son. Hearing *that* God, the God he experienced as a young man, the God that led him to reject the world of his childhood, is what makes Abraham the father of the Jewish people. It was to *that* God that we, the Jewish people, bound ourselves on Mount Moriah, precisely by believing that the pain and cruelty manifest in so many aspects of the world need not govern the world and need not govern our own internal lives.

Judaism does not begin with a human being who is the embodiment of love and goodness and full transcendence. It begins with a human being who is conflicted, who hears different voices, who has trouble knowing which really is the voice of God. It begins in the real world, the world of empires and ruling classes and parents who become the instruments for delivering to children the legacy of unresolved pain and hurt, as well as the possibilities for transcendence and freedom and love. Here Abraham stands out as the being whose life gives us the barest hint, yet enough to be a message of hope, that it is possible to break the chain of necessity, that we do not have to pass on to the next generation what was done to us. And for this reason, Abraham is our father, the founder of the Jewish people.

WHAT MAKES MUTUAL RECOGNITION POSSIBLE?

What actually happened when Abraham lifted the blade to plunge into his son? Was it the look in his son's eyes that suddenly awakened Abraham? A look of terror, fear, shock, betrayal? Or perhaps a look of trust and faith that whatever his father was doing must be all right? These looks would have been similar to what other children had given their fathers before they were brought to the slaughter, and yet those looks had not changed anything. What was it that allowed Abraham to understand the look from Isaac as the look of another human being? What made it possible for him to see Isaac as someone whose right to live and right to his own experience of God was just as legitimate as the message of the *elohim* who had told Abraham to sacrifice Isaac?

Whatever that Force is that makes possible this moment of transcendence, this breaking of the repetition compulsion, is what I call God, or what the Jewish tradition calls YHVH, the not-to-be-pronounced four letters that later Christian texts mistranslated as "Jehovah." God is the Force in the universe that makes transcendence and freedom possible.

Every fiber of Being, every cell in the universe, every moment, is permeated by the thunder and fire of this Force, a passion and energy that pulsates through all Being. Sometimes we experience it as the breath of all life, and the liturgists have talked about it as the soul of all life. Each word is wildly inadequate to describe it, and so my teacher

Abraham Joshua Heschel used to talk of it as the Ineffable. It is this aspect of Being which transcends all our categories and defies all our expectations, because its essence is radical freedom and necessarily beyond all our categories. It is this Force toward health, toward goodness, toward holiness, that does not obey the "rules," does not act in a lawlike manner, but rather enables us to break the expectations, to transcend the patterns of the past toward what could and should be.

For the past hundreds of years human thought has been dominated by a model of science that sought regularity and public observability in all phenomena. That which was not subject to public verification and repeatable experiments was seen as unworthy of our public attention, and perhaps even meaningless. No wonder that the radically unique, the aspect of freedom and transcendence and the breaking of repeatable cycles, seemed to violate science and thus to have no legitimate place in the public discourse of sophisticated and serious intellectuals. But in the past hundred years, especially toward the end of the twentieth century, this model of science has begun to break down. Particularly in areas concerned with human behavior, scientists and psychoanalytic observers are now beginning to modify previous theories that overly emphasized the pulls toward pathology and the repetition compulsion in human life. For example, psychiatrist Joe Weiss and his colleagues at Mount Zion Hospital in San Francisco have argued that we can best understand the behavior of psychotherapy clients as the unconscious drive toward psychological health that seeks to overcome the patterns of the past—a far cry from previous approaches to psychiatry that tended to focus more exclusively on the unconscious drives toward pathology. This pull toward health is part of what I am talking about when I discuss the God of transcendence. I imagine that people in similar fields will start to discover this health-oriented or transcendence-oriented aspect of human behavior. What they will be discovering is one dimension of the human behavioral consequence of being created in the image of God and having the capacity to hear God's revelation, the voice of God that makes us aware of our capacity to be free and to move toward the dimensions of our being that are most loving, caring, and other-recognizing.

Evil, violence, and cruelty are possible only to the extent that we fail to recognize the other as subject (or, in theological language, fail to recognize the other as equally created in the image of God). For Abraham to break the chain of necessity in which this evil is passed from generation to generation, he had to be able to see the other as godlike, as a being worthy of respect and awe. Transcendence, then, is not merely a political or ethical phenomenon—it is also a spiritual reality, an ability to recognize the God in one another. Transcendence includes understanding

- that we do not have to do what we have been taught to do;
- that we do not have to treat one another in the way we have been treated;
- that we are radically free to remake the world and remake our relations with one another;
- that in meeting one another we stand in front of a divine reality, a reality of another being as alive and spiritual and free and real and subject to pain and joy as we are, and hence a person who can be loved but who must not be made into an object or lessened in any way.

Recognition of our capacity for transcendence brings us face to face with the ways that we and others are embodiments of Divinity.

Yet human freedom also makes possible a misrecognition, and hence cruelty, distortion, and evil.

RECOGNITION AND MISRECOGNITION

Recognition—to be known and affirmed by an other, to be understood, seen, loved—is a basic human need. We need that recognition from one another and from God, and we need to be recognized by ourselves and one another *as* embodiments of God.

The force of this mutual recognition operates somewhat the way gravitational forces work: every single isolated being is attracted to every other, to the extent that each is filled with the spirit of God and capable of seeing the other as similarly filled. Our potential to be this way operates as a force from the future into the present, pulling us toward all that we can be, so that we become the kind of people who can potentially embody this spirit of God and hence potentially be drawn into the web of love that attracts all such beings.

But from earliest infancy we are faced with social arrangements and familial realities that undermine our ability to experience mutual recognition or to recognize the God within ourselves. Social theorist Peter

Gabel, in his public lectures and in an unpublished Ph.D. thesis, has given a cogent explanation of how this occurs. Most infants are *misrecognized* by parents. Parents deny their infant's reality in part because to recognize the freedom and subjectivity of the child would be to remind oneself of one's own freedom and subjectivity, which most of us deny in order to fit into the "real" world as currently constituted. The parents themselves have undergone a long history of being underconfirmed to the point that they now misrecognize themselves as beings who can be only what they have actually become. Growing up has come to mean learning to fit into roles defined by others, to adopt the traits and dispositions that make one acceptable to one's parents and the surrounding world. In this process we learn to accept the currently constituted world as fixed and immutable, and the futility of challenging it. As Peter Gabel has argued, we settle for distorted forms of recognition offered by our parents because we desperately need *some* form of recognition and emotional nurturance, even if it is bought at the price of becoming accomplices in the denial of our deeper need for authentic recognition. Buying love from one's parents through accepting their world as they construe it, the child constitutes for itself a socially validated identity. This necessary denial of one's subjectivity for the sake of acceptance often produces rage, the source of which the child cannot fully understand. Sometimes the child feels guilty or ashamed not to be appreciating all that it is being given by loving parents, and does its best to bury the rage that it doesn't understand. And when that rage emerges again, in school or in adult life, we sometimes interpret this as experiential proof that there "really is" evil in the world, since we know of our own "dark side."

The reason we are so willing to blame the evil in the universe on God, or on some innate disposition that constitutes our "human nature," is because of our immense fear of confronting the possibility that the actual evil we have experienced in the world is *not* necessary. In some ways, it's easier to deal with the pain that we've faced in our lives if we think that there was no other possibility, that this just *is* what it is to be a human being. It becomes much more painful if one recognizes that the pain need not have been there, and was. The brutalized throughout history have found it easier to think that the universe was intentionally imposing pain on them, rather than face the even more upsetting notion that their pain really resulted from the evil actions of others, and was *not* part of some unchangeable divine scheme that had transcendent purpose. It becomes even harder if one has to recognize that it is sometimes one's own parents who are the immediate conveyers of unnecessary pain. Hard, in part, because for most people throughout most of human history, the instinct to cry out in anger at parental abuse has been repressed through parental violence or threat of violence during childhood.

The thought that one's parents are acting inappropriately or cruelly has often been far too scary to entertain seriously. Moreover, since many children simultaneously intuit in their parents not only the cruelty but also a deep fear and vulnerability, there has been a desire on the part of many to "protect" their parents by justifying the cruelty, for example by developing stories about how one as a child really "deserved" to be punished, ignored, misrecognized emotionally, or in extreme cases physically abused, because of some alleged lack in oneself or some way in which one was essentially bad. People who have suffered emotional or physical abuse have often developed various metaphysical or religious conceptions that make it "appropriate" that there should be so much pain, so as to deflect their attention away from perpetrators whom it might be too painful to confront.

In my practice as a psychotherapist I've listened to some clients who denounce social-change movements as "naive" or "unsophisticated" because these movements fail to recognize the "dark side of reality," or "the inevitability of evil," or "the complexity of human motivation with its self-seeking and selfish dimensions," or some other attempt to pin the problems of the world on some innate aspect of human beings. Invariably, the client eventually uncovers some aspect of his or her own parents or other close figures who were perpetrating some kind of emotional or physical abuse; but even then, the client resists feeling anger and instead blames "human nature" or something of the sort. For many of these people, it was just too scary to notice that something wrong had been done to themselves when they were relatively defenseless, that it was done *not* because of something that they had done to deserve it and *not* because of some innate distortion in human nature, but because these particular parents had made these particular wrong or hurtful choices. It rarely occurs to them that, once they *do* allow themselves to see this, then they could move beyond anger to understanding and compassion for their parents as well, who were themselves part of social and psychological realities that made them under-recognized, enraged, and hence unconsciously ready to pass on the pain to their children.

Yet many people in our society don't get to this point, but are stuck in a depressive acceptance of their currently underrecognized selves, meanwhile nurturing hidden stories that they've told themselves about why they actually deserve little more than what they currently are receiving from the world. Much energy is invested in containing their rage—whose origins they don't understand and whose existence fills them with fear. They do their best to stay away from delving too deeply into their own only partly conscious feelings. Yet there is always a nagging sense that something is wrong, that this isn't all that life can or should be; and that is why societies based on misrecognition are always fundamentally unstable—because they depend on a denial that human beings are created in the image of God.

Our sense that something is wrong with the world gets expressed obliquely in the tremendous excitement people feel at the birth of new children. We sense that something new is happening. The child's world has not yet been fixed and deadened in the way that ours has. Even in societies where children's worth is measured in terms of their ability to help improve the material well-being of the family, the child's birth is often celebrated as a joyful event not just for financial reasons, but because it represents a deeper rebirth of hope.

Yet the very possibilities associated with childbirth also evoke terror, anger, and envy in us.

- The terror: that the world with all of its pain and frustration need not be the way that it is, and that therefore all of us who have built our lives to accommodate to that world are living a lie. To undo that lie would require not only a momentary flash of recognition but also a monumental and uncharted struggle against all the ways that the world's "normal" interactions have been constituted, all the ways that we make our livings and deal with others. So much easier, then, to repress that awareness.

- The anger: that to recognize this child you must invalidate and struggle against all that you have become—and what right does this being have to awaken those feelings and place upon you that kind of demand?

- The envy: that the child need not accept the alienated compromises that have so limited your own world.
- The resolution: not to allow yourself to be aware of this "reality"-transcending aspect of the child, to make sure that the child "fits into" the already established world, to ignore the being who is before you. And to be as detached from this child as your parents were from you, reassuring yourself that this level of closeness is all that could be, that its attempts to be recognized as a free and equal being are really not happening, and its manifestations of holiness are not really present.

The child grows up experiencing the misrecognition, and this becomes a constantly accessible background pain and sense of distortion that makes the world feel not quite right, a background pain that is often drowned out by the foreground pain of feeling that oneself is not quite right. A huge amount of adult energy is then expended on various techniques to drown out the pain one feels about not being quite right. Psychic numbing, denial, "not being able to understand" all kinds of things, and many other techniques are mobilized in defense so that one need not be aware of what one suspects is one's deepest truth—that one is not okay. Yet that hidden "deep truth" is actually not true, but a result of a process that people have gone through in their childhoods, the exposure of which would lead to real anger against parents, and eventually against the entire social order.

All this threatens to unravel when one is confronted with the anger in one's own child, since that child is now calling into question all the choices that have led to one's own current state of psychic numbing. Rather than allow the child to disrupt one's own pattern of accommodation, parents frequently respond with anger to the child's sense of injustice, thereby forcing the child to repress that awareness as the very condition of gaining love and approval. Desperate for whatever love may still be available if one represses one's anger, the child accommodates itself to the levels of falsity and misrecognition that are available. This, we are taught, is reality, and our task is to accommodate to it.

Accommodation to this conception of reality requires, in Peter Gabel's phrase, denying desire (our fundamental desire for connection and mutual recognition) so that the child becomes acceptable to adults as someone not threatening to tear their world apart. The price of getting the love available from parents is to deny, first to them and ultimately to oneself, that something is fundamentally absent and deeply unreal in the connection. And if essentially good parents nevertheless have this dark side, perhaps believing that God also has this dark side is not so strange. Perhaps it was God's dark side that not only asked Abraham to sacrifice his son but also ordered Moses to kill all the inhabitants of the Promised Land who might corrupt God's chosen people or keep them from their legacy.

To be sure, a part of us is also aware that something is wrong and deeply desires a different kind of world. Yet through most of human history the level of repression of desire has been so massive and total that we have never had much opportunity to experience it, and instead have accepted the world as it is with an automatic and depressed resignation.

Only in the past ten thousand years at best, and probably most noticeably in the past thirty-five hundred years, have societies evolved to the point where fundamental material needs are adequately met and human energies are available for less constricted and more fulfilling connections among people. The fundamental emotional/erotic need for recognition can now emerge more fully. But when it emerges, this need for recognition plays a subversive role, potentially disrupting the accommodations made to the world of oppression. The absence of recognition becomes the precondition for the possibility of class societies, for any one group oppressing another. Seeing one another as fully human, fully alive, fully embedded with the spirit of God, would make it much more difficult for us to enslave others or turn our back on their suffering.

It is in this context that Abraham enters history, aware that indeed something *is* fundamentally wrong, unwilling to accept idolatry. Abraham can sense something more in the universe, some greater potentiality than what may be manifest in the worship of what is—power, beauty, wealth, etc. In breaking the idols he is symbolically trying to break through to Terah, his father, to say: "This dead matter that is used to justify an oppressive social order is not real, and you and I don't have to remain stuck in it, do we?" The inability of his father to respond, to see the life energy and reality in his son and to say, "Yes, son, something more is possible," means that instead he has to see his son as the problem. For Abraham's father to break through social conventions would require a level of emotional, spiritual, and political aliveness and honesty that is too overwhelming and threatening. So Terah cannot recognize Abraham, and thus Abraham has to reject and transcend the world of his father.

THE TERROR OF BREAKING FROM CRUELTY

The legacy of pain and cruelty that is part of the history of human relationships reasserts itself as Abraham follows his dream. Yet what makes Abraham in touch with God is the extent to which he can imagine a reality in which that legacy of emotional and spiritual deadness need not govern his experience of the world.

Making this kind of break with one's parents and with "normal reality" is dangerous. Most human beings are too scared to make the break, and instead cling to their existing pictures of themselves and of the world as necessarily involved with pain, injustice, cruelty, violence, and evil.

The very thought that the world, including our childhoods, could have been different is so overwhelming that many people will do anything *not* to understand it. The very idea of thinking about childhood in this way gets dismissed as "psychobabble" by people too scared to consider the possibilities being discussed. The keepers of the established orders of cruelty are so desperate to avoid any consideration of an alternative way of creating society that they define as childish, stupid, or incoherent any view that envisions an alternative.

To be "mature" on their account is to learn to accept that the distortions and cruelty and lack of recognition we experienced as children are fundamental to how the world is. It's not that the world has some lack in it because human beings have not yet fulfilled their potential or have misused their freedom. Rather, the world's flaws are fundamental, created by God, part of the structure of necessity. Like moths drawn to the fire that will kill them, most of us are drawn into dreamlike states in which the evil of the world seems inevitable, and those who seek to eliminate evil are fools. No wonder, then, that every prophet is castigated, stoned, threatened, ignored, made into a sideshow, ridiculed, or otherwise discounted.

For those who remain loyal to their parents in this respect, who will not imagine that the way human beings connect with one another could be fundamentally different, the principle of evil in the world has substantive reality.

Out of loyalty to their parents and to their own lives lived in a spirit of resignation and compromise, those who limit their vision are furious at anyone who thinks that the world could be fundamentally different. The logic of their position leads them to side with those who believe that what is important about the Akedah is that Abraham unquestioningly brought his son to the altar in the first place—and that therein lies the glory of Abraham. And no wonder they would see it that way. In their own daily lives and their own childhoods it was precisely this self-sacrifice that was the cost of reconciliation with their own fathers.

Those who are committed to ontologizing evil and cruelty often embrace some variant of the notion that a mysterious paradox is governing the universe. Any theory that does not recognize this fundamental evil and cruelty will seem "simplistic" or "naively rational" or "post-Enlightenment consciousness" or "utopian" or "simplemindedly optimistic." Those who do not acknowledge the inevitability of the forces of evil are dismissed as dreamers whose naivete might lead to gulags or holocausts.

The conservative and neoconservative consciousness that has become a major force in late twentieth-century Western thought is in part a product of this dynamic, in part a product of the (quite legitimate) outrage at a world that seems to confirm their worst suspicions because it embodies in its activities the playing out of violence and cruelty. It's no wonder that the combination of a real world in which cruelty continues to reign and a childhood experience in which we are bound to this cruelty could produce a set of religions, metaphysical and political philosophies, that see all this violence and cruelty as "the nature of reality." This combination accounts for the contemporary popularity of pessimism and cynicism among both liberal and conservative theorists. Yet this way of looking at the world is the opposite of what was revolutionary and foundational to Judaism in the life of Abraham.

I am tempted to say that it was merely the external reality of oppression that led the people of Israel to reconstruct our memory of Abraham's story so that what we found most moving in it was the "recognition" that the world is governed by paradox and irrationality, and our faith in a God who governs despite the paradox and beyond our human understanding. Rather than making the Abraham who challenges God about Sodom and who dares to argue and bargain with God the paradigm for the father of our people, they may have chosen the Akedah as our founding moment precisely because they saw in this moment an affirmation of their own need to suffer the irrationality of the world. Yet I doubt that this choice was merely a failure of nerve precipitated by external reality. More likely, it was the reassertion of the loyalty to our parents that we all experience and to the lives that we have imaginatively and energetically created to sustain ourselves in the face of a loss we only dimly perceive and dread to confront.

And why be hard on ourselves? After all, Abraham himself, the revolutionary par excellence, was still loyal enough to the experience of cruelty and pain that he actually heard the voice of that legacy, the very thing that he had hoped to transcend—and he heard all that *as* the voice of God. Yet we must remember that Abraham's greatness, and the insight that we need to hold on to and build upon, is that ultimately he heard another voice of God, and that second voice allowed him to transcend the past and break the chain of necessity that always threatens to link generations in an embrace of cruelty. The Force that makes possible that break, the force that makes possible recognition of our common humanity, that is the Force we call God. It was at such a moment of recognition that Abraham discovered God, and it is in testimony to the possibility of such moments that Jewish renewal seeks to reclaim the voice of God who told Abraham not to continue the violence, cruelty, and evil in the world.

CHAPTER THREE

MOSES AND THE REVOLUTIONARY COMMUNITY

THE FEAR OF DEATH

Not every ancient culture is suffused with a fear of death. There are some cultures in which death is accepted and integrated into the ongoing life of a community. For some ancient peoples, the group or clan, not the individual self, was probably the source of each person's identity, and people probably didn't have the kind of differentiated sense of self that makes possible worrying about individual mortality. With the emergence of class societies, riven by sharp divisions and oppression, the harmony and integration of clan-based communities began to dissolve, and individuals began to distinguish themselves from the larger societies in which they lived. As this individuation took place, people began to identify themselves as separate beings with separate fates—and to worry about their personal survival.

While there may be some level of sadness that individuals feel when faced with the prospect of leaving loved ones and community, and that the loved ones and community feel when they lose an individual, the desperation and denials of death that have become virtually synonymous with the human condition in the past several thousand years are not built into the structure of necessity. When people feel happily integrated in a society that has a spiritually and ethically rich communal purpose, they tend to be less traumatized or obsessed with their own individual deaths and more concerned about the survival of the community. To the extent that people feel unfulfilled, oppressed, or divorced from a framework of meaning and purpose provided by their community, the fear of personal death may take on much greater importance. In such societies people become invested in myriad ways of overcoming death. They look for an understanding of the meaning of life. They might build businesses, corporations, or empires; write books and songs; create religions or philosophical systems to assure themselves that somehow they will be able to transcend the meaninglessness of the world as currently organized.

Societies become death-oriented to the extent that people accept the alienated status quo as unchangeable and believe that the only meaning they can find must be purely personal. In that case, death threatens the meaning of one's life—so many seek to sustain meaning through personal immortality. Moreover, to the extent that existing systems of evil and cruelty appear to be unchangeable, one can hope only to find a more caring and loving world in some other transcendent reality.

Moses grew up as part of the ruling elite of a death-oriented society. Egypt had become the greatest empire in the world and, in the process, the greatest exploiter and oppressor of peoples. Faced with the pain and suffering that their social order inflicted on the vast majority of the population, Egyptian rulers developed a theory of personal immortality. The construction of the pyramids provided a religious guarantee that in a future life the rulers of Egypt would enjoy the same power as in this one, built on the backs of thousands of slaves whose lives were filled with pain and suffering (some of whom were killed and placed in the pyramids so that they could serve as slaves when the rulers came back to life).

Moses' genius was in being able to see through the most elaborate and powerful system of organized oppression that the world had yet known, to understand the lot of the oppressed, and to identify with them. His moral brilliance was in being able twice to renounce the good life available to him, first when he slew an Egyptian who was mercilessly beating an Israelite slave (thus creating the circumstance in which he had to flee the palace and leave Egypt); second when he left his life in Midian to return to Egypt to lead his fellow Jews to freedom. His spiritual brilliance was in recognizing that the God of the universe is a God that makes possible our transcendence of slavery and oppression and our ability to create a very different kind of world. Numerous scholars have attempted to identify Moses' achievement with that of the Egyptian Pharaoh Ahkenaton, who had introduced a kind of monotheism to Egypt. Yet Moses' contribution was not in identifying the right *number* of gods, but in his conception of what God is like.

Moses' God is acutely attuned to the suffering and pain of the world and will make change possible. Death is not necessary for liberation from pain and oppression; the cruelty of the world can be dealt with and meaning can be built in *this* world.

SALVATION ISN'T ONLY INTERNAL

The God revealed to Moses at the burning bush passionately insists on saving the entire people of Israel from their fate as slaves. God is available, actively calling to us from the fire of the burning bush—a fire that does not destroy but energizes—to join in transforming the world. Our task is to hear the voice, to recognize God's availability to us, to make space for it in our lives. This mystical experience is tied to an ethical and political awareness in a way not typical of most mystical systems.

Moses' path is a unique blending of the spiritual and mystical truths with an ethical and political awareness. What Moses understands is the true nature of the universe: that spiritual enlightenment and moral obligation to struggle against oppression are not two separate things; they are inextricably united.

Some repressive orders create "spirituality" as a separate part of one's being, split off from life, or narrowly restricted to special experiences. Religious practices and specialists in spiritual or mystical experience emerge, and these specialists validate the social reality that allows economic and political oppression, the denial of mutual recognition, the creation of unjust social relations, and the repression of our ethical sensibilities. When this oppressive "spirituality" artificially separates us from our deeper knowledge and sunders the inherent unity of ethical and spiritual reality, we begin to experience the world with a diminished sense of awe and wonder. As a result, we are less willing to sing the song of joy at creation, less able to resonate with the splendor and grandeur of Being. And as this reduction happens, we are more able to fit into spiritual, mystical, and religious systems that provide a narrowly restricted place for our awe and wonder, a restricted language, a delimited set of rituals. Spirituality that was once part of the totality of our experience, intrinsic to our moral sensibilities and our sense of love and connection to every human being, gets split off, narrowed in focus, and created as a distinct arena. Humanity becomes depressed, its language loses its musical tone and becomes more monotone, as this diminished spirituality attempts to reconcile people to a world of oppression.

It is this ethical/spiritual unity that is reclaimed by Judaism. The split between the ethical and the spiritual is not real; it is a mistaken or idolatrous view of the universe. Political struggle for human liberation is not some realm separate from our spirituality, but rather potentially a vehicle through which we get back to the fundamental unity of our spiritual and ethical being. The isolated, narcissistic, materialistic, cynical individual of our day is a momentary distortion that can and must be overcome precisely so that we can be more attuned to our nature as created in the image of God.

Human beings have the capacity to restore this ethical and spiritual unity. The God of the universe has made it so that transcendence and transformation of the world are both possible and necessary. The obligation of those who are spiritually alive, then, is not to pursue their own paths, but to become involved in the struggle, return to Egypt, fight the pharaoh, change the consciousness of the slaves so that they can come to see themselves as potentially free, and lead them through the process through which that transformation can begin to happen.

This is a break with alienated forms of spirituality that do not connect human beings directly and immediately to the struggle for liberation. But this liberation is not narrowly political—it is a liberation from the artificial division between our ethical and spiritual beings, and hence also from religions that validate the grandeur of the universe but make peace with oppressive social realities that keep human beings from actualizing their capacities.

The actualization of those capacities is accomplished not only through social transformation, but also through our individual spiritual and psychological work. There are moments in our lives when the focus on individual spiritual and psychological growth may require so much energy that we cannot fully engage in the social and political struggles. So Moses goes to Midian and for twenty years lives far from the struggle. Living in the desert, raising a family, caring for animals—all may have helped him deepen his own spiritual and psychological readiness for the next stage of spiritual development, when he could integrate his own personal growth with his larger task of being part of the struggle for liberation.

I emphasize this moment because it can sometimes sound as if people committed to revolutionary movements think only in collective and political terms. Deepening one's individual psychological and spiritual resources is an important part of the process of serving God— though given the individualist biases of the contemporary world, we are always in danger of making that part the totality.

THE GOD OF TRANSCENDENCE

Moses finds God, YHVH, at the burning bush. And when he understands that God is asking him to return to Egypt, he is sorely afraid of the task. He argues that he is inadequate. Irrelevant, God retorts; to be the liberator one need not have any specific skills, not even communication skills (Moses stutters!). Moses tries to imagine the difficulties he will have explaining this God to the people who have been enslaved for hundreds of years. Give me your name, at least, says Moses. He wants something concrete to hold on to, something that will make sense to the people. But God responds with a message that shatters Moses' expectations and gives us a deep sense of what we are dealing with. Says God, *Ehyeh asher Ehyeh*. Tell them that Ehyeh sent you."

In the King James Bible, the English translation is "I AM THAT I AM. Tell them that 'I am' sent you." But although this translation is permissible—the ancient Hebrew sometimes uses the future tense to indicate present tense—an equally good and contextually sounder version is to understand that the future tense is being used intentionally, so that the passage should best be understood as "I shall be whom I shall be. Tell them 'I shall be' sent you."

Similarly, the four letters written as the name of God in Hebrew, YHVH—*yud, hey, vav, hey*—traditionally pronounced "Adonai," is a provocative way of indicating the future tense for the verb "to be." HVH—*hey, vav, hey*—can indicate the present tense of to be. So *yud, hey, vav, hey* may be an attempt to say the unsayable within the language—that that which is shall be transformed and be more fully.

These formulations indicate a unique concept of God. Moses is not the first person to recognize spiritual reality. But he is one of the first to hear a voice from the fire of God's passion that requires us to struggle against existing systems of oppression. The ultimate Force governing the world, the Force that has created the entirety of Being, is the energy that presses for transcendence toward a world in which all Being manifests its fullest ethical and spiritual potential, a world in which human beings recognize one another both in our particularity and in our ability to manifest ethical and spiritual possibility. That Force exercises a spiritual pull within all Being to move beyond what it is to what it ought to be. This God is not some fixed entity with a fixed essence, something that can be put into some set of existing categories and delimited. Nor is this God some "order" or principle of regularity of the sort that seventeenth- to nineteenth-century science tried to establish as the ultimate nature of reality. Rather, the God of Moses is a Force that transcends all limits and makes it possible for us to do the same. This God is the Force that makes for the possibility of possibility.

The transcendence made possible by this God is available not just to spiritually talented individuals, but to *all* people and for an entire society. Individual and social transcendence are inherently linked, because spirituality is not some split-off or separable realm, but permeates every aspect of our being and our life together. Conversely, don't expect many individuals to be able to sustain a spiritual life at a higher level of development than the rest of society, because the only way a person can do so is to separate from the rest, turn his or her back on the pain and suffering of others. The kind of spirituality that is thereby achieved is a false or deeply flawed spirituality because it is arbitrarily and hurtfully separated from the kind of ethical awareness and connection to others that the truth of our being demands.

Buddhists sometimes encourage us to "be here now," to live in the present moment and allow ourselves to be fully present to it. To be connected to the God of Israel is also to be present in the moment; but to *really* be present is to be alive to the way in which this moment is pregnant with the possibilities of transformation, bursting with the energies that make for transformation.

The "possibility of possibility" is not some concept of randomness. To say that the God of creation is the God of freedom is to say that, at its core, every part of the world is fundamentally endowed with freedom and transcendence as its essential ingredient. We may not yet fully understand all that is entailed in that concept of God, but Torah and the Jewish tradition are meant to give us some hints of what that meant at one historical moment so that we might extrapolate to other moments.

One meaning is this: If you thought Egypt (or any subsequent system of organized injustice) was based on the fundamental nature of reality, an order that could not be overthrown or overcome because it was an expression of the gods, forget it! No system of oppression is divinely sanctioned or has a chance of lasting. Every oppressive order is based on forcing or convincing human beings to be less than they can be, less than the image of a God of freedom and transcendence and a unique ethical/spiritual unity. No matter how powerful it appears, every social system that does not recognize, promote, and enhance the expression of God within us will turn out to be fundamentally unstable and will eventually be replaced. This insight is the center of the Jewish religion.

THE WAY THINGS ARE IS NOT
THE WAY THEY HAVE TO BE

In its heart, Judaism is a proclamation to the world that the way things are is not the way things have to be. The capacity to transform our world into one of justice and kindness, a world in which our own ability to embody an ethical/spiritual unity is nurtured and enhanced, is a constituent element in how God created the world. Hence, the central story of Judaism is the story of a people who are enslaved and who, because of the principle of freedom that governs the universe, are enabled to become free and to embody the unity of our ethical and spiritual natures.

The Jewish religion is built around this founding story of emancipation. Holy days do not commemorate the conquest of Canaan, the dedication of the Temple, the creation of the Davidic monarchy, or the various military victories of the Israelite kingdom when Jews were enjoying and living their hard-earned freedom. Instead, every Shabbat, once a week, the Jewish people sit and read a portion of the story of liberation. The central religious holiday, Shabbat, reminds us of two closely related realities: *zeycher le'ma'aseh b'ereyshit* (in remembrance of the events of creation) and *zeycher le'tziyat mitzrayim* (in remembrance of going out from Egypt). These two realities are intrinsically connected, because the God of creation is the God of liberation from Egypt.

The central mantra of the Jewish people, the prayer called "Shma," is usually translated: "Hear, O Israel, the Lord our God, the Lord is One." At first glance it doesn't seem to say much—perhaps that we are monotheists, not much more. But in Hebrew the words *Adonai Eloheynu* have deeper meaning if we understand that *Adonai* (YHVH) refers to the aspect of God that embodies the capacity for freedom and transcendence, while *Eloheynu* refers to the aspect of God which is the God of nature, the God who created the universe. In that case, Shma has a very serious and deep meaning: it calls upon us to witness that the God of nature is the God of freedom, that the Creator is the principle of transcendence toward all that the world and human beings can and ought to be. Or, to put it in other language, that the division between spirituality and ethics and politics makes no sense, because the Force that we've come to worship in the realm of the spirit is actually the Force that makes possible and necessary the moral/political transformation of the world.

These ideas sound terrifying to modern ears because spirituality can be used to justify oppressive social orders. In fact, many of us have fought to keep these two realms separate because we didn't want existing forms of oppression to get the benefit of spiritual sanction. But any form of oppression or stunting or misdirecting of human capacities for love, caring, freedom, and creativity are contradictory to the highest spiritual truths of the universe, *not* sanctioned by those truths.

We in the modern world have seen spirituality used in very destructive political ways. When we see some West Bank settlers quoting Torah as justification for random murders of Palestinian civilians, or as proof that the world will always be against us, or when we see God invoked as the basis for settlers' claiming land and water rights without regard to the impact on others, we begin to wonder if we wouldn't be better off with a secularized politics in which spirituality plays no role. But the fact is that that is not an option. Human beings distorted by a history of oppression always have used spiritual categories to justify acts of cruelty. That was true in Abraham's time and in Moses' as well. If all the people committed to healing the world were to stop using religious language, that would *not* stop the others from using it and appropriating the valuable truths accumulated in the religious traditions as a buttress to their cruelty. There is no good reason to cede that language and those truths just because they continue to be misused. On the contrary, there is every reason to insist on developing another way of understanding spiritual reality, one that does not abandon the spir-

itual/political continuum, but one that insists on a different understanding of the message that Moses brought with him to Egypt: that the
gods that were used to sanction cruelty were not the real God. When
Moses discovered *that*, he had discovered the same God that told
Abraham that he did not have to pass on the cruelty to Isaac.

BEING GOD'S WITNESS

In the Torah scroll, the last letter of the first word of Shma is written
large, and the last letter of the last word is written large—together they
spell *eyd* or witness, as though to remind us that the Jew's goal is to be
witness to this reality.

"What's really at stake here? So what if the God of nature is the God
of history? Around this you build a religion?" Yes. Because it is a
powerful claim when we start to explore its consequences.

First, the idea leads to the possibility of creating history. If it is
possible to remake the world in accord with a notion of the good, then
the central human story is about how we are doing in any given
historical period in relation to what we could and should be doing.
History is not simply the endless repetition of themes that are necessarily always the same. Instead of eternal recurrence of some natural
cycles, we can tell a story in which events become in part a consequence of choice. Nor is history simply an endless gathering up of
neutral facts: the Jewish notion of history presupposes that there is
some purposefulness, not only in what actually happened but in what
could have happened. If human beings have the capacity to live lives of
transcendence toward the good, then the extent to which they don't,
the reasons why, becomes a story from which we can learn.

A sense of history is thus the first consequence of the concept *Adonai
Eloheynu*.

The second is an incredible optimism about the world: ultimately,
good will triumph. This is *not* some narrowly Pollyannish view that
humanity is moving steadily toward good, or that some political party or
religion will bring about good, or that some vanguard exists that fully
understands the real laws of history. When Jewish theology gets reduced to these simpleminded views of progress toward the good, it is
easy to dismiss it as naive post-Enlightenment fantasizing. As Abraham
Joshua Heschel used to point out, the naive faith in science or an
inevitable and linear "progress" was definitively disproved by the reali-

ties of Nazi and Communist domination, not to mention the international "immiseration" caused by three centuries of Western imperialism imposed upon Third World societies. The belief in progress has all too often functioned as a convenient cover for ruling elites. The result is that most of us bear the inconvenience and cost of their "progress" as they reshape the world in ways that deplete the ozone, consume the earth's resources, and commodify culture and human relationships.

Judaism, instead, proclaims a more grounded optimism. Psalm 92, recited as the *main* psalm for Shabbat, and hence repeated in both the evening and morning services every Shabbat, affirms such a grounded optimism: "An empty-headed man cannot know, nor does a fool understand this: When the wicked bloom like grass, and all the evildoers blossom, it is so that they may be destroyed forever . . . the righteous will blossom like a date palm, like a cedar in Lebanon, he will grow tall . . . they will be fruitful in old age, they will be full of sap and freshness." The world is not simply neutral, a blind reality in which anything can happen. Evil may triumph in the short run, sometimes masquerading as progress or as the forward march of history, and the short run may be thousands and thousands of years. Ultimately, however, the God energy in the universe will cause a tilt toward the triumph of the good. In the post-Holocaust era it is easy to make this message seem silly, shallow, fanciful, or just another instance of human hubris. Yet it means something deeper and truer.

If the universe has at its core the reality of freedom, transformation, transcendence; if what governs the universe is not some force that ensures the triumph of the status quo; and if human beings are made in the image of this Force for transcendence—then we should use our energies to change aspects of the world that we find oppressive, immoral, or unfulfilling. The world could and should be radically remade in accord with our own best understanding of the good.

Torah proceeds to give us a sense of how that good was perceived by our ancestors. They saw their task as directly connected to remaking the social order. *Tzedek, tzedek, tirdof,* Torah proclaims: Justice, justice shalt thou run after (pursue). And love your neighbor as yourself. Don't oppress the stranger—use one standard for yourself and for the other. Take care of the powerless, the orphan, the widow, and again the stranger. Don't be oppressive to animals. Redistribute the land. Don't withhold the wages of those who have done work for you. Make sure the poor have enough to eat. Don't repeat the ways of the oppressor.

Torah predisposes the Jewish people to be sensitive to the oppressed. We were slaves, and we are enjoined not to forget it, and to keep that in mind when we deal with others ("you know the heart of the stranger, for you were strangers in the land of Egypt"). A Jew who remembers this cannot shut her ears to the cry of the oppressed or avert her eyes from the hungry, the homeless, the sick, the poor, the refugees and immigrants, the children who are effectively without parental guidance, the people who are so alienated that they've been driven to alcohol or drugs or other attempts to deaden their minds, the lonely, the emotionally distraught, or the physically or culturally or intellectually impaired.

Of course, people have always had a tendency to feel the pain of these others. But over and over again they have been taught that there is no point in investing too much energy in these causes—after all, the pain of humanity has always been there and always will be. What we see is all that can be.

The Shma proclaims that history is *not* over. It is a matter of faith for the Jew that there can be no end to history without the triumph of the good. We can always tell a false messiah, because the only messiah that would interest us is one that actually brings a triumph of good in the world. Until that happens, our task remains to proclaim the possibility that the world can yet be transformed, must be, and that we will help make that happen.

In later ages, as Jews felt defeated by history, some attempted to transform this view into a more "evenhanded" position in which good and evil would always be in contention, there would never be a triumph of one over the other. But this is certainly not the view of the Bible. Not that the Bible has any simplistic notion of a quick or easy victory for the forces of good. On the contrary, it tells the story of Jewish history in a complicated and nuanced way that does not glorify our heroes but reveals their self-destructive flaws. But neither is there any "ontologization" of evil as Evil. The attempt to transform Judaism into a support system for contemporary political conservatism or pessimism about the long-term possibilities of the triumph of good requires imaginative interpretive jumps that violate the thrust of much of the Biblical texts.

The third consequence of Judaism's claim that God is the Force that not only creates but also assists us in transforming the world is that we are all required to engage in the struggle to change the status quo. Moses is proclaiming a religion in which freedom is possible in *this* world, and consists not only of some changes in individual consciousness. The call to be free is not only a personal and private matter but also a collective and communal one: "Proclaim liberty throughout the land, to all the inhabitants thereof" (Leviticus 25:10) is an unequivocally revolutionary message.

The fourth consequence is that the physical world is so infused with the spirit of God that it participates in the rebellion against oppression. The account in Exodus focuses on plagues and gives the impression that God is an external power who is intervening in nature this one time to save the Israelites. But Torah goes on to proclaim a much fuller version of this notion, in a portion that the later rabbis understood to be an elaboration of the Shma and so attached it in the prayer service: *V'haya Eem Sh'moa*. This section tells us that built into the order of nature is a moral imperative: if people obey God's commandments, create a moral and just order, then the world will work fine. But if they recreate oppression, straying from God's commandments, then there will be ecological catastrophe. Nature is not some neutral arena; it embodies a moral/spiritual reality that cannot long coexist with oppression.

Every fiber of Being is a moral/spiritual/physical continuum, and at every moment a moral/spiritual Force is pulsating through all of Being, aspiring to transcend what is and achieve what ought to be. To believe in the God of Israel is to believe that this is what the world is like. It is a total reorientation to reality, a reorientation that shatters the fixity and "thinglike" Beingness that emerges from a scientistic account of the world. While few scientists have actually endorsed the popular ideology that the world is fixed, lawlike, and governed by an eternal recurrence and circularity of all Being, ideologists and justifiers of the status quo have attempted to use the mantle of science to create a popular consciousness that thinks of the world in these rigid terms. To the extent that people think that the world is fixed and unchanging—except according to natural principles over which human beings have no sway, and over which ethical principles have no impact—they will be more willing to accommodate to this fixity of existing social arrangements.

The claim that there is a God, that this God is YHVH, the Force that makes for the possibility of transcendence of that which is toward that which ought to be, and that YHVH created and runs the universe, shatters for all time the complacency and safety that rulers have felt about their ability and right to run the world.

OUR INNER RESISTANCE TO THE MESSAGE

Other religions share with Judaism the notion that the universe legitimately generates awe, wonder, and radical amazement. But our awe is a response not only to the grandeur and magnificence of the universe, but also the overwhelming recognition that we humans, created in God's image, are charged with healing the world, and have the possibility of transforming toward a moral order. In encountering God they had recognized that this possibility is built into the very foundation of the universe.

This God of freedom and possibility is the good news that Moses brings back to Egypt. Not surprisingly, the Israelite slaves do *not* quite "get" it. It does not fit into their categories, their experience as slaves in imperial Egypt. Although the leaders of the people are ready to believe the message as conveyed to them by Aaron, Moses' brother, who translates the message in a way that the people can hear, they become understandably despondent when Pharaoh increases their burden in response to Moses' first appeal for freedom. The Israelites are impatient, and the increased bondage imposed by Pharaoh in response to their willingness to listen to Moses seems to convince them that nothing is really possible, that the dream of freedom is really just a delusion that will only increase their pain. The first response of the enslaved is cynical realism.

So it is with all of us. Part of the reason we cannot take seriously Torah's message of transcendence and transformation is that we are fearful that it is merely an illusion, and if we act in the world as though things could really be different, we will merely increase our own pain and discomfort, antagonize those with power who will make things worse for us. These fears make the Israelites resist Moses' message.

Every one of us knows how reassuring some connections—or common interests—with the powerful can be, and how terrifying it is to find ourselves heading in a direction at odds with them. Whether we have few material comforts or many, we know that if we decide to challenge the way things are, we will be in considerably worse shape. Our job security will disappear; our friends will feel that they are taking a big risk by remaining our friends; we will be made fun of, not only by those who have power, but by those who are aspiring to power. Some will say that we are crazy, others that we are merely misguided, others that we ourselves are power-crazy. And when we really start to seem like a threat, when we become successful enough so that ruling elites start to worry, we will face overt repression, physical assault, imprisonment, expulsion, torture, or death.

Jews, like anyone who has ever contemplated becoming a union activist, social-change organizer, or critic of the established order, ask whether the risk is worth taking, whether enough can be accomplished to make it worth the personal pain. Sure, things are not good the way they are, but to challenge them might be to do nothing more than to bring down upon ourselves the personal ire of the powerful. Judaism is trying to tell us that it's worth the risk!

This was what faced every Israelite as each asked him/herself, "Should I join this group of people who are going to the wilderness as the means to escape slavery? After all, they have no plan, no sure way of finding economic security or food, no place to go. Do I become one of the homeless and landless to follow an ideal? Do I risk the fleshpots of Egypt for the uncertainties of a life of commitment to a principle and a vision that may not be actualized in my lifetime?" When put this way, it's no wonder that it's not always so easy to take seriously the message of transformation and transcendence inherent in the belief in YHVH.

There's another dimension to why this is so overwhelming. The Biblical conception of God works to undo the sense of safety derived from our daily routines. It suggests that the physical world is infused with transformative possibilities and operates according to spiritual and not just material concerns. *Yir'at ha'Shem,* the fear of God, is really a recognition of the fact that we are surrounded by and enmeshed in a set of spiritual realities that far transcend our capacities to understand.

The seeming fixity and predictability of the world may be an illusion. To the extent that we have drawn our security from seeing the world as predictable and potentially under our control, the notion of a God that allows for and requires transformation seems threatening. That instability may seem even greater when we recognize that every fiber of our being is permeated with this God energy, that the innermost being of every cell in our bodies is pulsating not to the rhythm of fixed regularity but to the song of divine freedom and transcendence. Contemplate the consequences: that our health as individual beings may be intrinsically linked to the health of the total human enterprise and the degree to which it has become a true embodiment of divine energy (i.e., the degree to which we have succeeded in becoming partners with God in healing and transforming the world).

It's clear why this message should be horrifying to ruling elites whose ability to dominate has been sustained in part by their ability to convince us that existing systems of oppression are inevitable and unchangeable. But why should it scare the rest of us? Because most of us have adopted a strategy for coping with our own experience of alienation and frustration of our highest spiritual capacities that involves accepting this frustration as a natural part of reality. Nevertheless, the alienation and mutual nonrecognition continue to cause us pain. So our solution has been to recast ourselves in our own minds and in our own experiences as separate beings who really can exist without mutual recognition and without fulfilling our own needs for spirituality and loving connection. Thus, our emergence as isolated individuals, able to stand on our own, seeking our own fulfillment, imagining that we can develop rigid boundaries that will both separate and protect us from others (but that actually function to contain and repress our own awareness of our need for others). In a world in which we have given up on the possibility of healing the pain of others, or significantly relating our lives to their fates, or participating with them in the kind of mutual recognition for which we hunger, the best self-protection is to deny the need and imagine ourselves to be self-contained, well-boundaried, and delimited beings who can achieve fulfillment and salvation on our own and without regard to what is happening to anyone else. In this mode, we become fearful of anything that might threaten those boundaries or essentially link us to others, since we have come to believe that it is precisely in our detached and self-contained selves that we have a chance to achieve a personal salvation, whereas we have long ago given up on the possibility of collective or social salvation.

Now enter Judaism, with a fluid and progressive account of the world, an insistence on the fundamental interdependence of all human beings, and an account of the fundamental unity of all Being. Just when we have gotten the world into neat and contained categories in order to reconcile ourselves to its alienation, Judaism proclaims a oneness that is permeated by a transformative (divine) energy that moves us to transcend our alienated separateness and to become partners with God in transforming reality. The false solidity we had constructed as part of our strategy for dealing with alienated reality suddenly is in danger of melting beneath our feet.

No wonder, then, that God appears to Moses not as a mountain but as a voice coming from the fire, a bush that is not consumed but burns with intensity and overwhelming power. No wonder that Jewish religious experience seems to be entering into the dangerous and uncontrolled to people who have made their peace with a world of alienation and who are intent on finding a personal solution within such a world.

To think of ourselves as made in the image of a God who is the Force that makes for transformation and possibility is to destabilize not only the world, but even any fixed conception of ourselves. At the core of our being lies possibility, and the core of human nature is the possibility of human nature in any historical period being radically transformed. Judaism forces us to confront the falsity of all those notions that attempt to reify human reality and hence provide a degree of predictability so that we can shape our lives to fit the contours of a world dominated by alienation and oppression. Judaism dissolves the false security some people seek in religion. Instead, we stand trembling before the revelation of God. This is not a God that makes the world totally orderly and predictable. It is not a God tamed and made safe by Enlightenment rationality—it is the God that is experienced through the thunder and lightning of that incredible moment at Sinai when an entire people was confronted by a revelation that shook it to the core.

CHAPTER FOUR

SOMETHING HAPPENED

SINAI AND TORAH

Something happened.

It may not have been a specific day or a single moment in which the revelation of God's will to the Jewish people took place. The Torah may have been compiled by a redactor in Ezra's time (circa 400 B.C.E.) rather than written by one prophet at the time of the Exodus. It may itself be the product of conflicting traditions and derive from alternative sources. Yet what it records, buried in the myths of a people trying to recount its own development, is an event monumental and transparently true: that at some point in our history as a people we "got" it. We together received and accepted a message that we have a special obligation to live in accord with a transcendent view of the world.

This "getting" it was not simply the enlightenment of a single soul or a small group of special enlightened gurus, philosophers, artists, wise men or women, spiritual seers, or mystics. The remarkable claim of Torah is that an entire people got it at the same time, and in a sense all stood at Sinai together. And as the Midrash wisely adds, not only those living at that historical moment, but also all future generations were at Sinai, so that all of us heard the message together, and all of us can remember how we heard it.

Had only a small spiritual elite been enlightened, it might be easy to fudge the story. But here we have an entire mass of people claiming that they've been through something together. Moreover, they tell it to their children with energy and commitment and veracity so intense and special that those children in turn tell the story to their children, who in turn tell it to their children, so that one generation tells the next for three thousand years (or maybe "only" twenty-four hundred years). And they tell the story in a way that is very different from mythic history: They tell it with the details preserved, with the faults of the people preserved, with every betrayal and failure and human weakness preserved.

The very way that this story has been told from generation to generation is good evidence that something happened, and that something happened to an entire people, not just to a few people.

But there is another way to look at the story: that the something that happened was the telling itself. The very fact that this kind of story has been told, has taken root, and has held the moral and spiritual imagination of a people for twenty-four hundred years is itself the story of a revelation. The ability of a people to grasp, hold, imaginatively transform, and yet remain loyal to a story of liberation may be the very thing that happened.

Speculation about the historical details of the Exodus has led some scholars to develop an alternative account to that found in the Book of Joshua. Biblical scholar Norman Gottwald suggests that most of the tribes living in the hills of Judea never experienced the Exodus. Rather, they were engaged in creating a relatively independent life for themselves, free from the oppressive order of the established cities that dominated much of the land of Canaan. At some point a group of nomads from the Sinai desert entered the land and eventually succeeded in uniting these different tribes in a struggle against the city-states that had previously oppressed them. This group of nomads, largely the tribe of Levi, had a set of Moses stories that eventually became the dominant stories of the other tribes that joined in a loose federation to struggle against the city dwellers. Eventually the tribes succeeded in conquering the cities, and slowly the Moses stories became the dominant stories of the entire people.

If some variant of this account were true, would it undermine our claim that "something happened"? Not at all. Not only would we still maintain that the Moses group got it and that event was Sinai, but also we would say that the other tribes who accepted the telling of Moses' story got it too. This process might have taken place over the course of five hundred or eight hundred years, but eventually a very large number of people got it.

Now *what* they got was very different from, say, an account of miracles or plagues, although that may have been a part. Unique about this claimed revelation is that these people and their descendants personally understood something about the world that obligated them in a deep and lasting way—obligated them to become witnesses for the possibility of transformation in the name of a God of transcendence. Whenever they got *that* understanding, we call it Sinai. All who read Torah and hear within it the voice of God commanding them to join the Jewish people's efforts to live lives committed to healing and transformation have similarly received the revelation, and can reasonably tell their children that they too were at Sinai.

But how can we convey what really happens in these revelatory moments? What we can do, at best, is speak about the human experience of revelation, what it felt like to us, or what kinds of language we attempted to use in describing an experience which wasn't like other experiences, didn't fit into the words or categories we normally have. The dominant metaphor developed from that experience was hearing. We heard something, and what we heard we attempted to write down.

The central mantra of the Jewish people is not "Read, O Israel" or even "Study, O Israel"—though both of these are very important elements in the process. It is "Hear, O Israel." Listen. The command implies that still one can hear, that the revelation is still happening. So when the Midrash says that each person heard it differently, the message is that we will not all hear it in the same way. Nevertheless, each of us is hearing the real thing. And *that* has very profound consequences—because it empowers each of us in a way that challenges every orthodoxy, including the orthodoxy of the Jewish religion.

The revelation's sound waves are still reverberating through the universe. In Psalms it says that a thousand years are like a moment in God's eyes—something that must be true when we recognize the billions of years that have elapsed since the universe began to expand. If so, we are really living only a few moments after Sinai, still living in a moment when we can experience the aftershocks of the first sound waves, when the universe is still pulsating with that revelation. If we check the history of the human race, we find that in this same historical period, from approximately 1200 to 200 B.C.E., many other peoples had sages arise who claimed to have gotten a new revelation or a new way of understanding the world. In their own ways, other peoples may have been picking up on the same event in the life of God that the Jewish people call Sinai. The Midrash unintentionally makes this point when it says that the revelation went out in seventy different languages.

Something happened, and it shook the Jewish people very deeply. It turned us into a group that would play a vanguard role for much of subsequent history. Out of the experience of Exodus and Sinai would emerge a small group of people whose descendants would take these insights and spin off other religious traditions, including Christianity and Islam; and later, psychoanalysis, Marxism, and other liberatory traditions of the modern world. Something happened to make this group conceive of itself in such a way that it would make a contribution to the world out of proportion to its numbers, a contribution that would build upon the realization that the oppression and evil in the world could be overcome.

So, for our purposes, let us call whatever happened the revelation at Sinai.

The central insight at Sinai is this: the God of the universe is the God of freedom and transcendence; the God that has made possible the liberation from Egypt; the God that ensures that the way things will be need not be the way they have been; the God that enables us to break the chain of negativity and pain that links the generations.

The specific way Torah insists that human beings can break the chain of cruelty is in our treatment of the powerless, the widow, the orphan, and most particularly the stranger. The thought repeated, in various formulations, more frequently than any other is this: When you come into your land, do not oppress the stranger; remember that you were a stranger in the land of Egypt.

Why would we be tempted to oppress the stranger? Precisely because the children of Israel function psychologically like all other human beings, by repeating the behavior generated by earlier traumatic events, but now from the position of being the agent who is inflicting it rather than suffering from it.

But as in the Akedah (Abraham's story, discussed in chapter two), Torah says, "No! don't do it! You don't have to do it. You can break the chain of suffering, you can transcend it. You do not have to pass on the pain that was delivered to you to the next generation, or to the people over whom you have power, or to the people with whom you have contact. You do not have to recreate Egypt! The logic of oppression that has ruled every society is not the only possible way things could be. In fact, the universe is governed by another logic. And so, you must not oppress the powerless; one standard of behavior must be adopted for you and for the powerless; not two."

Torah provides a concrete form and way of life that embodies the call for mutual recognition, for transcendence, and for seeing others as created in the image of God. Much of Torah legislation is concerned with finding concrete ways to embody God's transformative message in the best possible manner that could have been envisioned in the ancient world.

Unfortunately, Christian polemicists who were interested in establishing that the Torah had been "superseded" by a "New" testament succeeded in popularizing interpretations of what the Torah was about that essentially reduced the enterprise to a bunch of sterile and oppressive laws. Ironically, many Jews today have never read through the Torah with a commentary aimed at highlighting its revolutionary message. Without understanding the historical context of its injunctions, we can quickly misunderstand some of its precepts, particularly when we read them through the eyes of a Christian culture whose interpretation already presupposes the false dichotomy between love and law. For Torah Jews, love becomes empty emotionality unless embodied in a way of life. Many of Torah's seemingly opaque or ritualistic moments read quite differently when understood in the context of the meaning of the various rituals in relationship to the constituted cultural realities of a people emerging from slavery in one society and confronting the class structure in another (Canaan).

There is nothing that is more frequently cited as reflecting insensitivity of Torah ethics than the injunction "An eye for an eye, a tooth for a tooth." Yet even this statement that seems to embody insensitivity actually provides an impetus for change. Other societies allowed or even encouraged people to seek revenge completely out of proportion to the pain inflicted upon them ("You insulted me in public, so I will kill you in response to avenge my honor"). In contrast, the "eye for an eye" concept demands a fair and equitable relation between the crime and the punishment: don't take two eyes for one eye; don't kill a whole family if one member of that family killed someone in your family. Equally important to remember is that other ancient legal codes linked the price for inflicting injury upon another to the class status of the injured party.

Injuring a poor man was less costly than injuring a rich man. By asserting an eye for an eye, Torah insists on equal dignity for all human beings. And it rejects the idea that a money value can be placed on human life—a life for a life, not money for a life. It also spurns vicarious punishment (e.g., killing the son of the person who killed your son).

Torah also demands that wealthy people meet their social obligations to the poor at the risk of physical punishment. They must not harvest the corners of their fields, so that the poor can take this food. Moreover, recipients of public sector assistance must be treated with dignity.

There are some aspects of Torah law that seem progressive even today. Perhaps most fundamental is the Torah law mandating redistribution of wealth, which details how land is to be allocated equally among the tribes and families. Then it orders that every seven years all debts are to be cancelled and every fifty years, the Jubilee, all transfers of land ownership that have occurred in the past fifty years are to be annulled. In this way, society returns to its original equality. The redistribution suggests that because human beings are fundamentally equal, all made in the image of God, no one has an inherent right to rule over others or to exercise the power over others that unequal ownership of property would entail. Redistribution is to be achieved not "from above" through some centralized government, but "from below" by the action of each tribe and each family.

We have no historical record of whether the Jubilee was actually implemented in ancient Israel or how it worked. But the Torah injunction is clear and revolutionary. If implemented today, it would provide the basis for a totally different economic world, one in which principles of justice and fairness would have far greater power.

Torah assumes a level of collective responsibility for the problems facing a society. When someone is found dead in the fields, the elders of the nearest city are held accountable for the crime, and must publicly proclaim "our hands have not shed this blood," and must offer an atonement sacrifice, since they are seen as having failed to provide shelter or food for the murdered stranger, or alternatively as not having provided employment or charity for the assailant, which led him to become a murderer.

There is no question that the Torah tradition embodies gender inequality. So it is all the more striking to note that it is also the first tradition to forbid marital rape. As Daniel Boyarin explains, "far from treating a wife as a piece of property or a mere object for the satisfaction of her husband's sexual desire, talmudic law may be the first legal or moral system that recognizes that when a husband forces his wife, the act is rape, pure and simple, and as condemnable and contemnable as any other rape."[1] Moreover, if a wife has agreed to sexual intercourse in one instance, the husband cannot assume that she continues to agree moments later to repeated acts of sexual intercourse, but must know explicitly that she wishes it.

Likewise, the Torah tradition insists that sexual relations between husband and wife be accompanied by loving feelings. So if a husband hates his wife, is drunk and can't pay attention to his wife's sexual and emotional needs, or even if the couple has had a fight and not yet made up after it, sexual relations are forbidden.

BEING COMMANDED

The recognition we had at Sinai created for us an obligation. Once you see things in a certain kind of way, there is no going back. As with any new level of awareness, you can hide from yourself, try to lie to yourself, but only at a very high cost and with great inner turmoil. This is the high price of any vanguard in consciousness: they cannot *not* know what they do know, and knowing what they do know always separates them in some way from those who do not share their understanding. As one Midrash recounts, it felt to us as if Sinai itself were being held over our heads, that we were coerced into the Covenant.

Knowing that the world both can and ought to be changed gave the Jewish people a sense of being commanded.[2] The written Torah that we have is the record of the moment in history when the Jewish people understood that their laws and conduct must embody mutual recogni-

---

[1] Daniel Boyarin, *Carnal Israel* (Berkeley, CA: University of California Press, 1993), p. 114.

[2] Contemporary philosopher Immanuel Levinas extended this insight to all our encounters with others—to encounter the other, to look at her or his face and recognize there the presence of God, is to put ourselves unconditionally in the place of the other without expecting anything in return. Martin Jay further explains that such encounters force us to suspend the sovereignty of our own egos and to enter into a nonerotic love of our neighbors that expects nothing in return.

tion. It was all an elaboration of the first commandment: the critical task is to recognize God—to recognize God in one another, God in everything—and then to act in the world in a way consonant with that understanding.

Being commanded is not a lowly conditon of powerlessness, but an elevated state. Only someone capable of recognizing God can feel commanded, because being commanded is being in touch with the most profound role—being a partner with God in healing and repair. The Talmud draws this lesson explicitly: It is better to have done the good deed because one was commanded than to have done it without having been commanded. So, being focused on *mitzvot* (commandments) is not like being in an inferior state of consciousness in which one is merely acting out of fear or out of routine. Rather, it is a higher consciousness, a recognition of ourselves as our highest possible selves, as God's agents in the universe.

No wonder, then, that the Jews delight in Torah. The psalmist proclaims, "How I love your Torah, all day it's my meditation." We dance with the Torah on Simchat Torah, we proclaim our joy with Torah, we are defined through Torah. Its *mitzvot* are, in the words of the evening prayers, "our life and the length of our days." This joy in being commanded seems foreign to the contemporary sensibility, which sees command as a repudiation of autonomy and creativity. But for the Jews, our autonomy is exercised precisely in encountering the deepest truth of the universe and hearing it. Just as we are not enslaved nor our autonomy violated when we recognize the truths of science or mathematics, our autonomy is not denigrated when we recognize moral and spiritual truths. Of course, certain conclusions about how we should act necessarily follow, but these requirements are not constraints. They free us to be our deepest

---

Thus, the deepest truth of our subjectivity is not its "being for itself" as Sartre would have it, but rather its "being for the other." Our most fundamental self is expressed not in our ability to act in a ferocious and unguided Faustian fashion, but rather in our ability to be ethically alive responders to others, compassionate caretakers of others and of the world—to be able to achieve mutual recognition with them, so that we see them and they see us as ends rather than as means, as embodiments of holiness and deserving of dignity and freedom, as infinitely precious and sacred.

selves. Mutual recognition valued by Torah, far from weighing us down, liberates us, makes us joyful partners with one another and with God.

And this point was recognized by the rabbis of the Talmudic period, as was written in The Ethics of the Fathers (Pirkei Avot 6:2): "As it says, 'The tablets are the work of God, and the writing is the writing of God engraved (*harut*) on the tablets.' Don't pronounce it *harut* [engraved] but *herut* [freedom], for no one has freedom but one who is engaged in Torah." The deepest freedom is precisely to act in accord with our highest understandings of the truth of the universe.

Capitalism extols itself because it has made possible an endless array of choices for consumption, and each of us gets to make whatever choices we want as long as we have the money to back up the choices. The underlying assumption is that the more choices we have, the freer we are.

But being free to be who we really are is a very different conception of freedom, because we really are, according to Torah, beings created in the image of God, who have received a certain revelation about the world. Once having seen the world in a particular way, we are stuck with a certain kind of recognition that shapes and determines our consciousness. We are *not* free to choose any morality we wish, because we have come to see that there is a right way for the world to be and that we have the task of making the world that way.

In short, the kind of covenant we have entered into with God is not like the choices offered to us by the capitalist market. Our freedom is constrained by our being. Or, to put it another way, our highest freedom is our ability to recognize who we really are, to recognize our relationship with God, and to open our ears to hear God's revelation; and by being open to God, we learn what God requires of us. Hence, the strange rabbinic imagery of us entering freely into a covenant while the mountain of Sinai is being held over our heads. This conception of liberation has little in common with countercultural fantasies of endless opportunities to gratify one's desires. It stands at odds with postmodern attempts to deny an objective foundation for ethics, though it need *not* deny the postmodern description of the way the self has been fragmented so that we find it harder to experience ourselves as commanded by anything that transcends the media-induced tastes of the moment.

We are not trading one form of slavery for another.[3] To understand that we are servants of YHVH—the Force that makes transformation of the world possible—and that we have an obligation stemming from the fact that we are created in this God's image and that we have heard this God's commands for love and justice, is not to reduce us to yet another form of slavery.

When Torah tells us that we are slaves to YHVH, this is *not* a claim analogous to announcing that Pharaoh X has been substituted for Pharaoh Y.

To be subjugated to this God is the deepest freedom, because this kind of subjugation is a joining and participation in the process of transforming and healing the world. The conservatives seek reassurance that the punishing parent is still in place, that the distortions in the world are really ontological, and that some system of oppression and unequal power is really necessary. But Torah's conception of God's kingship tells us just the opposite: that the only real power governing our lives is the Force that makes it possible for us to leave systems of oppression and start over, creating something fundamentally different and new. Torah insistently warns us not to go back to Egypt, and not to repeat the ways of Egypt—yet that is precisely what Jewish conservatives think is the only mature path.

If the revolutionary aspect of Torah defined *all* of Judaism, then everyone would agree that within Judaism there lies the basis for a liberatory worldview that guides us in our struggles to heal and repair the world. But of course, the conservatives can find some supporting material for their views in the Torah. The truth is that within the Torah there are other voices that provide a basis for those who have never really been able to leave Egypt, for those who wish to carry with them the notion that some form of subordination and oppression is neces-

---

[3]Jon Levenson at Harvard University makes the most compelling case for this mistaken view in his *The Hebrew Bible: The Old Testament and Historical Criticism* (Cambridge, MA: Harvard University Press, 1993). Levenson argues that the covenant is fundamentally similar to covenants throughout the Middle East, and the Israelites have merely replaced one ruler with a more powerful suzerain. He misses the qualitative difference between being slaves to a capricious human and being slaves to a God whose will is revealed in a covenantal book that is voluntarily accepted, and whose continued acceptance depends on the voluntary will of the community.

sary. We have seen Torah used as the justificatory basis for chauvinism and cruelty, particularly by some right-wing fanatics in Israel who quote Torah as they spread hate and provide ideological support for acts of violence against Palestinians. They refuse to see that within Torah there is yet another and more liberatory voice. Torah is a record of the struggle between these two voices in the consciousness of those who received God's revelation.

CHAPTER FIVE

THE STRUGGLE BETWEEN TWO VOICES OF GOD IN TORAH

In the last chapter I argued that Torah laws give a concrete form to the project of mutual recognition and transcendence. But the Torah also contains rituals, ways of thinking, and injunctions which are insensitive, chauvinistic, or even cruel. How can a Jew deal with these aspects of the Torah?

THE VOICE OF CRUELTY IS NOT THE VOICE OF GOD

Torah is filled with the voice of God as I have tried to describe, a voice of compassion and transcendence. But it is also filled with another voice, which mirrors human distortions and accumulated pain. Just as Abraham had trouble getting the land of Haran out of him, so the Jews had deep trouble getting the spiritual, ethical, and emotional legacy of Egypt out of them.

If, as I have argued, the accumulated pain and cruelty is passed from generation to generation, reinforced by the dynamics of nonrecognition and the desperate attempt to achieve connection by acting in ways that stay loyal to what our parents have taught us, then the people of Israel, like all peoples, will be hearing the voice of God in ways that are often mixed with the voices of pain and distortion. Our job is to distinguish the one from the other. To the extent that we are ready to hear God's voice, we can find it in Torah. But to the extent that we are morbidly drawn to our own tendencies toward cruelty and pain, those will be the resonant voices we respond to in Torah. How could it be otherwise?

Torah itself gives us some hints at the limited nature of the receivers of the revelation—as though perhaps it were partly conscious of the problem. From the moment that we understood the revelation, we began running from it. According to Exodus 20:15–16, the people were trembling and distanced themselves (*amdu m'rachok*), and then turned to Moses and said, "You speak to us and we will listen; but God should not speak with us because we will die." It is simply too much to stay in the full presence of what is being asked of us; and so we retreat. Let it be turned into language that is mediated through the limited consciousness of another human being.

The tradition says that "this is the Torah which Moses put before the children of Israel, by the mouth of God, by the hand of Moses." God may have transmitted, but it was Moses who received. Moses was a limited human being like every other human being. So what he heard was a limited revelation, the revelation receivable through the conceptual apparatus of a remarkable person, but a person born and raised in Egypt, looking at the world through its assumptions and its language even as he rebelled against those assumptions and that language.

In addition to Moses' limitations, we have another set of distortions: those imposed by virtue of trying to make a Torah that would be applicable to the specific realities of the people. The medieval Jewish philosopher Maimonides was alert to this issue in his own interpretation of many of the rituals that were developed by God. Moses is up on Sinai for forty days, but when he tarries to return a few hours late, the children of Israel lose faith that he will return, and demand of Aaron as follows: "Up, make us gods that will go before us . . ." (Exodus 32:1). So Aaron makes a calf from their gold rings, and the people say, "These are your gods, Israel, which brought you up out of the land of Egypt."

The people are hungry for the ways of Egypt. They are limited beings, and they can make only so much of a leap in one generation. Maimonides believed that many of the detailed rituals within the Torah were given by God in order to elevate our historically conditioned needs by placing them within the liberatory context of the fundamental insights of Judaism. The rituals are accommodations to the historical limitations of the people—they are not wanted by God as ends in themselves, but as a means to make it possible for limited human beings to "get" the fundamental points by teaching it to them through ritual behaviors that satisfy their needs. They give the people some degree of being "regular," with a "regular" religion that doesn't *only* demand that they stay true to the message of transcendence, but *also* gives them some less overwhelming tasks.

But there are more serious limitations to the message of transcendence, moments in which Torah seems to propagate ancient social practices and attitudes that embody the pain and cruelty of existing social systems. Sexism is the most striking and upsetting example.

This distortion shows through most clearly in the passage in which God tells Moses to prepare the people for the revelation. "And the Lord said unto Moses: 'Go to the people, and sanctify them today and tomorrow, and let them wash their garments, and be ready against the third day; for the third day the Lord will come down in the sight of all the people upon Mount Sinai. And you shall set bounds to the people around about, and say: Take heed to yourselves, that you do not go up into the mount, or touch the border of it; whoever touches the mountain shall surely be put to death; no hand shall touch him, but he shall surely be stoned, or shot through; whether it be beast or man, it shall not live; when the ram's horn sounds long, they shall come up to the mount.' And Moses went down from the mount to the people, and sanctified the people; and they washed their garments. And he said unto the people: 'Be ready against the third day; come not near a woman'" (Exodus 19:10–15).

Where does this "come not near a woman" come from? Not from God, according to the text; Moses simply understands from the standpoint of his conceptual apparatus that when God asks the people to sanctify themselves, this must mean that the injunction is addressed to the men and not to the women; and that contact with women undermines this sanctity.

It's quite clear in this instance that these are assumptions Moses brings into the communication—Moses receives God's command through his own sexist framework.

If we understand the "we" to be the community of males, thereby excluding and marginalizing women, then we can say that the primary form of distortion within the Torah is the distortion of exclusion, lack of concern for, and intuitive sympathy with the other. And the tension exists as a contradiction within the text itself. On the one hand, there is the recognition that we are all equally created in the image of God. The revolutionary implications are there in the text: "male and female created He them." And the rabbis of the Talmudic period, commenting on the notion of *tzelem Elohim*, the image of God, say explicitly that the purpose of this emphasis is precisely to communicate that everyone is equal, that no nation could possibly say that it is on a higher plane or closer to God.

And yet the text itself continues to reflect a different voice and sensibility as well, one that embodies the fear and denigration of the other, and the desire to pass on to others the violence that has been done to us, the common practice for those living in a world of oppression. The children of Israel are enslaved and then subjected to genocide as Pharaoh orders the death of every newborn Jew. The degradation and humiliation that this causes us as a people is deeply embedded, and though Torah does its best to undermine the process, it is at the same time, and in important ways, a product of that very process. So at times Torah externalizes anger at the other, falling into the pattern of non-recognition that it itself most seeks to transcend.

The Israelites had gotten at least as far as anyone else in their contemporary world in overcoming cruelty and recognizing the other. The Torah tells us that when the Israelites left Egypt, it was not simply the blood descendants of Abraham, Isaac, and Jacob who became part of the people—it was "a mixed multitude." The Jewish people are not composed, then, of people who were racially pure or born Jewish—we are composed of this mixed multitude that wandered together in the desert. The great challenge of transcendence is specifically focused on the relationship to the non-Israelite, the *ger*, the person who is the outsider. Over and over again, Torah shows us an ethos of caring and concern for the other, for the powerless, for those who are in no position to defend themselves. Moreover, the revolutionary claim that Torah makes about human nature, that we are *all* created in the image of God, is the locus classicus of the politics of inclusion. Counter to every document of exclusion, there is in Torah a voice that insists on the sanctity of the other.

And yet there is another voice that we can hear clearly in Torah. It is precisely in regard to the other, the outsider, the non-Israelite, that the legacy of pain and cruelty acted out against us reasserts itself and is heard by some as the voice of God. The book of Deuteronomy, claiming to be recounting Moses' speech to the Israelites in accord with the will of God, makes clear that one of the tasks is to dispossess and destroy the peoples of the land to which they are coming, the land that God promised them.

In one sense, to come to the new place, to create a new reality, it was necessary to uproot the old way of life, to make no compromise with the oppressive world that already existed. One might hear this notion as a revolutionary demand: Make no deals; don't allow yourself to flirt with the dominant culture; create something totally different. But when that kind of insight gets translated, as it does in the Torah, to the demand that the peoples of the land be utterly destroyed, then we have, under the guise of fighting for a righteous cause, the reemergence of the cruelty and pain that had been inflicted upon the Jewish people in Egypt.

THE VOICE OF CRUELTY IN TORAH: "SHOW NO MERCY"

The triumphalist tone of Moses' account of the march of the people of Israel toward the Promised Land already marks this deterioration in moral sensibility. Sihon, the king of Heshbon, would not allow the people of Israel to pass through nor sell food or water to them, but instead fought against them. "And the Lord our God delivered him up before us; and we smote him, and his sons, and all his people. And we took all his cities at that time, and utterly destroyed every city, the men, and the women, and the little ones; we left none remaining; only the cattle we took for a prey unto ourselves, with the spoil of the cities which we had taken" (Deuteronomy 2:33–35).

But lest we think that this is a momentary aberration flowing from the passion of the battle and the anger at having been attacked, Moses goes on in Deuteronomy to tell the people exactly what they are expected to do to the Hittite, the Girgashite, the Amorite, the Canaanite, the Perizzite, the Hivite, and the Jebusite—the seven nations that live in the land that God is now giving to the Jewish people: "Thou shalt smite them; then thou shalt utterly destroy them; thou shalt make no covenant with them, nor show mercy unto them" (Deuteronomy 7:2). *Loe techanem*—thou shalt show no mercy.

The Book of Joshua carries forth this spirit, rejoicing in the defeats and destruction of the people of the land, assuring us that this is really the spirit of God and the continuation of the legacy of Moses. And that same spirit manifests itself again when Samuel, prophet of God, turns in fury on King Saul, who has failed to kill Agag, the king of the Amalekites, despite the allegedly clear command of God that he do so. Samuel picks up the sword and himself beheads the Amalekite—supposedly showing thereby his vigilance and commitment to God. It is an action that recalls a similar act of violence in the Torah itself, when Pinchas kills an Israelite and the Midianite woman with whom he is having sexual relations—to show that the Israelites are not to have sexual contact with "the enemy"—and is rewarded by God with the right to have his branch of the Levite family become the high priests.

It matters little for the sake of the present argument if all this was written much later than other parts of the Torah tradition, written so much in the style of the late prophets that some people believe that the whole book of Deuteronomy was a creation of Jeremiah or his followers. Or if it was written by a people of Israel who were becoming enslaved and defeated by those around them, or by people in Babylonian exile, or by people recently returned from exile in the time of Ezra. It matters little if the whole story of the conquest was a later fabrication, as has been forcefully argued by some historians, an attempt to give strength and a sense of purpose to a people who were experiencing themselves as powerless and unable to defend themselves.

Actually, these considerations *would* matter if our task were to judge *them*, the people who put this book together, or the people who heard God's revelation in this way. But that is not my purpose in raising this issue. I confront these passages and the entire "Joshua tradition" not to judge those who adopted it, but to say in the most unequivocal terms: *This is not the voice of God*, but the voice of pain and cruelty masquerading as the voice of God.

There is no point in trying to hide from ourselves the cruelty and insensitivity in these passages. Nor is there any point in pretending that it was a momentary aberration. All through Jewish history some people have been hearing God's voice in this way, building on these passages their own understanding of the essence of Judaism. Furious at their vulnerability and powerlessness, outraged at the immorality of those non-Jews who periodically murdered, raped, and pillaged them, some Jews adopted a Torah of cruelty that distorted the Torah of love and compassion. Unable to imagine that the non-Jew was himself or herself a victim of oppression, seeing only their power and the hurtful and destructive way that power was used against the Jewish people, some Jews embraced those strands of the tradition that refused to recognize the non-Jew as really deserving of the dignity that Torah seemed to confer on them in claiming that we were *all* created in the image of God. So, for example, the sixteenth-century compendium of Jewish law, the Shulchan Aruch (Yoreh Deah 158), reasserts a talmudic injunction forbidding Jews to save the life of an idolater or of a Jew who brazenly rejects the kosher dietary laws or someone who does not believe that the dead will be resurrected someday. It's not hard to see how nonrecognition of the other as created in the image of God is a slippery slope: one starts with the idolater, and it is only a few steps to taking nonobservant or nonbelieving Jews to be the enemy as well. Right-wing Israelis who have physically attacked peace activists continue this distorted process.

This sensibility, this denial of the other, really *is* in the text. The text really does record two different kinds of voices of God. The redactors or composers of the Torah, like the halakhic authorities of later ages, reflect both those voices in the text and do not recognize, or at least do not tell us that they are recognizing, the conflict between these two voices.

Those who redacted the Torah and the Joshua tradition incorporated this cruelty into the revelation as they understood it, because when they listened to the voice of God, part of what they heard was the transcendent message of Sinai, and part of what they heard was the distorting influence of the legacy of pain that infused their consciousness. By the time we get to later elaborations of Jewish law, there are some who argue that Jews do not have an obligation to save the life of a non-Jew. The voice of cruelty appeared at some moments and within some sectors of the Jewish world to be more powerful than the voice of healing and compassion.

Jews in subsequent generations have built on this tradition of anger and denigration of the other, used it as their own basis of fantasied compensation for the actual experience of powerlessness and humiliation in their daily lives. They were responding to the voice of pain and cruelty within, not to the call of God. Through the ages, and culminating in the religious Right wing in Israel today, these passages from Deuteronomy, Joshua, and Samuel have given the voice of cruelty an apparent divine seal of approval. The massacre of twenty-nine Muslims at prayer in Hebron in February 1994 by an Orthodox Jew was an outgrowth of a culture of violence among some "Modern Orthodox" Jews that builds on these texts, using them as their own historical precedent to legitimize the way that they too can identify their own inner cruelty with the voice of God.

FINDING THE "NICE" QUOTES

The approach of many of the rabbis throughout Jewish history and of many of the more humane religious voices in Israel today has been to try to counter these quotes with other quotes, to find textual bases in which to root a more humane and sensitive attitude toward others. For example, countering rightists who cite the injunctions to kill the inhabitants of the land as justification for contemporary policies toward Palestinians, they've pointed to those interpreters of Halakha who claim that "idolaters" refers only to the original seven tribes of Canaan, and hence that there really isn't anything to worry about in injunctions against idolaters since none exists anymore.

Religious rightists, on the other hand, have accused these religious humanists of ignoring the texts, and they have a legitimate argument. If you accept the defining position of contemporary orthodoxy, that the texts are themselves holy and the embodiment of God's will and word, then you must take seriously the parts of the text that seem to be in conflict with your sensibilities. The religious Right makes this point when it says that the religious humanists are really embodying a set of Western ideas and parading them as Judaism. It would be more accurate to say that there are conflicting voices and strands within the tradition. The voice of cruelty and fanaticism and intolerance and oppression sometimes *can* be heard in our holy texts, alongside the voice of transcendence and compassion. The religious rightists, in emphasizing one strand, are no more or less "authentic" than Jewish renewalists who emphasize the other. What *is* a distortion sometimes engaged in by the Right, however, is to attribute the ideas of compassion and caring for others to Western humanism or post-Enlightenment optimism, when these values so clearly come from the Torah.

INEVITABLE DISTORTIONS

Talking about the struggle within our tradition between the voice of transcendence and the voice of accumulated cruelty is not meant to be any denigration of Torah. If Torah embodies this struggle between two voices, if some of what is identified as God in Torah is really the voice of accumulated pain, it is nevertheless a document which provides us with a way of hearing the voice of God and, from that insight, being able to learn to critique the voice of accumulated pain. The extraordinary thing about Torah is not that it contains a voice of pain—after all, it was limited and distorted human beings, we and our forefathers and fore-mothers, who *received* Torah, so naturally we would receive it through our limited and distorted receptors—but that it is not *only* the voice of pain, and that for the first time in human history a human community consciously acknowledges itself to be hearing, commanded by, and committed to a different kind of voice, a voice of love, justice, and transcendence. Respond to *that* voice!

How Do You Recognize the Voice of God?

The voices of God can be found in those parts of Jewish tradition—Torah; Midrash; the stories; the Halakha; the humor; the way of being human in the world—that tend to lead you to believe that the world can be changed from one dominated by pain, oppression, patriarchy, and evil to one in which human beings can live together in love and justice.

Whatever parts of the tradition help you to connect with the recognition of the other as created in the image of God, whatever tends to give you confidence and hopefulness about the possibility of joining as partners with God in the task of healing and repair of the universe, those are the parts of the tradition that have been revealed, that have the mark of God in them. Every part of the tradition, the Halakha, the stories, the humor, or the ways of being in the world that tend to make you doubt the possibility of human beings living that way is *not* the voice of God, but the voice of the accumulated pain of history, masquerading and parading as wisdom or profundity, but reflecting only our collective disappointment and impatience that the healing of humanity is taking so long.

Is This ALL Judaism Is About?

No. Judaism shares with many other religions a recognition of the grandeur of the universe and reflects the quite appropriate human response of awe, wonder, and radical amazement. Our contemporary inability to respond to the world in this way is one of the great losses of human history—and is the precondition for the destruction of the ecological foundations of human life. Reclaiming a sense of celebration and joy at the wonders of creation is another dimension of Jewish renewal.

So too is the recognition that we are surrounded, enmeshed in, and constituted by levels of spiritual reality that we can only barely apprehend. The world is not reducible to the material universe as described by science. It is pulsating with the fiery and noumenal reality that is sometimes described by mystics, alluded to in poetry and music, glimpsed through drug-induced or meditation-induced moments of transformed consciousness. Jewish renewal is interested in shaking loose from the carefully contained and antiseptic forms of religious observance that Jews adopted by attempting to fit into Western Christian societies, so that it can reclaim this Biblical Judaism. Yet in so doing, it connects with a reality that is also approached by other religious traditions.

What is unique about Judaism is that it entwines this sense of awe, wonder, amazement, and this spiritual reality that surrounds us, with a vision of the God who not only created the universe but also is the Force that makes possible an ethically guided universe. Many non-Biblical religions separate these two dimensions and celebrate creation as the central reality. Judaism, on the other hand, insists that these two elements are inseparable: the Force that creates the world is the same Force that makes possible the triumph of goodness.

The antireligious secularist makes a powerful challenge at this point in the argument: "Once you've abandoned the notion that God's revelation is responsible for the entire Torah, aren't you simply reduced to picking what you like from the Torah? And if you are doing that, in what sense are you rooted in the Torah? Moreover, why even bother with the Torah in the first place; why not just start from your own insights about what you like?" My answer: because in Torah we find God.

I've tried to argue that the Torah can best be understood as the record of human beings' encounter with the Divine, including the record of the ways that our understanding of that encounter has been limited by who we are and who the people were who first had that encounter. The struggle between our capacity for transcendence and compassion, on the one hand, and our tendency to embody and pass on the pain and cruelty of the past, on the other, is the central drama of human life and human history. That it finds expression in the Torah should be no surprise, nor necessarily a basis for discounting the divinity and holiness of the Torah tradition.

There's a part of many liberals that would have been more comfortable with a Torah that manifested only transcendence and compassion, and that had no pain and cruelty. Yet such a book would have had little to do with the reality of the human experience. The Torah is a useful guide to life because it is both a record of grappling with reality from the standpoint of God, and a record of the way that we are still in the struggle. To be Israel, the very word implies, is to *yisra* (struggle with) *El* (God). That wrestling is never a finished product, but a path which a people has chosen to be on.

Some people yearn for a Torah that would feel more like the completed teachings of "a perfect master," along the lines of various Eastern religious gurus. But we have a Torah that is an ongoing process, in which each generation unpacks its meaning by allowing itself to hear the voice of God within it in the way that that generation can hear. Some generations merely accept the texts as the received tradition, and to the extent that they treat these texts as "holy" fetishes that can't be struggled with, they transform them into idols. The essence of the process of renewal built into the Torah is to take these words, *va'chie ba'hem*, and *live* through them, which is to say, make them alive and life-giving and life-nurturing. Jewish renewal is a central part of the process through which this takes place.

This is very different from a guru's enlightenment. Many who relate to the guru traditions exhibit a certain passivity, a willingness to let others do the interpreting, a waiting for others to provide the meaning and suggest the roads with which to find the highest truths. The over-reliance on authority, be it the authority of a given explicator of the Torah or a given Hasidic spiritual master, has always engendered resistance in the Jewish world. The Jewish world has been characterized by a degree of contentiousness and disagreement that has guaranteed a spirit of independence of thought and action. Although the contentions often take place within the normative framework of Jewish religious tradition, the spirit of that contention, embodied in a long history of disputes about what exactly the tradition *is*, has created much space for alternative ways of looking at the world. But in the process, the tradition must not be radically discontinuous with the world it seeks to transform. "*Loe bashamayim hee,*" says a verse of the Torah about the Torah—it is not in heaven, but very close to us. And that very closeness permits for distortion.

But if there is distortion built into the Torah, then aren't we better off relying on our own intuitions and not basing ourselves on a tradition that encompasses the voice of pain and cruelty?

Any liberatory tradition will necessarily incorporate the distortions and limitations of its period. There is no Archimedean point from which one can build a solidly healthy and transformative vision: every vision is necessarily partial and partially distorted. Consider some other liberatory traditions, such as psychoanalysis, Marxism, and feminism, to name a few that have been recent contenders. When one looks at each of these closely, one will find a set of distortions in some of the founding literature, based in part on the historically conditioned limitations of the people who were the initial theorists and founders. Moreover, each tradition has been used at various points as an instrument to repress rather than liberate by at least some of its practitioners.

Our Torah documents the history of human efforts at transcendence, and records the interaction between those attempts and the distortions that emerged in their midst. We may not yet have a total vision of the good, but we do have a vision of what has been bad, and we do have some solid intuitions that have been gleaned through the history of the human race and have contributed to the emergence of a liberatory perspective. We as a human race know that it is wrong to create needless suffering, and though we do not fully agree on what is needless at any particular historical moment, we nevertheless feel confident that there is some substantial content to this insight.

What the Torah also gives us is not a single criterion for determining what is God's word, but a sense of how people heard that word in the past, and evokes in us the confidence to criticize the Torah in the name of Torah. And that, in fact, has been precisely what three thousand years of Jewish commentary has been about—the critique of the Torah from the perspective of Torah, but done in the form of commentary.

DOES THIS ACCOUNT GIVE HUMANS TOO MUCH AUTHORITY?

If we say that two voices are contending in Torah, don't we ultimately leave the whole matter up to human beings to determine what is the voice of God and what is the voice of accumulated evil?

Yes. But that is not a new situation. We always have had to rely on human beings when understanding the Torah. We had to rely on human beings to determine where God wanted the Temple, and when an action is killing and not murder, and which are the real prophets and which the false. We had to rely on human beings to tell us that when the Temple was destroyed what God really wanted was prayer instead of sacrifice, in defiance of the plain meaning of the words of the text. The rabbis of the talmudic period understood what they were doing, and they spent a great deal of their time trying to find "prooftexts," however stretched the interpretations of them, upon which they could hang their own particular approach. Yet they understood that what they were doing was giving *their* interpretation, not *the* interpretation. When they changed the laws requiring sacrifices into the basis for a requirement of prayer, they knew that this didn't appear in the text. Perhaps they might have been tempted to claim that they were prophets, hearing a new revelation. But they made no such claim. They were changing the plain meaning of the text based on their best ability to understand, in light of their own intellects and spiritual intuition, what would be the best way to keep the enterprise of Torah alive in their own circumstances. Hundreds of years later, those who followed these talmudic rabbis attributed to them and their work a holiness that at least many of the talmudic rabbis would have dismissed as silly, pretentious, or idol-atrous. In imagining that these rabbis were on some higher plane, later generations could excuse themselves of the responsibility of opening their own ears to the call of God and to the need to reunderstand the text. Yet that attribution of a higher status to previous generations, and the selective process of choosing *which* of the interpreters of the past will be the ones we choose to respond to, *is* an act of interpretation every bit as subjective as the talmudic rabbis'.

We are always interpreting what God really wants, selecting which interpreters and which texts of the past to find decisive, and no set of written words is ever going to explain itself. So the notion of relying on fallible human beings is a shock only to those who have hid from themselves the degree to which even the most orthodox of the Ortho-dox rely on a long set of interpretations that seem to go directly counter to the obvious meaning of the texts.

And this is why the objection to the enterprise that says, "You are merely reading your own set of values into the text rather than really responding to what is there," is always either a deep misunderstanding or bad faith. The moment one chooses a rabbi, a *yeshiva*, a *posek*, a theory of literary interpretation, a hermeneutic style, one is already approaching texts from a particular discourse or framework. Read the Midrash and its frequent attempts to prove that the patriarchs were really observing Torah laws before they were given to Moses (e.g., that Abraham's serving butter and lamb together to the visiting three angels wasn't really a violation of *kashrut*) and you get a dramatic demonstration of how very ancient is this process of rereading texts.

Coming to the text with one's own set of conceptions, questions, language, and needs is inevitable. Attention is always and necessarily selective. All that exist are the Torah scrolls, scribbles on the page, and then interpretations of those scribbles into words, and interpretations of those words into meanings. The *ta'amey hamkirah*, the symbols that taught us how to sing a sentence and where that sentence actually ends (because the text has no punctuation, no commas or periods or question marks), was the first interpretive venture, and ever since there has always been selective attention in constructing the meaning of the text. Biblical scholars often imagine themselves as merely detached and objective readers unpacking the nuances, complexities, and contradictory elements of the text. Yet this style of reading is itself a political choice. All too often, the enterprise of Bible scholarship becomes the enterprise of taming the Bible so that it no longer sizzles with revolutionary power. The ability of one group of interpreters to portray its reading as objective scholarship, apolitical, and a rejection of "selective attention," is a fact about power, not about Torah.

Every position is inevitably shaped by interests and cultural baggage—but that doesn't preclude serious grappling with the text. I've often found myself astounded by what I've discovered as I've tried to uncover the complexities and nuances of a particular formulation—the clever wordplays, the economy of language, the playfulness, the hidden meaning in poetry, the layers of meaning—and this is part of the joy of studying the Torah. There is much pleasure and excitement in studying the texts—and though one always brings one's self, no matter how pious or Orthodox a self it is, one can find within the text formulations and insights that challenge and argue with that self.

Just as the answer to the question "Who is to say what we are to do when the Temple gets destroyed?" must be answered, "*We are*," so too a similar answer for the question "Who is to decide which is the voice of cruelty and which the voice of God?" *We*, the people who accept the

Torah; who hear in it the voice of God; who feel ourselves commanded by Torah; and who accept the responsibility for preserving, observing, and passing on the tradition to the next generation; *we*, who in this process become the current historical embodiments of the people of Israel, are the ones to say which is the voice of cruelty and which is the voice of God, using our best efforts to understand the tradition, ourselves, our distortions, our historical epoch and *its* distortions.

Could we be mistaken? Sure. But when you attune your ear carefully and open your heart appropriately, it doesn't seem so very hard to discover which texts seem to speak to the most loving and other-affirming places in your being, and which texts seem to speak to the angriest, hurt or hurtful, vengeful, and oppressive parts of your being. The more profoundly we become aware of the ways that our own past, our own inner distortions, and our own loyalties to past ways of thinking and feeling are currently shaping us, the more we are able to distinguish between the parts of what we hear when we listen for God's voice that are shaped by our own personal legacy, and the parts that seem actually to represent a voice of love, caring, compassion, and holiness. The value of what we have learned through psychoanalytic thought, Marxist thought, feminist thought, critical theory, music, art, poetry, and meditation is that these methodologies assist us in detaching ourselves from our conditioned psychological inheritance, distancing ourselves from the chains of anger and cruelty that are passed from generation to generation.

So here is how we listen to the voice of God: using every intellectual and emotional and spiritual tool at our disposal; refracting what we think we are hearing through the community of others similarly committed to hearing God's voice, constantly engaged in prayer and meditation to help us recognize new forms of self-deception; reminding ourselves in humility that no matter how hard we try, we are self-deceptive in the way we apprehend reality, asking for God's guidance, aware of the ways that others who have honestly asked for this guidance have nevertheless been shaped by their own inner legacies of anger and cruelty; and doing our best to stay true to what we hear or what we get as we open ourselves to God's presence in the universe. Using those intellectual and spiritual tools, and retaining the deep humility of knowing that what we hear is likely to be only a partial getting of what God wants us to get, we then approach the texts to listen to where we hear the voice of God and where we do not. If not everyone agrees with what we have gotten or the way we've identified God's voice in the text, that doesn't make us any worse off than anyone else who has ever approached these texts and this tradition.

"No, you *are* worse off, because your Jewish renewal is saying that some parts of Torah are not the voice of God, whereas in the past the founders of Rabbinic Judaism did not say that any part of the tradition wasn't really God's word; they only changed the interpretation or meaning of God's word." A reasonable objection, but it doesn't hold. Because what they were doing, in effect, was saying that they had gotten a new revelation of God's word that gave them the right to change the original meaning to their own meaning. And that was at least as dangerous an assumption as saying, as I do, that the original voice was not the voice of God, but only the way God's voice was heard by somewhat limited human beings, and that we, another group of very limited human beings, must try to hear God's voice as best *we* can—and that will entail, in part, determining for ourselves where in Torah we really think we are hearing the voice of God.

This is not to deny the holiness of the text. The Torah is holy precisely because it so strikingly preserves for us both voices, shows us the contrast, forces us to choose. In the very process of coming to grips with the voice of God and the voice of cruelty, we become sensitized to the fact that this same struggle is going on inside us at all times, and that at every moment we are forced to make choices about which part of our being we are going to give priority. Choosing how to read the Torah, and where in it to find the word of God, becomes a central part of our own inner *tikkun*.

Ultimately there is no escaping this obligation to put our full selves into the process. If we think we've escaped this by trusting some *rebbe* or authoritative teacher or *posek*, we've merely deceived ourselves, because in making the choice of *which rebbe* or authoritative teacher or *posek* to pay attention to, we have made the same intuitive choice.

Maybe we are distinguishing the voice of God from the voice of pain on the basis of our contemporary Western values: democracy, egalitarianism, feminism, etc., and hence simply picking and choosing on a contemporary Western value-basis what we like and dislike in the Torah. If that's true, it doesn't distinguish our actions from those in any other moment in Jewish history. What people heard at previous moments as the voice of God was based on the contemporary values of *those* times as well. What else were the rabbis doing, for example, when they decided to modify the elimination of loans during the sabbatical year? When they used their own understanding of what the Torah was trying to accomplish, and decided that their methods were better than those described in the Torah itself, they could just as easily have been accused of substituting the values of *their* contemporary society for the values of Torah. They thought they knew what would be best, and they read the Torah to conform to their judgment. Doing just this, using one's best possible judgment, *is the tradition.* It is obvious from reading the Talmud that they selected texts to justify the interpretive choices they had already made—choices that in their own minds were totally consistent with Torah—but choices that were not articulated in the Torah itself.

How do we decide which is the voice of God? This is a many-sided process. In part, this judgment emerges from our intuition or our ability to tune in to the reverberations of Sinai that remain available to us. But it is not intuition or listening alone. God created us with rational capacities and as part of a community of rational communicators, and so whatever we intuit must be subject to challenge, argument, and doubt. And we must do our best to overcome those factors that might distract or modify our choices. As Rabbi Israel Salanter and a wide variety of Hasidic teachers have insisted, we have to be aware that our own egos may distort our perceptions. We have to overcome what Jewish tradition calls *negiah,* the way that our own interests may touch on a matter in ways that make us unable to see it clearly. We can go through therapy to clear up the ways in which we may still be dominated by the legacy of cruelty from our own past. We can study with those who seem to us to have made progress in their own inner struggles against accumulated pain and anger. We can study the long history of Jewish interpreters and look for the ways in which they tried to interpret texts to highlight what they thought was God's voice and what they thought was the voice of distortion. We can engage in acts of kindness and compassion to deepen our own sensitivity to the pains of others. We can put forward tentative assessments of what we hear in the text that we think is holy and what we hear that we think is not so holy, and then compare them with the assessments of others. We can decide to join with others in an interpretive community and abide by the judgments of that community (but first we have to make the decision about which community to join or *which* people share enough of our sense of spiritual sensitivity to God to want to build such a community with them).

We must always keep ourselves open to rational questioning and rational critique, and we must insist that all people, created in the image of God, are part of the community of discourse whose concerns and critiques of the way we distinguish the voice of God from the voice of cruelty must be taken seriously. It is within this context of ongoing intellectual and spiritual struggle, always open to new doubts about our own possible distortions, always sensitive to and trying to compensate for the complex psychological, social, and ideological factors that may be inclining us in a particular direction, that we make what may be called a leap of faith, as we decide which is in fact the voice of God and which is in fact the voice of cruelty.

Does this leave us with a charismatic religion based solely on individual judgments, personal intuitions, and claims to direct access to God? If so, we might soon be indistinguishable from the crackpots on the corner who are constantly telling us that they hear the voice of God and who use that to validate every possible nonsense. What distinguishes us, as Rabbi Tzvi Blanchard points out, is precisely that our listening to the voice of God is always done within the context of a tradition that we accept, an interpretive community whose historical and current realities provide a framework for assessing our current encounters with God's voice. Faith does not isolate us from the demands of reason or self-doubt, nor from the responsibility of engaging in ongoing rational dialogue with the community of rational communicators. Abraham Joshua Heschel once said to me that he knew the Bible was sacred because he could hear God's voice in the texts. To know that, he *already* had some sense of who God was. Yet that sense was not something that popped into his head whole cloth, but rather was a product of a life enmeshed in a particular community of discourse, of study, and of *mitzvot*.

So when people object to this enterprise and say, "Who are you to say what is the voice of God and what is the voice of cruelty?" the only possible reply is: "A member of the Jewish people; part of a community that has been struggling with these texts for thousands of years; a contemporary inheritor of the wisdom and the techniques and the passion and the experience of our people; a community of people that developed psychoanalysis and Marxist analysis in part to deepen our abilities to recognize and compensate for our own distortions, now engaged in trying to do in this generation what Jews have done in every generation: open our ears to God's revelation, whose sound waves are still pulsating through the universe, and our eyes to God's Torah and to the interpretive community that grapples with Torah, that takes it seriously, and that will try not to allow it to be hijacked either by the legacy of cruelty or by the arrogance of those who think they have all the answers."

We confront this task with humility and a prayerful request to God, repeated in the Shachreet service each morning: "Enlighten our eyes in Your Torah, and cause our hearts to cleave to You, and unify our hearts to love and stand in awe of Your Name."

Prayer is no afterthought. Throughout this book I have argued that God is the Force that makes possible our ability to transcend our history and to recognize one another. And it is the God energy within us, the way that we are created in God's image, that gives us the ability to recognize God's voice.

It is this same God who is constantly pulling us toward transcendence of our own constituted ways of being and understanding reality. We move toward our newer conceptions of God *not* because we wish to be chic and modern, but because we are pulled in that way by God. Thus, Jewish renewal in every generation is made possible because of God's energy in the world.

OVERCOMING EGO DISTORTIONS

On both the individual and communal levels, those who think that they are "getting" the truth must be especially vigilant to deal with the distortions of ego. On the one hand, I reject moral or spiritual relativism, which assumes that anyone who thinks that they are getting some special insight must necessarily be self-deceived. I believe that in each historical moment there are some people who are specially tuned to some aspects of nature, social reality, ethical and/or spiritual truths, and that those people are both blessed (because of the joy of receiving these messages more clearly), cursed (because they often put themselves into positions of special vulnerability in relationship to others who feel angry that they have not been similarly blessed), and deeply responsible (to the rest of the human race to do their best to share what they have gotten and to embody it as much as they can).

Yet having this special role can also lead to wild ego distortions. And this has at times happened both to the Jewish people and to individual Jews, just as I've witnessed this same dynamic happen to many people involved in the healing and repairing professions, Marxists and other social-change activists, feminists, psychotherapists, and anyone else who in some way has vanguard consciousness, with something to teach that others need to learn. The absorption in self-importance sometimes undermines our ability to function as healers.

There are three parts to the remedy: first, more genuine self-love. Self-delusional importance, narcissistic self-absorption, and excessive attachment to the ego are often signs of a person or a people that has not gotten enough love and caring. Particularly when one is doing the kind of healing work in which the Jewish people or social-change activists are involved—healing that requires challenging existing social arrangements, systems of selfishness, and ideologies that insist on the inevitability of contemporary forms of social and psychological distortion—the world can often respond with severe battering, and after a while one can come to feel very unloved and unlovable. The compensatory nature of narcissistic self-absorption and focus on one's specialness ("the chosen people," on a social level; "the perfect master," "perfect healer," "Messiah," "fully analyzed analyst," or "most brilliant intellect or artist," on the individual level) is often a cry of despair or an appeal to be noticed and loved. The solution here is *not* to shake the person or people involved with a rebuking attitude: "Get a hold of yourselves: shame on you; wake up to reality." Nor should the individual do that to herself: "I've got to overcome my narcissism and make myself less selfish and self-centered." Rather, the cure here is healthy narcissism, encouraging the battered healers really and deeply to learn to love themselves, accept themselves and their limitations, understand more fully why they are not getting the love from a world dominated by forces that feel threatened by them, and providing opportunities for them to engage more fully in the kind of deep self-affirmation that will obviate the need to spend so much psychic energy reassuring themselves and others of how special they really are.

A second part of the cure is to increase one's connections and love to others. On the individual level, this can mean committing oneself to an other, allowing oneself to be absorbed in caring for and giving to them, even at times losing oneself in them. Nothing is more curative for excessive self-importance than this experience of really getting deeply into an other. On the collective level, this same direction may be useful. Occasionally the Jewish people need to dedicate their energies to learning about the cultural realities, history, religious and spiritual lives, and psychological pains of other peoples. Imagining ourselves into their situations, allowing ourselves to care deeply for their pain, coming to see how fundamentally similar all human beings really are, can contribute to the process of healing our own delusional self-importance.

Finally, a healthy diet can include daily spiritual work aimed at letting go of ego. Daily prayer and meditation can be very useful in this regard. To pray, one must suspend one's sense that one already knows everything, and instead allow oneself to fall under the influence of ancient rhythms and ancient formulations. To meditate, one must allow oneself to sit and "waste time," learn how to "do nothing," how just to be with oneself in order to go beyond one's self.

A perfect focus of meditation is the Shma prayer itself. In recognizing God as the Force that makes for the possibility of transformation of that which is to that which ought to be, one recognizes that the burden is *not entirely on us*, that we are not the center of the universe, and that although we have a task, there are also powerful forces in the universe that have been at that task for a long time before we arrived and will be there a long time after we are gone. We are privileged to wake up to the beauty and grandeur of the universe, to hear a bit of God's song being sung by the universe, to pass on to the next generation the bit of it that we get, and perhaps to embody it in the institutions and social practices we develop. But if we allow ourselves to see the world as filled with God's glory and already pulsating with God's message, we can tame our own self-importance.

Detachment from ego does *not* mean detachment from a commitment to our role and our task. But it *does* mean detachment from our inflated sense that the world is depending on our every move. Having a perspective on who we are and who we are not can be attained through deep meditation over the Shma and over the history of the human race. A little of that perspective, ordered systematically every day into a period that we set aside for prayer and meditation, can be brought into our consciousness, allowing us to breathe more deeply and calmly, to remain more in touch with the rhythms of our own bodies and the rhythms of the planet on which we live, and to take the time to notice the needs and pleasures of those around us as well. Part of the process of letting go of the anxiety produced by our feeling that *everything* depends on us was suggested by our rabbis centuries ago. They recommended that we keep a piece of paper in one pocket reminding us that we are but dust and ashes, and in the other pocket a paper reminding us that it was for our sake that the world was created. Keeping both in mind may give us a better perspective. So, too, it can be helpful to remind ourselves of how many others among all the nations of the world are increasingly drawn to the task of healing and repair. The world is filled with good and decent people, and increasingly they are involved in the same kind of renewal work in their own communities that we seek in Judaism.

But in case we haven't fulfilled this need for detachment, Judaism has one massive dose of it already set aside for us each week: Shabbat. In a later chapter I shall address how Shabbat works. Here I merely want to highlight that Judaism builds into our lives a full day out of every seven that will be devoted to gaining perspective, a twenty-five-hour meditation on who we are.

And this is also why humor and play are so important, and so central to a rich spiritual life. It's only when we can learn to play with who we are, to laugh and sport and frolic, that we can get the distance and perspective we need lest we become so self-intoxicated that we undermine all that we seek to accomplish. That's why the Hasidim taught that it's a great *mitzvah* to be full of joy. Jewish renewal must constantly seek ways to enhance joy in our lives, recognizing that through joy, humor, and play we are likely to make ourselves ever more deeply open to God's energy.

Yet here too there is an excess to be avoided. I have met people whose major spiritual work is focused on overcoming their ego or on learning detachment. In my personal experience I often find these people to be the most attached and ego-centered of any, because so much of their energy is focused on themselves and whether they have gotten to the truest, deepest, or most authentic level of spiritual being. Learning ego reduction and nonattachment can be very important, but it should not drown out or replace the other aspect of a healthy spiritual life: the energies devoted to healing, repairing, and transforming the world so that God energy can flow through every human interaction and every social institution. In this sense, being God's witness and fighting for world transformation is itself a form of ego reduction. If coupled with the three activities proposed here, it can be a central element in a spiritually healthy life.

CHAPTER SIX

COMPASSION FOR WOUNDED HEALERS

THE SECOND REVELATION

If the first great truth of Judaism is the discovery of God as the Force that makes possible the transformation of the universe, the second great truth is that we, the people involved in bringing this message, are wounded healers. We are severely limited beings, weighed down by our legacy of pain, anger, violence, and cruelty. And yet this is all that there is to heal the world: these limited human beings that are you and I and everyone else. There is no alternative.

This is the problem that every group of healers and transformers faces. When Jesus said, "Physician, heal thyself," he was on to something—the fact that the healers are always themselves part of the problem, and must work on their own limitations. But he was also deeply wrong, because by implication he was suggesting that it was possible to be some other kind of healer, a fully healed one. And this is impossible in the world as currently constituted. So every group of healers and transformers will be severely limited—the psychiatrists, psychologists, and social workers; the feminists, Third World activists, Marxists, and other social-change agents; the prophets, gurus, and spiritual teachers; the artists, writers, and poets; the spiritual leaders; the political leaders; the leaders of the Jewish people.

While we can recognize the distortions in our tradition and in our-selves, either we have to give up entirely, leaving the world exactly as it is, or we have to figure out a way to work with what we have, moving from our limitations to a healing that can be done only by limited beings. Hence, Torah's revelation of the need for compassion.

Perhaps this sense of a beaten-down and deformed people is the deepest truth behind the midrashic claim that the Jewish people leaving Egypt were all handicapped. As Rabbi Tanhumah son of Rabbi Abba says (Numbers Rabba 7:1), the people taken out of Egypt were a broken people, physically and, adds Rabbi Tzvi Marx in his landmark study *Halakha and Handicap*, "undoubtedly mentally as well." The physically healthy family of Joseph had been transformed into a handicapped people. And though the handicaps talked about by the Midrash are physical, the text of the Torah itself makes clear that they were not mentally or spiritually healthy either. On the contrary, it is precisely this recognition that provides God's justification for the decision to keep this generation in the desert until they die off, so that a new people could enter the Promised Land forty years later.

Return with me to the moment of revelation, the moment in which a people "gets it" that the world can be different, a people that has just experienced something that turned the entire world upside down, showing the inevitability of oppression to be a lie—a moment that subordinates the lawlike regularity of nature to a higher spiritual and moral order. The psalmist can declare that when Israel left Egypt, "the sea saw it and fled, the mountains danced like rams, the little hills like young sheep" (Psalm 114:2–3). They have personally experienced the fundamental truth of the universe: the possibility of possibility. They are overwhelmed by it, excited by it, and momentarily they understand that they have to embody this understanding in how they treat one another, in the way they conduct their lives, and they must tell this message to others, teach it to their children, shout and rejoice about it.

Yet it is only a moment later that they get scared. It's too much, the burden of this knowledge. And so they want to retreat from it, go back to Egypt, or at least recast their lives as loyal children of Egypt, dancing around the golden calf and doing their best to recreate a relationship to gods with which they are familiar. These are not people who have lost religion—they still have the consciousness, shared by other nations, that the world deserves to be celebrated. But they have lost the memory that the God that created the world is also the God that makes the transformation possible.

According to the Torah account, God's first reaction is anger. Perhaps this people should be replaced. But eventually a different response emerges. Urged by Moses to reconsider, God establishes the other side of His/Her being, the side of compassion.

SURPLUS POWERLESSNESS LIMITS TRANSCENDENCE

It was the side of God that demanded human transcendence that led God to be angry at the Israelites' failure to be what they could be. Yet God quickly recognizes that there are limits to human transcendence. In every generation people can make great strides forward, but absolute transformation is not possible. The reason: even when external oppression is gone and human beings appear to be free to act in accord with their highest selves, they still face the debilitating psychological effects of oppression and the internalization of cruelty. There is more than real powerlessness standing in the way of human improvement. There is also what I call surplus powerlessness, the degree to which individuals have internalized their powerlessness and become convinced that the way things are now is the only way that they can be.[1]

To the extent that human beings believe that reality is fixed and nothing can be changed, and that they themselves simply are the way that they are and unable to do things differently, they accept a world that is radically flawed and try to accommodate to it, rather than attempt to change it. Indeed, they become fearful of anyone who would suggest that change is possible, and become committed to the belief that such change could only threaten their own value and worth. Having worked out a way to receive the minimal level of recognition that they do receive, and remembering that the recognition that they got in their childhoods was "an achievement" rather than something that they received by virtue of their intrinsic worth, they quickly become terrified that any serious change in the status quo might threaten the always inadequate but nevertheless "all that we can get" level of recognition. Moreover, in every historical period there is a thickly embroidered set of ideas that are described as "common sense," which

---

[1]See my *Surplus Powerlessness* (Atlantic Highlands, NJ: Humanities Press International, Inc., 1991).

are in fact the summary set of expressions by which people reassure one another that what is is all that could be, and that one is foolish to try anything else. In most historical periods, this common sense is also dressed up in more formal garb—in the forms of religious, metaphysical, or (in the latest incarnation) scientific beliefs that serve to reinforce this deep conviction that nothing much can be changed.

But surplus powerlessness is not just some set of ideas about the world—it is also intertwined with a complex set of feelings about oneself. Most human beings are deeply committed to the picture they have of themselves as beings who do not really deserve to be more loved, more free, more conscious, more able to actualize themselves in daily life, more joyous, or more fulfilled than they actually are. They have internalized a picture of themselves as the kinds of persons who deserve whatever happens to them. Our surplus powerlessness, then, is a product of the complex intertwined beliefs we have about the world and the feelings we have about ourselves.

Of course, the whole point of the Jewish story is that this is *not* the whole picture. Despite the powerful dynamics of surplus powerlessness, human beings are created in the image of God, have the capacity for transcendence, and hence can never be fully stifled and contained within the legacy of pain and cruelty. This is what the experience of the Exodus and the revelation of Sinai helped clarify. Yet the story of the golden calf helps us to remember that at any moment the amount of transcendence is limited. Sinai is a moment of dramatic illumination. But when one comes down from such a moment, the life we lead takes over again, and things do not change automatically just because the illumination has happened. The deep structuring of surplus powerlessness makes the patterns and distorted consciousness embedded in the institutions and social practices of daily life difficult to dislodge.

COMPASSION AND LIMITS

So the process of change is slow, cumulative. The good news is that it is possible. But the demand for transcendence must be balanced by *chesed*, compassion. Though I use the word compassion as the best available English translation of the word *chesed*, the Hebrew term does not have the same sappy, nonjudgmental connotation that it has come to have in contemporary psychobabble. From the Jewish standpoint, *chesed* means lovingkindness, understanding others' complexities, recognition of the inner and outer obstacles we all face in receiving or giving love, recognition, or care. It does *not* entail an end to moral or spiritual demand, or an end to obligation. Jewish compassion does not obviate our personal responsibility to the *miztvot*. Rather, it helps us understand and accept the limitations of human beings, to not utterly reject them, to recognize that we are but flesh and blood, that we are weak and vulnerable and to some extent trapped in a social reality that we did not construct and which is hard to transcend. *Chesed* is not acceptance that allows a complacent reconciliation with one's own personal reality ("I'm okay, you're okay"), but the acknowledgment of what is and where it has come from so that one may move more effectively toward what ought to be. It recognizes the constraints upon us so as to encourage a lovingkindness and gentleness in our dealings with others.

Developing *chesed* for others or for oneself is not always easy. Particularly after the moments of illumination, one wants the world to have changed already, to be all that it could be. We see this clearly with Moses.

Moses, having pleaded with God to save the people of Israel from divine destruction, is angry when he has to confront the spectacle of the people worshipping the calf. Incensed, Moses organizes the tribe of Levi and, in the name of God (but without there being any textual indication that God actually authorized this in any way), they proceed to kill three thousand people from among the Israelites. Here is the irony: Moses becomes, in this moment, the very thing that incenses him—the limited, partial being whose own past, with its attendant angers, suddenly rages out of control. In the name of being true to the revelation and its vision of breaking the legacy of cruelty, Moses responds in a negative and cruel way.

It is after these bloody events that the text tells us that Moses asks God to "show me your ways" and then, a few sentences later, "show me your glory." Moses seems to be asking for a direct and unmediated experience of God—and this even the highest prophet cannot have. God offers to pass by Moses and show him that which is after God, God's back side, or more correctly, God's effects in the world. God invites Moses to gaze in the same direction in which God is gazing.

This account of the mystical union provides us with one model of the loving relationship among God and beings who embody God's presence. Non-Jewish instances of mystical union often aim at fusion with the spirit of God, coming to know God's essence through looking into God's face. But Moses is told, No, that's not the way. The way to know God is to look out onto the world the way God looks out onto the world. Moses is to face the same way God faces, and to see God's effects in the world.

So what is it that Moses sees? It is described in the words that are uttered as God passes before him: "YHVH, YHVH, the God of mercy and kindness, long-suffering and abundant in compassion and truth; preserving compassion for the thousandth generation, forgiving iniquity and sin; but not clearing away all the guilt, remembering the sins of the fathers to the children and grandchildren to the third and fourth generations." Or, to give the deeper meaning–drenched interpretation of Jewish Renewal Rabbi David Wolfe-Blanke: "YHVH, YHVH, expanding force of kindness, merciful womb, graceful giver, long-stretched web, many-faceted jewel, maestro of generosity, and dispatcher of truth; funnel of kindness to thousands, tolerator of distortion who puts up with intentional error, shoulders omission, and cleanses."

Just as we previously confronted God as the Force that makes for transcendence, now we are made aware that the universe is governed by a power that makes compassion possible, preserving compassion and keeping it alive even when the objective circumstances might not warrant it, out of a commitment to the earlier generations that may have done some acts of kindness and goodness that allow that compassion to thrive in the world (Chasdai Avot). Many ancient religions saw the world as hostile and threatening, full of demons that thwart human plans, or governed by gods that intervene randomly. The God of the Bible here reveals Him/Herself as having established a world in which there is a relationship between what happens today and what has happened in the past. Yet this is not simply the cause/effect relationship of karma—a one-to-one correspondence between what one does and what happens. It is through the generations that the goodness or badness of what one has done gets manifested in the world. Human beings' acts have consequences that shape the lives of the generations to come.

But the Force governing the universe does not pass on the good and the bad equally. Acts of compassion are amplified so that their consequences are felt for a thousand generations. It is this amplification that explains why parents, no matter how frozen in their internal emotional life, are unable to extinguish totally in children the desire for mutual recognition and confirmation. Almost always the parents communicate some level of recognition, no matter how subtly and unconsciously, that keeps alive and passes on to the next generation a sense of possibility and freedom that is never fully extinguished. These moments in which the child is quietly and unconsciously affirmed as a being are not totally predictable by any rational calculation of cause/effect; or, to be more accurate, they are predictable to the extent that one understands that the universe works in accord with God's description to Moses—that S/He accentuates the moments of compassion and loving to the thousandth generation.

Some moderns have been shocked at the down side: that the negativity gets passed on to the third and fourth generations. The good news here is that it's *only* three or four generations, as opposed to the acts of love and compassion that are amplified to the thousandth generation. It's not that the negativity does not get passed on beyond those three or four generations, for as we have seen, we have all been tied to a chain of negativity that links generations from the distant past. But the Force that governs the universe makes possible a transcendence of this chain, and the negativity can be overwhelmed by the possibilities created by a universe whose primary Force is committed to compassion.

Realistically, most human beings are going to exercise only very limited transcendence, and will have a strong tendency to fall back into previously-learned and socially reinforced patterns of negativity.

INTERNALIZED OPPRESSION AND JEWISH PSYCHOTHERAPY

Compassion for others depends on our ability to generate compassion for ourselves. We too are wounded healers. We too are filled with distortions that will limit our ability to see clearly and tempt us to accept as inevitable elements that we have inherited and that have been shaped by the transmission of cruelty throughout history. Recognizing this is the beginning of compassion. It is the dialectic between transcendence and compassion that shapes Jewish destiny.

Jews have often unfairly blamed themselves for the reactions of others toward us. We have internalized as self-blame the anger that others have projected upon us, so that we devalue our Jewishness, accept distorted accounts of Judaism, and subtly feel bad about ourselves. Developing compassion for ourselves and fellow Jews requires a complex understanding about psychological dynamics and also about the ways throughout history in which external oppression has shaped our being. (Ironically, the whole field of psychotherapy has been pioneered by Jews, most of whom have had little understanding of their own Jewishness and little comprehension that the ways that they saw the world were shaped by internalized oppression. So they taught about the necessity of forgiving one's parents, but rarely understood how those parents and *their* distortions were in part shaped by the internalization of external oppression, particularly anti-Semitism.)

Part of the deep attraction many Jews have to Yom Kippur, the Jewish Day of Atonement, is connected to our sometimes unconscious recognition that the Jewish project in the world is overwhelming, and one at which we will often fail miserably. Part of Yom Kippur's message is that the God that makes possible and demands transcendence is also a God that mandates us to be compassionate toward ourselves and one another. It is as wounded healers that we will bear witness. That we will *not* be the full embodiments of our own highest ideals is not a license to abandon personal or communal responsibility—hence we repent our sins, our failings, the ways that we have missed the mark. But we also affirm a God that accepts this reality, that can forgive, and that can urge us also to embody this same approach of compassion in our own daily interactions with one another.

THE DIFFICULT CASES

Compassion is not always easy.

The Book of Jonah, read in synagogues on Yom Kippur, reminds us that compassion must be extended to the enemies of the Jewish people. It's easy to have compassion for our friends who screw up. But what about those who really wish us ill? To develop compassion for them does *not* mean acquiescing to their will, or allowing ourselves to be physically hurt by them. It *does* mean keeping in mind at all times that they too are created in the image of God, and that the distortions in them that lead them to wish us ill are the product of a world of pain and cruelty that shaped them in this particular way. We don't have to condone their behavior to stay in touch with their fundamental humanity, to remind ourselves of how much we have in common with them, and to remind ourselves to ask whether some of the things that most annoy us about them may also, in slightly different form, be true of us as well.

Compassion is even harder when we find ourselves confronted with wild distortions among those who seem to share some of our ideas or experiences. We feel more betrayed, because these people are on our side. Let's take what seems like a particularly difficult case for me at the moment that I am writing this book: that small segment of Israeli settlers who have murdered, physically attacked, or terrorized Palestinians, or those who support policies based on the assumption that Palestinians are essentially evil or less than fully human—and then announce that they are doing all this in the name of Judaism. Some of these people have physically assaulted people I know in the peace movement. Some have personally made threats against my life because of the role I've played as a public supporter in the United States of the Israeli peace movement. Compassion does *not* mean that we accept this behavior or that we fail to publicly confront it. But it *does* require that when we confront these people we try to understand the pain in them that leads them to act out in this kind of way, just as we might also seek to understand the pain in a member of Hamas who is driven to similar or more destructive acts.

In remembering that these people are created in the image of God, we remind ourselves that their tendency to demean others and see them in stereotyped ways is something that could yet be overcome, that they could yet change, that they could yet respond to a reality of love and trust no matter how badly bruised they have been by life and by ideologies of hate and violence. We must remember that even if they never change, the spirit of God resides within them; *their* humanity must not be demeaned even as we combat the ways that they demean others. This is not always easy for us to accomplish, but it is the injunction of a God of transcendence and compassion.

One thing that helps develop compassion: listen to the stories of those whom you might be tempted to demean. Listen to their stories about their own childhoods and what they went through, their experiences in the world, and the stories that permeate their culture. Allow yourself to imagine yourself in their shoes. And then bring in as much information as you can from psychology, sociology, feminism, etc., to help situate their stories in the larger picture of the human race and its struggle to become more fully itself (which is to say, more fully infused with God's spirit). The more we hear the stories, and the more we understand the context, the more we see that those who are our enemies are themselves fully human and fully deserving of respect. And the more that we can project that attitude toward others, the closer we can get to becoming who we most fully want to be.

All this can sound very sappy if compassion replaces political struggle. This is *not* my intent. We can energetically confront the xenophobia of the Nation of Islam and its anti-Semitic leadership, or the moral bankruptcy of policies that allow some of the world's peoples slowly to starve to death while others live in unprecedented luxury and self-indulgence, or the craziness of a world economy that allows some corporate interests slowly to destroy the environmental life-support systems of this planet—and struggle to change the policies and politically isolate the racists, anti-Semites, and homophobes. But we will be most effective, and most spiritually centered, when we approach these struggles, imbued not only with righteous indignation but with a deep compassion for those with whom we must struggle, constantly keeping in mind their fundamental humanity.

Here, too, we need some compassion for ourselves. To have compassion for those who hurt us is very difficult. A Jewish-renewal consciousness encourages us to strive for this goal. But it must also encourage us to have compassion for ourselves for the ways that we do not yet fully embody the compassion in which we believe. We are, after all, wounded healers, and our compassion is likely to be less than perfect.

PART II

GOD SHATTERING:
THE RETREAT FROM GOD
IN JEWISH HISTORY AND
CONTEMPORARY JEWISH LIFE

Staying true to the message of Torah—that there is a Force that makes for the possibility of transforming the world from that which is to that which ought to be, that that Force is the central Power and Creator of the universe, that the repetition compulsion leading us to pass on to the next generation the cruelty and pain that have been done to us can be broken, and that the conveyers of this message will themselves necessarily be flawed human beings who deserve compassion for their failures even as they strive to transcend them—has been extraordinarily difficult throughout our history as Jews.

In this section I will explore what happens when Jews start to abandon the Jewish project, become more "realistic," and do their best to fit into the world as constituted. From the very beginning of our history, Jews have been trying to run away from the responsibility and the terror of being witnesses to the possibility of healing and transformation. We have been "reluctant witnesses," and our reluctance has grown even more intense in the modern world.

The pain of the Holocaust and the surge of pride at the creation of the State of Israel have both, in their own ways, undermined the Jewish people's ability to be witnesses to the possibility that cruelty and pain, power and arrogance and self-interest, need not define reality. The most typical explanation of the twentieth century goes something like this: Stuck in an idealistic expectation that the world could be made better, Jews were unprepared for the reality of the triumph of evil in Europe; luckily, some Jews had already abandoned the older ways of looking at the world, had become realistic, and had set in motion the forces that would create the State of Israel, a state founded on a cold and objective assessment that the Jewish people must follow the power- and self-interest–oriented examples of other nations, become like them, and thus protect Jewish interests; and since we've been doing that the Jewish-people have become powerful and respected once again.

In this section I propose another way to understand the Holocaust and Israel that is more in tune with a Jewish-renewal perspective on

Torah and the tasks of the Jewish people. In particular I show how a progressive Jew today might still believe in the prophetic injunction that it is "not by power and not by might, but by My Spirit" that redemption will come. In light of that prophetic injunction, I rethink the Holocaust and Zionism, and then proceed to suggest a way that Jewish renewal could translate its message into a meaning-focused language that could make a significant contribution to the larger world's political discourse.

CHAPTER SEVEN

How the Revolutionary Message Got Repressed and Abandoned

An Overview of the Discrediting of Judaism

I've just told you that Judaism is terrific. So then why would people run away from it? This is a central question, but it requires telling a complicated story.

As we have discovered thus far, the exciting news from Judaism is: the world can be radically transformed from what it is to what it ought to be, and the fundamental spiritual reality of the universe makes this transformation possible.

The difficult news is that we can understand these words but have trouble embodying them and staying true to them as we actually face our own lives.

The sad news is that there are parts of our unconscious that are deeply committed to denying this truth, to rejecting God, and to remaining depressively attached to the inevitability of pain; and there are enough people acting on that depressive attachment so that the rest of us will continually wonder whether our belief that things could be otherwise is merely wishful thinking.

This is the central dilemma of faith. No set of actual changes in the world has ever been sufficient to dislodge and replace our depressive attachment to cruelty, violence, and pessimism. We have never had the kind of miracles that we actually want, namely the kind that over-whelms us and forces us to believe, the kind of miracle that Job demanded of God, the kind of miracle that eliminates the need for faith. There never will be such miracles.

So we will always remain stuck in the fact that the evidence is inadequate, that maybe the Red Sea split because of wind conditions, that maybe the plagues were just natural events, that maybe the real truth is the moment of Israel's reversion to the golden calf and Moses' reversion to patriarchal anger. To have faith is to recognize that there will never be decisive proof, and to believe that the reality is both—both that the tendencies to reversions to idolatry, to despair, and to cruelty and violence are always present, and that those tendencies can be dramatically reduced, reshaped in ways that are less destructive and hurtful, and eventually overcome.

Jewish history can be read as a dialectic interaction between three realities:

1. the tendency of Jews to stay faithful to the revolutionary mes-sage, developing customs, stories, religious practices, legal ar-rangements, and ways of relating to the world that provide testimony to the possibility that the way the world is is not the only way it can be, and with that a spirit of optimism, humor, intellectual and emotional courage, ethical and spiritual sensi-tivity, generosity of heart, and refined capacities to love others that tend to accompany a belief in the possibility of a God of transcendence;

2. the tendency of Jews to disbelieve their own story, and to embody within themselves and their societies all the markings of cruelty, paranoia, self-doubt, powerlessness, pettiness, lust for power, defensive self-aggrandizement, and pessimism that are endemic in patriarchal societies;

3. the accommodations to power and to evil that are imposed by a world full of hostility to the Jewish message, a world that wants to "teach the Jews the lesson" that things really can't be dif-ferent because all that can possibly reign here is cruelty, pain, and deception, and that anyone who thinks differently must be a fool.

If Judaism's uniqueness can be understood as its fusing of a sensitivity to the grandeur and wonder of the universe with the spiritual force of transformation, then the process in which Judaism got discredited for many Jews had two moments. First, the splitting off of the revolutionary message, so that it moves from foreground to background; second, as Judaism becomes more like other religions, concentrated more on celebrating the world than on changing it, it is discounted, made into something purely subjective, removed from public life, and finally dismissed in the modern world by many Jews as irrational residue.

The process through which Judaism got transformed into merely a religion, and then abandoned by many Jews, has been facilitated by some Jewish leaders, teachers, scholars, and rabbis who felt that the cost of staying true to Judaism's revolutionary message was unbearably high. As Jews came into contact with the surrounding cultures, and particularly after we were exiled from our homeland, it seemed almost impossibly demanding to emphasize our message that the world could be fundamentally transformed. That message seemed to be at such odds with the "common sense" experience of how the world is as to be hopelessly naive and utopian. Never once recognizing that common sense in a world of oppression is merely the congealed wisdom of people who have been beaten down over and over and over again, and hence merely a reflection of the current level of internalized powerlessness, Jewish leaders throughout the ages have sought to preserve the Jewish people by helping them accommodate to reality, in the process often forgetting that the whole purpose of Jewish existence is to be witness to the possibility of transforming that reality.

Jews, then, have been torn between their revolutionary message and their perception that their survival needs depend upon toning down or even "spiritualizing" that message so that it will not be offensive.

No wonder, then, that you didn't hear this transformative message too clearly. When you read a Jewish text, hear a bit of Jewish humor or folklore, participate in a prayer experience, study a halakhic ruling, or explore social or religious practices of the Jews, you must always ask yourself to what degree the author or conveyers of the texts or the originators of the practices were themselves interested in remaining committed to the revolutionary thrust of Judaism, and to what extent they saw that as unrealistic and had already begun to ask questions, frame experience, develop conceptual frameworks that had subtly or not so subtly moved away from that thrust and began to assume that in this world nothing much could be changed. When you read the Jewish tradition with this question in mind, you will begin to see that many practices or worldviews that emerge throughout Jewish history are conscious or unconscious attempts to grapple with this issue. And you will encounter a deep ambivalence, sometimes even within a given writer or thinker or social movement, reflecting the tension between the desire to stay loyal to the revolutionary message and the desire to be practical and survival-oriented.

It is this deep ambivalence that also helps account for the fact that few people in the Jewish world speak about this issue directly. Part of the reason is that it's too scary to fully confront the meaning of our revolutionary heritage, with its powerful injunctions to change the world. Part of the reason is that the people who passed on Judaism themselves partly forgot and partly repressed the message. Part of the reason is that it is hard to take seriously the message of Judaism because we've had so many experiences of the world being dominated by cruelty and pain that it seems incredible to believe that things could be different.

One way that this ambivalence manifests is that the message remains, but since people see no immediate way to act on it in the world, they embed the message in a set of religious rituals, hoping that the rituals will keep the message alive. Later generations, still seeing no opportunity to act on the message in their world, begin to invest their passion in refining the details of the rituals or in the intellectual process of understanding the law, so that eventually much of the message is minimized, camouflaged, or otherwise played down so that even when it *was* told to you, it was told in ways that didn't make that much of an impression. They didn't explicate the message, but rather invested their energy refining the ritual practices.

But why all this ambivalence? Because staying true to this message has been extremely difficult. In telling the story of the ways Jews ran away from that message, I mean no disrespect, because the Jewish people were facing extremely difficult circumstances, and the choices that were made were often made by very dedicated and principled people who were doing their best. In telling the story of the ways Jews ran away from Torah, or tried to accommodate it to "reality," I want to emphasize that need for compassion and sympathy for those who ran and those who sought accommodations. There was plenty to fear.

Ironically, although the radical nature of our message may not be so clear to us in the Jewish world, it sounded very clear to those outside who found it offensive or threatening.

WHY THEY HATED THE JEWS

No one likes a party pooper. But the Jews disrupted the party that the ruling elites of the world set up to celebrate their own power and good fortune.

Every ruling elite of the ancient and medieval world, and many in the modern world, justified their rule by ideologies whose central message was that the world could not be changed, that the social world is fundamentally like the physical world, and that both are governed by immutable lawlike processes; and that those in power are in power because they are supposed to be, and those who are out of power are ordained to be, and that nothing human beings can do will alter the fundamental structure of the world.

Along come the Jews with a very different message: "The world can be fundamentally changed. Every system of oppression, no matter how powerful it appears to be, can be overthrown. In fact, we were part of overthrowing one, and we have watched as many others (Babylonia, Persia, Greece, Rome) have been overthrown. So nothing in the social world is fixed. And ordinary people can be central in those changes. We know that, because we did it ourselves. We were once the most degraded of all social statuses—slaves—and now we are free. And that transformation was made possible because there is a God in the universe that makes possible the transformation from slavery to freedom. So don't be fooled by any ruling group that tells you something different, because we are living proof that everything could be opposite to what it is."

This is not a side message buried somewhere in the midst of a full panoply of tales about the world. It is the central story. Four of the five books of the Torah are dedicated to telling the story of this process and of the legislation that grew directly out of that experience.

Moreover, the entire way of life of the Jewish people is dedicated to telling the story. Every week they proclaim a one-day Shabbat, on which they will not work. This is the first recorded workers' holiday. On it, Jews must do no work, "neither you nor your family nor anyone who works for you, nor any animal, nor any visitor, or anyone who is within your gates." Jews enforced this in the ancient and medieval worlds in the one way that they could: they proclaimed their willingness to die rather than to work on Shabbat. In so doing, they carved out an inviolable space that the employer could not impinge upon, and thus created the notion of workers' rights in the most powerful of ways. On each Shabbat they read a portion of the story, until the entire story is completed, and then they read it again and again.

The major holidays are also focused on this same story. And the minor holidays like Chanukah and Purim are elaborations of later struggles in which the Jews pursued this same path.

There is, then, a relentlessness to this people. Oh, yes, they share with other peoples the concerns of other religions: the celebration of nature; the standing in awe and wonder at the grandeur of the universe; the concern with noting the life cycle of the individual and of the cosmos. But subtly intertwined through all of this is the same melody: that the world can be radically transformed, and that the Power that runs the universe is the Power that makes that possible.

Moreover, the Jews create legislation and social practices that are so deeply radical in their impact that they potentially undermine the social basis for any system of oppression.

First, there is the reality of building a religion around a set of holy writings and then encouraging people to study those writings. The result is that Jews had one of the highest levels of literacy in the ancient world (qualified thus because we do not have accurate data from China), and with it the ability for ordinary people to gain access to knowledge that elsewhere was restricted to ruling elites and their hired scribes, philosophers, and playwrights. There is a corpus of social legislation that unequivocally promotes the cause of the poor and the other (the *ger*, or stranger, of whom it is written in the Torah: "You should love the stranger"). There is the insistence in the Torah that all are equal before the law—including the *ger*. Law is built not to sanctify privilege but to insist on one standard that is to be applied to all. Finally, there is the economic legislation which requires an end to debts every seven years and a radical redistribution of the land every fifty years, back to the original position. These are notions that are radical for our world today, and would make a tremendous impact if they were adopted in the modern world. How much more so in the ancient world.

As the story of Purim recounts, the Jews understood that their refusal to bow down to constituted authority was the source of their trouble. Not that Jews consciously saw themselves as a revolutionary vanguard. Nor did ruling elites regularly articulate their opposition to the Jews in terms of their role as revolutionaries who might spread their ideas to the masses (though the story of Pharaoh in Egypt and the story of Haman in Persia seem to indicate that the Jews in the ancient world sometimes attributed this consciousness to those who oppressed them). But even though they didn't use the language of revolution, the Jews made it very clear that they regarded secular power as limited and subject to higher authority. In their Aleynu prayer, said thrice daily, they announced to the self-declared "King of Kings" that their God was the King of the King of Kings. Jewish liturgy and theology was provocative and troublesome to the powerful.

There was no doubting that these were the most cantankerous people of the ancient world, the ones most involved in rebellions against constituted authority, the ones who were willing to fight against Rome even when they had no visible chance of winning, the trouble-makers par excellence.

So why should it be a surprise that ruling elites found the Jewish religion a scandal and the Jewish people offensive? Long before Christianity had its own special complaint—that Jews had not recognized Jesus as the Messiah or son of God—ideologues of the ancient world were identifying the Jews as a problem people.

The ascendancy of Christianity further intensified the problem. To the extent that rulers of late antiquity, the Dark Ages, and the feudal period based their claim to legitimacy on the truth of Christianity, the Jews were an even greater offense. Particularly in the first few hundred years after the death of Jesus, the Jews tended to be particularly provocative in detailing how they had had firsthand experience of this individual and had not been all that impressed. It was a troubling message that could best be responded to by insisting that the Jews themselves had been abandoned by God, superseded in their chosenness by the Church. But Jewish communities seemed to be still flourishing. So the ruling elites re-created the appearance of abandonment and devastation for the Jews, and it was for this reason—as well as to ensure that the Jews' subversively radical perspectives on the world would not be heard—that the ruling elites began to adopt repressive legislation designed to impoverish, oppress, isolate, and degrade the Jewish people.

Equally important, because they held control over every avenue through which ordinary people could get information about others, ruling elites did their best to turn the native populations against the Jews. Every possible abusive characteristic was attributed to the Jews: they were sexually overcharged and likely to rape the women or seduce the men; they were robbers who would manipulate and insidiously take advantage of you, leave you penniless, bankrupt your whole society, destroy your crops, undermine your well-being; they were liars who spread stories that would deceive you; they were murderers who might kill your little child and use the blood in mysterious religious rites just as they had already killed the son of God; and they were devils who had the most uncanny way of tricking you without your even knowing it. No wonder, then, that without even knowing any Jews the population gradually became ferociously anti-Semitic, often exceeding in anger and violence the ruling elites that had originally stirred up this anger.

Ruling elites sometimes found useful economic functions for the Jews as moneylenders and traders, so they did not necessarily want the total elimination of the Jews. But the racist anger that they helped to foster in the general population took on a life of its own and became a force that ruling elites could not always control. It is thus with all racisms and ethnic hatred—they can become far more powerful than originally intended by those who fostered them. The racist anger allows populations to express in distorted form their upset at living in a world in which *their* fundamental humanity is not recognized, and in a socially sanctioned way that forces no confrontation with the constituted authorities. The result: far beyond the limits prescribed by law, native populations began to adopt the hatred of the Jew which became the hallmark of Western "civilization" for much of the past two thousand years. The Jewish people became the mistaken target for all the legitimate anger at oppression. And once that pattern is firmed, there is a "surplus of hatred," hatred not based directly on anger at oppression, but rather hatred that is generated by the racist stereotypes and stories themselves.

It is not my intent to tell the history of the ensuing nineteen hundred years of oppression in any detail. What I do want to emphasize is that classical anti-Semitism cannot be understood as some irrational hatred that has no grounding in the needs of those with power.[1]

---

[1]Of course, Jews were not the only group of "others" that were hated or scorned in the ancient world. As I've argued earlier, whenever one group decides to conquer another, it must find a way *not* to recognize that other as fundamentally human, else the oppression would feel inappropriate. So the Greeks and later the Romans had a vested interest in seeing all those who were non-Greek as fundamentally barbarian. But Jews came in for special abuse in the writings of the ancient world, and at least one dimension of this specialness was connected to the threat that they posed.

THE JEWISH RESPONSE

No one likes to be unliked, and even less to be oppressed. The Jews were no exception. So, when faced with the reality of the responses that their religion was eliciting from others, many Jews did their best to downplay the revolutionary aspects of their tradition. Faced with the overwhelming imperial powers of the ancient world, Jews tried every possible form of accommodation. For some Jews, this meant placing the God of the Bible alongside other gods, trying to show that they could serve them all. For others, it meant taking the sharp edges off of the revolutionary aspects of Judaism by confining it to the world of ritual.

Perhaps the central ritual of the ancient world was the sacrifice—the ritual offering of an animal to the deity. The collective ritual meal that followed allowed for an instant redistribution—instead of being consumed by the killer of the animal alone, it was now to be shared by everyone participating in the celebration. When the Jews tied this ritual to the celebration of their liberation, purposefully sacrificing the lamb that had been held sacred by the Egyptians, they were proclaiming that religion could become an arena in which the false claims of the oppressor would be exposed.

Yet the ritualization of Judaism could also quickly lead away from the revolutionary message and into an absorption in the details of ritual life. How easy to turn an eye away from the Biblical injunction "Justice, justice shalt thou pursue" and instead focus exclusively on questions of ritual purity or other details of the law. This, of course, was one of the central complaints of the prophets who appeared in the eighth and seventh centuries B.C.E., and who denounced what they saw as a perversion of Judaism that was taking place in the daily life of the people.

For the prophets it was nothing less than a catastrophe that the Jewish people were using the language of the tradition but missing its essence. Having established a society in which they had power, the ancient Israelites were now acting the way that the other nations acted, and had set up a society in which the ordinary evils of other societies appeared. Violence and cruelty were once again becoming regnant realities, and all this supposedly in a society embodying Jewish values! For the prophets this was a scandal, and with every ounce of their being they denounced the perversion built into this accommodation with the way the world normally operates.

"Woe to him that buildeth a town with blood/And establisheth a
city by iniquity!" cries the prophet Habakkuk (2:12).

"There is no truth, nor mercy, nor knowledge of God in the land./
Swearing and lying, and killing, and stealing, and commiting
adultery!/They break all bounds, and blood toucheth blood"
(Hosea 4:1–2).

> As a cage is full of birds,
> So are their houses full of deceit;
> Therefore they are become great, and waxen rich;
> They are waxen fat, they are become sleek,
> Yea, they overpass in deeds of wickedness;
> They plead not the causes, the cause of the fatherless,
> . . . the right of the needy do they not judge.
> (Jeremiah 5:27–28)

It's important to understand that these prophets did not see themselves as radicals attempting to remake the religion, but as conservatives attempting to bring back the people to the essence of the religion.

The prophets were the first creators of the Jewish-renewal movement. But were they really renewing some previously existing reality?
Probably not. It's doubtful that the Jewish people had ever actually
embodied and lived by the fullest meaning of the revolutionary tradition in Judaism. Its injunctions to love your neighbor as yourself, to love
the stranger, to pursue justice, were *always* heard by people who were
hearing other and conflicting messages at the same time, people who
inevitably found it difficult fully to embody these demands. Some of the
prophets imagined that times had been better in the days *before Jews
had power,* in the time when Jews lived in the desert after leaving Egypt.
In that moment, fresh from the defeat of Pharaoh, the Jews had
followed God into an unknown land, and it was because of our early
faithfulness that these later moments of unfaithfulness to God's message would ultimately be forgiven.

Inevitably, as with every subsequent attempt at renewal, including
this one, their interpretations were also in part redefinitions of the
tradition, selectively choosing what was important, downplaying the
rest. In fact, it is precisely this process of selective reinterpretation and
redefinition that is the Jewish tradition. But every generation feels

threatened when this happens, feels that it is aimed against them, identifies with the accepted practices of Judaism, and wildly resists the new effort at renewal. The first such cycle began with the priests of ancient Israel who were confronted by prophets who denounced the way that current ritual practices were being separated from what they took to be the essence of Judaism.

"Is this not the fast that I have chosen, to relieve the oppressed . . . ?" cries Isaiah, proclaiming the word of God. To Isaiah it is obvious that the whole of Yom Kippur, the Jewish Day of Atonement, Judaism's most solemn ritual occasion, is a farce unless it is reflective of a deeper social and individual transformation that leads people to feed the hungry, clothe the naked, untie the bonds of servitude, create a society based on caring and responsibility for the other.

Well, the answer to Isaiah's "is not this the fast . . . ?" might be, "Excuse me, but . . . *no*, that wasn't exactly how you put it in the Torah. As a matter of fact, when you stated that we should fast, you didn't quite mention that the real fasting was to end oppression."

My point here, of course, is not that the prophets were wrong to emphasize this element of the tradition. In my view, what they were doing is precisely what Jewish renewal is always about: they were giving a specific interpretation of the texts, a reading that would be denounced at once as one-tracked (because it seemed to be "too political"), and also as inauthentic and contrived (because it was "reducing" the complex religion to an undue emphasis on social transformation). But for the prophets it seemed obvious that the point of the whole enterprise was to be witnesses to the possibility of a very different social order. Only now, instead of having to focus only on the corruption of *other* people, they would have to address the corruption of the Jewish people, the way that their own society failed to embody the values inherent in the Torah tradition as understood by the prophets.

In short, what the prophets saw was that the Jews were becoming like other nations, becoming internally corrupt, abandoning the special message of God. The prophets were confronting an issue that would come up over and over again in Jewish history: Do all these fine revolutionary ideals have any application in the real world? For the realists of ancient Israel, these pious sentiments were very nice as ideals, but could have little to do with daily life in the real world. But for the prophets, the "real world" was an idolatrous world. The essential nature of idolatry is this: to see only what is before you, to be unable to see the potential for transformation, and to refuse to bear witness to the Power in the universe that makes possible that transformation. In this sense, Jewish renewal is the functional equivalent of the struggle against idolatry—it is the attempt to refocus Jewish attention away from the "real world" and toward a truer reality that encompasses the possibility of possibility.

What the prophets *also* understood was that when the mind is dulled to the possibility of transformation and the consciousness is habituated to cruelty and evil, the sensitivity to the grandeur of the universe is lost. For the prophets, one *cannot* recognize God when one is participating in an oppressive social order, so that ritual automatically becomes merely ritual, rote repetition that cannot move us toward the consciousness of awe and celebration.

There may be plenty of rituals that claim to address the realm of the spiritual, but very little likelihood that individuals can enter that realm if they have already managed to close their ears to the pain of the oppressed, to the injustice and cruelty of daily life, or to the cries of the hungry and the poor.

Faced with the legacy of pain, the prophets often fall into a language of talking about God that reflects a vision of an angry parent chastising recalcitrant children. It is not the attributing of emotions to God that I challenge; as Abraham Joshua Heschel pointed out, while the Greeks thought that emotions somehow lowered or denigrated a being, who ought to be moved solely by reason, Jews have always accepted emotions as a central and valuable part of human and divine existence. But the specific anger that sometimes gets attributed to God seems at points to move beyond the righteous indignation at oppression and to take on a vindictive and cruel aspect.

Though Jeremiah constantly bewails his fate at having to bring a message of doom to a people whom he loves so much, there are moments when the prophets lapse into a detailing of the destruction that will face the Jews because of their evildoing, or of the subsequent destruction that will befall the enemies of Israel as retribution for the evil that they do when they destroy the Jews, that read as though the prophets were almost enjoying the contemplation of this comeuppance. The anger that they felt at having their message ignored may well have mixed with deeply embedded patriarchal attitudes that made the prophets long for a kind of power over others even as they reminded people of the need to give up on looking to power for salvation.

Their self-righteous enjoyment of prophecies of destruction, picked up later in the tone of Christian and Islamic texts, becomes so deeply ingrained in the consciousness of moral vanguards that it may at times reappear in the struggles for Jewish renewal.

Anger as righteous indignation sometimes makes sense. It can cleanse us of inappropriate self-blaming and energize us to struggle against oppression. But anger as a reflection of our own inner frustration at not having our message appreciated may reflect an unhealthy attachment to our own ego needs. To the extent that we can become conscious of these tendencies within ourselves, we need to acknowledge them, understand the flawed nature of all who purport to advance the necessary ethical and spiritual struggles, and then seek ways to detach from the personal involvement that this anger and desire for power represent so that we can be more effective in serving others and in transmitting the message of Torah.

LOSING POWER AND LOSING HOPE: THE PULL INTO A NARROWER SPIRITUALITY

If the pull to accommodate to "reality" seemed powerful during the ages of David or Solomon or the subsequent kings of Judea and Israel, when Jews still had some substantial power, how much more so after the destruction of the First Temple (586 B.C.E.), the exile of the Jews to Babylonia in that same year, the return and rebuilding of the Temple, and the subsequent conquest of Judea by Alexander. The Greek account of a world dominated by power and politics certainly seemed more plausible, and faced with overwhelming imperial power, Jews chose many different paths:

1. The assimilators or Hellenists. There were some who systematically divorced themselves from the message of Torah. They saw no point in being offensive to the powers when they might serve their own interests better by playing up to them. While there were times when this strategy required a total abandonment of the forms of Jewish life, there were other times when the imperial powers could understand the value of keeping Jewish religious ritual intact as long as those who practiced it did not take seriously the revolutionary message of Torah. Why *not* allow these people to continue their sacrifices to

their God, reasoned some of the imperialists, as long as they do a good job of repressing the elements of their message that are potentially disruptive to our rule? Hence, both Greece and Rome could make accommodations to at least some of the priestly class that ran the Temple in Jerusalem as long as those priests kept to being religious and avoided a focus on the Torah tradition.

2. The confrontationists. Some Jews felt the need to fight against the imperial powers in order to keep the integrity of their religion. Unfortunately, too often the power of the imperialists was so great that those who struggled against it became transformed by the struggle, and became trapped by the logic of the imperialists. The Maccabees, whose struggle I will discuss when describing a Jewish-renewal approach to Chanukah, became the founders of a dynasty that often seemed to mimic the power-oriented regimes of the enemies. The moral and spiritual weakness of their rule opened the gates for the domination of Judea by the Romans. And the ruthlessness of the Romans elicited among some Jewish resisters (Zealots) a similar moral insensitivity. The ability of the Jewish people to combat Roman domination was weakened, as Jews turned upon one another in a frenzy of sectarian self-destructiveness precisely when they needed unity and a higher sense of shared moral purpose.

3. The spiritualizers of the Jewish message. Starting with Jewish Neoplatonists, but eventually spreading through much of the emerging community of rabbis and teachers, one response to domination was to assert that the actual world in which we live is not the real world in which the fundamental problems must be worked out. Increasingly experiencing themselves as powerless to reshape this world, overwhelmed by the might of Greece and then of Rome, the spiritualizers discounted their contemporary world by reconceptualizing it as merely material and counterposing it to some higher level of reality, a spiritual realm of which this world is only a mere hint or copy. For the Neoplatonists, the Bible itself became an allegory about some "higher" or spiritual truths. This world, irredeemably limited and corrupt, could be transcended—and the goal of life may well be to prepare ourselves to have the purity that will enable

us to find the kind of fulfillment we can't have in this world by participating in a world to come.

Spiritualizing themes are already being hinted at in some passages in the Book of the Maccabees, and they become increasingly popular as the murderous and oppressive policies of Rome increase. Rather than proclaim liberty throughout the land, as Torah had enjoined, spiritualizing Torah's message might provide a way to accommodate to Roman power. Option 1: If the struggle against Rome can't be won, we may not really need to struggle because the real battle is not in this world, and Rome's triumph is only the illusion of this world. Option 2: If we can't win the struggle against Rome, perhaps Rome would not feel so threatened by us if it realized that we are no threat, since our calls for liberation have nothing to do with *this world,* but are really about preparing our inner souls for a future world.

The corresponding interpretive strategy for Jewish texts is to turn everything into an allegorical reference to some other reality. The words of the Torah do not *really* describe this world and the struggles that need to be fought here. Rather, they are really "higher" messages about a different kind of world, the world of the spirit, which contrasts favorably to this merely demeaned and physical world.

The appeal of thinking about the world in this way is directly proportional to the extent that human sensibilities are overwhelmed by outrage at the way that the physical world is being remade by the oppressors. As tens of millions of people are subjugated and enslaved by the Roman war machine, as Roman values enshrine and embody a level of cruelty and callousness that surpasses all experience, ordinary human beings are drawn to religious conceptions that help them come to believe that God's kingdom is *not* of this world, that all that is happening here is a mere *prozdor,* or corridor, leading to a higher reality.

Spiritualization is *not* necessarily a total abdication of the Jewish message. But what it *did* do was to undermine the urgency of the ethical and political critique of cruelty, allowing Biblical religions to be appropriated in destructive ways by people who would no longer be forced to judge themselves by the Bible's demands for transcendence and compassion, since those demands too could be seen as spiritual rather than actual in this world and at this time. Spiritualization may have protected Jews from conflict, but in the process it also weakened the clarity of the Torah message.

CHRISTIANITY

It's not hard to see why messianic hopes flourished during the centuries of Roman oppressiveness. Many Jews took quite seriously the prophetic promise that there would arise a figure who would bring about a transformation of the world such that swords would be beaten into plowshares and the lion would lie down with the lamb and none would be afraid. Moreover, many Jews envisioned this messianic era as requiring a struggle in which the kingdoms of light and dark would fight with each other.

Jesus was one of many candidates for Messiah, and from the standpoint of most of the Jews alive at the time of his death, not memorably distinct from dozens of others of his time. Like all the others, he failed to meet the basic criterion of Messiah: actually succeeding in changing the world from the brutality and oppression of Roman imperialism. But what made Jesus memorable was that his disciples switched this job description for Messiah, spiritualizing it, and referring it to a future world. One could retain one's belief in God's ultimate goodness and good intentions to redeem the world by believing that the place where salvation would take place was not in *this* world, but in a far-off, spiritual realm.

The convenience of this way of thinking was considerable. Instead of having to fight against oppression, one could "Render unto Caesar what is Caesar's, and unto God what is God's." In short, pay the taxes because they are merely forms of oppression in this relatively unimportant world, whereas there is another, more important world in which we will be held accountable. And not primarily held accountable for what we *did* in this world (e.g., the degree to which we engaged in revolutionary struggle against oppression), but rather held accountable for some set of inner states, what we believed and felt. The religion built around Jesus after his death centered on a certain state of beliefs—and salvation was a function of holding those beliefs which would guarantee one redemption in a future spiritual world.

This way of thinking became popular even among Jews who did not believe that Jesus was the Messiah. There were many other comparable religious sects who believed that some internal state of mind or being would guarantee one salvation in some future world. The tendency to spiritualize reality became increasingly powerful as Jews became increasingly powerless.

But there were many other Jews who experienced this spiritualization of reality as a severe betrayal. Still moved by the central story of their religion, many Jews believed that Rome could and would eventually be defeated in *this* world. Some of these people were extremely unrealistic in the sense that they did not bother to take into account issues of strategy and amassing force. Outraged at oppression, they threw themselves against the Roman legions in a massive rebellion between 67 and 70 C.E., eventually provoking the Romans to destroy the Temple in Jerusalem. A similar and, for a while, more successful rebellion under the leadership of purported Messiah Bar Kochba and Rabbi Akiba led to the creation of an independent Jewish state in 133 C.E., only to be ruthlessly crushed in a brutal Roman repression.

The failure of these rebellions severely tempered Jewish enthusiasm for head-on confrontation with Roman power. But it did not lessen antagonism that the political activists felt against the Christians and other similar spiritualizers. For the activists, the real struggle was to be fought in this world, against the real concrete force that was Rome. Even if the specific struggles proved impetuous, one might reasonably maintain that Rome would eventually fall, in *this* world and not the next, and that the goal of those who knew this truth was to spread that message and organize alliances that might eventually hasten the day of that defeat.

Some Jews who thought this way saw the Christians as undermining the struggle by focusing attention away from this world and toward salvation in another world. Their anger at what they perceived as a Christian betrayal of the national liberation struggle was intensified after the defeat of 70 C.E., when the Christians began to use the destruction of the Temple as "evidence" that Judaism had been superseded by a God who had rejected the Jews because the Jews had failed to accept Jesus.

There was, however, a more sophisticated line of argument that some Christians could have advanced: Military rebellions against Rome were bound to fail, they could argue, because Rome has and will continue to have overwhelming military strength. But the Christian strategy is more powerful: we will win over the masses of people in the Roman Empire to a different form of thinking about the world, one which invalidates the importance of military conquest and power in this world, and instead focuses on salvation in the world to come. To the degree that these ideas take hold, Romans will be unable to marshal the inner strength necessary to keep their empire together, and Rome will eventually collapse.

The counter argument that might be made by Jews of this period would run like this: If you succeed in infiltrating Rome with your ideas, but do not change its institutional arrangements, you will eventually find that it is *you* Christians who are changing more than Rome. Rome may adopt your religion, but your religion may be remade in the process until it becomes more like the Rome that you were seeking to change. Thus, the only way to fight Rome is overtly, not covertly.

I have no evidence that this conversation ever took place in precisely this form. What I am trying to do, however, is to explicate the *logic* of the positions. In the first few centuries after the death of Jesus and the destruction of the Temple, a fierce battle of words took place between Jews and Jewish-Christians, and Jews were often quite rude and disrespectful of the fledgling religion and its rapid growth among the slave population of the Roman Empire. Precisely because they had known Jesus and not been so impressed, their ridicule of Christianity was infuriating to those who were moving from claims about Jesus as Messiah to claims about Jesus as the son of God. To many Jews, the Christians had been the ultimate betrayers, abandoning the national liberation struggle against Rome when they were most needed.

On the other side, many Christians ridiculed the Jews for continuing to believe that they were God's "chosen people," a phrase that began in these circumstances to take on a set of meanings that far surpassed its original meaning as a vanguard that had had the fortune to participate in the liberation from Egypt.

Many early Christians perceived themselves as a Jewish-renewal movement. Like earlier renewal movements, they saw Jewish institutions being dominated by elites who had often seemed to be using Jewish ritual as a substitute for spiritual involvement. Accommodating to the Hellenistic spirit of the times, many Jewish intellectuals distanced themselves from the spirit of Torah in order to better immerse themselves in the letter of Torah. Others saw their task as "nation building," worried more about the survival of the Jewish body and the Jewish community than about the Jewish soul. There were among the early Jewish-Christians many who felt that they were critiquing these distortions of Judaism and helping to restore the basic intuitions that had originally animated Judaism. So what are the limits of Jewish renewal and how did the Christians overstep them?

The simplest answer is this: Christianity overstepped the boundaries to the extent that it began to collapse the distinction between what is and what ought to be, between an actually existing human being and the Divine, and then, ultimately, between the need to change this world and the hope for a spiritual transformation elsewhere. A Jewish-renewal movement is one that revives hope in the possibility of possibility; a messianic movement is one that destroys that hope by equating some actually existing reality with the goal to which we are striving. So once Christians saw Jesus as somehow an embodiment of God, the task became narrowed to accepting that God's kingdom had already arrived, that salvation was already at hand, that we were already living in the messianic era. But this premature collapsing of the distinction between the "ought" and the "is" is precisely what is meant by idolatry—and that is what Jewish renewal comes to challenge.

The disciples who tried to portray Jesus as the Messiah and later as the son of God may have robbed the Jewish people of a set of teachings, some of which might otherwise have been incorporated into the Jewish tradition. Jesus appears to have been motivated by a distaste for the ways that the Jewish establishment of his time had become excessively fixated on religious ritual at the expense of remaining true to the heart of Jewish spirituality and Jewish love. In innovative and forceful ways he tried to confront that establishment and to validate the experiences and needs of some of the most oppressed elements in Roman-occupied and -dominated Judea. He may not have had an adequate understanding of the ways that the distortions in Jewish life were themselves the product of the attempts by some to accommodate and others to resist the Roman occupation. But nevertheless he had insights and ways of formulating Torah truths that could have served as an inspiration for many Jews. His insistence upon ethical and spiritual integrity, his message that in our individual lives and in the ways that we relate to whoever is the most downcast of the society, we must embody Torah's message of compassion, and his challenge to ritual separated from ethical sensitivity could easily have found a place in Jewish tradition had it not been joined to the metaphysics of messianism and then to a religion that oppressed Jews. Indeed, as we move away from the historical period in which Christians oppress and demean Jews, it will be possible for Jews to look at Jesus' teaching with fresh eyes, and to reclaim the Jewish Jesus as an honored teacher without having to reject everything he said merely because of the ways it was subsequently used hurt us.

A healthy appropriation of the Jewish Jesus will avoid the kind of reverential tones that one sometimes hears from Jews who want to emphasize interreligious dialogue so much that they talk of Jesus as a prophet and healer in order to show Christians that *now* we can be nice to him. More appropriate to treat him like other Jewish teachers, subjecting him to the same rough-and-tumble scrutiny, recognizing his limitations in the same way that we recognize the limitations of other teachers of the talmudic age, learning the parts that seem good, rejecting the rest, and not allowing an internalized conception of how this will impact on our relations with Christians to affect what is accepted or what is rejected. When we can come to that point, Jesus will regain his rightful place as a respected and sometimes insightful teacher of the Jewish people. Just as today many Jews read the Book of Proverbs and find occasional gems but also find lots of material that is not particularly inspiring, and some material that few of us would take seriously, so Jews freed of the legacy of anti-Semitism will read the New Testament with interest, occasionally gleaning useful lessons, putting it into historical perspective, open to some of its beautiful stories, and dispassionately rejecting other parts.

Freed from the necessity of *goyim*-bashing as a self-protective mechanism to defend ourselves against the denigration of our religion and tradition by the dominant culture, Jews can also recognize that there are groups of Christians, not only those in the liberation theology circle, who are remaking Christianity in ways that reappropriate the revolutionary voice of Torah. These Christians are our potential allies for Jewish renewal in the task of healing and repairing the world. In a world made safe through real and substantial tolerance, it will eventually be possible for us to engage in religious debate with these Christians without fearing that in the end they will once again drag us off to inquisitions or concentration camps. Those fears, grounded in our history, can and should be overcome so that we can respectfully engage with our brothers and sisters in different communities of faith. That kind of dialogue, not the mealy-mouthed "brotherhood" or "tolerance through avoidance of the difficult spots," is something that we should be seeking.

RABBINIC JUDAISM

Though most Jews did not embrace the other-worldly salvation of Christianity, they eventually did move far away from the transformative voice within Judaism. The national tragedy, beginning with the destruction of the Temple and escalating to the near genocide after the Bar Kochba rebellion, left an abiding scar on the consciousness of those rabbis who survived. Many who did survive were those who had managed to avoid politics when everyone else was being drawn into the national struggle. Now faced with the monumental task of reconstructing a Judaism whose spiritual center had shifted from Palestine to the Diaspora, the rabbis who went on to shape the Talmud adopted a strategy that neither totally spiritualized the world nor validated the struggle to transform it.

Instead, the major energy of Jewish religious life was sublimated into the creation of a detailed legal system for how one ought to live in a world that no longer existed—the Jewish world of preexilic Israel. The details of daily life became the focus of immense and careful scrutiny in the Talmud, but it was often a daily life that existed no place other than in the study halls and pages of this great document of the human imagination.

This was an escapism of a qualitatively different sort. On the one hand, there was no referent to much of what became talmudic discussion. There was no Temple in which to conduct the sacrifices whose details talmudists debated; there was no land on which one could exercise tithing or from which one could draw the food for the priests (*terumah*); there was no society that could impose death punishments on those who failed to obey their fathers and mothers. On the other hand, the solution was *not* to abandon the discussion of what such a world should look like, and *not* to focus on some other nonearthly plane. Rather, this was a "holding strategy," a way of maintaining direct continuity with the world in which Jews had at one point exercised some power, while at the same time recognizing that that world no longer existed but hoping that it would soon be restored.

Not that all talmudic speculation, or the Jewish religious law tradition that grew from it, was entirely divorced from the realm of power. In Babylonia and Persia, where most Jews sought refuge from Roman oppression, and later in various Mediterranean and European countries, many Jews were able to establish relatively self-governing communities in which "the law of the land" was based on talmudic and subsequent halakhic discussions. If many of these laws presupposed a reality that no longer existed, some were finely tailored to meet the actual realities of Jewish life in the Diaspora.

Rabbinic Judaism was one of the great moments of Jewish renewal. Faced with a religion that was centered on Temple worship and a world that had destroyed and would not allow the rebuilding of that Temple, the rabbis re-created Judaism around a new set of paradigms, with prayer, study, acts of charity and caring taking the place of sacrifice; and the home taking the place of the Temple altar. Judaism would be based on familial units in communal association since the larger world no longer provided space for a Jewish national reality. It was a move that was bold and daring—all the more so since the rabbis attempted to reread the holy texts and interpret them in ways that would allow them to portray this Jewish renewal as an extension of a tradition of oral law going back to Sinai. Much of the Talmud is a rather intellectually straining operation to find "prooftexts" from the Torah, or later from the Mishnah and various *brietot* (rulings of rabbis from the mishnaic period that had not been incorporated into the final version of the Mishnah), that would give an authority-basis for subsequent talmudic rulings. The reality was wildly expansive innovation; the legitimation strategy, however, was to claim continuity through a twisting of texts.

For our purposes, the most important question to ask of the Talmud is: "Where is the God of possibility and transformation in this text?" The answer is not simple, because any text that bases itself on a tradition that emerged from Judaism must itself contain many moments in which the revolutionary voice of Torah shines through. In hundreds of concrete decisions, the rabbis pushed forward social legislation that advanced the fundamentally revolutionary program of Torah. Compared to other legislation of the same period, talmudic discussions often have an unmistakable edge of liberatory consciousness based on its assumptions about human dignity. Moreover, the fundamental style of talmudic reasoning is one that empowers the reader even as it seems to privilege the text. David Kraemer, professor of Talmud at the Jewish Theological Seminary, talks of the subversive questions asked by Talmud. Over and over again the Talmud challenges the reasoning of past authorities or of Mishnah texts and demands more convincing reasons than the texts seem to supply. Instead of teaching a docile acceptance of authority, it creates a people used to asking "Why?" and "How do they know?" and "Is their reasoning sound?" These questions encourage rational discourse rather than submission to authority. Repeatedly, one is confronted with the fundamental reality that there is no ultimate authority, no high court to resolve most of the disputes. In practice, throughout the rabbinic period in subsequent centuries, different communities selected individuals whose opinions became authoritative for them. But these authorities were frequently in conflict with one another, nor was there an agreed upon procedure for resolving disputes. And this absence of authority is even more pronounced in the text of the Talmud itself. Despite frantic attempts to root various positions in authoritative quotes from the Torah or the mishnaic period, much of the Talmud is a set of arguments among different authorities, with no final resolution. Sometimes these disputes end with a phrase called *Teyku,* which roughly translated stands for the idea that this dispute will be solved when Elijah the Prophet returns to announce the coming of the Messiah.

The outcome, and in fact the message of the text, is one in which the readers themselves are forced to use their own minds, grapple with complicated arguments, and come to their own conclusions about what makes most sense. The process is one of empowerment of the intellect. While such a message is carefully hidden within a framework of studying authorities, it is a message that is communicated and has had a lasting impact on the Jewish people.

This empowerment is reinforced by a typical form of talmudic study: the *chevruta* style in which two people study a text together, offer their own respective interpretations, and try to share with each other their respective understandings. The process strengthens the sense of competence, intelligence, and entitlement to be a participant in what the tradition defines as a holy process: that of carrying on the oral tradition, participating in a conversation with the greats of all generations of the past. For much of the past two thousand years, there simply did not exist another community of people that democratically extended this kind of empowering experience as widely as did the Jews.

THE TALMUD'S RESISTANCE AND PASSIVITY

Rabbinic Judaism embodies many different political tendencies and orientations. Rabbi Akiba led many others to join the Bar Kochba rebellion (132–135 C.E.) in the hopes that armed resistance to Rome might work. But when this rebellion led to the deaths of thousands and the enslavement of tens of thousands more, the rabbis and their disciples who had not joined the rebellion shaped a more passive approach to resistance.

Rabbinic Judaism can be understood in part as cultivation of what James C. Scott has called "the art of resistance." The resistance may have been dressed in the form of compliance with a world that seemed too overwhelming to change, but it was resistance nevertheless. As Scott put it, "The greater the disparity in power between dominant and subordinate, the more arbitrarily it is exercised, the more the public transcripts of the subordinate will take on a stereotyped, ritualistic cast. In other words, the more menacing the power, the thicker the mask."[2]

What's important to understand when approaching Rabbinic Judaism is that even its holy text, the Talmud, was subject to scrutiny by ruling authorities (and later, under Church rule, it was sometimes burned in public), so that its formulations had to be coded and framed in ways that would get past the inquisitive eyes of those whom it was meant to oppose.

Rabbinic Judaism attempted to discount the validity of the powers of this world, while at the same time it resisted those who would discount this world and claim that salvation would come in some other arena. It was precisely this world, the world in which the forces of evil were triumphing, that would be the world in which good would ultimately prevail.

There are moments in the Mishnah where the injunctions are so clear that there can be little mistaking of the purpose. A Jew is forbidden to identify the property of a fellow Jew to the tax collector. A Jew is prohibited from testifying in or participating in the legal proceedings of a gentile court. Jews are enjoined not to become close with civil authorities. In short, don't collaborate with the Romans.

Nor should a Jew be allowed to connect socially with the oppressor. The talmudic strengthening of *kashrut* laws goes far beyond the Biblical injunction and includes a law that Jews not be allowed to drink the wine that is touched by non-Jews. The prohibition of this wine effectively prohibits Jews from any partway steps toward assimilation, since wine

---

[2]James C. Scott, *Domination and the Arts of Resistance* (New Haven: Yale University Press, 1990), p. 3.

was the accepted form of drink at Roman gatherings. The rabbis saw Roman social gatherings the way that 1960s radicals viewed gatherings of American imperialists—disgusting displays of the conspicuous consumption that accompanies the arrogance of power. From the rabbinic standpoint, one would be morally contaminated by participation in their social or religious life, and *kashrut* was extended to become a barrier to contact with this moral impurity. This was the first and most long-lasting grape boycott: a permanent way of saying that the Jewish people deeply disapprove of the culture and social reality of Roman society.

Indeed, one might argue that the entire enterprise of focusing on the laws of the Temple even when there was no Temple was a subtle way of saying, "We don't accept the present reality, it will be overcome, the powers that be will pass, and things that are wrong will be overturned." In this sense, the entire Talmud may be viewed as a refusal to accept the present order—a refusal that does not escape to another terrain, but one that insists that eventually this world can be made right.

And yet, the Talmud has within it a defeatist thread that belies the optimism of the Jewish past. While some of its most respected voices are those of rabbis who engaged in the struggle against Roman imperialism, those who ultimately compiled the Mishnah and redacted the Talmud were disciples of the rabbis who had *not* joined the active resistance and who reflected a more passive or defeatist attitude. The struggle with Rome or with other forms of oppression is rarely mentioned, except in passing, and except within a context in which the power of Rome is taken as a given and not much can be done to fight it (if this was too risky to write down, it could have been taught verbally to Jewish students who would have maintained a covert oral tradition that would have been written down hundreds of years later when things were safer). The world is as it is, the Talmud seems to be saying, and what we can do is to preserve as much sanity as possible within it. The subversive part of that sanity is that we concentrate all our attention on how to run a society that we don't actually live in—namely a society governed by Torah. But the nonsubversive element is that every discussion presupposes the current distribution of power and the practices that a world of unequal power generates. Rarely does the Talmud encourage us to struggle to change the world. In many places, in fact, it has a resigned and depressive attitude, as though the revolutionary flavor of the Bible had been abandoned. As such it was probably accurately reflecting the sentiments of many Jews during the period in which the Mishnah was codified and the Talmud constructed.

Alongside what I am calling a deep pessimism and depressive attitude in Talmud, there are other strains that keep alive our rejection of the world as constituted. I've already pointed out that some Hellenistic Jews used spirituality as a way to keep alive our sense of the inadequacy of the world as it exists by contrasting it with an imagined higher spiritual reality yet to come in a different and nonmaterial world. The Talmud incorporates some of this consciousness in some of the stories that it preserves. In the rabbinic period there developed a rich midrashic literature which reflected the Bible in spiritualized form, and shaped prayers and stories that focused attention away from the world of oppression. These midrashim often seemed to take the edge off of the pain of this world, directing our attention to a "higher" reality, even as they preserved our understanding that there was something deeply wrong with the world. To the extent that this literature presented a conception of spiritual reality as somehow separate from and achievable outside of the world of oppression, it reinforced a conception of Judaism not as the inspiration for political struggle, but as an alternative to that struggle. In so doing, it further developed escapist themes in Judaism that had originally entered Judaism during the days of Hellenistic oppression and which may have been necessary for survival during periods of relative powerlessness that Jews faced as they attempted to live as a minority in a world not yet committed to principles of tolerance and diversity.

No set of material as complex and multilayered as the Talmud can ever be summed up in the way I've tried to do here. The Talmud represents ideas and discussions that took place over the course of an eight-hundred-year period in Jewish history. It preserves conflicting political and religious orientations and insights, and yet presents them in a manner that reflects the concerns of the redactors as well as the need to get past the political censors of the non-Jewish cultures in which we lived. No wonder, then, that it has elements that are deeply subversive, continuing the revolutionary tradition of the Jews; and elements that are deeply co-optive, conservative, and accommodationist, reflecting a sense that many Jews had of what changes would be necessary in order to survive in the world that they actually faced.

THE AMBIGUOUS LEGACY: TWO THOUSAND YEARS OF DIASPORA ACCOMMODATION

The pattern of resistance and accommodation to a world of oppression, embedded in Jewish religion and in the communal institutions of Jewish life, continue from the talmudic period to our own day. It would be nice to tell the story simply as one of a pure and wonderful legacy of resistance to the external oppressors (Rome, Persia, Christendom, Islam, the emerging nation-states of Europe), sometimes forced to accommodate, sometimes able to preserve its moral integrity. But the actual story is more complex, because as I've tried to show, even within the pure core of Torah Judaism itself there has always been a struggle between the voice of God and the voices that embody the accumulated pain and distortion of human history.

Moreover, though the legal (halakhic) tradition embedded in Talmud, developed by the great medieval commentators, by Maimonides, and by countless generations of rabbis and scholars, has always had within it a core of resistance to the world as constituted, it often fails to articulate that resistance as a self-conscious part of what it is trying to do. Avoiding a conscious articulation of a revolutionary commitment may have been prudent and necessary for survival, but it also had the effect of allowing some generations of Jews to ignore the explosively radical meaning of the tradition they were carrying.

Moreover, the growing repression of Judaism in Christian Europe deflected Jewish attention away from the most radical meanings of their own tradition. Faced with a hegemonic religion that blamed the Jews for Jesus' crucifixion, and that scorned Jews for having failed to understand that Jesus was the Messiah and the son of God, it seemed to many Jews a sufficiently radical task to stay alive and remain true to the oneness of God. For many Jews, living in small enclaves, then ghettos, then *shtetls,* the idea of Jews playing a role in transforming the world could best be understood in metaphorical or spiritual terms, certainly not as a practical program for any real world they could imagine in a Diaspora that seemed likely to end only with the coming of the Messiah. Even for those Jews who lived in larger enclaves, who were granted limited self-governance by ruling elites, the notion of Jews really running any part of the world without being definitively constrained by the non-Jews around them often seemed utopian. Though rarely as powerless in the Diaspora as later Zionists would portray them, Jews nevertheless were far from conceptualizing themselves as agents of a soon-to-be-actualized political or spiritual liberation. No wonder, then, that the parts of the Bible, rabbinic literature, and halakhic tradition that seemed world-weary or world-wary often felt to many Diaspora Jews to embody more wisdom than the brusque and confrontative spirit of Torah or the prophets.

I won't pretend to sum up the complex realities of the two thousand years of Diaspora life, the important differences between the Judaism that developed in Persia and Mediterranean lands (Sephardic Judaism), and that which developed in Northern and Eastern Europe (Ashkenazic Judaism), or the many moments in which the utopian and revolutionary themes in Jewish thought found expression in Kabbalah as well as in mainstream halakhic thought, in the poetry of Spanish Jewry, or in the writings of medieval Jewish philosophy. But when all the complexities and nuances are taken into account, I contend that the revolutionary thrust of Jewish thought was necessarily subordinated to the survival needs of the Jewish people, and that gradually through the course of time, the revolutionary message of Torah and the renewal message espoused by the prophets receded into the role of honorific teachings rather than as serious injunctions for daily life.

To the extent that Judaism made accommodations with relative powerlessness in a world of oppression, it began to act and feel more like a religion than like a movement or way of life. And the kinds of people who came to the fore as leaders were increasingly those who fit this model: not the people charged with a vision, but merchants, traders, physicians, and somewhat-detached-from-the-world scholars and pedants. People began to compete with one another for recognition as scholars of a text rather than as transformers or healers of the world. Thousands of Jews in every generation became immersed in the details of the law, often using powerful and impressive intellects to explore issues that could have no possible application in their contemporary world. For some, that was precisely the point—study of Torah, Talmud, the halakhic tradition, was a dramatic rejection of "reality" without jumping into spiritual fantasies of some other world where real redemption would be found. But increasingly that passive protest-dimension was underplayed and even forgotten, and Judaism for many became a set of communal observances and restrictions, for others a source of fascinating intellectual stimulation. Far fewer Jews publicly praised Judaism for its ability to develop one's capacity for being a loving and spiritually developed being. Fewer still lamented the growing gap between Judaism's revolutionary aspirations and their own current lives in which the possibilities for Jews to be effective change-agents and world-healers seemed slight.

I want to quickly remind the reader that the developments we are talking about occur to a people who are being systematically oppressed, legally discriminated against, periodically murdered in small or large numbers, totally expelled from countries, and constantly harassed. I also want to insist that the spiritually deadening aspects of fascination with Halakha were sometimes overcome by individual teachers who were extremely well developed spiritually, and who found adequate sources of inspiration within the rich arena of textual study. Moreover, throughout the past two thousand years there were periodic upsurges of reform or revitalization, most notably among those who developed the mystical books and practices that came to be known as Kabbalah, and then later in the Hasidic movement in Poland beginning in the eighteenth century.

The Ba'al Shem Tov's Hasidic movement spread quickly to the poor and illiterate masses of Eastern Europe who could not hope to become part of the talmudic-study–oriented life of the *yeshivot* that dominated the Jewish community in the sixteenth, seventeenth, and eighteenth centuries. Enthused by a religious populism that validated their experience as equally precious to God, buoyed by a faith in the supernatural powers of the Hasidic *rebbes* who taught through stories rather than through elaborate talmudic legal arguments, many East European Jews momentarily tasted the joys of a religious tradition that had reclaimed some of its sense of revolutionary mission. All the sadder, then, when some of these *rebbes* began to create lavish courts at which they wielded immense power over the lives of their faithful, established dynasties ensuring that their successors would be chosen from their children rather than from the community of those who most faithfully embodied the religious enthusiasm and, finally, proved their own orthodoxy by imposing halakhic requirements on daily behavior at least as rigid as any against which the original Hasidic critique had taken aim. Initially an attempt to combine spirituality, joy, and celebration as antidotes to the sterile narrowing of intellectual life that flourished in many *yeshivot,* Hasidism eventually ossified as it scurried to defend itself against even more radical responses to the perceived deadness of Jewish spiritual life.

Hasidism, like Kabbalah before it, was a movement that sought to renew Judaism, to get back in touch with God, and to shatter the various protective shields we had developed, like the escape into a certain form of Talmud study, that not only kept us from having to experience the social world in all its ugliness toward us, but simultaneously kept us from being fully alive to the God of Torah. That they succeeded only for brief periods is largely a result of the physical oppression and fear that continually froze Jews into fixed patterns and sapped their spontaneity and creativity.

It is important to note that when Jews did feel relatively secure they were able to come closer to getting back in touch with the most alive and morally and spiritually engaging parts of their tradition. But in the past four hundred years, particularly in Western lands (though oppression in Arab lands escalated also), there has been a growing terror against the Jewish people. The result has been further cessation of religious creativity, spontaneity, and joy. The Inquisition and subsequent expulsion of Jews from Spain, Portugal, England, and France, the mass murder of more than 100,000 people by Chmielnicki in Poland and Eastern Europe, the development of overtly anti-Semitic movements among the populace—all these contributed to a growing belief that Jews were potentially vulnerable to genocidal assault.

The consequence was an intensification of fear of the other, a growing anger that needed to be repressed but which often manifested in depression, and the development of an aura around Judaism that seemed to portend melancholy, heaviness, a sense of imminent danger, a conviction that nothing would ever go right, a desperation about the future, and an emotional and intellectual rigidity. Look at those Orthodox Jews whose black clothes or gowns copy the finery of sixteenth-century Polish aristocracy, or whose sexual mores reflect the Christian fear of sex that paraded as purity in Eastern Europe, and you get a graphic representation of when Jewish life in our era began to freeze.

Add to this picture the manifold ways that Judaism was appropriated by emerging Jewish elites to sanctify class inequalities and patriarchal practices, and how the interests of the more successful Jews influenced the kind of scholarship and Jewish literature and culture that would be supported—inevitably playing down the most revolutionary aspects of the tradition and finding solace in its most accommodationist or other-worldly strands—and you begin to get a sense of Judaism forgetting or misunderstanding its prophetic strands, so that the Jewish-renewal energies that had traditionally been part of the Jewish experience would seem foreign impositions from outside rather than organic developments from within.

No wonder, then, that when the ghetto walls began to crumble and emancipation from legal restrictions against conversion became possible, some Jews rushed into various forms of assimilation. There were many whose flight was governed exclusively by fear, just as there were some who were so angry at non-Jews for what they were doing to the Jewish people that they clung to Judaism regardless of whether they found its religious practices spiritually fulfilling or morally engaging. But there were many who began the rush toward assimilation not because they found capitalism so alluring, but because Judaism was not a source of spiritual or moral guidance.

SOME JEWS JOIN THE SECULAR TEMPERAMENT OF THE MODERN AGE

By the eighteenth century some Jews were beginning to identify with a much more powerful counter to the spiritual vacuum of Jewish life—a growing secularism that was capturing the imagination of many in the non-Jewish world. For more than a thousand years, Europe had been dominated by regimes that based their legitimacy on the religious authority of Christianity. Christian religious law, much like Jewish religious law, authoritatively controlled economic life, not only sanctifying the ownership of land by the feudal aristocracy, but also severely limiting the degree to which individuals could engage in trade, the prices that they could charge for goods, the wages they ought to pay their laborers, and many other details of economic life. The notion of fair price and just wage, had they been determined by a wise and ethically sensitive Church, might have generated a considerable following. Economic life, after all, was said to be governed in the interests of the community guided by God's will.

But the reality was quite different, and obviously so. The feudal order might claim a special relationship with God, but increasing numbers of people began to see it as an elaborate system of rationalizations to give ruling elites wealth and power while the rest of the population suffered.

The language of community, the common good, and religion were all being manipulated for the private interests of the powerful.

This realization was most acutely obvious to those who were engaged in commerce and trade and manufacture, the artisans and shopkeepers and merchants whose interests put them in conflict with the restrictions imposed upon them by the Church. Having been proscribed from many other occupations by Church-inspired legal decrees, Jews played a role disproportionate to their percentage of the population in these growing "bourgeois" occupations. They often found themselves the target of attack from two directions—the bourgeoisie itself, angry at the Jews for seeming to be successful at these trading matters (a success due in part to the international network of Jews that made it easier for Jewish merchants to find hospitality and assistance in foreign ports); and the feudal aristocrats, whose disdain at the crude money- and profit-orientation of the bourgeoisie, often counterposed to the higher spiritual and cultural values of the aristocracy, could find most violent expression when directed against Jewish merchants and Jewish traders.

It was as part of this bourgeoisie that Jews first began to hear the arguments being developed to justify bourgeois "rights." Though originally designed as a way of protecting traders and merchants within the feudal order, the rising class of merchants, traders, and bankers fought for a new conception of public space, one in which all particular religious, ethical, and spiritual programs would have no place whatsoever. Public space should be constricted to that which could in principle be shared by everyone. People might disagree about ethical, spiritual, and religious issues, but these disagreements should be relegated to a private sphere. Public space should be dedicated to matters that are public, that is, on that which could be observed and confirmed by everyone, not by the few who claimed privileged access to spiritual truth.

That new way of looking at the world provided a new empirical epistemology and, consequently, a new ontology. That which exists is that which can be presented to the senses in a publicly observable and repeatable manner. Otherwise it is literally "non-sense," and has no claim on our attention and certainly no claim to be known. Starting from these assumptions, empirical philosophers tried to show how we could construct our understanding of the world through the building blocks of data presented to the senses.

Many Jews enthusiastically embraced the interests and self-justifications of the rising bourgeoisie. Not only did they share some of the economic interests, but also they had an unequivocal interest in creating a political realm separate from Christian power. After centuries of victimization at the hands of Christian elites and murderous mobs who justified their Jew-hating by reference to Christianity, many Jews felt certain that they would be the beneficiaries of secularization and the triumph of individual rights. Jews were rarely as powerless as the lachrymose view of Jewish history has suggested, but our oppression was significant enough to make many Jews greet the possibility of the free market with almost messianic fervor. If given a level playing field, in which one's own religious background no longer mattered and in which there were no outside interferences from the rules imposed by authoritative communities, Jews would certainly flourish. So a small but influential group of Jews embraced secularism in the eighteenth century. Hoping to embrace what was best in the rationalist ideals and universal rights, and mix them with what was best in Jewish culture, the *Maskilim* (or enlightened ones) sought to reconcile two worlds without fully abandoning Jewish religious beliefs. But those who followed the *Maskilim* internalized the perspective of the larger society that saw Judaism as an irrational hangover from primitive times.

Secularism became a mass movement in the Jewish world in the nineteenth century when the triumph of the bourgeois revolution actually led to the acceptance of Jews as equal before the law.

The euphoria at "emancipation" led many Jews to embrace the newly emerging nationalisms of the various countries into which they were now being accepted as full citizens. For some, the absence of legal constraints led to a total abandonment of their Jewish roots. Conversion to Christianity was an option adopted by those who believed that such a transformation could assure them and their descendants a future safe from the persecution that had been Jewish fate. For others, Jewishness could be preserved only if carefully isolated from one's public identity. One could be a Jew at home, a Frenchman in the streets and stores and stock markets and voting booths. "To the Jew as an individual, everything," said one French official, "but to the Jews as a people, nothing."

For the majority of Jews still living in Poland and Russia, where legal emancipation had been only partial, these options were only distant possibilities—and yet many of them cheered for emancipation, yearned for it, and distanced themselves as much as they could from the

religious communities that seemed spiritually uncompelling and morally corrupt.

The enthusiasm with which so many Jews greeted the possibility of
leaving Jewish religious life cannot be attributed solely to a desire to
imitate non-Jewish trends. The reality of Jewish religious life was in fact
often stifling and repressive. Centuries of oppression, expulsions, murder, rape, and trauma had reduced Jewish self-confidence and narrowed communal vision in ways that made some Jewish communities
excessively focused on ritual laws, not only to the exclusion of the
Jewish revolutionary message but even to the repression of joy and
celebration. In the seventeenth century, restrictive norms of sexual
behavior and group coercion that had been prevalent in surrounding
Christian societies were absorbed into Jewish communal practice, and
then instituted as Jewish law, replacing the relative openness with
which some religious Jews had experimented in the hopeful centuries
when Jews lived under Islamic rule in Spain. But as the spirit of the
French Revolution spread throughout Europe in the nineteenth century, many Jews wondered why they had to be stuck in this kind of a
rigid and deadening past. Moreover, the headlong rush of some Jews
into assimilation had produced an even further rigidifying of the Orthodox religious community. Fearful that their children might be lured into
secularism or into the equally disquieting possibilities opened up by the
creation of Reform and Conservative Judaism, the traditionally observant religious community tightened its restrictions, fought vigorously
(and unsuccessfully) to keep its adherents from contact with secular
knowledge, and in other ways managed to make itself even less attractive than it needed to be.

But it would be deeply foolish to believe that Jews who were escaping
Judaism were simply making a rational choice for a better way of life.
Rational choice must be uncoerced. Given the context of Jewish history, the fierce two-thousand-year repression of the liberatory trend
within Judaism, the murder and rape and repression of Jews, the
systematic denigration of Jewish sensibilities and insights, the cultural
genocide against Jewish ways of being and thinking, the consequent
distortions in Jewish thought and Jewish practice, and the freezing of
Jewish religious life, it is ludicrous to describe the abandonment of
Judaism or the embracing of secularism as a product of rational choice.
Though each individual experienced herself or himself as choosing,
they were in fact choosing within a context that had been so heavily

manipulated by external forces as to dramatically reduce the chances that people *would* choose to remain within the Jewish religious framework. If most Jews did, nevertheless, stay, some stayed through ignorance of the choices, and others because they miraculously managed to find within Judaism the voice of God and some of what is enduringly valuable despite its externally fostered distortions. Yet for many who did remain within the fold, the Judaism that they were staying with was severely constricted, a Judaism whose renewal energies were preserved more in the text than in daily practice.

THE PERSISTENCE OF ANTI-SEMITISM AS A EUROPEAN HUNGER FOR MEANING

The first waves of secularism were associated with an almost manic euphoria that the years of oppression had come to an end. There might be some rearguard battles yet to fight, but the worst had finally been overcome now that feudalism had been defeated, and the new realm of secular nationalist states had replaced the old Christian civilization that had dominated life in Europe for fourteen hundred years.

Imagine the surprise, shock, disillusionment, and despair when Jews discovered that anti-Semitism had managed to survive its religious roots and had taken hold of the imagination of people for whom religious sensibilities in other respects had largely faded, and even of people who were embracing the same secularism, nationalism, and faith in the new bourgeois epoch.

The persistence of anti-Semitism, most dramatically symbolized to the Jews of Europe by the Dreyfus case in France, seemed to transcend the normal categories of analysis. Though there were Christians and progressive secularists who rallied to Dreyfus, the willingness of supposedly enlightened secular Frenchmen to embrace overt anti-Semitism sent a deep chill through even the most committed champions of secular enlightenment.

In my view, the persistence of anti-Semitism is perfectly understandable. Racism and other forms of demeaning the other are intrinsically necessary for any oppressive social order, either to justify dominating and exploiting some group ("they deserve to be dominated, because they are really so much less human than we") or, in oppressive societies whose system of oppression does not depend solely on coercion but also requires some degree of participation and consent of the governed, to explain why the society's claims to offer salvation or fulfillment don't seem to be working so well ("there is some Other that is screwing things up, otherwise this society would feel much more fulfilling or appear to be much more holy or much more spiritually and ethically centered, and that other is group X").

Through most of European history, the Other of choice has been the Jews.

Ironically, it was precisely because Christianity's appeal was based so much on its ability to provide a higher meaning and purpose to life than that available through Roman imperialism or through the kind of brutal life available to many in the wake of the breakdown of the Roman Empire that Christianity needed the Jews. Christianity spoke to a need for a moral and spiritual community based on the assumption of human worth and dignity, and it was that fundamentally Torah-based insight that made it (and not any of the other contending metaphysical systems) become the foundation for European religious systems. Christianity offered people a validation of hope and an experience of community and connection that stood in sharp contrast to the brutality of Rome, and later to the insecurity of the early Middle Ages.

But as the Church itself became aligned with oppressive orders, first in Rome, later in feudalism, its ability to portray itself as embodying spiritual and ethical values declined. Though needs for fulfillment might be postponed for generations, or projected onto a heavenly realm that would come with death, eventually its own teachings—particularly those rooted in revolutionary conceptions of Torah that seemed to validate human beings, a kinship with the Divine, and hence a dignity that was far more pronounced than that which existed in the mythology of pagan cultures against which Christianity contended—would lead to subversive expectations for a more just and fulfilling social order. Unable to respond to those needs, more and more becoming part of the problem itself as the Church became more deeply invested in existing systems of power, the Church could channel people's anger over unfulfilling lives against the Jews.

Though the origin of racism or anti-Semitism may have society-stabilizing functions, eventually these ideas take on a life of their own. Even when these practices no longer serve specific societal interests or needs, organized systems of demeaning the other eventually permeate mass consciousness, become embedded in folk wisdom and folk hatred that may persist for hundreds of years, even at times when the rulers of a given society may no longer particularly practice the racism or Other-demeaning in question.

Of course, blaming the Jews doesn't change the fundamental realities of unfulfilling lives, and eventually all racisms and Other-blaming ideologies are insufficient to contain popular discontent. Eventually, many people began to support the ascendancy of a new class as it struggled to dislodge the feudal order and create a new kind of freedom for the individual. Had the transformation from feudalism to capitalism involved a real liberation from oppression, there might have been a real chance of extinguishing anti-Semitism through a process of education and mass therapy, so that after a few hundred years this pathology might have disappeared. But when the new capitalist societies revealed themselves to be less fulfilling than their advocates had promised, ruling elites were once again in need of an Other to deflect popular anger, and since there had been no educational or therapeutic campaign to uproot the legacy of popular anti-Semitism, it was not so surprising that some sectors of the ruling elites would turn on the Jews. Moreover, Jewish enthusiasm for the newly emerging order, since it opened the doors of emancipation from the ghettos, made them one of the most visible and enthusiastic articulators of the virtues of the new regimes. Having little understanding of how other sectors of the population might possibly experience the new order as oppressive, and might identify the Jews with this newly oppressive order (and exaggerate Jewish power within it), Jews found it difficult to imagine that the persistence of anti-Semitism had anything to do with "oppression," certainly not capitalist oppression, because for most Jews the new capitalist society seemed to be the embodiment of liberation from oppression. Instead, many concluded that anti-Semitism had some metaphysical characteristic that made it impervious to social change. Anti-Semitism began to feel almost as though it were an ontological fact about the universe: the non-Jews simply hate us, always have, always will, and we'd better figure out what to do about it.

There were four characteristic responses to the unexpected continuation of anti-Semitism after emancipation: assimilation ("if we can be more like everyone else, fit in a less offensive way, not be noticed, give up what is distinctive about us, become 'true' Americans, they'll stop finding us a threat and they'll let us alone"); internationalism ("if we can get rid of all national identities and all religious identities and all forms of particularism, there will be no basis for anyone to hate us");

Zionism ("the non-Jews will always hate us as long as we have this peculiar status as a People without a state, so we need to get a state and an army of our own"); further rigidification of orthodoxy ("the non-Jews hate us because we are trying to be like them and we've been abandoning God; the only way to stop that process is to build tighter walls, intensify restrictions on Jewish life, and fight against all those Jews who are diluting Judaism"). The last, the further rigidification of orthodoxy, had the effect of driving more Jews away. Faced with the option of a Judaism with an orthodoxy that seemed increasingly obsessed with the details of religious practice, millions of Jews sought escape, either through assimilation or through the creation of religious movements like Reform and Conservative Judaism, which gave some recognition to the possibility that Jewish law would have to accommodate to the realities of life in the modern world.

ASSIMILATION

For some Jews the only solution was to try harder to fit in. In the past 150 years many Jews made a valiant effort to eliminate everything that distinguished them as Jews. The beards were cut off, skullcaps removed, distinguishing dress of all sort was abandoned. By mid-century American Jews were having plastic surgery to change what they imagined to be their distinctive Jewish noses or large breasts. If they could learn not to talk too loud, not be too aggressive, physically look like others, celebrate Christmas, act like everyone else, then perhaps they would protect themselves and their children.

The assimilatory strategy did not work very well in Europe. Though Jews quickly succeeded in business and the professions, the persistence of anti-Semitism was far deeper than Jews had imagined. The Nazis had an almost religious obsession with the Jews, so that even those whose families had converted to Christianity a generation or two before were searched out and murdered. And even in the half century since the Nazis were defeated, anti-Semites persist in Europe, sometimes attacking those Jews who are most assimilated, sometimes flourishing even in the virtual absence of any Jewish community.

In the United States, on the other hand, assimilation had a much better shot. Though its Christian roots guaranteed that anti-Semitism would strike resonant chords in America, the actual history of conquest of the country had produced two other "others"—the Native Americans and African-Americans. Indeed, the subordination and exploitation of black people has been so severe and vehement throughout most of the twentieth century that Americans have needed a racist system of thinking that could allow them to justify to themselves the continuing inequalities and degradation of black life. What better idea than to blame the victims themselves, to imagine that there was a "culture of poverty" that had created distortions in black life, and that it is now the black people who can be rightly blamed for the continuation of their lower economic and social status. This same way of thinking had been used against Jews in Eastern Europe, in Germany, and in the United States in the earlier part of the twentieth century.

The oppression of black people as the Other of choice in America— along with American anger against gay people, Japanese, and Arabs— has allowed many Jews to imagine a much more complete assimilation for themselves than had been possible in Europe. Jews might feel free to fit into American society, as long as they do not call attention to themselves or insist that others pay attention to their needs or their experience.

In this context, assimilation could offer a variety of options: a) totally abandon Judaism as a religion and adopt a thoroughgoing secularism, abandoning one's Jewishness as a mark of ethnic or national identity as well; b) become secular religiously but still maintain an identity as a part of the Jewish nation or ethnic group; c) keep one's Jewishness in the private sphere and emphasize Americanness in public. Or one could be Jewish in public, as long as that public Jewishness involves emphasizing aspects of Jewish life that fit into the American experience and do not rock the boat or challenge American economic, political, or social practices.

The key to assimilation in America has been the absorption of the dominant values of the larger society: materialism, selfishness, acceptance of the economic and political status quo (although with a cheerful reformist ethic that envisions making the worse aspects of capitalism slightly more humane), pessimism about fundamental social change, and individualism. One could be extremely observant of Jewish ritual, perhaps even be a bearded Hasid, and still assimilate in this sense. Many of the most Orthodox synagogues in America are, by this definition, fully assimilated, although their members observe many of the details of religious law. They have learned how to fit in and "make it" in a world governed by corruption and selfishness, and they them-

selves accept the cruelty and pain of the world as a given, seeing their
primary task as securing for themselves and for the Jewish people the
best possible deal within this "reality." It rarely occurs to them that the
spiritual realm is not meant to be something separate that is available
on Saturdays only, or that the God of the Bible would enjoin them to
struggle to reduce poverty, homelessness, materialism, and the ethos of
selfishness.

SECULAR JEWISHNESS

Not all secular Jews sought assimilation. In fact, at the beginning of the
twentieth century a very vibrant Jewish life was built around a secular
Jewish identity. For some, the essence of that identity revolved around
preserving Yiddish culture. For others, the identity was built around
socialism and world transformation. Often fiercely antireligious, the
Jewish secularists developed a rich array of newspapers, schools, community organizations, and political activities that spoke to the needs of
many Jews in Eastern Europe and to many Eastern European immigrants to the United States.

Secularists broke the stranglehold of the ultrareligious in Jewish
institutional life, and helped legitimate the rights of individuals to think
and act for themselves beyond the contours of the community's strictures. And that helped create the social and intellectual space for
Reform and Conservative Judaism and for the kind of renewal I am
advocating in this book.

Emboldened by the enlightenment liberalism that validated the importance of rationalism and individual autonomy, Reform and Conservative Judaism could look back through Jewish history and Jewish texts
and discover there a Judaism that had been much more alive than the
rigidified orthodoxy that had become the dominant form of Jewish
religious life in the nineteenth century. Conservative and Reform
scholars were able to rediscover within Jewish texts a rich and vibrant
heterodoxy, a commitment to the sanctity of the individual made in the
image of God, a strong commitment to democratic process in talmudic
decision making, and even an insistence on the right of individuals to
find their own paths to God. But what they could not buy in the
program of enlightenment liberalism or Jewish secularism was the
attachment to an empiricist epistemology that denied the reality of
the spiritual and that reduced ethics to a merely subjective expression

of emotion or personal choice. In short, they rejected secularism and forged authentic and new routes to Jewish spirituality.

What is striking is that the secular Socialists and Yiddishists were largely unable to perpetuate themselves throughout the twentieth century and create a sustainable Jewish culture that could be transmitted to subsequent generations. Though tiny remnants of these traditions remain alive, and there are periodic revivals of interest in Yiddish or in secular Jewish socialism, these communities have largely faded. Unable to draw on the rich religious heritage of the Jewish people, its rituals and prayers, its complex mechanisms for transmission of spiritual truths, the explicitly Jewish progressive secular movements have largely disappeared.

In their place, a different kind of secularism has triumphed in the last half of the twentieth century—one based largely on the same individualist principles and conceptions that are part of the culture of contemporary capitalism. Not all secularism is necessarily conformist or accommodationist. Yet in today's world, much of it is just that—an attempt to fit into the mainstream of American culture, a deeply secular culture wrapped in a religious veneer. Though Jewish secularism could in principle be communitarian and committed to humanitarian principles that are rooted in Jewish history and tradition, they were unable to withstand the corrosive community-destroying impact of American ultra-individualism. Absent the community-generating realities of actually living together in a particular geographical location, American Jewish secularists have been unable to generate much more basis for ongoing Jewish identity than fundraising for Jewish communal institutions or vicarious identification with Israel. Only in Israel, where geographical contiguity and national identity generate their own forms of obligation, has a Jewish secularism sustained itself for future generations. And even there, Jewish secular culture increasingly attempts to mimic and outdo Western materialist and individualist culture. The distinctively Jewish flavor of the early years of Zionist settlement (the Yishuv) has largely given way to a society that speaks Hebrew and observes Jewish holidays, but has failed to develop Jewish culture that is distinguishable from the increasingly homogenized international culture imposed on the world by Western corporate and media hegemony. Secular Israelis judge themselves by Western standards in everything from academic life to music to city planning to psychotherapy to industry because they have not developed a distinctively Jewish approach to these or most other areas of life. The reality of secular Jewish life in America or Israel has little in common with the high ideals of the secular Jewish Socialists of the late nineteenth and early twentieth centuries, whose transformative vision included building a distinctively Jewish culture.

Indeed, I would argue that secularism easily falls into this pattern because it does not have a different worldview with which to confront the materialism and individualism of capitalist societies. Unwittingly, many liberal secularists have implicitly weighed in on the side of an empiricist epistemology and a materialist ontology that have contributed to "disenchanting the world" and the denial of the validity of ethical truths. If the ultimate test of reality is that which can be presented to our senses, or that which can be subject to verification or falsification through publicly observable criteria, then reality gets shrunk to very narrow proportions.

The intellectual outcome of this process is a world in which most of subjective experience, most ethical and aesthetic and spiritual life, is relegated to the sidelines as something that is questionable at best, "soft," not *real* but *merely subjective*. We are allowed to have these "non-real" experiences in our private lives, but we must be cautious *not* to bring them into our public and shared lives. Public life is purged of all communal meaning—it becomes an arena solely for individuals to pursue their self-interests. The "common good" becomes a quaint and outdated concept, reminiscent of the "commons" that had been enclosed so that individual owners could pursue their own profits while millions of people went poor and hungry. What is to be taken seriously is the pursuit of power and money, and all else is to be relegated to a private arena that should keep its nose out of public affairs. Privatization and individualism are the results—because by what possible standard does anyone have the right to impose his or her moral views on the common space if every moral view is subjective?

Equally important, a secularist embrace of empiricism eliminates the foundation for hope that transformation is really possible. If what is real is that which can be presented to our senses, then the empirical evidence gives ambiguous foundation for any belief that the world can be fundamentally transformed into a world based on mutual recognition, love, caring, justice, and peace. Secularists are hard-pressed to sustain the belief in the possibility of transformation, so it becomes difficult to convince themselves that it is worthwhile to sustain commitment to the struggle under circumstances like those that exist in the late twentieth century in which there are no powerful transformative movements that might plausibly deliver a reordering of our society. It is no surprise that it has been the religious Left that has been most successful in sustaining transformative commitments, not only because that religious Left has been able to mobilize ritual and commitment to community and transcendence of individualism in ways that the secularists have not, but also because the very belief in the God of the Bible is a belief in the possibility of transformation. Without that belief, secularists are often overwhelmed by the "facts" (that is, by the reality that transformation has not yet happened and it is not immediately obvious from whence the transformative forces might arise).

Moreover, the secularists are less likely to notice the one place from which I believe the transformation will arise, namely from frustration with the denial of the meaning needs. Secularists, particularly to the extent that they have an empiricist worldview, have been notoriously tone deaf to the crisis of meaning, hence unable to see that this crisis of meaning may provide the very foundation for liberation that working-class and Third World movements failed to supply.

How Jewish Secularism Increased Jewish Vulnerability

It's easy to understand why many Jews would embrace secularism's efforts to empty the public square of all religious and ethical worldviews. After all, our experience in Christian and Islamic societies had taught us that when the public square *was* committed to a particular worldview, it was often one that demeaned Jews. If religion seemed to be the official validator of feudal forms of oppression, what better way to identify with the forces of liberation than to overthrow all vestiges of religious belief and practice?

Many Jews became the vanguard of struggles to keep religion out of the public sphere. Aware of the oppressive nature of some religious practice and the way that religion functioned to sustain hatreds and irrational fears of the other, Jews often enthusiastically embraced the most radical extensions of First Amendment guarantees of separation of Church and State, fearful that any weakening of the division might soon lead back to a sanctioned anti-Semitism. To the extent that these separationist struggles inhibit dominant groups from imposing a particular religious conception on minorities, they deserve our continuing support.

Jewish secularists enthusiastically embraced enlightenment liberalism with its promise of democracy, rationalism, education, individual rights, and the notion of community composed of self-determining individuals who freely choose the degree to which they wish affiliation to any larger unit. Some of these ideals played a role in the development of the halakhic community, but they were never explicitly acknowledged as such, and once articulated by the secularists, they were often resisted by the Orthodox. In retrospect, we can now recognize that the Jewish world benefitted greatly from the articulation of these ideals.

Many Jews embraced enlightenment with the same religious intensity with which their ancestors had embraced Judaism. They imagined that the triumph of democratic forms, the freeing of the individual from communal restraints, and the purging of spiritual and religious matters from the public arena would bring about a full emancipation of human life. Many Jews retained a private sentimental attachment to their Jewishness, but in public life they espoused a universalism that sought the elimination of all particularities.

There were downsides to the secular religion of enlightenment liberalism.

To end the coercive use of spirituality and religion, secular separationists sometimes assaulted the validity of the ethical and spiritual. Hence the rigid division between a public sphere in which only objective, morally neutral truths are allowed and a private sphere (the family, personal life, or religious communities) in which the "merely subjective" concerns of individuals and groups would be appropriate.

Emptied of values and spirituality, public space becomes merely technocratic and easily manipulated without restraint by the most powerful forces in the society. Corporations can set the public agenda by arguing that *their* goals, the maximization of consumable goods and progress made possible by the unrestrained development of science and technology, are publicly verifiable. People may have whatever private goals they wish as long as they are kept out of the public arena, but the goals of production and consumption are shared public goals. The proof is the market: the ultimate democratic mechanism, because it allows people to make their own choices. Public space should be limited to assisting the market to achieve its ends, which are ultimately the democratic choices of hundreds of millions of individuals.

Secular Jewish Socialists resisted this argument by pointing out that the market gives unequal power to some because of preexisting inequalities in the distribution of wealth and income. But when the defenders of the status quo insisted that equality was a Socialist value that should be banished from the public sphere and like all other religious and ethical values should play a role only in private life, secularists often found it difficult to explain why they had a right to privilege this value when they had fought for a public sphere free of all values. Despite valiant efforts by John Rawls and other liberal theorists to privilege values like equality and tolerance, the effect of their campaign for an empiricist metaphysics and a neutral public realm left them with little ability to mobilize popular campaigns for equality.

So, the freeing of public space from values and spirituality left the world impoverished and more easily dominated by market forces.

Similarly, enlightenment liberalism's lionization of the individual. The Jews became involved in a fierce pursuit of individual rights to ensure that no one can impose upon us the religious traditions of the majority, but those same rights have been appropriated by others to allow the unfettered pursuit of self-interest. A generalized triumph of selfishness and me-firstism has become the dominant quasi-religious commitment of most Americans in the twentieth century.

Nothing could fit the needs of a competitive market society better. The goal of the merchants, bankers, manufacturers, and traders had always been to free their economic system from any external constraints. To the extent that Jews have become champions of a secularism that undermines any objective ethical basis from which to critique the free operations of the market, our struggle for Jewish emancipation was unwittingly being achieved through the triumph of a philosophy that could have destructive consequences for much of the world.

Those who feel positive about the consequences of modernism and the competitive market have good reason to feel good about the role of Jewish secularism in all this; but those of us who have more mixed feelings about the specific ways that the market system has operated—particularly in regard to the way that it has contributed to the destruction of the ecological support systems for the planet and the homogenization of thought, emotion, and art—must be less enthusiastic, not about the fact of Jewish emancipation, but about the way we were allowed to achieve it.

We were presented with secular and antispiritual social movements for democracy and individual rights, which had emerged in a struggle against feudalism. Rather than imagining a different possibility, a democratic movement that could validate the ethical and spiritual truths of our tradition, most Jews were so grateful for the chance to be accepted by non-Jews in *any* joint venture that they enthusiastically embraced the secular enlightenment liberalism that was being offered, and even became its most outspoken advocates. The tragedy of contemporary Jewish history is that the only way available for us to achieve liberation from previous systems of oppression has been to identify with a secularist form of thinking that belies the deepest truths that we have been fighting to preserve throughout our Jewish history.

Yet the individualism and antispiritual empiricism embraced by some secular Jews run counter to the needs and aspirations of many other Jews, and many non-Jews. The sanctification of the individual and choice as the highest goals of life run counter to the actual experiences of most people on the planet. Despite the frantic attempts by the ideologically dominant forces in the society to convince us that the only thing we want is our own individual well-being, and to teach us that it is "human nature" to be narrowly self-interested, most of us feel most fully alive when we are connected to others, recognized by them, and in reciprocal loving and caring relationships. Moreover, we want to be related to others as part of larger communities of meaning that transcend the individualism and selfishness of the competitive market and give our lives a higher moral and spiritual purpose. Yet these "meaning needs" are harder and harder to gratify in the modern world, in part because of the ruthless denigration of ethical and spiritual thought, in part because of the near-religious status given to the individual in pursuit of self-interest.

The crisis of modernity has been particularly difficult for those who are *not* experts at changing themselves into the kinds of beings whose talents will always sell in the market. Because technological change requires continual change in the skills and talents that one can sell, there is a growing insecurity and fear that in the next set of changes we will be left out and discarded. Romanticizing a past that was often stifling, patriarchal, and oppressive, many of those who are most marginalized by the rapid change of modern life begin to wonder if they would not have been better off in a society based on something else besides individual achievement and self-interest.

Quite reasonably worried if anyone will be there for them, to care for them when they are weak or vulnerable, to provide love, and to enjoy commitment to shared ethical and spiritual values, growing numbers of people have viewed the triumph of modernism with mixed emotions. On the one hand, they are fascinated by the technology and astounded at the diversity of consumer goods suddenly available to large numbers of people. On the other hand, they are stunned by the decline in social solidarity, the growth of selfishness, and the absence of institutions that could challenge or at least mediate between themselves and the avarice of the marketplace. If their worth as individuals, and their ability to survive economically, are dependent solely on how well they are doing in the competitive market, many people will see that they are not doing so well, and that by these new market criteria they are actually next to worthless. And as an ethos of selfishness increases, people will see that they have no one to count on. The triumph of "individual rights" will mean little to people who imagine that this new freedom has become a codeword for isolation, alienation, selfishness, and the breakdown of loving relationships that existed in the framework of families and communities. It was *this* that was blamed on the Jews.

Our desperate attempt to get out of one system of oppression—instituted by feudal orders that validated a role for religious and ethical systems in the public sphere, but did so in a way that was destructive to Jews—led to our being placed in yet another form of vulnerability, in which our championing of secularism and individualism would become a target for popular anger more appropriately directed at ruling elites (because, after all, it was not the Jews who created modern secularism and it was not the Jews who had created or who were the primary beneficiaries of the competitive market system and all its attendant distortions). Because the secularism that emerged often went hand in hand with a materialist empiricism that seemed to deny the very ethical and spiritual concerns that working-class and lower middle-class people have sometimes believed to be their only bulwark against the unlimited exploitation of the competitive market, Jewish secularism opened yet another avenue for people to hate the Jews. Antimodernist and anticapitalist reactions, totally understandable given the context of the nineteenth and twentieth centuries, could get directed at the Jews who seemed to be the quintessential group embracing contemporary secularism and fighting to keep ethical and spiritual values outside the public sphere.

Of course, many secular Jews joined Socialist movements that were as much concerned with attacking the distortions of capitalist societies as were movements that preached reactionary nationalism and anti-Semitism. Yet from the standpoint of many who were attracted to the Right, socialism was only a more extreme version of the forces that had broken down traditional communities, leaving people vulnerable and without adequate protection. The passionate antireligious and anti-spiritual dimensions of twentieth-century Socialist movements, their adherence to social norms that seemed disrespectful of family and traditional communities, and their apparent culmination in Stalinist Russia with its extremes of oppression in the name of freedom and equality, made it hard for many Westerners to believe that these Social-ists were anything but an embodiment of the most fearful aspects of modernism.

It does not follow that Jewish secularism must be abandoned. But secularism, whether espoused by Jews or non-Jews, needs to be re-constituted in ways that can acknowledge the ethical, spiritual, and psychological concerns that have often been ignored or denied in the various materialist forms of secular thought. Most human beings have the need to transcend the individualism and selfishness of the competitive market and to root themselves in communities of mean-ing and purpose that link them to some higher ethical and spiritual goals than are traditionally validated in secular thought. Secularists need to address the ways that society systematically frustrates these meaning needs, and then to develop a "politics of meaning" that aims to achieve societal transformations aiming to eliminate those aspects of our economic and political life that frustrate our meaning needs, even if that political movement simultaneously rejects traditional re-ligious or theocentric formulations about how to approach spiritual reality.

HOW RELIGION GOT DISCREDITED

The triumph of secularism is an understandable consequence of the corruption of communities of meaning. Medieval Christianity was eventually unmasked to many Europeans as a system more concerned to provide economic and political power to a ruling elite than to service the spiritual needs of the European masses. And by the time political emancipation was available to the majority of Jews, Judaism itself had begun to appear less like a movement for human emancipation than like a hierarchical system of patriarchal authority that had made its peace with class divisions in the Jewish world and that was run by a small elite of scholars, rabbis, and community big shots who were more concerned about the details of whether their food was kosher than about whether their world was humane and caring. As religious communities were exposed by skeptical secularists as systems of privilege serving the self-interest of religious leaders, disillusionment about the core ideas of religion abounded. And to the extent that the religious faithful become engaged in the capitalist market, adopting its ethos of selfishness in public economic life, the ideals of their religion seem less and less serious, more and more merely an ideological sideshow that doesn't really govern their lives. No wonder, then, that increasing numbers of people begin to question whether religion is anything more than a cover for self-interest. They hear the fine words about love and justice, but also they see that the practice of religious communities often seems no different or higher than the practice of anyone else. "If all that people care about is their self-interest," people begin to reason, "then why shouldn't I go for my own self-interest, and abandon all the restraints put on me by religious communities if that interferes with my self-interest?"

As one system of meaning after another is similarly unveiled as being little more than a cover for self-interest, as capitalism and communism and every other system are unveiled as higher orders of selfishness, a despair sinks in throughout the society. Many people come to believe that there is nothing worth fighting for but oneself—because that is all that people really do fight for, and it would be naive to believe that there is some higher good.

Yet systems of selfishness and cynicism are themselves covers for the inequalities of a class society. While convincing each person to struggle for his or her own good, they fail to notice how the belief in selfishness itself becomes one of the causes for why most people never will achieve their own good, because to do so requires living in a society based on caring and mutual connection. Our need for mutual recognition and connection with others becomes even more difficult to fulfill when we are surrounded by human beings who have learned to be cynical, distrustful, and narrowly self-interested.

So we get the dynamics of the twentieth century: people alternately attracted to systems of selfishness and cynicism, as antidotes to previous illusions about communities of meaning that have been exposed to be fronts for privilege; then slowly growing sick of the kind of alienation and loneliness produced by this selfishness, so that they are once again attracted to compromised communities of meaning which will eventually be exposed as less than they promised. This alternation—between periods of frenetic involvement in the competitive market and the pursuit of individual gain and power, on the one hand, and periods in which people are so desperately in flight from the alienation and estrangement of the competitive market that they are willing to plunge without careful, critical thought into various pseudo-communities that promise the human connection, recognition, and ties to higher purpose that are transparently not available through enlightenment liberalism—produces, on the other, a deep, spiritual and political crisis that has been the backdrop to world wars, genocide, and the destruction of the life-support systems of the planet.

The solution is not a secularism and rejection of higher meaning. That simply does not work because it ignores our fundamental human need for meaning and ethical and spiritual foundation. Rather, what is needed is a renewal of the religious and spiritual and meaning communities, so that the inner corruption, patriarchy, and reality of self-interest are transformed and the communities become fuller embodiments of their own highest ideals. These communities need to transcend the cynicism within themselves that has lulled their own participants into spiritual and ethical unconsciousness.

The renewal forces within any community of meaning are those who testify to the possibility of this transformation (*tikkun*) of the world, who insist that cruelty is not destiny, and who actively seek to move beyond ritualistic invocations of their ideals to actually imbue daily life with the ethical and spiritual sensitivity which they profess. Happily, there are renewal energies flourishing within all the major religious traditions and many of the secular communities as well.

The disenchantment of the world—the elimination of spiritual and ethical categories; the triumph of empiricism, materialism, and ethical cynicism—has led to a narrow instrumentalism: everything viewed from the standpoint of what the individual can get for him- or herself. That consciousness, in turn, has led not only to the looting of the earth's resources with potentially devastating consequences to the whole human race, but also to the elimination of hope in transforming the world.

What I've argued in this first section of the book is that Judaism provides a metaphysics of transformation and healing capable of grounding a response to the contemporary triumph of cynicism and despair. Judaism is a movement that has been going on since we Jews pushed our way out of slavery some thirty-two hundred years ago, and its foundation is the possibility of transformation. "Yes," the cynic might respond, "but look at the Jewish people and Judaism today— they no longer embody this consciousness of Judaism as a transformative movement. All the more reason to give up on transformative movements—they simply don't work. So let's accommodate ourselves to the reality of contemporary selfishness and stop pretending that something else is possible."

This is precisely why Jewish renewal is so important—because if it can succeed in getting Judaism reattached to its original and most radical message, it can provide one concrete example of the possibility of a community that could sustain itself through time with a transformative message relatively intact. I've insisted that this is not all there is to Judaism, and that in focusing on this aspect we may be tempted to underplay the other spiritual dimensions to Judaism and to Jewish life, particularly those aspects concerned with celebrating and standing in awe of God's presence permeating every ounce of Being. Yet the articulation of this transformative message is extremely important because renewal in the Jewish world would inspire a new sense of confidence in the possibility of possibility.

This confidence, however, has been severely strained by the Holocaust and the experience of the State of Israel.

CHAPTER EIGHT

HOLOCAUST, EVIL, AND THE CONSERVATIZING OF JEWISH SENSIBILITIES

The genocidal destruction of European Jewry and the creation of the State of Israel have been the defining realities of the Jewish experience in the twentieth century. The joyfulness of Judaism, its affirmation of life and a God of possibility and transformation, have been hard to sustain when the Jewish people themselves have been so significantly traumatized by the murder of one third of our people. Fifty years later we are just beginning to get to the point where we can address the pain and the distortions in Jewish life and thought generated by this trauma. Jewish renewal requires a healing of these psychic scars.

Let's start by remembering that the scars are not the fault of the victims. If Jewish life has been distorted by the pain inflicted by others, we need to reaffirm as a first step in the process of healing that we Jews did not deserve what happened to us. We did not deserve to be punished for sins we did not commit; we did not deserve to be hurt. What happened to us was outrageous, a violation of our humanity and a desecration of God's image that resides within each of us.

The first response to the Holocaust was psychic denial (which, of course, is the normal reaction of survivors of trauma). Jews officially acknowledged it, but then went on about their business of building the State of Israel or obtaining political influence or financial success in the United States without seriously pausing to deal with the trauma, confronting it in any serious way as a community, or creating mechanisms for public grieving. In Israel, Holocaust victims were encouraged to forget the past and put their attentions on the problems of the present and future. There were even some tendencies within Israeli culture to see the victims as shameful or blameworthy ("they walked like lambs to the slaughter," or references to them as soap)—and in any event, the very existence of the new state was the real answer to the Holocaust, a statement that Jews would from now on be strong and powerful in response to potential oppressors. Israelis shunned excessive grieving and saw those focused on the Holocaust as stuck in a past that needed to be transcended quickly. Jews in other countries restrained their anger at the failure of non-Jews to respond, fearful that they might provoke new waves of anti-Semitism.

But while the emotional realities of the Holocaust were being avoided, denied, or subverted by a focus on current strength (possibly even invulnerability), the anger and pain that were not being expressed directly were being channeled into intellectual responses to the trauma, or what I'd prefer to call intellectualizing of the pain. Intellectualizing of the pain took two main forms: distrust of God, and distrust of humanity.

DISTRUST OF GOD

How could God have allowed Auschwitz?

This was the cry of pain that led both to a widespread defection from religious belief and to a spate of efforts to develop a post-Holocaust theology.

If God had the power to intervene, but did not, what kind of evil being must this God be?

As Eliezer Berkowitz points out, the problem is not a new one. The wrongful death of one Jew raises the same problem as that of the wrongful death of six million. The classical theological problem of evil is no less intractable than the problem of Nazi evil.

But the Holocaust makes the problem of evil unavoidable. People must face the issue not only on an individual basis in their own lives, but also as a social problem confronting an entire people. And this makes certain kinds of pious answers seem much less plausible. For example, "God has mysterious ways that we don't understand" might be plausible against a background of thinking that in general God is doing good in the world. But when confronted with six million murders, to people, it seems equally plausible to conclude that "there is no God," because the goodness of God's works no longer seems so overwhelming.

In the past, Jews dealt with the collective disasters of Jewish history by assuming the blame. The Musaf prayer for every Jewish holiday states this theme unequivocally: "Because we sinned we were exiled from our land, and are no longer able to fulfill the commandments of providing sacrifices . . ."

Now, one could object that it was *never* true that this could be an adequate explanation. After all, the argument might go, the Babylonians would have conquered us no matter how we had been treating widows and orphans (a reason proffered by the prophets), and the Romans would have defeated us even if there had been no groundless hatred among Jews (a reason proffered by the rabbis). But there is something to be said in favor of this kind of self-blaming. Most other peoples of the ancient world simply disappeared when their countries were conquered, their temples destroyed, and their majorities led into exile or slavery. Having felt that military defeats proved the inefficacy of their gods, they saw no point in maintaining their previous identities, particularly if they were offered the chance of assimilating into the victorious culture. The Jews, on the other hand, interpreted their *defeat* as proof of the power of their God, because God, through the prophets, had warned them that they had no absolute right to the land of Israel or to God's protection—that all that depended on their willingness to live up to the Covenant. In this sense, self-blaming became an instrument of self-preservation, a tool of empowerment in face of overwhelming force. Though we could not stand up to the power of the Romans, we could have power on a higher level, by explaining their power as *really* part of God's power.

Some ultra-Orthodox Jews actually tried to use this line in explaining the Holocaust. The Jews had abandoned religion and become secularized in Germany, the Jews had violated their arrangement with the gentiles by trying to regain their land (through Zionism), the Jews had tried to hasten the coming of the Messiah—these were some of the specific sins that were adduced to "explain" why God let the Holocaust happen.

But most religious Jews have found these explanations about as persuasive as those offered by some ultra-Orthodox Jews every time there is an auto accident in Israel involving the death of children ("their parents had a defective mezuzah on the doorpost of their house"). To most religious Jews it seems like a betrayal of the honor and dignity of the lives of these Jews and a wild demeaning of God to find some real or alleged sin in which these people engaged. There simply is no conceivable sin that could come close to justifying genocide. To think that God willed the brutal and senseless murder of more than a million children is to think that God is either a sadist or mad.

Some kabbalists, when faced with the expulsion of the Jews from Spain, described a *hester panim*, a hiding of God's face in history. God had voluntarily contracted His/Her presence in order to make room for the world and for the creation of human beings, and it is this purposeful self-contraction and dimming of His/Her own brightness which makes the creation of the world and its evils possible. The *tsimtsum* (voluntary contraction) of God is a dynamic ebb-and-flow, a kind of breathing of God's energy, so that the withdrawal is followed by *hitpashtut*, God's embracing or expansion. The dimming or covering of the brightness of divine light, which is lessened so that it will not blind or burn the human world it created, will be there, as sixteenth-century Jewish kabbalist Isaac Luria stated, "according to the measure needed to give them [the created worlds] light or life."[1] The divine contraction was a cathartic, cosmic process the kabbalists called "the breaking of the vessels" (*shevirat hakelim*), a shattering explosion of the divine light, and the sparks of that light flew either back into its divine source or downward to the earth. In this way, the good elements (the divine sparks) came to be mixed with the vicious elements (the *klipot* or shells), and humanity's task is to fix the world, *tikkun*, through a constant effort of raising the holy, scattered sparks to their divine source. Living a life of *mitzvah* is the way to bring about this *tikkun*.

Part of the process of *tikkun* is for human beings to invite God back into the world. The moment that we are unable to see godliness reflected in other people, we reconfirm God's hiding. But to the extent that we create a kinder, spiritually and ethically more sensitive world, God's presence is allowed to shine through the faces of each of us, so that Her/His presence in the world can be more fully experienced and known. It is, of course, not the fault of the Jewish people that God's face is hidden—the hiddenness of God is a reflection of the collective

---

[1] Mordechai Rotenberg, *Dialogue with Deviance: The Hasidic Ethic and the Theory of Social Contraction* (Philadelphia: Institute for the Study of Human Issues, 1983).

history of the human race, our sets of choices, the degree to which we have been hiding from one another. But when God's face is hidden, all people, including the Jewish people, suffer. And that is why we all have a stake in making God's presence more obvious by fostering the conditions in which God can shine through each of us.

Even if we don't accept the kabbalistic framework, the notion of God voluntarily limiting Her/His presence in the world gives us a contemporary version of a parental picture of God, reassuring us that God cares and providing a rational reason for God not to intervene. If God is a parent, then S/He may have revealed Her/His good intentions at an earlier moment (through liberation from Egypt), given us Her/His instruction and wisdom about how to live (Sinai), but then eventually come to understand that if we are to be fully grown up we need to develop an autonomy that is only possible by allowing us to make our own mistakes without constant interference from divine aid. Like a parent who joyfully watches her child exercise her freedom, God watches as we develop. And if we stumble, fall, even hurt ourselves, it may take every inch of self-restraint for God not to intervene immediately. But since God wants us to develop real autonomy, S/He understands that the whole process will be subverted if S/He interferes in this kind of way. So God will be watching over us, crying over our pain, but precisely because God respects us, respects our possibilities to be embodiments of the divine likeness, God cannot allow the luxury of intervening, because in the long run that would cripple us, perpetuate our childlike nature, make it impossible for us to develop the maturity and independence and autonomy that could allow us to be full partners with God in the healing and repairing of the world.

It is precisely because God respects our dignity and our potential embodiment of divinity that S/He will not any longer interfere with the world and its evil.

This conception is not some modern invention. The Talmud records a story that shows the rabbis dealing with similar issues, and assuring themselves that *they* have the right to change God's Torah in accord with their own sensibilities precisely because God withdrew from the world in order to allow this kind of human freedom. The story goes like this: Rabbi Eliezer was in a dispute with other sages about a point of law. Said Rabbi Eliezer, "If I am right, let the walls of this building incline." The walls inclined. The sages were not impressed. Said Rabbi Eliezer, "If I am right, let the heavens darken." The heavens darkened.

The sages did not budge. Finally, Eliezer said, "Let a voice come from heaven." A voice came from heaven and said, "The law is according to Eliezer." And the sages said, "No, the law has been given to human beings to interpret, and it shall be according to the majority of sages. So Eliezer's position is not the law." On that day, the Midrash continues, God said, "My children have transcended me." (The Hebrew *ba'nie nitzchuni* has also been translated that my children have "won against me"; others read, have "become my victory"; but all read it to mean that God rejoices in children who have thus declared their independence.) And this story is at least sixteen hundred years old. So human dignity, seen as depending upon freeing onself from a parent-child relationship with God, has a substantial pedigree in Jewish thought.

I believe that the accumulated evil in the world, manifested in the Nazis, is not some product of God's choice, but rather of a set of human choices. Having been given the freedom to choose, some human beings made choices not to recognize one another as human beings. Perhaps this was at the moment of initial scarcity when, driven by hunger and the fear that one's own children or family would starve to death, some human beings took food from others forcibly, used violence, imposed their will for the sake of obtaining nourishment. Probably not sharing the same language or customs, they allowed themselves to perceive the other as "Other," not fundamentally the same as oneself, not really sharing in that which deserves respect or caring. And that misrecognition of the other allowed for "power over," for inflicting violence, for domination and subordination to one's own program or will. This was the shattering of the vessels, the creation of pain and humiliation and anger, that would be passed on from generation to generation. And in each generation it got worse—in each generation people allowed themselves to treat others even more as though they had nothing in common, and in each generation the compounded psychic wounds and pain intensified, so that finally even slavery, mass murder, imperialism, and racism became possible. Not that the fundamental divine spirit in each human being had been extinguished, but that a legacy of accumulated pain and hurt had become so overwhelming, and that pain had been so fully embodied in economic, political, and social institutions governing daily life and reinforcing the insensitivity of each person to another, that there were moments when it became almost impossible for human beings to hear the voice of God in the world.

Every human being is born into a preestablished world that is the product of this long history of distorted choices. Through their first encounters with parents, significant others, social practices embedded in social and economic institutions, a language shaped to a world of domination and exploitation, teachers charged with conveying a culture laced with these distortions, and a culture whose "common sense" reflects this history of pain and distortion, children are taught to fit in. Each of us develops a self in this context, best understood by envisioning a set of psychic chains going from our own hearts and minds through our parents and backward in time through hundreds of generations of ancestors, each linked to past generations through these chains of negativity and pain, but also through cords in which the positivity and goodness and caring are passed on from generation to generation. There are moments when the pain becomes so overwhelming, the fears so intense, that human beings seem to be acting only out of the collective memory of anger, frustration, and humiliation. But those moments pass, somewhat. And they can pass even more if we use our collective energies to figure out how best to bring a *tikkun* into the world. This process of *tikkun*, of healing and repair, is within our collective grasp, but it is not at all inevitable that we will grasp it. It remains a permanent possibility, a possibility attested to by our claim that there is a God in the world.

One can, of course, accept much of the picture painted in this last paragraph, and nevertheless reject the notion of there being a God. For some Holocaust survivors even this picture seems too generous to a God who remained silent. What kind of a parent, they ask, would allow their children to be murdered in front of their eyes? Perhaps a parent might endure watching some hurt befall a child—but if the parent saw the child being murdered, and *could* stop it, how could there be talk about allowing the child to develop its own maturity?

One response here might be to suggest that God does not see the Jews as Her/His only children, but as one of many groups of children. And not all the Jews were destroyed, just some Jews. And God may have decided that the cost of freedom requires that some of Her/His children be destroyed.

But, we may respond, what could one possibly mean by "just some"? The minimizing flavor of that remark cannot be allowed in the discourse of a people whose prophets taught us to be outraged when even one widow or one orphan was being neglected, whose rabbis taught us that "anyone who saves one life among the people of Israel, it is as though they had saved the whole world!" If this is the kind of parent God is, then we reject such a parent! Or we see such a parent as an unworthy model—so we reject any need to learn from Her/His Torah, because it comes from a source that is too deeply accommodating to evil.

Another possibility remains for those of us who wish to testify to God's reality in the world: suggest that God cares very much, but simply lacks the power to intervene, or has constructed a world in which divine intervention is impossible. A God that has the wisdom to communicate truths about how we ought to live, truths which, if we lived by them, would make us able to accomplish a genuine *tikkun* of the world, would not be a useless God, though certainly less wish-fulfilling than a God who is our cosmic bellhop, doing our bidding if we behave right or if we offer the right sacrifices or right combination of prayers. This conception of God abandons the Greek notion of omnipotence, but it doesn't make God irrelevant or unimportant.

Nor, based on this interpretation of God with limited power, would the claim of the Shma be an empty one. In saying that there is a Force in the universe that makes for the possibility of the transformation of what is to what ought to be, we would not necessarily be claiming that whenever we want to make the transformation, this God will assist. Rather, we would be claiming that the way that the world was constructed allows us to overcome the distortions and pain within it, and that there is an energy in the universe that will help us know what transformation is necessary, and that will empower us with the strength to move in that direction.

Though every set of words about God necessarily limits and distorts a reality that transcends all language, we have only words, so let's try to paint a verbal picture here about this relationship. Imagine that God is like a sun, pouring out life-giving and transformative energies into the world, and that we are like moving and self-transforming plants who have the ability to receive God's energy into our cells when we face toward the sun. We might like to think that each moment that we receive God's energy is like an individual act of generosity and personal care, but more likely that energy is a permanent feature of the world, and what makes us feel charged up is the degree to which we've figured out ways to turn toward it. Part of the goal of Jewish renewal is to figure out ways to turn collectively toward that energy.

But when we've turned away, the world may seem very dark, our own energies for transformation may feel very depleted, and our memory of God's energy may seem very dim. We may have little more than the words of the prayers to remind us that there is something toward which we might turn. If we turn with anger, demanding that somehow this energy act in an immediate and personal way to become involved in our lives as a caring parent would, we will find ourselves deeply disappointed. Indeed, the anger of our disappointment may make it harder for us to receive whatever positive energy *is* being transmitted to us, energy that might be utilized to build the kind of social movement that would prevent a recurrence of the brutality of the Nazis. We see God's energy not as an alternative source of salvation, but as the Force that may make it possible for us to align with others and build a transformed world.

In this account of God, the Torah claims that are embodied in the second paragraph of the Shma prayer called *V'hayah Eem Sh'moa* make good sense. That prayer talks about the world not working if we do not live according to God's *mitzvot*. Perhaps the prayer is telling us something about the fundamental construction of the universe: that when we turn away from God's energies and act in hurtful and destructive ways, the physical universe itself rebels. We can see this in relationship to the ecological crisis of the contemporary period: because human beings have estranged themselves from the moral and spiritual sensitivities of Torah, they act toward the world as though it were a resource to be endlessly exploited rather than a treasure from God which we are charged to preserve. To the extent that we continue to abandon Torah sensitivities in the way we relate to the physical world, the physical world will not work—there will be an ecological catastrophe, and, in Torah's words, we shall perish.

This description of God's relationship to the world is more distanced than many people had hoped, but it may better correspond to our actual experience. God has built into the structure of reality a set of rewards and punishments, and has then communicated Her/His schema to us. It's not that God then intervenes at any particular moment, but that S/He has set up the world in such a way that it can work in the long run only if people act to maximize their own capacities to be godlike— compassionate, just, caring, loving, alive, conscious, free; maximizing beauty and goodness, joy and expansiveness, reflection, wisdom, and transcendence. Holocausts happen because a world that has thwarted these capacities for millennia generates human beings so distorted and so full of rage and pain that they are unable to recognize the spirit of God in one another. We are the inheritors of such a world, and it seems disingenuous to blame all this on God rather than to see the ways that human beings have been victims of the accumulated historical residue of humanly constructed systems of oppression—victims who then become oppressors.

In thinking of God in this way we are beginning to move away from the "God as parent" pictures to a "God as nourisher and sustainer and guider of the universe," but differently from the traditional conception. God can no longer be related to as the Force that is going to intervene to straighten things out when we create evil. We need God in order for us to be infused with a divine spirit, divine wisdom, and divine energy. But God needs us in order to complete the task of bringing divine spirit into the world. What God does is ensure that this possibility of transformation continues to exist, and that when we engage in the struggle we will find resources to make our triumph possible (not inevitable). I will return to this concept in the last chapter of this book. For the moment, my contention is only this: the Holocaust does not force us to be totally cynical about God.

We have every right to be enraged at what happened to us as a people. Not only in the Holocaust, but throughout the past thousands of years. Our families have been murdered, raped, brutalized, dispossessed, humiliated, oppressed, despised, vilified, and rejected. There is every reason for us to want a world that has treated us this way to change. But it does not follow that we must be angry at God. God may have had nothing to do with it. We could be angry that there isn't a God like that about whom it would be appropriate to be angry, but that anger ought not to lead us to deny or play down our joy and love for the God that actually does exist.

DISTRUST OF HUMANITY

Those post-Holocaust thinkers who were not transfixed with the death of God were often involved in proclaiming the death of "man." According to this line of reasoning, the Enlightenment brought a belief in the inevitability of human progress coupled with a virtual deification of the role of science and technology in bettering the human condition. Yet Germany, one of the most enlightened and scientifically advanced societies on the face of the earth, produced this barbarism. So our belief in "man" has proved to be mistaken.

Though this line of thought first gained prominence through the writings of Will Herberg and other Jewish theologians and social theorists in the late 1940s and 1950s, it remains a recurrent theme in contemporary Jewish thought. Listen to the rightly respected Rabbi Edward Feld of the Society for the Advancement of Judaism, a starship congregation of Reconstructionist Judaism, in his *The Spirit of Renewal*:

> [After the Holocaust,] all optimistic liberalism evaporates. Any simple trust in the basic and inevitable goodness is forfeited, any faith in the long-range victory of a general and progressive meliorism is dispelled. We now know the depths of humanity's capacity for evil. We are different because of the Holocaust, terribly different.[2]

The literature of disillusionment abounds. No doubt, there were some people who really did hold the naive picture of an inevitable progress toward human perfection. Yet the total dismissal of optimistic liberalism seems a bit overdrawn. The Holocaust refutes only the most simplistic forms of liberalism. It is possible to draw a more complex version of liberal optimism that accepts the human capacities to transcend the evil of the world without committing to the notion that those capacities will be actualized at every historical moment. On the contrary, in the struggle to transform the world there would be many moments of reversion, in which the embedded patterns of the past will reassert themselves.

In fact, it's precisely as one comes closest to creating fundamentally new ways of being that older and more self-destructive behaviors sometimes emerge with greater force than ever. It's often helpful for individuals to go through this moment with a therapist who can interpret the reemergence of past patterns as an indication that the client is making a last-ditch effort to hold on to the past, *not* a sign of the inevitability that that side of the client's personality will always triumph. In the presence of this reassurance, the client may be able to

---

[2]Edward Feld, *The Spirit of Renewal* (Woodstock, VT: Jewish Lights Publishing, 1991), p. 93.

summon the strength to persist in developing new ways of behaving, despite the "evidence" that change seems so unlikely. Analogous processes occur when people seek significant social change, and the belief in God—as the Force that can reassure us that the sought-for liberation is really possible—may potentially undermine those tendencies within us to settle for much more modest changes than we know are needed.

One way we get convinced to settle for less change than is needed is by allowing the view that the world can and should be fundamentally changed to be equated with the view that that change can take place overnight.

I do not hold the naive view that human beings are going to jump suddenly from where they are into some harmonious and egoless and evilless communitarian purity. The process of change may take hundreds of years. Some radical theorists in the past, particularly those associated with Communist parties, imagined that "the kingdom was at hand" and total transformation imminent—perhaps to sustain themselves through moments of intense persecution and oppression. I can sympathize with their desire for such total and immediate transformations, just as I understand how many of my contemporaries in the 1960s, desperate to see an end to the suffering of the Vietnamese and the poverty and oppression of African-Americans in the inner cities, latched on to visions of instant revolutionary transformation. Far from ridiculing such people, I want to honor them for the intensity of their commitment to overcome the oppression in the world, and their heartfelt desire to envision a more caring reality. It's a tragic fact that that need sometimes led people to overlook the tendencies within transformative social-change movements that lent themselves to totalitarianism. We can honor the need without accepting every political tendency or movement that justifies itself in terms of that need. Here, as elsewhere, it is exactly the critical exercise of our Enlightenment-sponsored Reason that teaches us to distinguish between potentially destructive and potentially liberatory responses to our need to end the world's suffering. We can still believe in radical social change, even though it may take many, many generations to accomplish. In fact, we Jews have been at this for a long time.

There is something very misleading in the argument that the Holocaust was the outcome of the progress of Reason. It was not in the name of Reason or Science that the Nazis took power, but in the name of defeating a universalizing Reason and rejuvenating a particularist religion of Blood and Soil. Conversely, the forces that defeated the Nazis—the United States, Britain, and the Soviet Union—were themselves governed by various forms of liberal or Socialist ideology, the very ideologies that Nazism supposedly discredits. It is useful to remind ourselves that it was these believers in progress who eventually dismantled the death camps.

I would argue that the particular forms of rationality and science that emerged in Western Europe made a triumph of evil possible because they were too detached from a moral worldview, precisely to the extent that they sanctified a radical division between the "real world" of empirically validatable science and the "merely subjective" world of emotions, values, and aesthetics. This kind of separation creates a form of public life in which intellectual activity is devoted not to eradicating human pain, but to "value-neutral" pursuits of accumulating more knowledge and new techniques. Value neutrality almost always ends up meaning that the people with knowledge sell their labor power to those with the greatest economic and political power, and the questions that they are paid to answer are those posed by and responsive to these interests. Reason is thus shorn of any substantive means of critiquing social reality or devising a more humane reality, and instead becomes subordinated to the goals of powerful elites. Reason becomes handmaiden to the powerful rather than a vehicle of liberation or a path to happiness, and in this role becomes discredited among many people who then become open to various irrational schemes. In Weimar Germany, people were in great pain in their daily lives. Yet the "responsible authorities" and all who worked with them—the intellectuals, the artists, the professionals, the opinion-makers—seemed to be going along their merry way, not really addressing that pain, not seeming to care much about it, and hence seeming to be indifferent or even callous to the experience facing millions.

Some people think that to avoid this callousness, it is a good idea to reject rationality or science or progress. More accurate to say that the dominant kind of ethically and spiritually detached rationality that was validated by ruling elites and established in the universities, publishing houses, and other institutions of public life was a god that failed. What was missing, from our perspective, was a kind of morally and spiritually engaged knowing, a knowing infused with a *tikkun* energy, reason committed to liberation. This same dichotomy allowed science and technology to be harnessed to the largest intentional genocide of world history. Lacking a serious tradition of ethical and spiritual guidance, a neutral and value-free science quickly adopted the goals of mass murder just as it could adopt to any goals that had been assigned to it. Some scientists resisted, but all too many, themselves schooled in the empiricist tradition that had banned values just as it had banned spirituality and religion, served the Nazis just as they would later serve Stalin or the West. It is not human reason that failed, but rather the evisceration of reason produced by the separation of knowledge from values; the teaching of technique rather than wisdom, of how to go along rather than how to critique power, and of respect for authority that ought to be challenged; and the sanctification of cynicism and self-interest without regard to the pain of others.

Just as the Holocaust cannot be used to justify an abandonment of God, neither should it be used to justify a rejection of belief in the self-transcending ethical and spiritual capacities of human beings. Rather, it should lead us to ask, Which human needs have been frustrated in the contemporary world that would allow people to join in the kind of violence and craziness to which the Nazis gave voice? And how do we build a society that promotes caring and empathy rather than moral insensitivity or callousness?

WHY FASCISM SOMETIMES TRIUMPHS

Were feudal societies nothing but oppression, and liberal capitalist societies nothing but liberation, it would be unlikely that there ever would have been a successful Fascist movement. The reality is more complex. Within feudal societies there were compensatory elements for oppression: the sense that everyone knew their place and, within that place, was relatively taken care of; the experience that people had of being part of a community that saw itself as having some larger meaning and purpose that transcended self-interest; the relative closeness to the rhythms of nature; the predictability and orderliness of daily life; the feeling that extended families and communities would provide shelter and emotional support for neighbors.

It's easy to exaggerate these features. When one factors in the irrationality of hierarchical feudal and patriarchal societies, the corruption of the Church, the use of ideas of community and spirituality to cover naked self-interest, the unpredictability of arbitrary authority, the lawlessness of the powerful, the abject subjugation of women and

children to irrational male whims, and the relatively low level of crea-
ture comforts, the compensatory elements of feudal life seem slight
indeed, and the struggle to overthrow it seems exceedingly rational.

Nevertheless, as the promise of liberty, equality, and fraternity embedded in the bourgeois revolutions of Europe began to create a new
system of class oppression parading as "modernization," landowning
elites who continued to struggle against the rising bourgeoisie began to
encourage a romanticized and very unrealistic picture of a lost harmony
that had been exterminated by the forces of modernity. As the enclosure
movement swept through Europe, eliminating communal lands and
turning everything into a commodity for sale, more and more Europeans began to identify modernization with homelessness, alienation,
powerlessness, and subjugation to inexplicable market forces. These
market forces pushed many people off the land and into the big cities,
where they either sold their labor power to the highest bidder or slept in
the streets. There were few supportive communities to fall back upon.

The Church itself was under attack; its ability to take care of the poor,
the orphans, the powerless—always compromised in practice, but
nevertheless officially part of its mission—was increasingly undermined by a civil society that sought to restrict its power. In its place
grew a bureaucracy that was fundamentally impersonal and largely
inhumane. Old ways of life, traditional means of social interaction,
traditional families, informal communal support institutions—all were
being eroded by the market and derided by a new intelligentsia that
taught suspicion of all established traditions and glorified the new
regardless of its moral or spiritual worth. All that had been solid seemed
to be melting into air. Shared meanings and goals were dissolving into
the crassest individualism and self-interest.

Reaction against all this was legitimate and reasonable. To hunger
for a community of meaning and purpose that would transcend the self-
interest of the market and that would root human beings in webs of love
and mutual concern and embed them in a framework of shared stories
about the past and the future—all this was legitimate and reasonable.
But the Left and progressive social-change forces were unable to
articulate this reaction to modernization in a language that would
speak to these legitimate "meaning" concerns. Instead, the Left offered
a language of rights and economic entitlements that addressed some of
the economic consequences of modernization but neglected the feel-

ings of dislocation, confusion, alienation, spiritual and moral hunger, and lovelessness that were causing so much pain.

Because the Left was itself without the truths that it might have learned from Judaism, because it was in part a product of Jews who had abandoned their Jewishness, taking with them the social-justice ethos of Torah but rejecting the spirituality and meaning dimensions of Judaism, it could speak only to a narrow band of needs, could not even recognize the pain that most people were in, and reduced everything to material oppression, it was in no position to reach and mobilize the very "masses" upon which it pinned its hopes for social transformation.

It was in this context that a reactionary nationalism—linked to feudal and capitalist elites and articulated by a coalition of street hoodlums, defeated army members, lumpen proletariat, and opportunistic professionals—coalesced around a Fascist ideology that glorified irrationality and feeling, valued national and ethnic particularity, rejected intellectualism and all forms of universal moral or religious ideals, thrived on patriarchy, and rejected modernism for an idealized and romanticized picture of a past that had never been.

Yet Fascists had no intention of transforming the basic economic realities that were at the heart of much of the alienation of the contemporary world. So fascism could not deliver on its promises. And, like every such ideology, it would need its identified Other to blame for its own failures. The Jews were the obvious target.

In their desire to repudiate the newly emerging modernist order, German nationalists glorified the old order of things, which the Jew was seen as helping to destroy. The very Napoleonic conquest that tore down ghetto walls and freed the Jews was for many Germans the embodiment of an alien spirit that simultaneously uprooted feudal arrangements and imposed bourgeois norms by force of arms. Suddenly the ninety states that had once been part of Germanic experience were forcibly united into one Germany. In the process, the small communities that had given people a sense of greater contact and familiarity with the forces that ruled over them were undermined. As Zygmunt Bauman points out in his prescient book, *Modernity and the Holocaust*, the rapid social and political advancement of the Jews seemed to symbolize the quick turning over of the old order that was so painful to many Germans. The transformation of the Jewish situation in Europe was one of the most visible signs that the old ways were changing overnight, that nothing could be counted on. The very changes that seemed so hopeful and progressive from the standpoint of most Jews were perceived by many non-Jews as a further undermining of the traditional communities, in which their needs had been taken more seriously than in the "free" markets of the emerging capitalist society.[3]

Of course, the older Germanic communities that were being obliterated or forced to merge into larger and more homogenized units were communities that excluded Jews, so Jews cheered on the very disintegration of German particularity that had oppressed them.

From the standpoint of many Jews, the farther from tradition one could move society, the better. The more one could embrace universal as opposed to particularistic identities, the better. Not that all Jews were unambiguous in their embracing modernity. Some Jews agreed with Volkish thinkers who perceived modernity as a destructive force that threatened traditional communities with disintegration. Even the Jews who wholeheartedly embraced modernity set up subcultures in an attempt to preserve elements of their identity and culture (through Jewish community centers, the Reform movement, or various intellectual groupings or institutions). And some Jews were early critics of the capitalist society, providing the insights and leadership for Socialist and Communist movements. Nevertheless, on the whole Jews were perceived by others as cheerleaders for modernization, and few Europeans believed that Jewish progressives sympathized with their fellow citizens on the emotional, spiritual, or ethical price of modernization.

Some Zionists tended to *agree* with some of the German nationalist criticism of Jews who participated in the moral degeneracy and extreme individualism of capitalist society. For these Zionists, however, the problem was not, as some anti-Semites proposed, that there was some essential feature of Jewishness that led in this direction. Rather, it was the particular distortion that Jews are forced to play in a society not their own. Jews, they argued, need homeland and a richly embedded particularistic culture just as much as Germans, and the only way to get it was to leave Europe altogether and reclaim their ancient homeland in Palestine. These Zionists recognized what German Jewish Communists

---

[3]Zygmunt Bauman, *Modernity and the Holocaust* (Ithaca, NY: Cornell University Press, 1989).

and Socialists would not: that the language of rights and economic equality could not adequately address the range of human needs.

But most Western European Jews were not Zionists. In fact, most Jews were either Communists and Socialists who opposed the capitalist system and the huge bureaucratic state, but who did so in the name of *further modernization* and an extension of more rights; or part of a much larger group, who identified uncritically with the modernization that had taken place, benefitted from it, did not think in political terms about their situation, and dedicated most of their time to advancing themselves within the context of their newly achieved freedoms. To these Jews, politics was a boring diversion from real life—and why bother getting involved in endless ideological disputes?

I am not suggesting that it was legitimate for Europeans to blame the distortions of modernization on the Jews or to allow themselves to be manipulated into anti-Semitism, but rather that Jews were in a vulnerable position in which those who benefitted from existing class relations could easily manipulate the popular resentment against modernization and unfairly channel it into resentment against Jews.

The Jewish bourgeoisie were also the major advocates of Western ideas of liberalism, rights, and the elimination of the old order throughout Poland and much of Eastern Europe. As Zygmunt Bauman notes, the "national spirit" of Poland and other Eastern European communities, as well as the established interests of landed elites and the Church, were seen as threatened by modernization.[4] The Jews seemed to be the vanguard of those forces based on industry and finance that would undermine the old order.

The role of the hated Other had a history rooted not only in Christianity but in the Jewish economic position in late-feudal and early-modern Eastern Europe, in which Jews were increasingly put in the position of being the public face of oppressive economic arrangements. In Poland in particular it was often the Jews who were the tax collectors, foremen, land managers, superintendents, and tavern owners, who were in visible positions of authority over the lives of the Polish peasantry. From the standpoint of many ordinary Poles, the Jews *were* the ruling class, because the Polish peasant rarely had access to the lives of the Polish nobility. It was this "intermediate" role as the public face of

---

[4]Ibid.

systems of oppression that was repeated in much of Western Europe, where disproportionate numbers of Jews were the lawyers, doctors, university professors, accountants, small-businessmen, journalists, teachers, and others whose tasks it was to mediate between the larger social system and the working people. Jews imagined themselves as having the ears of ruling elites, and they often fought hard to acquire these intermediary positions. Yet their position was one of great vulnerability. The Jews insulated the nobility from popular discontent, because the anger appropriate for the ruling elites could easily be deflected onto the Jews, who did not have real power and yet who appeared to the masses to be the people who were really running things. It was this fundamental distortion of reality that led to what some have called "the socialism of fools," the willingness of people to channel their anger at a social system into irrational anti-Semitism.

After the Nazis were defeated, the United States created Western Germany to serve as a buffer against possible Communist expansion. Former Nazis were given positions of power and the whole process of denazification was curtailed. The Soviets engaged in a similarly distorted process by creating East Germany. In order to give credence to this rapid relegitimation of German society, in order not to force people to look too deeply into who had collaborated with fascism and why, it became popular for Western political scientists and journalists to talk of Nazism as though the society had suddenly fallen into the hands of some irrational force in 1933, which then equally magically disappeared in 1945. There was much talk about the hypnotic or charismatic quality of Nazi leadership, the authoritarian character structure of Germans, or, on a more religious level, the reemergence of evil as a force in history.

What tended to be ignored in all this were those aspects of the German situation that could also account for the appeal of fascism in other countries in Eastern Europe, in Britain, in France, in the United States, and in South and Central America. While there were certainly regional variations, the recurrent appeal of Fascist movements cannot be accounted for simply in terms of a character structure or the persistence of evil. Instead, it makes more sense for us to realize that many of those who are attracted to Fascist movements have legitimate complaints about the society in which they live and the way that it frustrates their fundamental human needs. It is precisely because these complaints have not been adequately addressed either by elites of wealth and power (who would have to change the fundamentals of their society) or by the progressive social-change forces (who would have to expand their conception of politics beyond the struggle for economic entitlements and political rights) that people turn toward various right-wing, reactionary, or overtly Fascist movements that *do* address the issues, though in perverse ways and with disgusting solutions. The resurgence of fascistic and neo-Nazi forces at the end of the twentieth century replays these dynamics once again.

In Germany, it would have been much more effective if instead of thinking that one could fight fascism merely by pointing out its anti-liberal and racist consequences, its violation of rights that liberals held in high esteem but which were coupled in others' minds with the erosion of communities of meaning, or its links with ruling elites who had no intention of dismantling the alienating features of capitalist life, the anti-Fascist forces had begun to speak about what was legitimate in the resentments against modernization, and had been willing to develop a politics of meaning that spoke to the desire for community, caring, ethical and spiritual vision, and rootedness in history. In short, you can't fight fascism with an economic program alone, because fascism thrives on much more.

WHY DID FASCISM COME TO POWER?

Much of my family had been murdered during the Holocaust, and much of my childhood and teenage years was devoted to answering the question, "How could this have happened?" I was disturbed that the Jewish community narrowed that question to the details of how it could be that others let the Holocaust be carried out from 1939 to 1945. From my standpoint, the important question was, How could people have let the Fascists come to power in the first place? It might have been very difficult to resist the Holocaust effectively once the full energies of a major industrial and military power had been mobilized for genocide, but there was nothing inevitable about Hitler's ascension to power in the first place. If we ever want to be sure that this won't happen again, the key is to understand what made possible this attraction of so many previously decent human beings to a philosophy so deeply ingrained in racism and hatred. I originally developed my ideas about the need for a politics of meaning when I was a teenager sifting through various other accounts and finding them inadequate.

I found little of use in the most widely accepted accounts of fascism's appeal. Communist accounts blamed capitalist expansionism, based on the need of every capitalist society for new markets and raw materials. But since the world markets were already dominated by other capitalist states, newly emerging capitalist societies like Germany and Japan were forced into conflict with the existing imperialist states. Western Cold War discourse, with its talk of a sudden irrational force that had descended upon Germany in 1933 and had been magically lifted in 1945, or of a German "authoritarian personality structure" that had made Germans susceptible to the appeal of fascism (and which would subsequently be used to explain the attraction of some to communism), seemed of only limited use if one's goal was to learn from what happened to prevent its recurrence.

Much more instructive was the brilliant question asked by Wilhelm Reich, a psychiatrist who actually worked in Germany in the late twenties and early thirties, seeking to use his psychological knowledge to break the hold of the growing Fascist movement. "What," asked Reich, "are the legitimate needs that the Right is speaking to in distorted fashion?"

Reich thought the thwarted needs were sexual. He imagined that fascism was building on the sexual repressiveness of German society, and that the best way to counter that was to build a series of what he called Sex/Pol clinics aimed at spreading information about sexuality and encouraging a less repressive attitude toward sexual desire. Reich was denounced both by Communists (who thought his question was too psychological) and by psychoanalysts (who thought his involvement in politics was too antipsychological), but the Fascists understood the potential power of his approach and he was forced to flee Germany shortly after they came to power. But from my standpoint, Reich's answers were far too narrow. Reich missed the larger context in which sexuality was repressed—the frustration of the meaning needs that went hand in glove with the particular form that modernization was taking in Western Europe. It was not sex alone that was being repressed, but rather sex as one expression of a much more fundamental human need: our need for connection and recognition. By offering a pseudo-community that could address the alienation, loneliness, and sense of abandonment that were products of the way that modernity was structured in the capitalist market, the Fascists seemed to understand people much more deeply than Socialists and Communists, who were offering economic goodies but little more.

I use Peter Gabel's term "pseudo-community" because in fact the Fascists would not challenge the actual operations of the capitalist market that were causing the alienation, loneliness, and sense of abandonment (those who wanted to do so were eliminated shortly after Hitler took power). So, after the parades and national celebrations were over, people went back to a work world that was not fundamentally different, and once again experienced the pain and alienation that they had before. Why wasn't the system working to eliminate this pain? The answer typically supplied by Fascist movements is to find some Other— the Jews (though also homosexuals, gypsies, and Communists).

In talking about the frustration of meaning needs, I do *not* mean to suggest that the hard-core Nazis can be talked about in these terms, or that their racism and anti-Semitism can be reduced to a search for meaning. The pathological nature of many of these people should not be underestimated. These kinds of pathology-ridden people turn up in most advanced industrial societies but only rarely come to power. The question I am seeking to answer is *not* about them, but about the masses of Germans who did not always rally to fascism but instead slowly moved toward it in the 1930s, and then may have moved away from it in the fifties and sixties. It is these people who eventually became Fascists and thus enabled fascism to come to power who concern me, because their transformation was not inevitable and might have gone in a different direction had there been a politics of meaning that addressed their needs and provided liberal or progressive answers. A progressive social movement that seemed to understand their pains without resorting to anti-Semitism or chauvinistic nationalism might have prevented Hitler from coming to power, and hence might have prevented the Holocaust.

Had the Left not been divided between Socialists and Communists—each speaking a language of economic reductionism that totally ignored the hunger for meaning and purpose that grew more acute as economic chaos deepened in the 1920s, each unable to accept that noneconomic needs for community and connection (promised by the Fascists' alluring dream of national solidarity) would mean as much if not more to most people than a slight increase in their material well-being—but instead understood the need to unite to address the deprivation of meaning, it might have been in a position in the 1920s to head off fascism long before it came to power.

Jews could have been central to such a movement, instead of playing the roles that they actually did play: either as individuals trying to make it in West European societies, often without any "political" awareness (which, in effect, meant being unaware of the huge amount of suffering and pain that many ordinary people were experiencing, which would lead them to be open to Fascist politics); or as liberal supporters of modernism and champions of liberal capitalist society (again, largely ignoring all the signs of deep unhappiness that were surrounding them, just as many of us are doing again today in American society); or as supporters of Socialist and Communist movements (embracing a narrow economic viewpoint that blocked them from understanding the crisis in meaning that accompanied economic dislocation).

Imagine, if you will for a moment, what a difference it might have made had Jews not lost the revolutionary perspective embodied in what I have been calling the voice of God in Torah. Instead of letting the long history of our oppression distance us from others to such an extent that their pain seemed too distant for us to understand, we would have stayed attuned to them as people created in the image of God, just like ourselves. In that case, we would not have been able to ignore the clear signs of their pain, and would have interpreted their responsiveness to fascism not as a further proof that the goyim can't be trusted, but as an indication of how very deep that pain had grown. We would have then asked ourselves, What is it about the contemporary world that makes people so frustrated? Had we not also assimilated into the contemporary empiricist framework of thought, we would have held on to our understanding of the spiritual and ethical needs that were being systematically frustrated in the modern world, and would have recognized the crisis of meaning. Of course, I tell this story in part to show how overdetermined it was that Jews were not in a position to develop a politics of meaning. It was the very history of oppression that distanced us from Torah, made it difficult for us to imagine the pain of those who were oppressing us, led us to scurry into secularist intellectual frameworks that obscured the meaning dimension of human needs, and hence disempowered us to deal with the dynamics that would lead to the victory of our enemies. Far from blaming the victims, my account here is meant to show how virtually unimaginable it would have been for Jews to be in a position to have developed a politics of meaning to combat fascism.

Not that the rest of the society would have welcomed them in any event. The Socialists and Communists and other Left or progressive forces were themselves so infected with anti-Semitic residues that Jews typically had to prove that they weren't too Jewish to gain a hearing in these circles. Often it was other assimilated Jews who enforced a mindless universalism in the Left that required Jews to abandon all special interest in their own people and its fate. As a result, anti-Fascist work on the Left in the 1920s rarely involved attempts to teach the German working class what was wrong and destructive about anti-Semitism. Indeed, the Jews in the Left would have been embarrassed by such a focus, worried that such a focus would only give legitimacy to the claims of the Fascists that the Left was a Jewish conspiracy, and hence played down all focus on specifically Jewish issues and concerns. Given these dynamics, had Jews been successful at maintaining a Torah-based revolutionary perspective that addressed the meaning needs, they still would have faced almost insuperable odds against being listened to.

So why even begin to speculate "what if the Jews or the Left had understood the meaning needs and developed appropriate strategies to deal with them"? Because by thinking this way we can see that Nazi victory was not the victory of some inevitable or inexplicable "radical evil" that is endemic to human reality. Rather, by thinking in these meaning terms we allow ourselves to imagine how history might have been different, and hence to reaffirm the Jewish-renewal message of the possibility of transformation. The categories one brings to understanding human reality are always a function of what one's goals are. From the standpoint of Jewish renewal, the goal is to reaffirm this possibility of healing, repairing, and transforming, and from that standpoint one picks explanatory hypotheses. It was through this line of reasoning that as a teenager I developed the ideas about a politics of meaning, ideas that I would later come to understand might have relevance not only to Germany in the twenties and thirties, but to the United States and other countries at the end of the twentieth century.

NEVER AGAIN

This has been the rallying cry of a generation that is determined to learn from the Holocaust.

Never Again should lead us to apply the questions we've been asking about the Holocaust to contemporary realities: How do we address the unmet needs of people that, unless addressed, lead them to be open to anti-Semitic, racist, sexist, or homophobic movements?

Never Again should lead us to conclude that we have a moral obligation to fight against racism and national chauvinism *before* they get out of hand.

Never Again should lead us to reject those who pretend that economic security is sufficient grounds for security as a people. Jews were economically secure in Weimar Germany, perhaps even flourishing compared with other sectors of the population. But Jewish oppression cannot be reduced to economic oppression. Jews are a constantly available target for the frustrations and anger of people who are manipulated by ruling elites. Those on the Left who think that Jews have "made it" simply have not learned the lesson of history. But similarly, those on the Right who think that Jews can make a private deal with systems of oppression should also pay careful attention to the Holocaust. When push comes to shove, ruling elites will turn on the Jews, use our particularity as a focus for anger. To the extent that Jews remain loyal to the God of Israel, the God of possibility and transformation, we will always remain a potential threat in the eyes of ruling elites. Many Jews may forget that the logic of Judaism is a logic that testifies to the possibility of transformation, but those in power rarely forget it. In the back of their minds is always the sense that the Jews will be disloyal. This is not because they are being paranoid or racist, but rather because they hear within Jewish culture the covert messages of how the world can be changed; and intuitively if not consciously, they grasp that there will always be something subversive about Jews as long as they remain committed to their religious tradition. For this very reason, anti-Semitism remains a perpetual possibility in a world of oppression. And for this same reason, it is always objectively in Jews' interest, regardless of our subjective awareness of it, to be engaged in the struggle to change the world and eliminate all forms of oppression. The most deluded Jews are those who imagine that there is a private solution for Jews. There is no solution to the Jewish problem that is not a solution to the larger problems of the world.

Never Again means not only never again to the Jews, but never again to anyone, to any people, to any culture, to any religious, racial, or ethnic grouping.

It is particularly unnerving to be writing this book at a historical moment when national chauvinism is reasserting itself in many parts of the world, and when those proclaiming "ethnic cleansing" as their goal persist in murdering Bosnian Muslims. It is also troubling to be writing this book when Jewish extremists are using Never Again to justify acts of violence not only against Palestinians and African-Americans but even against fellow Jews. Never Again means very little if it does not at minimum lead people to engage in demonstrations and public political action designed to force their governments to mobilize resources to prevent ethnic hatreds and genocide.

The Abandonment of the Jews and Subsequent Jewish Paranoia

There was nothing secret about Hitler's plans. He talked about them in *Mein Kampf*, his manifesto written in the 1920s.

The Left was well warned about the anti-Semitism that was at the core of Hitler's plan. Yet it did virtually nothing to counter the growing anti-Semitism in the society or within its own ranks. In fact, many of the left-wing parties in Europe were filled with anti-Semites.

Jews in the Left were often reluctant to raise this issue, perhaps subconsciously aware that their non-Jewish comrades were unwilling to campaign seriously against anti-Semitism. But since they didn't want to stand out as Jews or seem to be parochial, they never really grappled with this issue. The tragic denouement: when the armed struggle actually began, many working-class people refused to side with or defend the Jews. Even Resistance forces battling Hitler sometimes turned their backs on Jewish communities seeking arms and assistance in the same struggle. Jewish comrades were betrayed, abandoned, or even actively turned upon by people in left-wing organizations whose anti-Semitism came to the fore. Partisan groups sometimes joined in hunting down Jews even as they hunted down Nazi collaborators.

The Allies did little for us. The United States shut its doors to refugees from Europe. Boats of Jewish refugees were turned away— some of them eventually sank in turbulent seas and the passengers drowned. Pressure on Roosevelt from American groups to bomb the concentration camps or railroad tracks bringing victims to the camps was ignored.

Some of the most prominent Palestinian leaders identified with the Nazis. The entire Arab world successfully pressured the British government (at the time, the occupying colonial force in power) to prevent any Jewish immigration to Palestine.

The peoples of the Third World had little to say. Focused on their own liberation struggles against British or French or German colonialism, they rarely raised a voice or lent a hand to Jews seeking support, refuge, or attention to the ongoing genocide.

In short, the world turned its back. Though the Allies eventually defeated Hitler, they didn't engage in the struggle because of the desire to save Jews, and they did little to go out of their way to focus specifically on ways to stop the genocide, though many Jews urged them to do so.

No wonder, then, that the Jews felt abandoned and betrayed. No wonder that most people who went through that experience realized that in the world thus constituted, the Jewish people needed a state and an army, and could not and should not depend on others.

But there has been a bad consequence of all this. In the ensuing half century many Jews took a paranoid turn. Enemies were everywhere. No one could be trusted. Every non-Jew might turn upon us. Even in the 1990s I have heard sermons in American synagogues that blithely equate Arafat with Hitler, as though some Jews can't tell the difference between a threat coming from the leader of one of the most technologically sophisticated and economically powerful states in the world, and the threat of a leader of a dispossessed minority.

No one who knows the facts of the Holocaust can *blame* the Jews for feeling this way. But those of us who care about Jewish survival can recognize that this kind of paranoia can be self-destructive. It leads Jews to push away as potential enemies people who might actually be either neutral or our potential friends. Even when paranoia is justified in some cases, in other cases it can become self-fulfilling, generating the very antagonism that it supposedly warns us about.

JEWISH P.C.

The paranoia goes into full force around the issue of criticizing the policies of the State of Israel. Much of the American Jewish press actively vilifies anyone who raises these criticisms. I've personally listened to sermons in Reform and Conservative synagogues that I knew to be bastions of liberalism on other issues suddenly degenerating into the most vicious forms of Jewish political correctness, assailing anyone who dares question Israeli policy. I've witnessed Jewish intellectuals like Ruth Wisse and Cynthia Ozick impose Jewish P.C. categories and demean other Jews who identify with the Israeli peace movement. As a result, morally sensitive people throughout society are forced to silence their criticisms, fearful that they will be labeled "anti-Semitic." There is a great danger for Jews here—the danger that eventually all this pro-Israel P.C. will blow up in our faces, that people will no longer allow themselves to be silenced, and that they will express anger at the Jews for having heavy-handedly repressed a serious public discussion of the complicated issues surrounding Israel and the Palestinians.

We've already experienced some of this reaction in another form—among Jews themselves. There are tens of thousands of Jews who have walked away from the Jewish community precisely because their objections to Israeli policy have been stifled by Jewish P.C. Whenever they've raised criticisms they've been told, "Remember the Holocaust," as though past Jewish suffering was a warrant for *any and every* policy of the State of Israel. The consequence has been the alienation of morally sensitive Jews who should have become the leadership of the next generation of the Jewish people.

Jewish P.C. extends to every conversation about the Holocaust. Whenever other peoples face mass murder and the systematic wiping out of hundreds of thousands or even millions, some Jews insist on raising the point that this isn't like *our* genocide. Of course, they are right. Since the settling of North America there simply has not been a major nation committed to using its powerful resources toward the systematic annihilation of another people, and willing to pursue that even when it is self-destructive to its other survival needs. But harping on that fact, on the uniqueness of our suffering, only separates us from others. It's the same problem that we encounter with oppressed groups in the United States. Each of them has such a deep commitment to focusing on that which is unique about their suffering that they have little energy left for helping others see what they have in common. Yet the real salvation for the oppressed will come only when people begin to feel a common bond with them. And that will not come from these groups' *only* emphasizing how *different* they are from everyone else, but rather also how similar they are.

From the standpoint of Jewish survival, the real goal should be to help Jews tell their story in a way that makes it possible for others to identify, and for Jews to see the suffering of others as something that

potentially builds common bonds. Yet it is precisely one of the continuing consequences of the pains of the past that we become blind to the
pains of others, unable to hear *their pain and their cries* because we are
so overwhelmed with our own. No one can *blame* the victims who are so
overwhelmed by their pain, but those of us who deeply care about our
people want to see that pain alleviated quickly, not only because we
want to make room for healing, but also because we want to prevent the
pain from blinding us to our own self-interest.

Israeli philosopher Adi Ophir predicted that eventually a Judaism
will emerge whose primary focus is on the Holocaust. It would have its
own commandments: "I am the Holocaust. Thou shalt have no other
Holocausts before me. Remember the Holocaust to keep it holy." His
exaggeration highlights a tendency that has distorted Jewish life. It
sometimes feels to younger American Jews as though the only place
where there is real energy in the Jewish community is in commemorating the Holocaust and searching out real or imagined enemies who
might, on further stretch of the imagination, threaten us once again.

THE 614TH COMMANDMENT:
DON'T GIVE HITLER A POSTHUMOUS VICTORY

Jewish theologian Emil Fackenheim formulated this commandment,
and it is one that makes intuitive sense to the generation of survivors.
But what this means in practice depends on how you understand what
it would actually mean to give Hitler a posthumous victory.

There are some right-wing Zionists who have come to think that the
commandment means that our highest goal must be the physical
survival of the Jewish people. They have justified every activity of every
Israeli government, as long as the government claims that what it is
doing is being done in the name of Jewish survival. If that means
shooting Palestinian children who are throwing rocks, if it means
imposing severe restrictions that violate human rights, even if it means
(as on rare occasions it has) actual torture of suspected anti-Israel
activists, well, that's what it takes not to give Hitler a victory. So who are
we to question? Those whose worry is limited to the physical survival of
Jews are often willing to abandon concern about preserving the Jewish
soul.

If Jewish survival is concerned only about the physical survival of people with Jewish genes, there are ways that this can be assured without a Jewish state or Jewish religion. People with Jewish genes can survive by assimilating into the population as a whole, changing their names, learning how to act and talk like non-Jews, and adopting the attitudes and lifestyles of non-Jews. The entire Jewish population of Israel could be brought into the United States and other Western countries—assimilated, and then disappear—and no one would have lost their lives.

So the issue is, Jews want to survive *as Jews*, with a distinguishable set of Jewish values, and to continue to play our role as witnesses to the possibility of healing, repair, and transformation.

But there's a great danger that the Jewish people's Holocaust trauma will convert us to a people with a different set of values. Instead of testifying to the existence of God's energy in the world, there are some powerful forces in the Jewish world that have been recasting Judaism as the religion that testifies to the existence of evil in the world; that sanctifies the notion that it's a dog-eat-dog world and no one can be trusted; that people should give up utopian hopes and focus more narrowly on their own immediate self-interests; that a narrow realism based on what is must replace an optimism about what could be; that Jews should become a people like all other peoples, with the same morality, the same willingness to sacrifice others for our own advancement, the same willingness to be brutal, and the same determination to get ours without regard to the consequences to others.

This would be the triumph of Hitler. If the Jewish people no longer testify to the possibility of the transformation of the world; if their existence is no longer based primarily on carrying that message to the world; if Jewish survival becomes a matter of preserving Jewish bodies espousing the values of militarism, national chauvinism, suspicion of others, cleverness in advancing our self-interests *über alles*, nostalgia for a romanticized past, religion without moral sensitivity, toughness to show that we can't be pushed around, smartness separated from ethical passion, insistence on our wounds as a way of closing our ears to the pain of others—then Hitler has won.

This is the danger of Holocaust museums and Holocaust fascination. The story must be told. But some who tell it do so in a way that validates pessimism about the possibility of transforming the world. They ridicule meaning-oriented social-change movements precisely because the

Nazis also addressed meaning issues. Instead, using the Holocaust as their warrant, they embrace the cynical logic of self-interest that is the common sense of the contemporary society. In so doing, they merely return us to the same alienated and cynical individualism, which eventually creates a hunger for community so desperate that people are willing to embrace the very totalitarian or fascistic forms of community from which this liberal individualism was designed to protect us. They reject all serious commitment to *tikkun*, and insist that any totalizing project of *tikkun* must necessarily lead to a reappearance of Radical Evil. The transformation project is dismissed as utopian and probably destructive, and instead the task of the Jew is to be witness to the possibility of Radical Evil.

As I argued earlier in this book, Jews have known about evil people for a long time. Pharaoh gave us a first taste of genocide when he decided to kill all our first-born males. Our history began in the face of the pyramids—temples that embodied the death religion of ancient Egypt. Judaism was created in rebellion against those who transformed evil into Evil. Judaism came into existence to testify to the fact that cruelty is *not* destiny, that the evil in the world can be dramatically reduced. It was not a dualistic religion that said there are two contending forces—the force for Good and the force for Evil. No. Judaism proclaimed that it was the Life Force, the Living God, the Force that made for the possibility of the triumph of good, that actually created and ran the universe.

I don't blame anyone who has trouble holding on to the faith of Israel. To hold that faith is to hold it despite history, in the face of oppression. And it has always been thus.

But I do blame those who identify their pessimism and cynical realism with Judaism, when it is in fact only the latest restatement of the very ideology against which Judaism came into the world to combat. In so doing they give Hitler a posthumous victory, thus violating the 614th commandment. Jewish renewal is committed to preserving the God of possibility and of rejecting the religion of pessimism and cynicism based on an ontologization of Radical Evil. There are evil people and evil acts. There are institutions and psychological practices that embody and pass on evil from generation to generation. But there is no Radical Evil working behind these phenomena and making them happen. Our testimony as Jews is to a very different Force in the universe.

THE NEOCONS AND JEWISH CONSERVATISM

The Holocaust has cast a shadow over many Jewish thinkers for fifty years. Many became deeply cynical about human beings and about the possibility of changing the world in any positive direction. The ontologization of evil reached its most vulgar expression in *The New Republic* and *Commentary* magazines. It pervaded the consciousness of a whole generation of Jewish intellectuals, and persists as a theme among many of those who head American academic, intellectual, and cultural institutions. These people, Jews and non-Jews alike, have become the guardians of public opinion, ensuring that anyone who thinks that fundamental transformation of reality is either possible or desirable is unveiled as a fool—superficial, naive, deluded, or otherwise intellectually or morally impaired.

It is no surprise that this kind of Jewish intellectual would rise quickly to power in America. The ruling elites who ran such institutions got the message that *they* wanted the world to hear: that any schemes for fundamental transformation of society must necessarily be discarded and the people who hold these schemes must be dismissed. Ruling elites have always wanted intellectuals, artists, and cultural mavens to reinforce the status quo. What could be better than to find a whole generation of people who are going to tell this story from the standpoint of their own experience as an oppressed minority? Understand the irony: the very group that has always been a threat because of its testimony to the possibility of transformation was now supplying the world with a generation of intellectuals who would testify to the *impossibility* of transforming the world! It was almost too much to ask—a whole generation whose primary mission was to attack "the God that failed." No wonder these people were given plenty of opportunity to "make it" in American society.

In the first two decades after the Holocaust, these disillusioned Jews spent much of their energy denouncing fellow Jews who had remained connected to communism. And given the slavish loyalty of American and Western European Communist parties to the disgusting and repressive regimes of Eastern Europe, exposing the fallacies of communism was easy—one need only have looked at the actual regimes that claimed to embody its theory. The conservatives refused to acknowledge the considerable hostility toward the Soviet Union articulated by early New Leftists, or Irving Howe's, Michael Harrington's, and other Socialists' critiques of Communist totalitarianism. Nor have most conservatives in subsequent decades grappled with the far deeper religious critique—that communism had a distorted conception of what it is to be a human being since it did not validate people's ethical or spiritual needs—because the same critique might equally apply to the materialism of contemporary capitalism.

In the ensuing decades, the disillusioned Jews spread their conservatism much farther, repudiating those Jews who had become involved in the civil rights and antiwar movements, and subtly aligning themselves with the antiblack racism in American society.

The Jewish neocons championed an American foreign policy dedicated entirely to combatting communism and supporting the current government of the State of Israel. Every issue was refracted through the lens of these two concerns. *Commentary* magazine, the flagship of the neocons, championed a distinction between authoritarian regimes (those that did not support communism) and totalitarian regimes. The most repressive regimes in the world (merely authoritarian) could be supported as long as they could be seen as allies in the struggle against communism (totalitarian)—because allegedly the totalitarian regimes would never change internally (imagine the consternation when Gorbachev came to power, and then the confusion when the Russian people themselves, and without any outside military intervention, dismantled the Communist system), while authoritarian regimes would. Every excess of the Israeli government was justified, and anyone who criticized it was deemed either an enemy of the Jews or, if they were Jewish, a self-hating Jew.

Jewish neocons played a prominent role in attacking affirmative action (never mind that Jewish women have been some of the primary beneficiaries of this social policy) and other liberal social programs that benefitted African-Americans. They championed Reagan's cutback of programs for the poor, supported policies that actually resulted in a net increase of wealth for the richest sectors of society and a decrease in the wealth for the poorest sectors, and generally tended to support the unrestricted operations of the capitalist market as the cure-all for societal ills. Moreover, the neocons helped legitimate among Jews a form of argumentation that had been much less prominent in the earlier part of the twentieth century: the argument from narrow self-interest.

Through much of the nineteenth and twentieth centuries, Jews in Europe and Western societies had aligned with liberal and progressive social-change movements, partly because these movements supported programs that served the interests of most Jews as they moved out of poverty and into working-class jobs and then into the middle class, partly because these movements opposed fascism while mainstream centrist and pro-capitalist parties made many compromises and accommodations with the Fascist regimes until World War II actually began, partly because the social-justice agenda of these movements reflected Torah values. But as many Jews moved into upper-middle-class earning in the 1960s and 1970s, and as the religious community increasingly focused its attention away from the moral imperatives of Torah and onto an obsession with details of ritual practice, Jewish liberalism came under fire. Neoconservatives focused Jewish attention on the abandonment of the Jews during the Holocaust and argued that since no one was there for us when we needed them, we have no moral obligation to be there for anyone else. Jews should recognize that this is a world based on self-interest, and the smartest thing Jews can learn from the Holocaust is that Jews should ensure that Israel is strong and the Jews are in positions of influence in Western circles. Liberal attention to eliminating poverty, homelessness, hunger, and unemployment were increasingly perceived as distractions because most Jews no longer face these problems as personal issues.

Neocons rarely raised the question of what Jews might do to head off the rise of fascism or anti-Semitism in the future, since the ontologization of evil made these kinds of things seem inevitable. Ironically, while these conservatives were doing their best to win power and influence among American non-Jews, their philosophy stemmed from a fundamental distrust of non-Jews, a sense that they would always turn against us.

Not that the neocons were completely wrong to worry about the persistence of anti-Semitism. But that persistence was based on two things: first, the fact that ruling elites rightly suspected the revolutionary impact of Torah. This, of course, could be dealt with by most neocons, who were *not* religious and who were all too happy to abandon Torah's subversive message. But it was ironic when some Orthodox Jews also embraced neocon thinking, unwilling to notice that in so doing they were really abandoning the voice of God in Torah; and second, the fact that it is often convenient for ruling elites to use the

Jews as a target of anger more appropriately directed at the larger economic and social system. Yet it was precisely this system that the neocons were embracing, the system whose malfunctions would then be blamed on the Jews all the more easily, since the neocons among us had become its chief apologists.

The neocons were particularly impactful in the Jewish world in the 1970s and 1980s because they provided a justificatory framework for those American Jews who were attracted to the ethos of selfishness in American life but had previously felt constrained by a Torah ideology that preached concern for the poor and the oppressed. To be sure, the interests of the wealthy and the fundraisers had played a disproportionate role in shaping Jewish communal life for centuries. But by the 1960s and 1970s a small number of Jews were reaching commanding positions in industry or commerce in the larger American society, and they were bringing along with them a coterie of Jewish professionals (lawyers, business managers, accountants), and supporting the advancement of Jews in media where they placed advertising revenues. Because they had more to give, because they wanted influence and power, and because some of them continued to be motivated by some of the best charity-oriented Jewish traditions, these Jews gave a significant amount of money to the synagogues, to the Jewish community federations, and to other institutions of Jewish life. Their propensity toward more conservative politics on economic issues—including issues like affirmative action or how much tax money should be spent to alleviate the worst impact of the economic system that was benefitting them so much—could have created a potential crisis for Jewish professionals whose original motivation for doing this kind of work was based on a high degree of idealism and caring for others. Neocon ideology helped make it possible for Jewish professionals to feel that they could remain "idealists" but reject that part of their former liberalism that called upon them to give priority to caring for others outside the Jewish world.

The neocons argued that no one had cared about us during the Holocaust (all too true, though still this neglects the significant numbers of people who were involved in acts of rescue that saved the lives of tens of thousands of Jews); that we are still in danger of annihilation (largely false in the late twentieth century, though always potentially true as long as we live in a society that needs a scapegoat); and that liberalism is distorted because it focuses exclusively on the needs of others and never on Jewish needs (almost totally false, since within the

Jewish world it has been the Left that has played the major role in creating the State of Israel, through its Socialist-oriented Labor party; since the Jewish Left has often argued that fighting poverty, oppression, and racism is not only morally correct, but also good for the Jews; and since societies where these problems fester typically have become societies that are open to anti-Semitic movements). Neocon ideas were given further legitimacy by the right-wing governments of Menachem Begin and Yitzhak Shamir, who constantly used the imagery of the Holocaust to justify the continuation of the Israeli occupation of the West Bank and Gaza, and who portrayed the Jews as an embattled people whose very existence would be endangered should Palestinians be given any rights to national self-determination. The near-universal condemnation of Israel's invasion of Lebanon in 1982 and the ensuing several years' war that left hundreds of Israelis and thousands of Lebanese dead or wounded further accelerated this contention that no one really cares about the Jews, and that hence we should stop worrying about everyone else and worry more about ourselves.

This contention, of course, would ease the way for former liberals to justify turning their attention away from the social programs that were designed to ameliorate the worst effects—accelerating inequalities of wealth, and hence the acceleration levels of misery, crime, and social pathology—of the competitive market. Now these former liberals could refer to our aloneness as Jews, see contemporary reality through the exclusive focus on the Holocaust, and conclude that selfishness and shutting one's ear to the suffering of others would be acceptable and even quintessentially Jewish behavior. Rabbis and Jewish scholars could find precedents and texts and interpretations of holy writings that would warrant this emerging selfishness, and in so doing they could provide a very spiritually and emotionally welcoming home to the new group of businesspeople and professionals who need to find a way to justify to themselves their participation in the increasingly ruthless operations of the larger capitalist society. Some of the people most prominently identified with the large-scale mergers, junk bonds, and savings-bank failures of the 1980s—whose consequences were devastating to American society—were Jews who were playing a significant role in the institutions of the organized Jewish community. It never would have occurred to these institutions to question the moral role these people played in the larger society; "after all, they were benefitting Jews, weren't they, and isn't that all that counts?"

The path to selfishness was further eased by the growing tensions between blacks and Jews. When blacks began to move beyond civil rights struggles—which the majority of American Jews had enthusiastically supported—to Black Power, many Jews felt that their previous efforts on behalf of black people were being discounted or unfairly misrepresented as paternalistic and manipulative. Neocons were quick to highlight the voices of black anti-Semitism, and though these particular black people remained a very small proportion of the total black community, they nevertheless provided conservatives with further rationale for supporting tax cutbacks ("Why should I pay higher taxes to alleviate *their* suffering when they are acting in a racist manner toward us?"). Jewish fears of vulnerability were manipulated by neocons who warned Jews to abandon their liberal voting pattern and join the ranks of conservatives. Many did, and even those who considered themselves liberals and Democrats in the organized Jewish community adopted some of the assumptions and conceptualizations of the Right.

Jewish relations with African-Americans is one area where neocon fears began to be self-fulfilling. While Jews have maintained their self-perception as loyal supporters of blacks, and while the majority of Jews continued to support candidates for office who could be counted on to support social legislation sensitive to the needs of the black community, many African-Americans perceived Jews through the lens of mainstream Jewish organizations that had begun to adopt an insensitive view toward blacks by the middle 1970s. For twenty years, African-Americans heard mainstream Jewish organizations leading the struggle against affirmative action. They heard "Jewish leaders" attack progressive blacks as they began to achieve national prominence (most recently, candidates for positions in the Clinton administration like Johnetta Cole and Lani Guinier). They heard organizations like the Anti-Defamation League (A.D.L.) seem to brand as anti-Semitic everyone who had any criticism of the policies of the government of Israel. And then they heard Jews at *Commentary* and *The New Republic* magazines foster a blame-the-victim ideology that suggested that it was black cultural pathology that caused poverty rather than the other way around. Is it really any wonder that some of this would make some sectors of the black community more receptive to the hateful garbage being spewed by Louis Farrakhan and other black Muslims? The anti-Semitic response cannot be condoned, and should be combatted—but to protect Jewish interests it is also necessary to recognize that hateful or insensitive behavior by prominent Jewish leaders and spokespeople will have and has had an impact, and may be one of many factors that contributed to the rise of black anti-Semitism in the 1990s. Demeaning the other has consequences. Here neocon behavior has been facilitated also by the constant insensitivity of people on the Left and in liberal and progressive circles to legitimate Jewish interests. I have argued this case more fully in *The Socialism of Fools: Anti-Semitism on the Left.* Throughout the twentieth century, liberals and leftists have failed to confront anti-Semitism within their own ranks and have been unable to understand or give credence to legitimate Jewish fears that arose not only from the Holocaust but from subsequent anti-Semitic outbursts in ostensibly Socialist or Communist societies. Moreover, there was a complete ignorance of the history or contemporary functioning of anti-Semitism, a blithe and mistaken notion that Jews were now part of America's ruling elite, and an inability to understand the contemporary dynamics of Jewish oppression. Finally, so many Jews in liberal circles had rejected their Jewishness that some committed Jews began to feel that liberalism was a competing rather than a complementary worldview.

It never occurred to many in the organized Jewish community that by embracing conservative values they were actually embracing the legacy of Hellenism, a legacy that the well-to-do would find comforting but the morally and spiritually sensitive would find offensive and would mistakenly come to think of as the essence of Judaism! Yet for many Jews born after the Holocaust, the Jewish world began to feel so conservative and spiritually dead that they felt compelled to reject the Jewishness that they were being offered. They might come to a High Holy Day service, give their child a bar or bat mitzvah, or support a home for Jewish seniors. They might come to a Jewish arts show or book fair, a Jewish film festival, or a Jewish nostalgia fest, but Jewishness was increasingly a momentary form of entertainment for a growing number of American Jews rather than a serious commitment—because the Jewishness that had been shaped by conservative sensibilities seemed spiritually deadening, boring, and ethically obtuse. The neocons had undermined Jewish continuity and estranged the morally sensitive young from Judaism.

Increasing numbers of Jews began to distance themselves from the Jewish world in the decades of the 1970s and 1980s and in the first half of the 1990s—precisely at the moment when the Jewish institutions were most heavily controlled by conservative forces. Not all of those who distanced themselves became seekers of spiritual truths, or progressive political activists. There were many who became devotees of the me-firstism of the competitive market. Having recognized that the "bottom line" of selfishness in the competitive market is not fundamentally different from the bottom line of selfishness that seemed to run the Jewish world, many concluded that they could pursue the selfishness of the larger society more effectively without encumbering themselves with the restrictions of religious life or the burdens of learning Hebrew and strange rituals. Sure, they could hear in the Jewish religious texts a certain amount of idealism and an alternative logic. But the actual existing Jewish community was so filled with people speaking a language of self-interest justified by the pains of the Holocaust that there was little to hold the attention and loyalty of the next generation. Those who found the focus on self-interest offensive began to look to other political or spiritual traditions; those who found it persuasive sometimes looked elsewhere to find their greatest advantage; and some remained inside the Jewish world in part because they thought that within it they could make good business contacts. While it would be unfair to imagine that this was the totality of Jewish life or Jewish experience, it was dominant enough to shape the experience of tens of thousands of Jews.

Perhaps the most extreme version of these dynamics occurred in the sector of the Jewish world called "Modern Orthodox" (as opposed to the ultra-Orthodox sects). Often filled with Holocaust survivors whose new faith had become a demeaning of the other, or with American Jews who loved the way orthodoxy could provide a supportive community dramatically absent in the selfishness-dominated economic markets in which they made their livings, these Modern Orthodox could be amazingly successful in shutting their ears to the parts of Torah that enjoined them to "love the stranger" or to pursue justice (and not just for Jews, and not just for their type of Jews). Remarkably generous and willing to extend themselves to others if the others were fellow Orthodox Jews, participating in precisely those caring *mitzvot* (like inviting people home for a Shabbat or holiday meal or visiting the sick or making a conscious and sustained effort to introduce singles to one another) that were often absent from the actual practice of many Jews who espoused liberal ideology but rarely saw themselves engaged in acts of caring as Jews, these Orthodox Jews built a vibrant community full of song, dance, and adherence to the ritual aspects of Jewish law, but at the very same time, they were rejecting Jewish liberalism. Though a valiant minority of Modern Orthodox continues to present reasoned argument why authentic Jewish tradition may be far closer to the insights that I call Jewish renewal than to the conservatism that became a dominant framework for religious interpretation and practice, the emotional appeal of Holocaust imagery—constantly being reinforced not only by the Holocaust Museum but also by the release of movies, videos, and a continual flow of books that build on the fears generated by that tragedy—works hand in glove with the not-too-hidden desire of these Modern Orthodox to succeed in the economic world. What results is a Judaism that is at once rigidly traditional and chauvinistic in its internal life and wildly accommodationist when confronting the dynamics of selfishness and me-firstism of the competitive market.

Yet, despite all the ways that neocons have infiltrated Jewish life and thought, the masses of American Jews have remained loyal to liberal politics and principles. When the *Los Angeles Times* in 1989 asked Jews to identify what feature of their Jewishness was most important to them, twice as many indicated "social justice" than any other feature. Neocons had welcomed the 37 percent Jewish vote for Reagan in 1980, but while the rest of the country increased its support for Reagan in 1984, Jewish support declined to 30 percent and was even lower for Bush in 1988 and 1992. Neocons lamented, but the perception that Jews would have their consciousness determined by economic needs was as false when articulated by conservatives as when articulated by liberals. Though it might seem that on economic grounds alone, Jews should be more conservative, it is not economic grounds alone that shape Jews' consciousness. Jewish loyalties are determined by the needs most Jews have to be part of an ethically and spiritually grounded community of meaning and purpose—and for many Jews it has been the Torah, Jewish sources, Jewish history, and Jewish culture to which they have turned to find meaning. Many Jews have interpreted the Holocaust not as a license for the further passing on of the cruelty and harshness of the past to the next generation, but as a lesson about what happens when people turn their backs on one another. Many Holocaust survivors have become more, not less, spiritually sensitive and ethically alive, understanding that the only protection against future genocide is future sensitivity and caring. It has been the God of the Bible through which some of these people refract these historical experiences—and they have emerged with a fuller and more robust liberalism, despite the neocons' efforts to validate an alternative frame of interpretation of Judaism with conservative consequences. The struggle for the heart of Judaism continues to this day.

WHAT'S RIGHT ABOUT THE NEOCONS

The neocons raised three criticisms of the liberal consciousness with which I agree. One was the tendency of liberals to place all responsibility for social problems on social reality and to minimize individual responsibility. This critique, when directed at middle-class youth, has some plausibility. There was, particularly in the New Left of the sixties, a certain tendency to view the society as one giant bottomless cookie jar. Our task was merely to stick our hands in and pick out the cookies we wanted, and if we didn't get a good one, to blame the society. This focus on social reality can be debilitating when it undermines individual initiative. But the neocons took this critique in a racist direction when they applied it primarily to inner-city unemployed blacks, most of whom could not get employment no matter how hard they tried, were the last-hired and first-fired, or found part-time or wildly underpaid work. By minimizing the economic constraints facing most African-Americans, by not understanding that even the minority that systematically took advantage of welfare were often merely the products of generations of despair and hopelessness generated by an economy that provided opportunities for some but not for all, these Jewish intellectuals heaped contempt on a black population least able to defend itself. On the other hand, the Left's correct analyses of how economic oppression generates and sustains a distorted culture of poverty was sometimes coupled with a moral permissiveness. One can both understand that a certain economic reality produces and sustains a culture of crime and rip-off mentality, and know that the only real hope for a significant change will come from a change in the economic realities—and nevertheless oppose the resulting crime and condemn the moral degeneration. The Left often refused to take seriously the need to fight crime and oppose moral laxity, for fear that in so doing they would unwittingly play into the Right's racism. And this made them appear morally inconsistent as well as insensitive to the needs of many Americans traumatized by fears of crime and understandably angered by the glorification of violence, misogyny, and sexual irresponsibility that is manifest in some rap music and some sectors of black inner-city youth.

The neocons were also correct in criticizing the self-indulgence of some parts of the liberal world, the use of moral relativism to avoid all standards of criticism, and the willingness to put immediate gratification ahead of commitment to families, children, or communities. While I believe that these values are primarily rooted in the ethos of the capitalist market, it is nevertheless true that they have been adopted by people who consider themselves "progressive," making it seem that social-change ideas are merely a cover for self-centeredness. I shall argue below for a form of Jewish renewal that requires a more serious commitment to community, family, and tradition than is sometimes associated with liberal causes. But it remains particularly ironic that the neocons should be the ones to raise these criticisms, since the economic system to which they are committed rewards selfishness, espouses moral cynicism and "bottom line" materialism, shapes a consumer culture reinforcing the ethos of immediate gratification, and depends on the delegitimation of any objective ethical criteria by which its performance could be judged, critiqued, or restrained.

Finally, the neocons were correct to highlight the political correctness (P.C.) distortions in some parts of the liberal and progressive social-change movements, and the imposition of rigid political requirements on every part of life. Yet Jewish neocons pioneered this technique with their assaults on Jews who criticized Israel when it was under a Likud government (they shifted their line once their friends were no longer in power). The strict enforcement of Jewish P.C. about the Holocaust and about Israel, often to the point of labeling as enemies some of the Jewish people's most loyal children, has been mimicked by other oppressed groups in their own contexts and with their own criteria. For neocons to respond in outrage is pure hypocrisy. But the critique of P.C. is legitimate. Instead of engaging in reasoned arguments against language, ideas, or behaviors they found offensive, some leftists have attempted to use coercive techniques to ensure that the language and behavior are excluded from the public arena. In fact, any idea, no matter how subtly drawn or compassionately articulated, can be used as a club to beat others into submission (including the use of anti-P.C. as a way to discredit the legitimate insights and struggles of women, gays, African-Americans, and others). Ironically, an upsurge of anti-Semitic language by African-Americans on campus may soon lead some of these neocons to wish that to protect Jewish interests, a new code of politically correct language be enforced.

HEALING THE TRAUMA

As renewed conflict between Serbs, Croats, and Muslims in the former Yugoslavia demonstrates, historical wounds that have not been healed have a tendency to fester and erupt many generations later. The pain of the Holocaust has not been healed. All too often the way that the Holocaust is taught, the way it is commemorated, the focus on finding new candidates for Hitler, the insistence on reassuring ourselves that there was Jewish Resistance, the abstractions into discussions about evil, the focus on the historical details, the excessive attention paid to nutcakes who deny the very existence of the Holocaust, the reassurance of Never Again given to us by our toughness—all these work as ways to avoid dealing with the shame, the humiliation, the brutality, the pain, and the way in which all that has been unconsciously internalized.

A first step in the process of healing is for Jews to get over the delusion that the State of Israel provides the guarantee Never Again. There can be no such guarantee for any minority in this world, nor could we have such a guarantee if all Jews moved to Israel. Deeply dependent on the United States and other trading partners, Israel can't afford to be out of touch with the reality of an increasingly interdependent world. Nor can nuclear weapons provide that protection: they can assure that others will pay a price should (God forbid) Israel ever be destroyed, but they cannot assure Israeli survival against an enemy willing to pay the price. Nor does the attempt of American Jews to play up to ruling elites in America make long-run sense for Jewish survival. If American ruling elites continue to act irresponsibly toward the global environment, Jews, like everyone else, will inevitably pay the price, both in terms of a world population driven to violence by inadequate resources, and by an ecological catastrophe. The sad fact is this: There is *no solution to the Jewish problem that isn't simultaneously a solution to the world's problem.* There will never be an end to Jewish vulnerability until there is a world of justice, caring, ethical and spiritual sensitivity, mutual recognition, and ecological responsibility. Living with this vulnerability, and shaping a conscious way for the Jewish people to do their best to counter world tendencies toward fascism and other forms of global craziness or irresponsibility, is a first step.

A second step in the process is for Jews to create, both in Jewish communities and in smaller groups, a therapeutic process in which we can allow ourselves to reexperience and master the trauma. Jews need to disentangle, carefully and systematically, the ways that we have internalized the hateful images of Jews put forward by the anti-Semites; the ways that we have come to discount what is beautiful and powerful in our own tradition; the ways that we have come to see one another as unattractive or undeserving; the ways that we've overcompensated for self-degradation by pomposity, self-aggrandizement, arrogance, or aggressiveness; and the ways that we've learned to repress our righteous indignation. Then Jews need to express rage, not only at the Holocaust, but at all that has happened to us. Sections of the prayer book for Yom Kippur and of the Haggadah, where that rage was once expressed, have been excised or have been turned into mechanical readings—but Jews need to legitimate that rage, both in ritual and in the small-group therapeutic processes that are necessary. Next, Jews need to mourn, deeply, fully, sustainedly—both for others and for ourselves—for all that has been denied us; for the ways that our parents' and our grandparents' lives were distorted by anti-Semitism; for the ways that the Jewish state, finally come back into existence, has been so much less than it could have been by having been created in response to our oppression instead of in response to our highest ideals; for the ways that our lives could have been fuller had the six million European Jews and their children and grandchildren still been part of our Jewish world; for the ways that our fellow Jews have given up testifying to the possibility of healing and repair because of the deep cynicism that our suffering has engendered.

A third step is for Jews, having gone through this process, to call an end to it. It may take a generation or two to complete the process. Then we should learn from the wisdom of our tradition's message about death and grieving. At a certain point it becomes excessive and a sin to continue to mourn actively. At that point the Holocaust must be put into the same kind of religious framework as the destruction of the Temples. It will have its special day for focus: Yom Ha'Shoah. It will be mentioned on Tisha B'Ab and in lectures about Jewish history, but it must cease to be an obsession dominating and distorting Jewish life. That moment is not close, because we have not really begun to allow ourselves to grieve and to mourn. We've allowed romanticizations of our suffering to replace a serious and psychologically sophisticated grappling with the actual, complicated, ambiguous, and painful reality. We've allowed museums and television docudramas and movies to replace a personal encounter with all that we have lost. We've allowed Israel's strength to hide from ourselves our actual vulnerability. We haven't begun to get real about the Holocaust. That process must be completed, because the pain has kept Jews from being able to remain faithful to our function as testifiers to God's presence in the world.

One final cautionary note: Keeping alive God's message of hope and transformation could not possibly require that we deny the possibility that there may be future holocausts. We cannot hold a naive optimism that makes us unprepared for the actual cruelty that persists in human history. We should be insisting that the struggle against cruelty be taught in public and private schools, so that all people learn about the Holocaust and other genocidal or potentially genocidal struggles in human history. We should be insisting that people understand the roots of the Holocaust and the way the denial of meaning plays into the development of chauvinistic nationalism, racism, sexism, and anti-Semitism. We should be confronting and challenging moral relativism and the way it disempowers people to struggle against cruelty. We should insist that the larger society confront the meaning of the Holocaust—not as a pious show of concern for our victims, but as a serious commitment to understand and prevent genocidal acts, racism, and national chauvinism.

The task for Jewish renewal is to ensure that we don't confuse that genocidal cruelty with the voice of God, that we don't ontologize it and let it overwhelm us; that we keep alive an understanding that the evil comes from a complicated set of psychological and social practices that are embedded in specific social institutions and in complex forms of human behavior, and can be fought against and overcome; that the web of pain can be unraveled gradually; that the process of healing and repair is a task that we human beings can, with God's help, work to accomplish.

CHAPTER NINE

POST-ZIONISM

Israel was born twice in the modern world. In 1948, Israel was born in blood and tears, as the Jewish people crawled out of the gas chambers and crematoria of Europe. Those who founded Zionism had warned the Jews that there could be no solution to "the Jewish problem" without Jews becoming a nation like all other nations, with our own land, our own flag, our own army. The Holocaust seemed to vindicate them—and to set the course of development for the State.

The Jews leaped from the burning buildings of Europe. Some leaped early, before the fire was literally destroying millions of us. Others leaped at the last possible moment. And when we leaped, we landed on the backs of Palestinians. We did not intend to land on them, and we certainly did not intend to hurt them. But when we did hurt them, it was impossible for most Jews to acknowledge the pain we had unintentionally caused. Our own pain was too great.

"How can anyone compare their pain to our pain?" some Jews reasoned. "We lost one third of our people; they lost some land. We had no other place to go; they were surrounded by Arab and Islamic states where they could find refuge. And, in any event, they weren't really a full-grown people with their own identity, culture, literature, and history."

We felt that we had to deny them their pain, and even their identity.

And so Zionism became identified in the minds of millions of non-Jews with a form of oppression. The liberation of one of the most oppressed groups in human history had been achieved only at the cost of that group's becoming the oppressor of another group.

Those who reduce the meaning of Israel to the story of its relationship to Palestinians necessarily miss so much of what is wonderful and what makes Jews justifiably proud. A people that had been forcibly ripped from its land by Roman imperialists, then scattered and dispersed throughout much of Europe, North Africa, and West Asia, maintained its identity and its hopes to return to its homeland for eighteen hundred years—despite unbelievable levels of oppression, systematic harassment by Christian and Islamic civilizations, periodic expulsions of entire Jewish populations from a variety of European countries, countless episodes of being the victim of mass murder—and then finally was able to build a movement that would allow Jews to return to the land from which they had been exiled and attempt to rebuild a national identity. From being a people who were the objects of history, the Jewish national revival in Palestine allowed Jews to become once again the subject of their own history, freely choosing how to create themselves. The revival of the Hebrew language, the creation of a rich modern culture drawing from two thousand years of Jewish creativity but moving in new directions, the absorption of hundreds of thousands of Jewish refugees (many from Islamic societies), and the establishment of democratic institutions and a rich array of societal benefits far more generous than those available in the United States, all bespeak what is close to a modern miracle of social, intellectual, political, and cultural development.

Yet the wonder and miracle of Israel has been marred by the suffering its creation caused to hundreds of thousands of Palestinians. It was only in the 1990s that the people of Israel were able to acknowledge that Palestine had *not* been, as the Zionist slogan portrayed it, "a land without a people for a people without a land." The birth of Israel had resulted in the displacement of hundreds of thousands of people—and their subsequent suffering, indeed their very existence as a people, had been denied.

In the 1990s, Israel received a second birth, this time in joy and in peace. After decades of building itself into one of the world's strongest military powers, Israel chose a new direction. In 1993 it signed an accord with the Palestine Liberation Organization. Mutual recognition and peace were the central goals of that accord. In so doing, Israel had started on the path of post-Zionism, in which Jewish values could eventually triumph over the worship of power, and Jewish compassion could replace Jewish rage. Just as it took thirty to forty years for the Zionism born of pain to recognize its distortions, so it may take several decades for the transcendence involved in Israel's second birth to be fully manifest in the policies and realities of Israeli life. There will undoubtedly be many retreats from the full implications of recognizing that one's enemy can become one's neighbor, and even friend; that the way things are is not fixed; that evil can be overcome; that pain can be transformed eventually into joy. But in taking the first hesitating steps in this direction, Israel has begun the process of rebirth, potentially opening itself to a deep Jewish renewal. The scars in the psyches of Jews caused by our troubled relationship with Palestinians will undoubtedly persist for generations after a peaceful and mutually respectful relationship has been achieved. But as the peace becomes a reality in the next ten to twenty years, all that is marvelous in the achievement of the Jewish people may surface as a process of healing and repair takes hold.

ZIONISM

First Babylonian imperialists expelled Jews from their land; Roman imperialists did so again, in a much fuller and more destructive way, enslaving tens of thousands and killing hundreds of thousands of Jews. Arab imperialists, fully clothed in the ideology of Islam, made it almost impossible for many Jews to return for most of the past twelve hundred years.

Most Jews gave up the hope of returning, and though they prayed daily for the rebuilding of Jerusalem and for "our eyes to see God's return in mercy to Zion," most imagined that this would happen in an indefinitely postponed messianic future. It took secularists, often militantly rejecting the political passivity of religious Jewry, to turn this messianic hope into a practical political program. Recurrent anti-Semitism proved so intractable in the late nineteenth and early twentieth centuries that some failed assimilationists came to believe that nothing but a Jewish state and Jewish army could possibly protect the Jews.

Zionism was the national liberation struggle of the Jewish people.

Like all such liberation struggles, it has had its Right wing and its Left wing, its moments of barbarism and moments of transcendence, its ongoing distortions and its liberatory elements. Yet Zionist ideology must be seen in historical context.

Zionists tended to see themselves as having been vindicated by history. It was they who had urged people to leave Europe, waiting neither for Messiah nor for Socialist revolution. Their minions survived, while those who did not understand the necessity of a Jewish State and a Jewish army had perished in Europe, or in refugee boats sinking at the doors of European and American countries that refused to let them in.

Need they say more? Yes, they need. But let us start by acknowledging that the Zionists had a strong case, and that people who try to reduce the Zionists' case to nothing more than a bunch of Europeans looking to colonize some Third World peoples, or a bunch of chauvinist Jews insensitive to anything but their own needs, simply miss the complexity of the situation they faced and the obvious strength of the Zionists' argument in the face of the *real world* options as they actually existed at the moment.

A NATION LIKE ALL NATIONS

Am kechol ha'amim. The Zionists argued that Jewish life in the Diaspora was fundamentally distorted. Jews had become an unhealthy people, a people that lived off and preyed upon the majority population, a people that could not have self-respect, a people without backbone—weak, dependent, twisted. This was the inevitable result of being a powerless minority in others' lands. What was needed, the Zionists argued, was to normalize Jewish existence by making the Jews a nation like all other nations, and that required a homeland, an army, a life in which Jews would be the farmers and the plumbers and the policemen and the garbage collectors and the builders and the ditchdiggers.

Similarly, Jews' special intellectual and moral sensibilities were merely a neurotic product of oppression, a heightened alertness based on the necessities of survival. Jews, some Zionists argued, have traditionally thought of themselves as "chosen" for moral superiority, and this reflected a defense against their actual degradation in the Diaspora. But this moral superiority has never protected us from the non-Jews; it has only incensed them more. We need to stop judging ourselves by some superior standard. Let us be like all other nations, and that must mean being just as immoral and power-oriented as anyone else. The world may miss its oh-so-sensitive Jews, but since it rewards us with oppression, we may have to disappoint it. We Zionists want to build a different way of being, a way in which Jews can be free—and that means free also from the slave religion and slave morality that Jews forged in the Diaspora.

Many of those who critique the misuse of Israeli power today have been called "self-hating Jews." But in fact, it was the Zionists who were the classic self-haters, the people who despised what the Jewish people had become in the Diaspora. They adopted an extreme philosophy of *shlilut ha'golah* (negation of the Diaspora) as a way to explain to themselves how they could abandon their fellow Jews to the vicissitudes of history. As the Holocaust became more imminent, many of the Zionists in the Yishuv used this negation of the Diaspora to justify relative political and military quietude instead of seeking ways to organize Jewish rescue missions in Europe.

Their guilt was mostly inappropriate—once the decision was made to live in the Yishuv rather than to try to put major energy into organizing armed resistance in Europe in the 1930s, there was little that the Zionists could have done to stop the destruction of the Jews. But to reassure themselves, Zionists intensified their disparagement of European Jewry, imagining the destruction as the logical outcome of a failed Jewish civilization.

The bottom line in this world, the Zionists argued, is power. Jews have none—that's why they are being destroyed. Now Jews must get power and use it like everyone else.

Zionists' picture of European Jewry was filled with the imagery and sentiments of the anti-Semites. For cosmopolitan Zionists like Theodor Herzl and others who emerged from Austria and Germany, it was not so surprising that their perceptions of fellow Jews were mediated by internalized self-hate. Jewish traits were to be rejected—what we couldn't accomplish through assimilation, we might accomplish through normalization of existence in a Jewish state. It was more surprising that these same images gained an audience among Zionists in Eastern Europe, many of whom knew the richness of life in the *shtetls* and towns where a deep Jewish intellectual and cultural tradition flourished. Yet the distortions were certainly there also, and there is no question that some of them were the product of Diaspora oppression.

What seems striking in retrospect, however, is how deeply the Zionist enterprise itself imbibed anti-Semitic attitudes, and rejected that which ought to have been honored in Jewish life.

In a world in which moral sensitivity is too often absent, a cultural tradition that finds a way to preserve moral alertness and sensitivity to the other ought to be honored. Yet it was this very sensitivity that some Zionists rejected as being merely a product of the Diaspora-generated need to "please the *goyim*" by showing how much we would take their needs and make them our needs (just as women, blacks, and other oppressed groups have learned to do). It was our sensitivity to others that made us unable to concentrate on our own survival needs as a people, some Zionists argued, and it was precisely this that made life in the Diaspora so precarious. If Judaism makes us vulnerable as a people, if testifying to the logic of a different kind of world makes us the subject of hostility and oppression, is it not obvious that the only response is: "Let's give this stuff up because it's too dangerous"?

No! Another possible response is: "We've got to find a way to survive that is consistent with our continuing to take this role as witnesses to the possibility of a different kind of logic in the world. And if we can't do that, then there is no point to staying alive as a *Jewish* people.

"If our goal is physical survival, we can do that through assimilation, if not in Europe then in other countries of the world. But to be Jewish cannot be to aim to be like all other peoples. The people Israel are the people who entered into a covenant with God, and our task is to tell a certain story, convey a certain message, embody a certain kind of sensibility. If we stop doing that, we are no longer the Jewish people anyway, so why bother to fight for a separate existence?"

To many Zionists in the twentieth century this argument would have seemed ridiculously out of touch with the realities of the world. But from the vantage point of what actually happened, the way that the highest and most noble ideals of Zionism actually ended up creating a state whose moral code too often became one of worshipping power, the argument seems considerably more plausible.

THE PALESTINIANS

How wonderful if the Palestinians had welcomed the Jews back. Today there are many Palestinians who think it is possible to share the land, who believe that two peoples can coexist on one land. But when

Palestinians held most of the land and, through their Arab brothers who were the elites of the oil-producing countries, had disproportionate influence on British decision making, they did everything possible to block Jewish immigration. As Hitler's cloud spread over Europe they convinced the British government to enforce a blockade that made it impossible for European Jewry to escape to Palestine.

There was no talk of sharing then. Jewish anger at this history of Palestinian behavior toward Jews in the pre-1948 period is largely justified. The massacre of Jews in Hebron in 1929, brutal attacks against Jewish settlements in the thirties and forties, and some Palestinian leaders' political ties to the Nazis contributed to Jewish anger at Palestinians.

Still, it's important to remember that most Palestinians had little to do with the decisions being made in their name. They were largely illiterate peasants, working the land just as their families had done for generations (though many were new immigrants themselves, because as the Yishuv grew, so did the Arab economy, attracting tens of thousands of Arabs from neighboring lands who sought work). Their leadership was not democratically selected. The decisions were being made by the landowning class, many of them fearful that Socialist Zionist ideas would eventually radicalize their own workers, many fearful that the Yishuv would dispossess them of their great wealth. The information that they provided to most Palestinians came through the mosques and through informal Arab networks which were hard for Jews to penetrate, and hence it was hard for Jews to make direct alliances with the Palestinian people.

But the early Zionists did not place a very high priority on building such alliances from the bottom up. Many of them shared a European-style contempt for Arabs, coupled with a well-earned Jewish suspicion of non-Jews. They were the people who had rejected the visions of internationalism being offered by Jewish anti-Zionist Socialists in Europe. Socialist Zionism usually meant socialism for Jews. There could be a Socialist *kibbutz* or possibly even a Socialist economy, but this was to be a Jewish state and so its institutions would be Jewish institutions aimed at promoting Jewish interests.

Not everyone agreed. There was a Left wing of the Socialist Zionist movement that argued for the inclusion of Arabs in the Labor organization (Histadrut), in *kibbutzim*, and in the institutions of the Yishuv. There were Jewish visionaries like Martin Buber and Judah Magnes, who called upon Jews to build a binational state that recognized equally the rights of the Arabs. But they were a small minority. As fascism and anti-Semitism spread through the world, and Arab resistance to *any* Jewish immigration hardened, more narrowly nationalist and chauvinist sentiments seemed increasingly legitimate within Zionism.

And those sentiments were strengthened by Palestinian intransigence and armed resistance.

There is no fair way to tell the story of the ensuing struggle that does not blame both sides for massacres, insensitivity to the legitimate claims of the other, and a reckless indifference to the pain that their choices would cause to the lives of human beings. Zionists have tended to minimize their own responsibility, correctly criticizing Palestinians for not allowing Jews to seek refuge; highlighting that the Zionists were willing in 1947 to accept the United Nations mandate that would have granted both peoples a state; and pointing out that far too many Palestinians sided with the Arab states that invaded Israel in 1948, in an attempt to end all Jewish hopes for national self-determination. Palestinians rightfully argue that most Palestinians were not engaged in hostilities; that the vast majority of the hundreds of thousands of refugees created by the 1948 invasion were civilian noncombatants, some of whom had been systematically uprooted by the Israeli army; that hundreds of Palestinian villages were plowed over or turned into land given to *kibbutzim* or new settlers; that homes left temporarily by Palestinians in Jerusalem, Haifa, and other cities were unilaterally seized and given to Jews; and that many Palestinians who were willing to live in peace with the new state were prevented from returning to their homes.

In the late 1980s and early 1990s, a new generation of Israeli historians have discredited the old Zionist mythology that Palestinians voluntarily fled their homes in 1948 in response to the appeal by Arab states and leaders to quit their homes and the Zionist areas, to which they would return once the Arab armies had destroyed the Jewish state. It should interest those who worry that some Palestinians today imagine the creation of a Palestinian state as only the first stage in a process of total liberation, aimed at expulsion of the Jews from the remaining parts of Palestine, that Ben-Gurion's acceptance of the 1947 partition plan may have masked similar Jewish aspirations for eventual expansion of a Jewish State in the rest of Palestine. According to Avi Shlaim's *Collusion Across the Jordan*, Ben-Gurion actively conspired with Jordan's King Abdullah to frustrate the possibility of Palestinian statehood and to divide between themselves the areas earmarked for an independent Palestine.[1] In *The Birth of the Palestinian Refugee Problem, 1947– 1949*, Benny Morris argues that while Yishuv leaders, including Ben Gurion, wanted to establish a Jewish state without an Arab minority or with as small an Arab minority as possible, and supported a "transfer solution," the Yishuv never adopted a master plan to accomplish this during the 1948 war.[2] But neither "did Arab leaders issue a blanket call for Palestine's Arabs to leave their homes and villages and wander into exile. Nor was there an Arab radio or press campaign urging or ordering the Palestinians to flee [despite the fact that Arab radio stations and other press were monitored by the Israeli intelligence services and by Western diplomatic stations and agencies]. . . . No contemporary reference to or citation from such a broadcast, let alone from a series of such broadcasts, has ever surfaced." Indeed, Morris shows that Arab radio stations and leaders in May 1948 "issued broadcasts calling upon the Palestinians to stay put and, if already in exile, to return to their homes in Palestine."[3] There were some local Arab commanders who did order evacuation of women and children from war zones, or, as in Haifa, local leaders asked their communities to leave rather than stay in a potential or actual war zone. But most of the 600,000–700,000 Palestinians who fled in this period did so out of fear of being caught in a war zone, or because they were scared of Jewish attacks (according to Morris, "there were massacres of Arabs at ad-Dawyina, Eilaboun, Jish, Safsaf, Hule, Saliha, and Sasa"[4] besides the more famous massacres at De'ir Yassin

---

[1]Avi Shlaim, *Collusion Across the Jordan* (New York: Columbia University Press, 1988).
[2]Benny Morris, *The Birth of the Palestinian Refugee Problem, 1947–1949* (New York: Cambridge University Press, 1989).
[3]Benny Morris, "The New Historiography: Israel Confronts its Past," *Tikkun* 3, no. 6 (Nov./Dec. 1988), p. 99.
[4]Ibid., p. 100.

and Lydda). Jewish leaders in Haifa pleaded with Arabs not to leave, but in many other towns and villages Haganah commanders were happy to see mass evacuations, and sometimes used psychological warfare ploys that warned Palestinians that they might soon be in physical danger if they did not leave immediately. And as Palestinian leaders from some of the bigger towns began to flee, their example exacerbated fears among the rural Palestinian population.

Undoubtedly future scholarship may refine or question some of these points. Suffice it to say that the rosy picture of a voluntary Arab exodus in 1948, a picture still held by many Jews in the 1990s and taught in Jewish schools, must eventually confront the serious work of Israeli historians who now recognize that the Zionist movement played a significant role in creating the Palestinian refugee problem. To be sure, there were Palestinian massacres of Jews throughout the twenty-year period preceding 1948, and brutal attacks by some Palestinians against Jewish civilians in 1948 (think of the Palestinian reprisal for De'ir Yassin, in which Jewish doctors and nurses traveling to Haddassah Hospital on Mount Scopus were massacred).

Nevertheless, if Palestinians eventually accept an arrangement that concedes Jewish rights to retain all of the territory in the pre-1967 borders of Israel, they will be agreeing to something very substantial— the permanent loss of lands, some of which were taken by force in 1948 when Israel extended its rule beyond the borders allocated to it in 1947 by the United Nations (accomplished in part by refusing to allow the return home of hundreds of thousands of people who had fled a war zone).

Palestinians point out that over the course of the ensuing decades the Palestinian diaspora has grown to include several million people who see themselves as exiles from their land just as Jews were in exile from theirs. Zionists point out that more than a million Jews living in Arab lands fled in the face of persecution and a long history of oppression, so that in effect there had already been a transfer of populations, and that if the surrounding Arab states had settled the Palestinians rather than using them as a political football, then the problem would have been resolved. Palestinians respond that they didn't want resettlement— they wanted to return to their homes, just as Jews have wanted to return to their homeland for eighteen hundred years.

The historical arguments are complex. In the 1940s it was the Jews who were living in refugee camps when they weren't being murdered, and it was the Palestinians who closed their ears to the cries of the oppressed. Jews seeking to return could best be understood as terrified and traumatized people who inadvertently hurt Palestinians as we sought protection for ourselves.

But taking responsibility for the damage we unintentionally caused has been extremely difficult for Jews who saw themselves primarily as victims. How can a people that clawed its way out of the death camps and crematoria of Europe be blamed for the damage it has done to others as it desperately tried to survive? If the world tortures us, brutalizes us, murders us to the point that we are driven to moral insensitivity toward others, and then we act in hurtful ways, why not blame the world? Haven't we had enough of blaming the victim?

There's a problem, however, with this kind of argument. Jews are not the only victims in world history. And we don't accept this argument when it is used to excuse pathologies in African-American life or Palestinian terrorism or Serbian attacks on Bosnians. Compassion for the suffering does not bestow on past victims a blank check to engage in current acts of moral insensitivity. Oppression does not obviate moral responsibility—not for Jews; not for Palestinian terrorists.

The responsibility of Israelis toward Palestinians must include helping them achieve national self-determination, making restitution for that which was taken from Palestinians by force, and rectifying the consequences of a history of discrimination against those Palestinians who remained within Israel and who lived peacefully with their neighbors. Moreover, Israel must rectify the anti-Arab racism, the national chauvinism, and the demonization of the other that has played too large a role in Jewish consciousness. The responsibility of Palestinians toward Israelis is to acknowledge the long history of oppression that Islamic states imposed on Jews; acknowledge the morally unacceptable role that the early Palestinian nationalist movement played both in blocking immigration of Jews and in violent confrontations with the Yishuv that contributed to the creation of the Palestinian refugee problem; and accept a solution that will provide not only national self-determination for Palestinians but adequate security for Israel, a forcible repression of those Palestinians who wish to continue struggling for "liberation of all of Palestine," and a fostering of compassionate attitudes toward the Jews among Arabs. Palestinians must rectify the distortions in their own community that have led some to embrace antidemocratic, chauvinistic, and anti-Semitic attitudes. And they must acknowledge their own role in supporting terrorism that played into the worst fears of Israelis and thus helped perpetuate the conflict. Finally Palestinians should support demands on Arab countries for restitution for that which was taken by force when Mizrachim, or Sephardic Jews, fled their homes, fearful of the growing repression and overt anti-Semitism that was being whipped up by anti-Zionist elites.

THE OCCUPATION

Though Israel had every right to defend itself against what many perceived to be imminent attack by Arab states in 1967, it should never have occupied the West Bank for more than a year or two. Israeli Defense Minister Yigal Alon presented a plan for an Israeli defense perimeter on the Jordan separating the Palestinians from other Arab states, which would have been sufficient to protect Israeli military security and which could have been imposed unilaterally, but Israeli politicians found it easier to go along with a new state-oriented messianism that rolled through Israeli society and that insisted that the West Bank and Gaza were really part of Israel and must never be returned to Arab rule.

There ensued decades of Israeli occupation and growing Palestinian resistance. Daily life on the West Bank and Gaza has been filled with humiliation and suffering. There were moments when the material condition of Palestinians improved and when colleges and universities gave Palestinians under occupation advantages that few other Arabs had in conditions of self-determination. Moreover, the exposure to democratic and liberal Israeli cultural norms had a profound impact in preparing Palestinians for self-rule. But Israelis sometimes exaggerate the material benefits of the occupation. They might be sobered by Israeli journalist Amos Elon's report after visiting Palestinians in Jordan in 1994: "It is a reflection of the Israeli military occupation of the West Bank," wrote Elon, "that in almost every respect—urban culture, transport, sanitation, town planning, social institutions, cultural amenities, medical services, and education—the West Bank today lags at least twenty-five years behind Jordan."[5]

---

[5] Amos Elon, "Look Over Jordan," *The New York Review of Books* 41, no. 8 (1994).

Moreover, Palestinians were often humiliated by arbitrary searches and harassments characteristic of an occupying army. They were subject to arbitrary collective punishment: if one group of Palestinians engaged in a terrorist act, the whole population was disciplined, put under curfew, restricted in travel, prohibited from going to work, etc.

Under a series of Likud governments, Israelis were encouraged to form settlements on the West Bank. Cheap and attractive suburban-style housing brought tens of thousands of settlers to some of the plush areas within easy commuting distance of Jerusalem and Tel Aviv. In addition, a hard core of ideological settlers came not for the housing but because they believed that the conquest of the West Bank by the Israeli army was God's will. Not interested in finding good housing but in establishing the Jewish claims to parts of the West Bank that had little Jewish presence, encouraged by militant words from Israeli leaders like Ariel Sharon and Prime Minister Yitzhak Shamir, a handful of settlers would appear on a hill overlooking an Arab village, set up tents, and declare that they had founded a new settlement. Slowly they would construct a few houses and then, under protection of the Israeli army, would take adjacent land, vineyards, and water rights that had for generations belonged to the neighboring Palestinian village. Protected by the army, in which many of them served several months a year, and willing to defend their presence with guns and acts of intimidation, these "ideological" settlers spread fear and insecurity among the Palestinian population.

The occupation may itself have created the Palestinian people as a people. At the very least, it generated a growing cycle of violence as single acts of resistance provoked massive Israeli retaliations, which in turn generated new crops of young people willing to risk their lives to express their outrage at occupation. The Palestinian uprising (Intifada) that began in 1987 was the expression of growing frustration and inability to remain passive in the face of constant abuse. Palestinian teenagers, angry at the passivity of parents who had made accommodations to the torture, used rocks and bottles to battle fully armed Israeli troops—and sustained the struggle for years. They were particularly enraged as Israeli leaders explicitly acknowledged that their goal in expanding settlements was to "create facts" that would make any exchange of land for peace politically impossible for any future Israeli government.

The futility and immorality of the occupation gradually became clearer to the Israeli public, particularly after President George Bush made it clear that badly needed loan guarantees to help absorb and settle Soviet Jews in Israel would not be available unless Israel changed some of its West Bank policies. Yet when the Israeli Labor party came to power with a slim majority in 1992, it could not claim an unambiguous mandate for fundamental change. To achieve mutual recognition took courage, leadership, and belief in a different kind of logic. For the first time since its founding forty-five years before, Israel allowed itself to acknowledge that there really was a Palestinian people and that some process of reconciliation would be needed. The actual process involved a series of clandestine meetings with Palestinians in which time was given to moving beyond "the issues" so that the people involved could get to know one another as human beings, look into one another's eyes, recognize there the presence of a fellow being—a modern version, perhaps, of what happened when Abraham looked into Isaac's eyes. Suddenly they "got" it that the pain of the past need not and should not be passed on, that the repetition compulsion could be broken, and the Force that made that possible is what we call God. Which is why, hundreds of years from now, the reconciliation and mutual recognition between Israelis and Palestinians will be celebrated as a Jewish holiday, though today, wondering as we do whether the whole process will be derailed by acts of terrorism from settlers and from Islamic fundamentalists, we see it as little more than a first, feeble step.

The process may take a long time before it is completed. Provocative actions by settlers and by some members of the I.D.F. (Israeli Defense Forces) and border patrol predictably infuriate Palestinians and encourage the military wing of Hamas, the organization of Islamic fundamentalists, to take acts of retribution against the Israeli population. These, in turn, weaken domestic support for the peace process. So it's no surprise that when Dr. Baruch Goldstein, an American Jewish settler connected with one of those right-wing groups, entered a mosque, murdered twenty-nine Palestinians, wounded dozens more, and was subsequently hailed by some settlers as "a martyr, may his memory be for a blessing [sic]," many Palestinians asserted that even though Israel was withdrawing troops from Gaza and the tiny West Bank town of Jericho, more than one million Palestinians remained under Israeli military rule in the West Bank, and were subject to attack from Israeli settlers. They could not feel secure, much less free, until the most provocative settlements were dismantled.

Imagine the feelings that tens of millions of followers of Islam must have had as they watched television footage of Muslims being murdered in their mosque by an American Jewish settler in the West Bank. Then they watched as thousands of Jews dressed in religious garb mourned the murderer. That very same week the Rabin government publicly explored the possible inclusion in its government of a far-right party that supports "transfer" of Palestinians (ethnic cleansing) and whose leader boasts that the settlers would trap Palestinians "like drugged cockroaches in a bottle." Despite powerful words of condemnation of the massacre, the Rabin government declined to dismantle the settlements or to disarm the settlers—and instead military activity was once again directed against Palestinians. One does not need to imagine some innate hatred toward Jews to understand if young people growing up in the Islamic world who watch all this on television carry animosity toward Jews in future generations.

Many Jews seem unable to put themselves in the mind of the other, to imagine how they would feel as Palestinians. So, for example, many Israelis were stunned and disillusioned when the withdrawal of Israeli forces from Jericho and parts of Gaza did not end terrorism and did not generate massive Palestinian gratitude. They discount or ignore stories of West Bank Palestinians who report that their lives have become even more difficult as Israel simultaneously prevents them from developing independent economic institutions and closes off access to jobs they previously held inside the Green Line. Fearing new acts of Islamic terrorism, unable to understand that the one million Palestinians still under Israeli military rule fear that the continued presence of largely unrestrained Israeli settlers may indicate that Israel never intends to grant them full national self-determination, the Israeli population at times imagines that continued Palestinian acts of resistance and terrorism are proof that nothing short of the destruction of Israel would satisfy most Palestinians.

Unfortunately, some of the fear of what will happen should we loosen our grip on them is based on an unconscious awareness that the occupation has justifiably enraged many Palestinians. Though we feel comfortable thinking that we are merely facing yet another example of irrational hatred of Jews, some Jews suspect Israeli policies toward Palestinians may have produced hatred toward us that is based *not* on irrational religious hangovers, but on the actual oppressive, racist, and other-demeaning behavior of some Jews. Similarly, people in countries that never heard of Jews before are learning of Jews through television coverage of the occupation. This era may be one of the very rare moments in history when anger toward Jews is not simply a product of manipulation by ruling elites, but is engendered by the images of Jewish behavior conveyed to hundreds of millions of people around the world as they watch some Jews engage in acts of hatred and use language that demeans Arabs.

Not that it will be rational or reasonable for Palestinians, Muslims, or anyone else to hold these angers or to act on them. In doing that, they will be engaging in the same racist behavior of some right-wing and Modern Orthodox Jews: blaming the many for the outrages of the few. The fact is that Jewish haters are a relative minority, but they are a relative minority that has been allowed to have prominence because the rest of the Jewish population refuses to stand up to them, silence them, or take dramatic actions of caring toward their victims.

No act of terror against Jews is ever justified. And the actions of some of the settlers must also be understood in terms of their righteous indignation at Palestinian acts of terror against Jews. I am outraged at Palestinian acts of violence against Jews, not only because they perpetuate the cycle of hatred, but because they are killing my family, my people, and usually totally innocent victims, every bit as innocent as the Palestinian children so many of whom have been killed by the Israeli army. The victims of Arab terror, like the victims of Israeli settlers, are precious to God. I mourn them both. But it is not enough to mourn the dead—it is our obligation to break the cycle of violence. And for that, the most likely first step is to end the occupation, dismantle any settlement that is not prepared to live in peace within a society governed by Palestinians, and make restitution for some of the damage done by the occupation.

TORTURE

In the midst of the Intifada the Israeli Information Center for Human Rights, (B'Tselem) issued a report on the use of torture in the interrogation of Palestinians. Based on interviews with forty-one Palestinians who were interrogated by the G.S.S. (General Security Service, or Shin Bet), the report shows that a number of interrogation methods were routinely used that are prohibited by international conventions concerning torture and "cruel and inhuman treatment," as well as by Israeli laws banning the use of force to extract confessions or information. Virtually all were subjected to the following methods of interrogation:

- insults and verbal abuse
- threats of harm to the detainee and/or his family members
- deprivation of food and sleep
- prolonged periods of painful confinement in small closetlike cells (and in some cases, closets or refrigerators)
- being tied in painful positions for long periods of time
- violent assaults by "collaborators" to extract confessions
- forced physical exercise
- cold showers; enforced sitting on a wet floor for prolonged periods
- severe beatings on all parts of the body with fists, bricks, and other instruments

Detainees were often held for as long as two or three months without access to lawyers. Despite the self-promotion of the Israeli judiciary as an independent voice, the report did not find a single case where military judges used their authority to place restrictions on the Shin Bet, whether by allowing detainees access to lawyers or restricting the period of detention.

The report also charges that the Landau Commission, which had been created by the Israeli government to investigate previous allegations of misconduct by the Shin Bet, has contributed to the atmosphere of tolerance of torture by having condoned what it calls "moderate physical pressure." By removing the absolute moral taboo against torture, the Landau Commission opened the way to interrogation practices that are not allowed in other democratic societies.

Not one of B'Tselem's interviewees was found guilty or even suspected of the types of serious "hostile terrorist activity" for which the Landau Commission justified the use of "moderate physical pressure" in interrogation.

Of course, reliable information on such abuses is scarce, as the authors of the report noted. Victims' memories are not always accurate, and they can be suspected of exaggerating for political reasons. But it is important to note that not a single one of the torture victims was ever charged with or even suspected of committing an act of terrorism.

After two months of public controversy surrounding this particular report of torture, the Israeli newspaper *Ha'aretz* interviewed several key figures on the Israeli Right to hear their reactions. Rabbi Shlomo Goren, the former chief rabbi of the Israeli army, was quoted: "I haven't read the B'Tselem report. I don't know these people and I don't want to know them. They betray the people of Israel and the State of Israel; they're serving our enemies. Since they're traitors, they weren't created in the image of God. . . . I trust our Jewish officials. Jews are eternally merciful. They don't apply excessive force when there's no need to, and if they apply force, it's defensive force, force that should be applied so we don't end up with another Holocaust. The Arabs want to bring another Holocaust upon us." Limor Linyat, a member of the Likud Central Committee, was quoted as saying about B'Tselem, "It's hard for me to digest the idea that Jews would be a fifth column in their own country. I find it hard to understand how Jews go out and inform on other Jews. . . . The Right concentrates on the rights of the Jews. We established this State in order to safeguard *our* rights. The right to live in security, for instance. I don't suggest that we should trample on others' rights, but one must call a spade a spade: Zionism and rights don't always go hand in hand."[6] A central theme of many other responses quoted in the newspaper: It can't be happening here, but if it is, it must be all right, because Jews do this kind of thing only when it's justified.

It should be noted that the methods of torture used in Israel were less elaborate, less systematic, and less intense than those favored by more brutal authoritarian regimes.

Stanley Cohen, professor of criminology at the Hebrew University, writes about the various forms of justification that appear in public discourse: "There is no other way. . . . national security requires these methods. A second, more elevated version appeals to a sacred mission, a higher set of values that transcend the rule of law. A third appeal, deeply ingrained in the collective Israeli psyche, is to the Darwinian struggle for survival: It's us or them; it's our fate to be locked into a cycle of violence that has no end. And finally, a fourth line of defense is to

---

[6]"The Wrong Arm of the Law: Torture Disclosed and Deflected in Israeli Politics," *Tikkun* 6, no. 5 (Sept./Nov. 1991).

reproduce wholesale the self-image of the security services: good people doing their job as best they can under difficult conditions; somebody has to do the dirty work. . . . Every palace has its dirty corners."[7] Cohen, a member of the committee who investigated allegations of torture, admitted to feeling despair that at the end of the twentieth century he should have to try to convince Jews that torture is bad. "As with slavery, the only morally defensible position about torture is abolitionist." But, concludes Cohen, "in all societies at all times (and Israel is no exception), and for the vast majority of the population, the contours of daily life depend on ignorance, silence, and passive collusion."[8]

There was always the hope that once the matter had been brought to public attention, things would change. But according to the *New York Times* on August 14, 1993, two years after the B'Tselem report, there continued to be new instances of torture. Amnesty International, in a human rights report in July 1993, said Palestinians under interrogation are "systematically tortured or ill-treated" by Israelis.[9] The International Committee of the Red Cross, whose representatives regularly visit Palestinian prisoners, accused Israel of using interrogation methods that violate the Fourth Geneva Convention on treatment of civilians in occupied areas. The *New York Times* takes care to mention that the reported mistreatment is "significantly less severe than the torture documented in other Middle Eastern countries, like Iraq, Syria, and Turkey."[10]

Many Israelis have protested the continuation of torture. Israeli doctors have sought to prohibit any physician from cooperating with abusive interrogation and to require doctors to report abuse. Lawyers from a variety of civil rights organizations in Israel have fought to end the abuse. But many Israelis and many American Jews continue to deny the very existence of torture, criticize those who have exposed it as traitors or self-hating Jews, or else attempt to provide rationalizations for why torture by Israelis is different from torture by anyone else.

---

[7]Stanley Cohen, "Talking About Torture in Israel," *Tikkun* 6, no. 6 (Nov. 1991).
[8]Ibid.
[9]*New York Times*, 14 August, 1993.
[10]Ibid.

Hopefully, many of the concerns about torture and occupation will seem like ancient history to a future generation. Yet just as the issues raised by the conquest of the United States from the Native Americans, and the building of the United States through the enslavement of Africans, remain central to our understanding of contemporary reality, so it is likely that decades from now Israelis will be dealing with the issues of affirmative action, reparations, and other measures to clean up the mess created by the occupation and the original expulsion of Palestinians. Future generations will wonder how it was possible that Jews living in the late twentieth century, themselves the victims of racism and demeaning of the other, could have allowed the distortions in Judaism and in Jewish practice that are now the daily reality of life in Israel and that are justified in the United States. The answer, of course, is that it is precisely the degree to which we were the victims and were demeaned that we began to internalize our oppressors' ways of looking at the world, and that their distortions became our distortions. No, we were never mass murderers, and *no*, there is nothing comparable in horror or scope between what Israel has been doing to Palestinians and what was done to us. Our Torah, our history, our collective memory, prevented us from ever becoming very much like the monsters who oppressed us. And yet, to the degree to which our State became deeply distorted, and our religion not only closed its eyes to the suffering of others, but also, at least for some manifestations of that religion, actually seemed to justify the oppression of others, we can understand this as the result of the ways that we have not yet healed from what was done to us. Jewish renewal can teach us that the healing is possible, and that Judaism will in fact pass through and beyond this current moment and once again reclaim its connection to the healing and transformative Force in the universe.

SOLUTIONS

Lasting peace is possible only when the pain and fear of both sides are recognized and legitimated—when both sides can truly say: "I understand why you need to be fully recognized as an equal being, equally entitled to what you need as I am to what I need." Mutual recognition must mean that, or it becomes an empty concept.

The details can be left to the diplomats if both sides really remain committed to mutual recognition. Still it makes sense to ask what a political solution that takes mutual recognition seriously might look like.

We may see many different accords being reached in the years ahead. One side or the other may be forced by the political realities they face to enter into agreements that they ultimately cannot live with. So it's more important to formulate a solution that takes into account the real needs on both sides than to get a quick fix that ultimately doesn't work unless both sides admit that they are simply confidence-building interim measures aimed at creating a climate of mutual trust from which greater trust and deeper accords will soon emerge. Here I want to discuss the terms for a long-term agreement that could create peace for both sides.

The terms of a political solution must be these: Palestinians should receive the right to create a demilitarized state in the West Bank and Gaza, with representation in the United Nations, a flag, and all the trappings of independence.

The terms of the creation of that state should be included in its own constitution, in a treaty with Israel, and in the ratification agreement by the United Nations, and should include the following provisions:

1. The Palestinian state agrees to remain totally demilitarized for the next fifty years. The demilitarization will be enforced at the borders by the Israeli army, which is granted a strip of land separating the new state from Jordan and surrounding Arab states, on which the I.D.F. may station troops and weapons. In return, Israel grants the Palestinian state a strip of land connecting the West Bank with Gaza, on which the Palestinians may construct a highway to facilitate travel.

2. The Palestinian state, in the name of the entire Palestinian people, renounces all claims to land or property inside the pre-1967 borders of Israel.

3. The Palestinian state agrees to enforce law and order within its state, and to prevent rocket, artillery, or guerrilla attacks from being launched from within its territorial boundaries. It is given an armed internal police and border patrol that has the power to repress terrorism and restrain violent groups who seek to undermine the accord with Israel or who seek to use violence

against Jewish settlers within the Palestinian state. If it is
unable to prevent these attacks, it recognizes the *right* of the
Israeli army to enter Palestine to attack suspected guerrilla
bases, but not to station troops on its land.

4. Any Palestinians wishing to remain within Israel but to hold
citizenship in the Palestinian state may do so, but in that case
they cannot vote in Israeli elections. Conversely, any Israelis
wishing to remain within the jurisdiction of the new Palestinian
state may do so, provided they abide by the laws and court
decisions of the Palestinian state. They may vote in Israeli
elections and retain Israeli citizenship, but only if they give up
the right to vote in Palestinian elections. Israel will *not* provide
protection or economic support for Israelis living in the Palestinian state, and the Palestinian state will not provide protection
or economic support for Palestinians choosing to live in Israel.
Israeli settlers who refuse to abide by the laws of the Palestinian
state should be treated as criminals in the exact same way that
Palestinians refusing to abide by the laws of the Israeli state are
treated as criminals. Just as Israel has special opportunities and
advantages for Jews, so the Palestinian state will reasonably
have special advantages for Arabs, and those Jews who live in the
state will have to accept that inequality just as Palestinians
accept that kind of treatment within Israel proper.

5. Jerusalem shall remain under Israeli military control but shall
become the capital of both states. Citywide elections will elect
a government that provides basic municipal services. Jerusalem
will remain united as one city, but the Palestinians will be given
the right to raise their flag over a set of governmental buildings
in their capital, and will have free and unrestricted access to
those buildings. By providing a model of intergroup cooperation, Jerusalem will earn the Biblical reputation: "From Zion
shall go out Torah, and the word of God from Jerusalem."

In a world in which perceptions are often as important as the details
of the fine print, it matters greatly to the world's perception of Israel
whether it can find a place in its heart for a magnanimous gesture, or
whether even in making peace it does so in a withholding and resentful
manner.

The Jewish people have a rare opportunity to make a definitive statement about themselves on the world stage. That statement should be one that reflects confidence, moral commitment, and a testimony to the possibility of a different logic than that of cruelty, paranoia, and passing on to others what has been done to us. So it matters very much that a peace settlement be entered into with enthusiasm, energetic support, and a genuine openness not just to ending hostilities but to positively achieving peace.

Any political settlement will always remain weak and unstable unless there is a concomitant effort to build trust and peace between the two peoples. That is going to be a long-term project, requiring some of the same processes that are required for Jews to mourn the Holocaust described in the previous chapter. Both Israelis and Palestinians are going to have to give up their maximalist fantasies and accept that they have gotten the best that they are going to get. And they are going to have to allow themselves to grieve for what is lost—and not to pretend that they haven't given something up. Then they are going to have to be able to tell their stories honestly and in the more complicated way that acknowledges the truths of each other's pain.

Utopian? No. What is utopian is to imagine that the Jewish people could have a state in the middle of an Arab and Islamic world *without* making extraordinary efforts to build mutual understanding, firm lines of communication, and common interests. There is no set of military alliances sufficient to protect Israel in the long run from a hostile Arab world. The only real security for Israel lies in working out collective agreements based on mutual respect and understanding.

SETTLER VIOLENCE

Some Jewish settlers and Palestinian terrorists will do all they can to undermine the peace process in the years before a demilitarized Palestinian state is established. As peace gets closer, they will get all the more desperate, escalate violence, and give credence to the contention of some Israeli rightists that what we are facing is not a peace process but a terror process. Israelis who fall for this are willfully ignorant of the realities of Palestinian life even at the moments when they don't face anything as dramatic as the 1994 massacre in Hebron.

The reality for most West Bank Palestinians is a life always subject to the assaults of the settlers. According to the Israeli human rights organization B'Tselem, since 1988 settlers have killed sixty-two Palestinians (not counting those murdered in Hebron). In four of these cases Israelis opened fire under conditions in which they faced mortal danger, in three other cases they knowingly put themselves in danger, and in six cases there was insufficient information to establish the level of danger being faced. In the other forty-nine cases, Israeli civilians killed Palestinians in situations *not* involving mortal danger.

The B'Tselem report goes on to describe what Palestinians often face.

Using weapons supplied by the I.D.F., individuals and organized groups initiate operations against Palestinians and their property in order to intimidate, deter, and punish. In many cases these are planned operations, initiated and carefully planned by groups of settlers who are backed by the established leadership of the settlements.

The operations initiated by settlers against Palestinians include entering villages, shooting at houses and solar water heaters, sabotage and torching of vehicles, violent disturbances, blocking roads, smashing windows, destroying crops and uprooting trees, harassment of merchants and stands in the markets, including destruction of their wares and so forth.

The many rampages and other acts of violence by settlers against the Palestinians and especially the organized character of many of these raids attest to the fact that these are not merely criminal acts; they constitute ideologically and politically motivated violence.[11]

Exploring the role of the I.D.F., the B'Tselem report notes that "Frequently soldiers who witness acts of violence by settlers against Palestinians make no effort to prevent or put a stop to the incident, or at least to take the personal details of those involved and pass them on to the police. . . . There are cases in which soldiers not only do nothing to stop the violence by settlers, but themselves also join in. In many cases of settler violence the I.D.F. restricts the movement of the Palestinians, including by means of curfew, but takes no such action against the settlers. The rationale is to protect the Palestinians from the settlers, but the result is an absurdity in which the restrictions are placed on the victim but not on

---

[11]From an executive summary of the B'Tselem report, translated by B'Tselem and faxed to *Tikkun* magazine, 16 March, 1994.

the assailant. Despite its duty, the I.D.F. has shown protracted impotence in dealing with violence perpetrated by settlers against Palestinians. This is not a chance development but the product of the close ties between the I.D.F. and the settlers. . . . The I.D.F.'s recurrent failures in reacting to settler violence despite repeated warnings by politicians, reporters, and human rights organizations suggests that these failures are not the exception but part of the I.D.F.'s overall policy."[12]

In examining how the Israeli courts deal with those few instances of settler violence that are actually prosecuted, B'Tselem concludes that in comparing the punishments given to settlers with punishments of Palestinians for similar crimes, "the Israeli courts tend to deal harshly with Palestinians, while lightening the punishment of Israeli citizens who committed identical crimes. For the crime of stone-throwing, for example, Palestinians have often been sentenced in military and civil courts to one year's imprisonment, and in certain cases to much harsher punishments."[13] In conclusion, B'Tselem asserts that "the Israeli government has failed in its task of protecting the lives, persons, and property of Palestinians from repeated attacks by Israeli civilians in the occupied territories. The various authorities apply an unstated policy of tolerance, compromise, and failure in bringing about full justice where Israelis who attack the Palestinian population are concerned. Every branch of the government and legal system, individually and together, tends to view the many acts of violence by Israeli civilians against the Palestinian residents of the territories with an insufficient degree of seriousness. The Israeli government applies a double standard between Israelis and Palestinians in law enforcement in the territories."[14]

In an epilogue to the report about the massacre in Hebron in February 1994, B'Tselem argues that the information in its report "demonstrates that Goldstein's act [the Hebron massacre] did not emerge out of nowhere, but was, rather, a consequence of the ongoing anti-Palestinian incitement, and another link—the most severe to date—in the chain of violent acts perpetrated by settlers against Palestinians, including frequent illegal use of firearms, which, for the most part, went unpunished."[15]

---

[12]Ibid.
[13]Ibid.
[14]Ibid.
[15]Ibid.

It is this kind of activity that lies behind the Israeli peace movement's demands that the process of resolving the fate of the West Bank be speeded up and the most provocative settlements dismantled.

Some settlers have spoken openly about civil war and armed resistance to the Israeli Defense Forces should they be required to give up the settlements. Fearful of the political consequences of Jews fighting fellow Jews in Israel, the Labor government has backed away from dismantling the settlements, and so has left in place a political time bomb that is certain to make a final resolution all the more difficult. If the settlers are not forced to choose between being dismantled or taking active steps to reconcile with their Arab neighbors—including ending de facto segregation and making the settlements open to Arabs who might wish to live there, integrating their schools, and allowing impartial courts to adjudicate land and water disputes—they will remain a major factor preventing a serious peace.

Eventually some of these settlers may turn their guns on Israeli supporters of the peace process, whom they sometimes describe as "worse than the Arabs," or even on the Israeli army itself as it seeks to implement peace agreements. Some supporters of the settlers have already resorted to violence against fellow Jews, planting bombs near the offices of American organizations that support the Israeli peace movement. From the beginning of the Intifada, other staff members and I at *Tikkun* magazine have received death threats regularly from people who identified themselves as supporters of the settlers, because of our criticism of the occupation. The threats of violence faced by supporters of peace—in both the United States and Israel—together with the discourse in some sectors of the Jewish world that implicitly assumes that Palestinian lives are not to be valued equally with Jewish lives, that Jewish acts of terrorism need not be met with the same punishments given to the same acts taken by Palestinians, that Jews are somehow better because we apologize for our acts of terror while the Palestinians do not (a claim that misses the obvious asymmetry between the occupier and the occupied, and plays into the dynamic by which Jews "cry and shoot," that is, oppress and then claim to be better than those whom they oppress because they shed tears of regret at being "forced" to lose their moral purity and engage in these terrible acts which they supposedly never would have wanted to do but were forced to by "the necessity" of occupation), and that Jewish murder of Palestinians must be understood in light of our history but that Palestinian terrorism can never be understood in light of *their* history—contribute to the silence of the Jewish moderate Center, who are unwilling to confront the Right if that confrontation might involve violence, and hence do little to prevent the continuation of Jewish violence against Palestinians.

Two caveats: Most settlers moved to the West Bank for economic reasons (cheap housing) and their hostility to Palestinians is a legitimate product of their experience of feeling unsafe as they drive daily through contested territory. In 1994 some observers estimate that only twenty-five percent of the settlers are ideological, committed to staying at all costs, and committed to disrupting the peace process. Second, many of the settlers, even among the most committed to disrupting the peace process, are fundamentally decent human beings. If I vigorously oppose what they are doing and what they stand for, I do not wish to demean them, to deny that their way of seeing things has often emerged from their own experience (either of the Holocaust, or of hostility from surrounding Arab states, or of the threat that they feel from Palestinians), or to suggest that the fundamental act of living on the West Bank is illegitimate. I do not believe in principle that the West Bank should be *Judenrein*. Israel should immediately dismantle the most provocative settlements (those that have become the centers of opposition to peaceful reconciliation with Palestinians) and should require proof on the part of the other settlements that they are engaged in serious and sustained efforts to rectify past wrongs and are prepared to live in peace as a minority group within a demilitarized Palestinian state. But those who really do wish to live in that peaceful way should be given support, and Israel should insist that a peace treaty enable them to remain in the settlements, provided that the settlements do not discriminate against Arabs in housing (in other words, Palestinians are allowed to buy apartments in them just as Jews should be allowed to buy in any part of the West Bank), education, or employment, and provided that the Israelis live in accord with the laws of the new Palestinian state.

SETTLER JUDAISM: POWER WORSHIP AND THE IDOLATRY OF THE STATE

Although the settlers are only a small part of the Israeli population, the demeaning way that some of them talk about Palestinians, non-Jews in general, and even fellow Jews who are peace activists has had a poisoning effect on many other areas of Israeli life. And that impact is magnified worldwide because many of those most committed to holding on to the occupied territories at all costs are religious, root themselves in religious language, and use Jewish religious sources to defend their attitudes.

The settlers' organizations have been explicit in opposing Israeli Prime Minister Rabin's peace moves, and escalated their opposition after the signing of the peace accords in Washington in September 1993. At this very moment in which the Israeli government sought public support for the peace accords, faced with hostile reactions from Israeli rightists, a variety of American synagogues began to publicly "adopt" specific West Bank settlements to show political support. In January 1994 a group of prominent Upper West Side Orthodox synagogues in Manhattan organized a public rally in "Solidarity with the Settlers."

Too often I've encountered among the people at Orthodox synagogues where I sometimes *daven* (pray), and among people in Reform and Conservative synagogues where I've been invited to be the "scholar in residence," a willingness to cast Palestinians in the role of the latest embodiment of "those who in every generation arise and seek to destroy us." It is not infrequent to hear references to them as "Amalek" (the tribe that attacked us in the desert and whose memory we are commanded to wipe out), the "seven nations" which inhabited the land of Israel before the Israelites under Joshua conquered it and who the Bible tells us to uproot and destroy, or to the Nazis.

Even after the massacre at Hebron, I heard some people in the religious world argue that it may be appropriate to assume that every Palestinian is a potential attacker or terrorist, and hence that it is appropriate for Israelis to attack them first. They cite the Torah injunction that when one person is a pursuer (*rodeph*) who is seeking to kill someone else, it is legitimate to stop the *rodeph*, even with deadly force. Since the Palestinian people are themselves supporters of the terrorists, give them aid and comfort, they must be construed as collectively a *rodeph*, and hence it is legitimate to attack them.

Of course, the words of the Torah never state or imply any such collective *rodeph* status, never suggest that the family, friends, or supporters of the *rodeph* are liable to be punished or peremptorily attacked or killed. The extension of the danger from the individual terrorist to an entire people is a racist assumption. And yet, since this same kind of thinking was the basis for putting hundreds of thousands of people under Israeli military curfew after a terrorist attack or after a violent demonstration by a few groups of rock-throwing teenagers, it's not a surprise that eventually this way of extending responsibility and hate to an entire people would take root.

As someone who is often in the position of trying to convince unaffiliated Jews why they should recommit themselves to the religious tradition, it is particularly difficult to have to explain why it is that so many people in the religious world seem to have adopted hateful attitudes toward Palestinians, non-Jews in general, and even fellow Jews who oppose the peace process. Jewish religious leaders were for centuries among the most morally developed and sensitive beings on earth. Yet in Israel today a disproportionate number of religious Zionists have become advocates of the harshest sentiments in Torah, cheerleaders for the sensibilities of conquest as described in the Book of Joshua, and almost mute about the universalistic sentiments articulated in the Books of Ruth and Jonah. An inordinate number of religious Jews today root themselves in precisely those texts I've described as the residual voice of cruelty in our tradition. As I argued earlier in this book, the voices of pain and cruelty have always been there in our Torah along with the voice of God. Yet when we were powerless, those voices seemed relatively innocuous, the outraged cry of an oppressed group that could fantasize acting out power against various groups of oppressors. It is very different, however, when the oppressed suddenly come to power, have one of the most powerful armies in the world, replete with nuclear capabilities, and possess a standard of living far higher than that of most of the peoples of the world.

Replete with a full array of quotes from Deuteronomy, Joshua, Samuel, and those commentators and halakhists who have built on their legacy of religious triumphalism and demeaning of the other, ignoring or reinterpreting all the many parts of the tradition that call for an attitude of kindness, gentleness, and compassion, religious rightists have hijacked Judaism to such an extent that most other Israelis have come to think that "religious" and "politically right-wing" are virtually synonymous concepts!

Followers of the late Rabbi Tzvi Yehudah Kook, many right-wing religious Israelis, believe that the military victories of the Israeli Defense Forces (I.D.F.) are a reflection of the will of God. In this view, the conquest of the land of Israel, including the West Bank, is a direct sign of God's intention and will in history. It is therefore incumbent upon

Israelis to hold on to that land. To do otherwise would be to violate God's intentions and to bring upon the Jewish people a tragedy comparable to the destruction of the Second Temple.

In its most extreme form, some versions of Modern Orthodoxy in Israel devolve into a form that I call Settler Judaism. Settler Judaism holds that since the world is against us, abandoned us during the Holocaust, and hypocritically condemns us for violence more sharply than it criticizes others, we don't have to live according to a universal moral standard. God gave *us* the West Bank as our eternal inheritance and we have the right to do *whatever* is necessary to hold on to it. Anyone who trusts Palestinians or assumes that they have the same human needs and motivations to live in peace as Jews, or who doesn't realize that the only Palestinian motivation is to destroy us, is naive and likely to endanger the Jewish people. Indeed, our fellow Jews are betraying us by calling for an exchange of land for peace. These peace-oriented Jews are traitors and may be as dangerous to our future as the Arabs. The obligations to pursue justice and love your neighbor apply only to our fellow Jews, not to non-Jews, certainly not to Palestinians, and maybe not even to Jews who advocate the peace process.

Needless to say, Settler Judaism is the opposite of the Jewish-renewal Judaism that I have been exploring in this book, and it is far from the spirit of the morally and spiritually sensitive versions of Judaism that have predominated through most of Jewish history, a Judaism that typically saw God as siding with the oppressed and the powerless, helping the humble and the gentle and the kind. But all that, according to Settler Judaism, "didn't work." To be realistic in a post-Holocaust world, one must live by the gun and must fight for God's will, even if this means fighting against the majority of Israelis, who may not understand the sacred obligation thrust upon the Jewish people to safeguard the holiness of the land of Israel.

Settler Judaism was given a dramatic boost in the spring of 1994 when the former Ashkenazic chief rabbi of Israel joined some two hundred other rabbis and religious leaders in issuing an order prohibiting religious members of the I.D.F. from participating in activity that would remove settlers from the West Bank.

To be sure, these are *not* the only voices of religious Judaism in Israel. There is a religious peace movement that continues to testify to the voice of a compassionate God who commanded us to love the stranger, and there are some voices within each religious community that occasionally get up the courage to remind Israelis of the other voice in Torah, what I've been calling the voice of God. Modern Orthodoxy has within it morally sensitive and antiracist voices, and so does every other branch of Judaism.

Yet these voices have been relatively isolated within the religious community in Israel, often on the defensive. While those who support many of the principles of what I'm calling Settler Judaism have dominated the National Religious Party and received seats in the Knesset, Meymad (a political party closely identified with the religious peace forces) was unable to win even a single seat when it ran the much-respected, peace-oriented Rabbi Amital, head of the Gush Etziyon Yeshiva. Few Israeli *yeshivas* (post–high school religious training institutions) publicly identify with a peace-oriented Judaism, though there are many *yeshivot* which publicly identify with many of the principles of Settler Judaism.

Not everyone who supports the Israeli Right or who questions particular parts of the agreements being worked out by the government necessarily supports Settler Judaism. There are many who have legitimate security concerns, and those concerns are being addressed by the Israeli government. But alongside those legitimate concerns is a discourse of demeaning the other and a way of thinking about social reality that seems to me subversive of what Judaism has most often been about.

For example, some religious thinkers have argued that those religious peace activists who criticize Israeli policy—in regard to either torture, the imposition of curfews and six months of "administrative detention" without trial, legally sanctioned unequal treatment of Arabs and Jews, or de facto imposition of hardships on Palestinians in response to the actions of a small number of terrorists—are imposing utopian criteria for morality.

The religious peace movement frequently makes references to Torah injunctions like "One law shall be for you and the stranger who dwells within your midst," or "You shall love the stranger," or "Justice, justice shalt thou pursue," or hundreds of subsidiary halakhic rulings that would require a much more caring and charitable attitude toward the Palestinian population than one frequently encounters in many right-wing religious circles in Israel. Or it reminds people that the Book of Jonah, chosen by the rabbis to be read in the synagogues on Yom Kippur, is precisely designed to challenge the xenophobic nationalism that characterized some moments in the life of preexilic Israel.

Amazingly, some religious Jews who refer to the tradition as their justification when it comes to every other area of life find the tradition "outdated" when it comes to moral guidance. The moral codes of the past, they argue, are useless since they were developed a) by a Judaism that actually never had to worry about how to hold and wield power; b) before the Holocaust, from which we learned that the alternative to holding power is death; c) by people living physically outside the situation they were moralizing about; and d) by people holding on to a prophetic demand for a higher standard of conduct than God demands of other nations, a standard that made sense when God was involved in intervening in the world, but is no longer appropriate since God has withdrawn from the world and given to human beings responsibility for living morally. The new situation of the Jewish people in power, after the Holocaust and God's "no show," creates a new reality and hence the need for a new kind of morality.

But these arguments do not hold. The demand of the religious peace movement in Israel is that Palestinians be treated as human beings, that their lives be treated as equally valuable with Israeli lives, and that their attachment to their own land and willingness to fight for it necessitates some kind of historical compromise in which two peoples learn to live together in peace, even at the expense of dividing the land between these two peoples. Given these principles, the occupation is seen as self-defeating and untenable, and the horrible brutality used to impose it as an unnecessary use of force. While peace activists recognize that there will continue to be a danger of terrorism after any arrangement with Palestinians (just as there is likely to be a danger of Jewish terrorism directed against both Palestinians and Jews), there is no danger to the survival of the Jewish state posed by the creation of a fully demilitarized Palestinian state. Moreover, while there will certainly continue to be Hamas (Islamic fundamentalist) terrorists who will proclaim that nothing short of the full destruction of the Jewish state is acceptable, their appeal will decrease dramatically in the decades after a Palestinian state is created, if that state is created in a way that validates Palestinian dignity and if that state is supported to become economically viable. Fundamentalism's appeal would be even further undermined should religious Israelis begin to conceptualize joint activities of mutual help and concern with religious Muslims, and take steps to create contexts in which our shared religious sensibilities could be explored.

There is nothing about this position that can be refuted by the argument of the realists. First of all, the position is one that is advocated not only by religious peace activists, idealists, or people living outside the country and enjoying the moral luxury of not having to face the consequences of the moral path, but also by many former generals in the Israeli army and Labor party "realists" who helped build the state and defend it in the 1967 war. Nor is it a standard that is higher than that demanded of others. The demand that all people be entitled to vote for their own government is almost universally applied, has recently been universally applauded when instituted in South Africa, and where it is not (e.g., China or other totalitarian systems), there is considerable criticism by the rest of the world. Since few Zionists wish to impair the Jewish quality of Israel by giving West Bank Palestinians the vote inside Israel (where they would quickly become one of the biggest voting blocs), there is nothing utopian about giving them the right to shape their own demilitarized state.

But what is most troubling are the arguments made from the basis of "what others do" and "realism." One frequently hears the argument about Israel being judged by a higher standard. For example, torture that has been revealed in Syria or Iran or Iraq or Turkey or China is used as an excuse, and right-wingers argue that these other states are not being condemned, so Israel is being subjected to a double standard. Factually, they are incorrect since these other states are frequently criticized, and our knowledge of torture and other obnoxious anti-democratic behaviors in those societies helps account for why there is little support in the United States to provide them with the kind of financial support that the United States yearly doles out to Israel. But from a religious standpoint, this argument is subversive in the extreme to the original conception of the Jewish people.

Jews were never enjoined to make a sociological study of the morality of other nations, and then to conform to that morality. While it seems *illegitimate* for *others* to hold us to a higher standard than they hold themselves or the rest of the world, it is perfectly *legitimate* for *us* to hold ourselves to a standard not based on watching what everyone else is doing. That is precisely what having the Torah is about—having a special responsibility to bring to the world a way of living in accord with our understanding of God's revelation.

"Wait a second," someone may object, "that *is* utopian, because God's requirements as presented in the Torah are really impossible given the actualities of our real world. That's why the halakhic tradition has always had to make accommodations, and that's what is needed today." This seems a perfectly legitimate counter-argument to me, but it must be very carefully scrutinized. "Ought" always implies "can," so Israelis cannot be under a moral obligation to do something they cannot do. But this is also a very slippery slope, because what one "can" do is not a fact about the world so easily determined independent of one's beliefs about the world. I remember how for many years some Israelis said that they wanted to negotiate peace, but there was nobody with whom to negotiate. But when they decided to actually proceed, suddenly they managed to find somebody (the P.L.O.). What can be done is often a question of assessing whether certain risks or consequences are "acceptable," and that depends on one's moral worldview, and is not a fact independent of that worldview.

So judging a position utopian because it has difficult consequences is a quick way to eliminate not only the peace process but every other part of morality. One might make the argument that "Thou shalt not commit adultery" is equally impractical in modern Israel, given the new levels of moral relativism and sexual freedom that have swept the world. Or that "Thou shalt not wantonly destroy" is impractical to apply to the environment given the requisites of the international capitalist economy. In short, if one argues that it is utopian to act in accord with moral ideals in a world in which those ideals are usually *not* acted upon, then one might as well reject the entire Torah. Of course, my point about contemporary Judaism is that that is exactly what has happened in substance, and the reason we can't see this is that those who have been most active in rejecting the moral vision of Torah have nevertheless managed to hold on to various aspects of the religious practice, partly out of habit, partly because the community created around the rituals provides enough sense of connection and shared purpose that it feels good anyway, partly out of loyalty to parents and martyrs of the past whom they do not want to betray by abandoning the tradition.

Yet people who take the position I'm discussing here have substantively abandoned the God of Torah and the most central aspect of Jewish destiny: to be the people who testify to the possibility of a different logic in the world than the logic of cruelty and power.

"But," argue some, "the logic of power is the way the real world is constituted, and if we want to have a Jewish state, we have to play by those rules."

Again, there is some truth in this argument. I support Israel being a strong state and hope that democratic countries around the world will provide Israel with the military hardware, economic support, trade, and alliances to ensure its physical survival. In fact, part of my argument for why it's important for Israel quickly to forge a demilitarized Palestinian state is that such behavior will enhance Israel's military security and its ability to remain strong in the real world. But on the other hand, when this argument gets used, as it has been by some religious thinkers, to defend torture, discriminatory practices toward minority groups, or other behavior that violate Torah or moral norms, the argument seems less persuasive.

The trump of the argument is, "This is the only way to maintain a Jewish state." But what makes the state Jewish if in maintaining itself it must abandon any serious commitment to the moral guidelines and sense of mission that have been the defining characteristics of Jewish life? If by "Jewish state" you mean a place where lots of Jews live, then I'm in favor of there being such a state only if Jews can and are willing to live and be judged by the same moral standards that we should apply to the rest of the world. So if you tell me that that's not possible, then I suggest that if you were right (which you're not), then it would be premature to have a Jewish state. And if you tell me that for security reasons the Jews need such a state, but it won't be a state that can live according to the higher moral standards required by Torah, then I say let there be such a state, and let it be secure, because the Jewish people have suffered too much in history up till now to make their security depend on their morality. But please, please, please, don't call it a Jewish state. Call it a state of many Jews, but don't allow Judaism to be identified with that state. And certainly don't argue that Jews have no right to critique that state.

In short, the great danger to Judaism is its collapse into being a cheerleader for an existing reality. Judaism's contribution is precisely in its ability to provide a standard of criticism for existing reality, including, and particularly, Jewish reality. That is what it did traditionally. I sympathize with those who say that our people have been so traumatized by the Holocaust that it may take some time for us to be ready to return to the norms of Torah. That compassionate attitude has some resonance. But that is a world of difference from saying, as Settler

Judaism and many other contemporary forms of right-wing Jewish thought are doing, that Judaism's norms must be shifted to accord with the realities of the current State of Israel.

In fact, to reduce Judaism to a spiritual service station to a Jewish state is to reduce it to idolatry. Israeli philosopher Yishayahu Leibowitz may exaggerate when he refers to this as a form of fascism, but his reminder to think of any national flag as nothing more than "a *shmate* [rag] on a stick" should be a useful corrective to those who wax eloquent about the religious meaning of nationalism. The fundamental belief in Judaism is that the world can be transformed from that which is to that which ought to be. Over and over again the Torah insists that Jews have *no* claim to the land of Israel if they don't live according to God's moral law. Jews will be exiled and the land will literally vomit them out if through immorality they pollute the land. What the Jewish people actually do or think they need to do for national survival can never be equated to what God wants, because God's requirements are never reducible to a sanctification of the actual. Every attempt to reduce the tension between Judaism's utopian vision and an existing reality by changing Judaism is a betrayal of the God of the Bible and an emptying of the Shma of all its significance.

Unfortunately, many of the Judaisms that have emerged today do not proclaim, "Hear, O Israel, the Force that makes possible transformation is also the Force that created and sustains the world, and that Force permeates all Being and makes for a fundamental unity in the universe," but rather "Hear, O Israel, the God of the Jews doesn't have power to change the world anymore, so whatever seems good for the Jews in the short run is what we will now call God's will."

This abandonment of hope in God is based on an interpretation of the Holocaust. God didn't act on our behalf, say some Jewish religious thinkers, so God is in no position to make prophetic demands on us anymore. Or, in a more polite way, they say that God has given us the responsibility to interpret the law, and this has given us a new sense of dignity and adequacy so that we no longer have to respond to the old commands. On first hearing it sounds progressive and empowering, yet this notion of giving human beings a sense of adequacy and dignity can have a very reactionary meaning if it frees us from all transcendent responsibility to transform the world and allows a democratic community of Israel to decide that it no longer needs to live in accord with the moral vision of Torah.

In the last chapter I talked about a need to change our conception of God to one in which we can still hear God's command to heal and repair the world, still believe that the world has been constructed in a way that will allow for the *possibility* of the triumph of good should human beings make the appropriate choices as ongoingly revealed to us by Torah as we grow to understand it, and yet understand that this God is not the kind of heavenly father sitting and watching who could have intervened but chose not to do so. On such a construction, God did not abandon us. We as the human race failed to transcend the long history of negativity and cruelty that traps so many of us and leads us to act out in destructive and hurtful ways against other people. The lesson of the Holocaust is not that everything is permitted, but that the healing of the world is desperately necessary, and that we ought to change our lives to give that focus a much higher priority in the way we spend our time and resources. God's revelation to us through the Torah tradition, far from being irrelevant or outdated, is all the more relevant and necessary.

But what many religious Jews have been feeling is that "reality" (read, the Nazis) has taught us that Torah ethics are "impractical." In my view, history taught us the opposite—that the Torah ethics are all the more necessary, and that there is the greatest urgency for us to discover the political, economic, and social strategies that will make it possible for us to implement Torah ethics and to heal, repair, and transform the world. Yet those who justify an excessive reliance on force on the grounds that "this is the way of the world," though they may be living up to one aspect of the Zionist dream to make the Jews "a nation like all other nations," are actually undermining the central reason for Jews to remain Jews, namely their loyalty to the task of bringing the distinctively Jewish message to the world. And the reason that they are willing to compromise this task is because these religious Jews do not really believe in God anymore, or at least not the God of the Torah that I've tried to explicate here.

It is easy to understand this response. The Holocaust was too traumatic for them to continue to hold on to the way of viewing reality that emerged from Torah and was articulated by the Prophets. The reason why it may not be so obvious that these religious Jews are moving away from God is that a similar though less drastic move was taken by Rabbinic Judaism after the destruction of the Temple, the defeat of Bar Kochba's rebellion, and the acceptance of an almost permanent exile status by Jews. The rabbis were disillusioned with God, too, and the

Judaism that they fostered made far more compromises with existing reality than Torah had ever envisioned. Yet these rabbis of the talmudic era also retained a utopian and transformative dimension to their thought, embodied both in their interpretations of the Torah and in some of the ways that they developed Jewish ritual and moral law. What they did was to create a second stage in Jewish consciousness, a retreat from the optimism and hopefulness of the Prophets.

Today we live in a third stage, in which all hope for transformation has disappeared among some sectors of the religious community. These religious "realists" would be more honest if they simply admit that they no longer believe in the transformative possibilities of the God of the universe, and then either accept the god of some other religion or acknowledge that they are ritually observant atheists. But because they are attached to other aspects of the religious community, they have managed to construct a Judaism that no longer testifies to the possibility of possibility, but instead learns its lessons from the way the world actually operates. And in so doing, they've created a version of Judaism that worships the idol of state power, that is unable to criticize the actual beliefs and behaviors of the Jewish people, that turns the I.D.F. into God's prophet, that allows the moral standards of the Jewish people to be set by angry and vindictive men, and that as a result has little moral or spiritual attraction for those Jews who are spiritually and morally awake. This is Settler Judaism.

It is not that I wish to condemn these people as human beings, but that I want them to stop calling their accommodations to reality "Judaism." But since Judaism can be in every age only what the Jewish people decide it is, I have no right to make the demand on them but can only contend among Jews for a different vision of what Judaism is, and that's what this book is meant to do by proposing a return to the founding principles of Judaism through the process that I'm describing as Jewish renewal and incorporating and building upon those teachers, texts, and rituals that have tried to do this same thing over the course of the past thirty-five hundred years. Indeed, the Jewish texts and traditions may well be viewed as a record of the ongoing struggle between those who thought it possible to remain true to the transformational and revolutionary (*tikkun*) consciousness and kept remaking Judaism in light of that understanding, and those who thought that holding on to that vision was too utopian and who kept remaking Judaism in light of *that* understanding.

But from my standpoint, the *tikkun* consciousness requires that Judaism be an independent and critical voice that holds the State of Israel to the highest moral and spiritual requirements. It is precisely because I take seriously the mission of the Jewish people that I ask, What are the preconditions for the possibility of the Jewish people really becoming the light unto the nations? And the first part of the answer is, the Jewish people need to heal and repair themselves.

Still, that healing and repair cannot be done without larger world transformation. I've learned enough about the failure of the Stalinist fantasy of "socialism in one country" or of "socialism in one *kibbutz*" to understand that no healing and transformation on the micro level is possible without a healing on the macro level. The formation of a world economic and information marketplace makes it inconceivable that any one place is going to become a vanguard of healing and repair while the rest of the world wallows in moral, spiritual, and economic backwardness. The general level of pain will ultimately affect us all. The conclusion, of course, is not that we fall to the lowest level, but that we understand our task of healing as twofold: both to heal ourselves and simultaneously to be connected and concerned with healing others.

And this is not some utopian moral concern, but a very practical survival concern. Israel is not going to survive in a world that is driven crazy by hunger, ecological devastation, and systematic deprivation of its sense of meaning and purpose. It is utopian to imagine the fate of the Jewish people as somehow independent of the fate of the rest of the world. In this sense, Zionists who thought they could build a special solution to the Jewish problem were mistaken, not only because they turned their backs on the fate of millions of Jews who would perish in Hitler's genocide, but because the fate of the Jews of the entire world is inextricably linked to the fate of that world.

Israelis may fantasize that they have achieved independence and, mimicking the self-delusions of the fans of the international capitalist market, think of themselves as self-made and autonomous. But the economies and consciousness of the entire world are ever more interdependent and interlinked, and Israel's survival, like the rest of ours, depends on the health of the totality. When one understands this fully, one understands how misguided are those who have attacked Jews who worry about the fate of the rest of the world without worrying enough about the fate of Israel. There is no such separation—and we would be wiser to think of ourselves as needing a division of communal labor, in which some dedicate themselves to improving the well-being of Israel (a first step of which is combatting Settler Judaism and building the peace process), while some others work to improve the well-being of the rest of the world, knowing full well that doing that can only help the Jewish people. Instead of those world healers being pushed away, they should be proudly embraced as contemporary variants of how to live a Torah-serious life.

Similarly, if God's voice is being heard anywhere in Israel today, it may be precisely through those prophetic voices, more often secular than not, that talk about the possibility of reconciliation. It is these people who bear witness to the possibility of possibility, who insist that transformation and healing are really possible, who insist on recognizing the spirit of God even within the community of people who are officially construed as "the enemy," and who are open to finding ways in which we can live together in peace. Though pained by the continuing violence, by the rise of Islamic fundamentalism, by the chaos and confusion among those Palestinians who are attempting to run their new society, and by the various ways in which Palestinians have been inadequately sensitive to legitimate Jewish needs and Jewish pain, many of those in the Israeli peace camp are able to see how the distortions in the Palestinian world were produced and how they might be transformed.

It is these Israeli peace activists who are aware that what is is not all that could be, and though their secular language fails to testify to the Force that makes transformation possible, their substantive belief in that possibility puts them far closer to the essence of Judaism than those ostensibly religious people who are constantly preaching "realism" precisely because they don't believe that anything can be different.

Just as Rabbi Avraham Kook once saw secular Zionists as unconsciously serving God's will in opposition to the orthodoxy of his day that opposed Zionism, so today we might imagine that it is these peace activists and those who work daily in small acts of Palestinian-Israeli reconciliation and trust enhancement who are bringing God's energy back to Zion, bringing to fruition the hopes expressed in the daily prayer book: "May our eyes behold Your [God's] return to Zion in mercy." Up till now, we saw a return to Zion, but it is the peacemakers who are making possible a Zionism in which God's *merciful* presence returns to Jerusalem.

An Ethos of Kindness, Gentleness, and Sweetness

Those who hope to redeem religion in Israel will be engaged, in the years ahead, in trying to build a climate in which God's merciful presence is welcomed. It is time to put on a back burner our attention to the God who calls for the destruction of other people, the God whom Israelites cheered when the Egyptians were drowning, the God who is worried more about the sanctity of the land of Israel than about the moral quality of the lives of its inhabitants, the God whom we turned to when we were so hurt that we felt empowered when we envisioned this God as taking vengeance and ordering us to do the same. Not that we should deny that such a God played a role in psychologically saving us when we were weak, but that we are ready to move to a different way of thinking about God, returning to the God of love, kindness, and healing. Thinking about how to build a Jewish state that can embody and manifest *that* God is the strategic thinking necessary for the next stage in Jewish history. Let that be the main task of the Third Jewish Commonwealth.

It will not be easy. Jews have been pushed around a lot, so many Israelis think that toughness is simply contemporary realism. One of the most common phrases in daily parlance in Israel in the 1980s and nineties has been an expression that warns against "being a friar." A friar is someone who is moral without regard to the fact that the world is full of frightening and destructive people. It's an understandable worry for anyone who lives in the Middle East, because there are Islamic leaders (e.g., in Iraq or Iran) who really *do* have ambitions to endanger Israel's security (which is one reason why I believe that Israel must retain a strong and well-equipped military that is not weakened by the need to impose unjust policies on an occupied Palestinian population). Yet this fascination with strength and danger has had a distorting effect on daily life in Israel, which sometimes takes on a harsh and aggressive feel as people on the street sometimes treat one another as potential adversaries. All too often, Israelis feel that they have to protect themselves against one another, and that frequently influences how people treat one another. Thus the continued legacy of the hurt that has been inflicted on us by others and how it sometimes gets internalized and transferred onto those about whom we care the most.

Israeli society needs a deep healing that goes far beyond the specifics of the struggle with the Palestinians. The whole legacy of Jewish history lies heavily on the collective unconscious of Israelis. The rage that Jewish men have felt at being unable to defend themselves or their families against rape and genocide sometimes leads Israeli men to feel the need to prove their "manliness" and to show that they are not weak or "feminine" (which sometimes equates in their mind with taking love, caring, gentleness, or psychological sensitivity "too" seriously). The fear of trusting others, of being seen as weak, of suspecting that one will be betrayed unless one has one's guard up—these are the legitimate fears based on our own history. But they must be healed, because as they function at the present moment they make it difficult for Israelis to see where their real interests actually lie, what the real threats to it are, and they also make daily life in Israel less a place in which God's mercy and kindness can be felt. So Jewish renewal has as one of its goals to encourage the forces that will make such a healing possible in Israel.

Tens of thousands of Israelis in every walk of life will be involved in creating the mechanisms to make this renewal possible. Some will be schoolteachers, who will take the risk of presenting to Israeli children the details of how Palestinians were pressured to leave between 1947 and 1949 and what Palestinian life under occupation was like and how it bred terrorism and led some people to so despair of meaningful life in this world that they were attracted to fundamentalist views of salvation in another. Others will be journalists, writers, film producers, television writers and actors, and even political leaders, who will dare to challenge the dominant attitude that one must be "tough," and instead will model a way to be *both* strong *and* vulnerable, how to be realistic and idealistic.

Still others will be psychotherapists, who will develop groups and mass educational campaigns designed to create safety so that Jewish rage can be worked through.

Tens of thousands of Israelis will spend sabbaticals in the United States and other Western countries, and in the process learn what is good about living with others and becoming sensitive to their needs, just as tens of thousands of Westerners will spend a year in Israel, learning from the strengths of that society.

Israeli businessmen, trying to integrate Israel into a world economy, will find that it is in their economic interests to foster the development of more gentle qualities in the Israeli personality, so that Israelis can be more effective in their interactions with others.

A new generation of religious leaders, trying to save Judaism from the moral disrepute brought upon it by the generation that allied it with Settler Judaism and racist attitudes, will eventually turn to the very Jewish-renewal ideas that will likely be dismissed initially in Israel as too American, too flakey, or too naive.

Finally, a powerful women's movement will emerge and begin to reshape ways that people interact, adding a dimension of sensitivity, caring, and gentleness that has long been ridiculed in Israeli society. Some of these women will create a nonsexist version of Judaism that will open the doors to Jewish-renewal consciousness.

These are some of the things that may happen that could make Jewish renewal a reality for the Israel of the twenty-first century.

The Practice of Post-Zionism

Post-Zionists are Jews who fervently support the State of Israel, believe that its welfare and military security must be ensured, but who wish to see an Israel based on tolerance; an honoring of the multicultural realities of the people living within its borders; peaceful coexistence with a Palestinian state; an end to all religious coercion; separation of religion from state power; and a societal commitment to fostering ethical, spiritual, and ecological sensitivity.

Post-Zionists hope that Israel will develop into a Jewish country, but see the Jewishness of the state as measured by the degree to which it becomes an embodiment of the highest moral and spiritual ideals of the Jewish people. By its acts of generosity and kindness, by its ability to transcend the legacy of anger and pain that afflict all people, by the beauty of its music and art, by the joy of its people in celebrating the grandeur of the universe, by the degree to which its citizens become volunteers in assisting others around the world to create their own self-help projects and liberation movements and ecological sanity, by the self-evidence of its ability to be the place from which Torah emanates to the world, by the degree to which spiritually sensitive people of all religions are drawn to study and learn from this Judaism, and by its commitment to actively support all those engaged in the struggle to heal and repair the world—these are the ways that Israel shall be known as a Jewish country, instead of merely a country with a majority of Jews.

No one will excuse Israeli behavior or the claim "you can't understand it without living there," because people will be so drawn to Israelis and the kinds of lives they are living that many people will want to be there, and the world will demand that Israelis teach them how they reached this spiritually high place.

For any of this to come to pass, Israel must radically undo itself as a religious state. Nothing has done greater harm to Judaism or ensured Israeli hostility to Judaism than the power of religious parties—to exempt their students from military service and to impose religious laws governing marriage, divorce, *kashrut*, or Shabbat observance. Post-Zionists seek a secularization of the State of Israel so that Judaism might have a chance inside the Country of Israel.

But this does not mean that Israel should no longer be a Jewish state. Michael Walzer has argued that while a Jewish state cannot enforce a singular and uniform Jewishness, it can "express in public places and on public occasions—in its official calendar, its evocative symbols, its formal ceremonies, its historical celebrations, its school curriculum—a version of Jewishness common or potentially common to all the varieties of Jews."[16] But post-Zionists would want to be sure that all of the other religious and cultural traditions of the peoples living in Israel were also taught in the schools, recognized on the public calendar, and given honor in public discourse.

Israel should remain a Jewish state in one other important respect: it should be allowed to give special attention to the rescuing of Jews from persecution, and to special immigration rights for Jews. Israel must be understood in this respect as world-scale affirmative action for an oppressed people. I believe that the Law of Return should be phased out, but only seventy-five years after the last time anyone sees any visible sign of anti-Semitism in the world. Once anti-Semitism is gone, the special need for affirmative action for Jews in one particular country will be gone, and when seventy-five years have elapsed and we have some degree of confidence that it is not still simmering in the unconscious of some group, then the State of Israel need no longer privilege Jews. By similar logic, post-Zionists will also support affirmative action for Palestinians in a new Palestinian state, and will support the right of

---

[16]Michael Walzer, "What Kind of a State Is a Jewish State?" *Tikkun* 4, no. 4 (July/Aug. 1989).

that state *not* to give equal priority to the claims of Jews who may seek immigration or housing on the West Bank.

Inevitably, there will be a struggle between two kinds of post-Zionism. I have described earlier in this book the process by which people become disillusioned with communities of meaning and purpose that are eventually revealed to be smokescreens for particular selfish interests—and in their despair, become devotees of the capitalist market and its enshrining of the principle of materialist self-interest. There will be an Israeli version of this in a post-Zionism that urges Israelis to reject all ideologies and to put all their energies into building a high-tech society capable of playing a central role in the world's economy. As Israelis become more familiar with Palestinians, more repulsed at their own society's willingness to demonize them, some will be attracted to a new "anti-ideology" ideology whose elitist cynicism will feel like cosmopolitan sophistication. Judaism will have been blamed for the mistaken policies of the past, so many will be resistant to any new religious or political worldview, no matter how ethically sensitive or healing it might be.

There will be a competing post-Zionism, based in Jewish renewal, that will embrace the redemptive and liberatory aspects of Judaism, reject its racist and repressive aspects, and articulate a critique of the emerging world capitalist order, challenging the assumption of some Israelis that "making it" in the world economy will provide ultimate fulfillment or an adequate substitute for a community based on ethical and spiritual sensitivity.

These Jewish renewal–oriented post-Zionists will see and support the possibility of Israel becoming an embodiment of some of the best elements of the Jewish tradition, and in this sense becoming "the beginning of the flourishing of our redemption" (*reysheet tzmichat ge'ulateynu*).

At the same time, post-Zionists honor and support the efforts to build Jewish life in the Diaspora, seeing the Judaism that may emerge from Diaspora as equally important and valuable for the future of the Jewish people and for service to God. Post-Zionists hope that there will be a mutual exchange of spiritual, ethical, and psychological wisdom between Israel and the Diaspora; mutual respect; and healthy competition as both communities seek to become the proudest and most successful embodiments of Jewish spirituality and ethics; the most successful in communicating Jewish spirituality and ethics to others;

the most renowned for eliciting joy and wonder at creation; the most generous in their caring for others; the most successful in leading the struggles against the legacy of pain and oppression that in the past have left so many of the peoples of the world vulnerable to anti-Semitism, racism, sexism, and homophobia.

Post-Zionists are those who realize that the safety and security of the Jewish people, and of the State of Israel itself, ultimately depend on a healing of the pains and anger, and a transcendence of the legacy of cruelty. While insisting on Israel's security and strength, post-Zionists will be committed both to the struggle for Jewish self-interest and to the struggle for world healing, *tikkun olam*, not seeing the one as counterposed to the other.

When *tikkun* is allowed to reemerge on the agenda of Israeli society, it will become possible to think of Israel as a Jewish state not only in terms of its demographics but in terms of its substance. At that moment, a Jewish-renewal conception of God will become a major contender for the soul of the Jewish people. To the extent that Israel embodies a vision of transformation and world healing, its light and its message will provide guidance for others, and it will hasten the moment when all people will recognize their brotherhood and sisterhood.

CHAPTER TEN

A POLITICS OF JEWISH RENEWAL

Jewish renewal is part of a worldwide religious and spiritual revival, a product of the failure of secular modernism to shape a world that would satisfy human needs. The transformation of our conceptions of time and space in ways that have tended to make human beings appendages to an economic/political system focused on production and accumulation, power and control, has produced a world rich in things but poor in our human relations and in spirituality. It has generated an instrumental way of looking at the earth, which has produced ecological insensitivity and potential catastrophe. And it has reshaped economic and social arrangements in ways that undermine loyalty, ethical and spiritual awareness, and family ties.

Human beings need to be embedded in communities of meaning that transcend the individualism and self-centeredness of a competitive market society, that provide a framework which enables people to see their work and their family lives and their individual life stories as part of some larger framework of meaning, and that connects them to ethical and spiritual values in which they can believe.

There are huge dangers in this search for meaning. I have already shown how Fascists and other right-wing political and religious movements are able to speak to these needs and manipulate them in extremely destructive directions. Part of the continued appeal of right-wing forces in the United States and other advanced industrial societies is their ability to speak to the meaning needs.

The Left has been unable to speak to meaning because it is locked in an intellectual framework that does not allow it to take seriously ethical, spiritual, and psychological needs. Because the Left has uncritically supported the pseudo-scientific empiricist worldview, it tends to be blind to the hunger for meaning, and unwilling to conceptualize a program for social change that would address the failures of vulgar materialism and ethical relativism.

Even the most spiritually sensitive leftists end up having to divide themselves between a political world in which spiritual concerns are seen as flakey at best and usually suspect as potentially right-wing, and a spiritual world in which their deepest understandings of the world can be validated but in which their passion for social justice is given too little space.

While psychoanalysis is much closer to the meaning needs because it explicitly addresses consciousness, it has nevertheless managed to miss the boat. Psychoanalysis is threatening to the larger world precisely because of the revolutionary nature of its demand to understand how our current perceptions of the world have been shaped by what has happened to us as we grew up in a world of distorted relationships. To protect themselves from being seen as too radical, psychoanalysts have tried to prove that what they are doing is scientific and hence objectively justified, rather than assimilating it to the essentially Jewish, *tikkun*ish, healing and repair of the world paradigm. Psychoanalytic theory developed within an empiricist epistemology that validated self-interest or, in later formulations, a need for mutual recognition, but could not validate any spiritual or ethical needs as essential to human reality, except insofar as they are projections or deflections of more "basic" needs for ego-satisfying love. There have been very few psychoanalysts who have been able to see our need for a spiritually and morally significant universe as equally basic to human life as our need for love. For that reason, though I believe psychoanalytic thought to be indispensable as a vehicle in the process of human liberation, it ultimately falls short in its attempts to address the crisis facing the contemporary world, a crisis rooted in the deprivation of meaning engendered by the despiritualization and disenchantment of the universe attendant upon the rise of a competitive, individualist, market society.

There are important truths in both democratic socialist thought and in psychoanalysis that can play a role in healing the world. But what the world needs is some form of progressive politics of meaning, a progressive form of spirituality. Judaism provides a model that can be learned and replicated by others.

Judaism affirms both the deep spiritual truths about the world and our fundamental human need to be in tune with that spiritual world. Yet at the same time, its particular approach to spirituality understands God as the Force that makes for the possibility of transformation and that pulls us toward healing, repairing, and transforming the world in accord with a vision of social justice and love that is at sharp variance with the realities of the contemporary capitalist world, or with any other system of oppression.

So this Jewish-renewal version of Judaism offers an answer to the world's most pressing problem: how to satisfy the meaning needs without abandoning the economic justice and human rights–affirming aspects of the Left.

There are two possible roads we could take to implement this solution. One would be to develop a social-change movement that takes the central elements of Judaism and sufficiently separates them from the specific history and cultural tradition of the Jewish people so that the rest of the peoples of the world may become equal partners in shaping it. A second would be to attempt to convert people to Judaism. Let's consider each.

A JEWISHLY INSPIRED MOVEMENT FOR A POLITICS OF MEANING

There have been other attempts to separate Judaism from the history and culture of the Jewish tradition in order to make its insights accessible to people from different histories and cultural backgrounds. Among the most successful have been Christianity, Islam, Marxism, and psychoanalysis. In each case, important truths that could be found within Judaism were amplified, stripped of the limiting frameworks within which they had originally appeared, and presented to populations who badly needed these truths. Yet in each case, significant aspects of Judaism were underplayed or rejected, which limited the success of these mass outreach efforts. Early Christian evangelists may have brought the Ten Commandments and the Torah notion of "love your neighbor" to an audience that might have been reluctant to accept the ritual demands of Judaism, but in the process they may also have compromised excessively with a conception of God that abandons the revolutionary this-worldly aspect of Judaism and postpones salvation to a future world. Marxism caught the this-worldly, revolutionary dimension, understood Judaism's insistence that the present ought not to be dominated by the past, but abandoned the subjective, the spiritual, and the awe, wonder, and radical amazement that are necessary components of a transformative practice. Psychoanalysis also eschewed awe and radical amazement, and while it captured the subjective dimension and understood the need to free oneself from the repetition compulsion, it could not understand the necessarily interconnected nature of psychological and social liberation.

A Jewishly inspired politics of meaning would have the following characteristics:

1. It would explicitly help people understand the connection between the decline of meaning, spirituality, ethical sensitivity, and community on the one hand, and the rise of an individualistic, self-centered, materialistic, capitalistic worldview on the other. It would expose those who use the hunger for meaning as a method to advance new systems of inequality, privilege, or power for the few.

2. It would reject attempts to recapture meaning through the revival of feudal, patriarchal, sexist, homophobic, or otherwise repressive communities.

3. It would integrate the best aspects of democratic and liberal societies, including their insistence on a private sphere that should not be subject to political intrusion or political control. It would resist the tendencies toward "political correctness" or other forms of group totalitarianism in which the standards and moral insights of the community are forced upon the individual in every area of life.

4. It would campaign against the self-blaming that leads so many people to feel bad about themselves and aspects of their work and individual lives that are *not* their fault, but it would simultaneously resist the tendencies of political opportunists to obviate people of any area of responsibility for themselves.

5. It would recognize the complexities of human history and

psychology—the ways in which we are all embedded in complex webs of social relationships that make us both perpetrators of oppression and victims of it. It would avoid the
victimology of the Left and also the refusal to understand
oppression that characterizes some religious and right-wing
communities.

6. It would insist on the priority of eliminating poverty, homelessness, hunger, ecological threats, and inadequate health
care, shelter, education, physical security—for all the peoples
of the world. It would struggle against any tendency to privilege one group of people as having more of a right to these
than any other. At the same time, it would insist that politics
must also be engaged in *meaningful work* (work that serves a
higher moral purpose that has been democratically decided)
and *less alienating work* (working conditions shaped by the
workers themselves, and management democratically elected
by the workers). It would seek economic, political, and social
structures that reward caring and cooperation, and moral,
spiritual, and ecological sensitivity—replacing a world that
rewards selfishness and helps generate narcissism.

It would reject all attempts to claim that material needs are
more important than spiritual or ethical needs. It would es-
chew the tendency of leftists to think that people who are
relatively economically more secure are privileged and thus
are the oppressors, and instead recognize that any system that
sets people against one another and makes it difficult to
sustain loving relationships is oppressive to virtually everyone,
and that there are no real victors.

7. It would construct itself as a movement that seeks to embody
its values. It would create democratic processes that ensure
real participation, but simultaneously combat the tendency of
the weak to act out against their own leaders as surrogates for
acting against the really powerful. It would seek to nurture
and support people who take leadership or initiative—and to
resist the self-devouring and self-negating tendencies of the
powerless. To do this, it would create support groups for its
members apart from their explicitly political activities, so that
people would understand that part of their commitment to
larger change involves active participation in caring for one

another. And it would create a rich array of rituals, celebrations, and spiritual retreats aimed at focusing attention not only on the realm of politics, but on the shared sense of awe, wonder, and radical amazement. It would use Shabbat, Passover, and other Jewish religious holidays as models for developing a set of secular celebrations and ritual observances that would become a regular part of the social movement. But it would not seek to replace religion. Rather it would seek to bring religious traditions together in dialogue, to learn from all of them, and to selectively adopt ritual activities from each that seem to bind together a more universal movement. Unlike so many progressive movements in the past, which have made people feel uncomfortable with their particular religious or spiritual traditions, a movement for a politics of meaning would validate these other allegiances even as it attempts to supplement them.

8. It would see mutual recognition, love, and spiritual sensitivity as the highest goals of life, and would seek to ensure that the very movement that fought for these transformations in the larger world would achieve these in their own practice. But, learning from the experience of the Jewish people, it would reject utopian criteria for how much individuals or the social movement could be expected to fully embody the values it holds.

9. One of the most important insights of Jewish history: the vanguard will not fully embody its ideals; it will get scared, will run away from its own words. Because it will recognize that leaders, social-change activists, movement participants, are likely to be deeply flawed, this movement will reject the self-destructive dynamic in which we project onto our leaders utopian expectations and then are shocked and disillusioned when we find that they aren't really a different breed of humanity from the rest of us, that they too have selfish motives, ego needs, and at times are petty, self-aggrandizing, insensitive to others, or in other ways flawed. The vanguard will always be *wounded healers*, people who are inadequate— and the appropriate response to this inadequacy is a healthy measure of compassion, mixed with a healthy measure of pushing forward to achieve the ideals. This dialectic between

the God of compassion and the God of transcendence, central to understanding Jewish history and Torah, is also central to any successful social-change movement.

But it's not *just* leaders or the vanguard who deserve compassion. One of the central goals of this movement would be to teach people how to develop compassion for themselves and one another, and understand their own personal lives in the context of the social forces that shaped their options. Just as the women's movement helped millions of women understand that much of what was going wrong for them was based not on individual failings but on a sexist world, so a politics of meaning would help everyone to understand the ways in which their personal lives have been shaped by the society-wide selfishness and narcissism that undermines families and relationships and subverts communities. People who wish to be activists for meaning-oriented social change will have to begin by accepting themselves and their own families and cultural traditions and approaching others in a compassionate way. They, too, will have to work through their own childhoods and come to accept their parents not as evil people but as people who were doing their best, faced with an overwhelmingly distorted social and psychological inheritance.

In general, the movement would learn from the dialectic of transcendence and compassion, which is the central lesson of Judaism, and hence recognize that people in the politics-of-meaning movement will always be less than their ideals, and should be credited for their aspirations and not just scolded for their inadequacies.

10. It would *not* present itself as a Jewish movement. It would be open to all, it would not privilege Judaism or Jews, and it would attempt to formulate the insights it has learned from Judaism in a language that is accessible to people from very different ethnic or religious traditions.

A JEWISH ROLE IN THE POLITICS OF MEANING

Though a politics of meaning derives many insights from Judaism, Jewish activists may be one of the groups most resistant to it, since it would require them to forgive their own parents, their own people, and come to a compassionate grappling with their own Judaism. This remains a major stumbling block for many liberal and progressive Jews.

I've learned in my work as a psychotherapist that many Jews who have become activists in social change are not yet willing to see their parents, their families, or the Jewish community as another set of flawed victims of oppression, and hence to forgive them for the ways that they failed to be all that they should be. Precisely because Jews have articulated some of the highest and most wonderful values, precisely because our families and our communities have been able to understand more about the world than many others, we have often been disproportionately critical of them when they failed to embody their own ideals. The hypocrisy, the conformism, the sexism, the materialism, the self-interest, the self-aggrandizement, the chauvinism of the Jewish world have often been harder to forgive because these are people who *should* know better.

But that kind of judgmentalism must be abandoned once you consider the historical explanations I've presented for why the Jewish people have had such a hard time living up to our own knowledge, staying true to the revelation of Sinai and to the lessons of our own history. After millennia of genocidal violence directed at us, the Jewish people need to be celebrated and honored for the extraordinary degree to which we *have* held on to truths that we learned.

Any and every people can be critiqued. Our task is to generate not a blind acceptance of flawed realities, but an acceptance based on a renewal of the liberatory and transcendent aspects of a cultural, religious, or national tradition, and based also on a compassionate re-reading of the historical options facing people under conditions of material and spiritual deprivation. It is only from this compassionate attitude that we have any hope of transforming the world. Jews who cannot develop this compassion for their own tradition and their own people cannot heal the world.

JUDAISM HAS SOMETHING TO OFFER THE WORLD

The politics of meaning is intentionally articulated in a secular language that does *not* require one to be Jewish or to accept a particularly Jewish slant on "meaning." Yet the fundamental notion—that the world can be transformed from its current focus on selfishness to a focus on caring, and that to do so we would have to see ourselves as sharing a commitment to a set of ethical and spiritual values that transcend the narcissism and power dynamics of the contemporary world—draws upon the dual legacy of transcendence and compassion that emerges from Judaism.

There is more to Judaism than a secularized, progressive politics of meaning can offer. Judaism offers a rich tradition of attempting to embody a politics of meaning through thirty-five hundred years, and a unique approach to the fusion of spirituality and politics from which its rituals, its stories, its perception of human reality have flowed. As a living religious tradition, Judaism's attempts to hear God's voice in the modern world will continue to yield new insights from which the world could benefit.

There is nothing intrinsically particularistic about Judaism other than its historical legacy. But that legacy must be learned by every single child born into a Jewish family—it is not given by genes, skin color, or any physically intrinsic characteristic of a Jew. Anyone could potentially decide to adopt that history as *their* history, much as converts to the Left, to psychoanalysis, and to feminism have adopted the history of their movements. When the Jewish people left Egypt, Torah tells us, they left with "a mixed multitude." The message of liberation had spread to many people who could not claim to be descendants of the twelve tribes, but who wished to become part of the venture. Judaism remains open to people who wish to join that venture even today.

So another way to get people to become part of a politics of meaning is for them to join the Jewish people, get involved in Jewish renewal, and become part of one of the longest-lasting and most successful communities of meaning in human history.

JEWS SHOULD SEEK CONVERTS

If you have something good, why not share it?

The almost universal fear among Jews about seeking converts is based on a long history of oppression in which we were forced *not* to seek converts. In many parts of the world throughout much of the past two thousand years, it was illegal for Jews to encourage conversion. In some instances, the entire Jewish community was expelled from a city as punishment for one conversion. Even when it wasn't officially illegal,

Jews often understood that the likelihood of anti-Semitism moving from passive to active was intensified by the degree to which Jewish ideas seemed to be spreading and threatening ruling elites. Even the "spin-off" Jewish ideas like communism or psychoanalysis were likely to get the Jews in trouble.

This fear was not as operative in Biblical or early rabbinic literature. So the Talmud declares, "The Holy One, Blessed be He, exiled Israel among the nations in order to increase their numbers with the additions of converts" (Pesachim 87b). Or, as Resh Lakish tells us, "The convert is dearer than the Jews who stood before Mount Sinai. Because had they [the Jews] not seen the thunder and the lightning and the mountains quaking and the sounds of the horn, they would not have accepted the Torah. But this one, who saw none of these things, came, surrendered himself to the Holy One, and accepted upon himself the kingdom of heaven" (Tanchuma B; Lech Lecha 6). Leviticus Rabbah tells us that "when a person comes to be converted, one receives him with an open hand so as to bring him under the wings of the Divine Presence." The Halakha even accepts those who were converted "in order to marry, to advance themselves, or out of fear." And Maimonides later argued that toward father and mother we are commanded honor and reverence; toward Prophets to obey them, but toward converts we are commanded to have great love in our inmost hearts.

In my own experience, many converts often bring wonderfully creative energy into the Jewish world. They ask piercing questions that haven't occurred to Jews to ask, they are committed to the centrality of Judaism in their lives in ways that many born-Jews aren't, and they often have spiritual insights that can enrich the Jewish experience.

The greatest difficulty many converts have is that of joining a people. Many converts can get the idea of being part of a religion, understood as a systematic sharing of specific beliefs, but it is much harder to join a community whose shared history is central to its current identity. It is precisely here, in learning how to identify with and have compassion for the Jewish people, that the greatest challenge lies for those who would be converts.

It's easy to see what's exciting about Jewish ideas, but much harder to face the ways that the Jewish people don't always live up to or embody those ideals, and are seen to be people like everyone else. So converts can become disillusioned with Judaism and with Jews once they find out that we are just as screwed up as others; or converts can become chauvinistic, insisting that Jews are so much better than everyone else, supporting expansionist policies for Israel, acting out their own anger at their parents and their past by becoming *goyim*-bashers. Yet if converts can develop that sense of compassion for the Jewish people without becoming chauvinistically Jewish or identifying with right-wing conceptions that see no wrong with what Jews have done or currently do, then they will have taken the first step toward embodying an ethos of caring that can have importance for the entire world.

Resistance to converts in the Jewish world is usually inversely proportional to the degree of religious practice of the resisters. The most involved in religious practice welcome converts, usually quite warmly. To those Jews who are most conflicted about religious practice and base their Jewishness on a vague ethnicity, shared memories of childhood, and matters of style rather than substance, a convert represents a threat to the authenticity of one's Jewish identity, because the convert hasn't had that kind of childhood and probably hasn't shared the ethnic characteristics. So we hear frequent stories of nonobservant Jewish parents objecting when a child decides to marry a non-Jew.

Resistance to intermarriage by Jews who do not sustain the tradition may sometimes border on racism. If one doesn't observe Judaism and hasn't raised one's children to do so, there can be little grounds to worry about the religious affiliations of the grandchildren. Remember, it is not intermarriage that I am advocating, but conversion. Judaism has a rich and wonderful set of insights and treasures to offer the world, and those who wish to join with us and share the risks of testifying to the possibility of healing and transformation, using our cultural and religious apparatus to do so, should be enthusiastically embraced.

In the process, it is important to treat the non-Jew as a human being worthy of respect, rather than as a sinner who has repented evil deeds and now found the truth. Non-Jews should not be asked to repudiate who they are as human beings, or to deny the importance of their parents and their own cultural traditions, in order to become Jews. Parents who produced this person who now wants to identify with the Jewish people almost certainly have some wonderful things about them that ought to be honored and cherished.

In some communities there has been a tendency not to talk about a convert's previous life as a non-Jew, or to assume that converts must necessarily be ashamed that they weren't always Jews. This sensibility needs to be challenged. Rather, we should publicly honor the convert for converting. Some Jewish-renewal communities have begun to do this by organizing a ceremony to welcome the convert into the community. After the convert completes the *mikveh* immersion and dresses, s/he goes to a place in which the community forms a circle into which s/he is welcomed. Each person in the circle addresses the convert by her/his new Jewish name, offers words of welcome, and then the community says a prayer and joins in song and celebration of the happy event.

To seek converts does not mean to imitate the coercive or manipulative techniques of television evangelists or street-corner salesmen of religious ideologies—there need be nothing cheap or demeaning in the content or style of what we put forward.

Seeking converts is a huge psychological revolution for Jews. It assumes that we are safe enough not to get persecuted for doing this—a huge leap for a people that has been so persecuted for so long. It assumes that we need not continue a defensive elitism in which, to protect ourselves from the psychological degradation used by so many cultures that sought to demean us, we imagined our Judaism to be something so high that a non-Jew simply couldn't be expected to understand or respond to it—and hence could be seeking entry into our people only for some less noble motive (e.g., to marry or to get some kind of economic advantage).

Intermarriage is far less desirable, in my estimation. There are some instances in which it can be a creative mix of two cultures, and the tensions can produce individual growth and an exciting exchange of ideas and perspectives—in the rare cases when both people are really strong advocates of their own religious traditions, solidly knowledgeable about them, and not neurotically attached to them. But in all too many cases the people seeking intermarriage know only very little about their own religions, have deeply ambiguous feelings about them, and pretend that the differences between themselves and their spouses won't really matter. This is particularly unrealistic in cases where there will be children. The notion that children will be enriched by having two traditions to choose from has rarely worked out in practice. I've led group discussions involving children of intermarriage, and most of the stories I've heard have been of parents who foisted on children choices for which they were not ready, of confusing double messages about what is really important, and of children who found themselves without any larger culture with which they could feel emotionally solid. It's much fairer to the children to give them one culture, enthusiastically raise them within it, and then let them begin to make choices from the standpoint of that earlier foundation.

Intermarrieds ought to be seen as potential converts. Rather than being treated as betrayers, the intermarried couple that starts to attend synagogue or other Jewish religious observances ought to be enthusiastically welcomed. The degree of warmth, love, and caring that they experience in the Jewish world may not only entice non-Jews, but might begin a process of healing for the Jews involved as well, allowing them to strengthen some of the emotional ties to Judaism that may not have been fostered in childhood. Remember also that to the extent that intermarriage is occasionally a sign that Judaism was not central to the life of the Jewish member of the couple, the fault usually lies within the kind of Judaism he or she was offered, not in some defect of the person.

One caution: Not every intermarriage is a product of a rejection of Judaism. Given the failure of the Jewish community to take seriously the need to help singles meet one another, and given the sometimes neurotic feeling that Jews have toward one another, a particular individual may find herself in circumstances where it really *is* impossible to meet a Jewish partner who shares common values and who is emotionally available for commitment. That person may then have fallen in love with a non-Jew, sought to have him convert, and found resistance to the conversion. Rather than be made to feel that she has done something wrong, such a person should be treated with caring and respect by the Jewish community, her partner welcomed into the Jewish world, and efforts should be made to show that partner what it is that is exciting and nourishing about Judaism. But even if they never convert, the more love and acceptance shown, the better for our Jewish souls.

STOP THE *GOYIM*-BASHING

I don't need to be reminded of the many ways that Jews have been oppressed throughout history by non-Jews. It is totally legitimate for Jews to be angry about this history—and to say so publicly. Moreover, we ought to demand that non-Jews take responsibility for teaching the disgusting history of anti-Semitism. It should be taught in public schools and it should be taught in churches, in mosques, and in other public and religious institutions of any society or religious tradition that has previously oppressed Jews. Jews ought to avoid the obsequiousness that has sometimes led them to shape behavior to please non-Jews. We've had a long history of trying to straighten our hair, shorten our noses, lower our voices, and behave like our image of the proper WASP, so that we wouldn't be noticed or endangered. Jews should stop playing up to non-Jews.

Moreover, it's psychologically healing for Jews to have rituals in which we can publicly express our anger at this history of anti-Semitism, our anger at the non-Jews who went along with it, and our anger at those non-Jews today who do not acknowledge this history or actively work to rectify the consequences of this anti-Semitism in the contemporary world. There is nothing *goyim*-bashing about clear and deep expressions of anger by an oppressed group at the oppressors.

But there's a secret in Jewish life that goes beyond healthy and clear expressions of anger at oppression: that our contempt has been based on our outrage at our persecution and our inability to express that outrage in any straightforward way, and so we developed anti-*goyish* humor, stories, and a generalized attitude that non-Jews are less intelligent, less moral, and less deserving of respect than Jews.

These attitudes have no place within Jewish renewal or any Jewish life. They violate Jewish religious strictures and the fundamental notion that all human beings are created in the image of God. And they lead Jews to act in paranoid and self-defeating ways that sometimes create new antagonism from non-Jews.

Rooting out *goyim*-bashing from Jewish life does not require any compromise of what should be a total intolerance of anti-Semitism or any other form of racism. But fighting anti-Semitism is more likely to be successful if we can adopt strategies that affirm the humanity of non-Jews, that assume that most non-Jews will *not* join anti-Semitic causes, that they can be won to a "philosemitism" if we speak to their deepest meaning needs, and that non-Jews do not have fundamentally different needs or desires than Jews.

One aspect of rejecting *goyim*-bashing is to allow ourselves to be open to the truths and beauty in other people's religious, cultural, and national traditions. If Jews were to immerse themselves in the study of their own religious and cultural heritage, learn the texts and read the literature of the Jewish people, we would have a serious basis for engaging in what could be a richly productive multicultural, inter-religious dialogue. If we were securely grounded in our own tradition, we could allow ourselves to learn from others, even to the extent of adding insights from others to our own tradition. Where this becomes problematic is when those who are engaged in the enterprise really do not have the foundation within their own Jewishness, who engage in intercultural dialogue more to please the other than to share their own tradition, and hence come up with inauthentic insights or, worse, instant conversions to the wisdoms of other traditions without ever having tried the wisdom of Judaism. But when one is solidly grounded in Judaism, then the richness of other traditions need not be threatening or polluting in any sense, but can instead only deepen our understanding of the word of God. If God's word was spoken at Sinai, it may well have been heard in important ways by the many other peoples of the world, and it behooves us to learn how they heard it and whether their hearing can illuminate or clarify ours.

Jewish reconciliation to cultures and groups that were at one point our oppressors can become a model of reconciliation for the rest of the world. Jews are the quintessentially oppressed group of the modern world. Our ability not to allow that history of oppression to define our future may provide a path that others too will follow. In that sense, the positive steps toward reconciliation between Palestinians and Israelis currently being pursued may be a first step in realizing the adage of Torah coming out of Zion. In the twenty-first century the multicultural realities of a shrinking world will become a central defining fact of life. Groups will contend with one another for the status of being "most oppressed" and hence most in need of special treatment. Jews have played this number in relationship to Israel, demanding special treatment and different standards for judging its behavior. If we can move beyond this, we would be a model for others to do the same. Multiculturalism is oppressive when it becomes a zero-sum struggle for recognition. But there is a different model possible, one based on mutual recognition among cultures, a recognition of the ways each culture embodies the spirit of God refracted through the prism of different historical and cultural experiences.

Mutual recognition—the ability to see the other as created in the image of God, deserving of love and respect and caring, embodying in his or her being the very qualities of freedom and creativity and consciousness and holiness that pervade all of the universe—is the continuation of the process begun when Abraham recognized that he should not sacrifice Isaac, that the voice of God was the voice that told him to break the repetition compulsion, come to a higher level of awareness, and wake up from the pain-induced unconsciousness that makes us unable to recognize the God in all human beings.

The solution to the Jewish political problem is ultimately a religious solution: it is to have a world that recognizes God's presence in the world and in other human beings. This is our response to the Holocaust and our answer to the enemies of Israel. Rejecting the logic of pain, rejecting the notion that power or cruelty must necessarily rule the universe, the Jews must continue to proclaim the possibility of a different logic for this world. The mutual recognition that is necessary need not take place under the rubric of religious language, nor be connected with any particular religious or secular or national tradition, nor need Jews receive credit for the insight. What is necessary is only this: that the world be healed, transformed, and repaired in such a way that the cruelty that has been passed from generation to generation— often camouflaging itself as wisdom or finding refuge within the arenas of religion, spirituality, literature, philosophy, sociology, psychology, common sense, or even liberal or progressive politics—is replaced with a new spirit of caring, sensitivity, and aliveness to the grandeur of creation and the absolute necessity to treat one another and the world with compassion and gentleness. Jewish renewal is an attempt to develop that sensibility within the Jewish world, and stands in alliance with similar tendencies, whether officially called religious or not, within other religious and spiritual communities, political parties, aesthetic or literary persuasions. This is the only path to salvation for the Jews, and to believe in God is to believe that this healing and transformation of the world is possible.

Whether it be through a secular politics of meaning derived from Jewish insights or through a full-fledged Judaism blessed with renewal energies, the Jewish people have an important contribution to make to the world—and the world badly needs it.

PART III

GOD HEALING:
JEWISH RENEWAL
IN DAILY LIFE

Throughout this book, I have argued that the distinctive feature of Judaism has been its unique blending of spirituality and a liberatory political vision. To the extent that Jews abandoned the revolutionary vision that this kind of Judaism entailed, they lost the ability to sustain what was most alive within it. For a while, Judaism could coast on the remnants of its message embodied in its traditional practices, or it could mimic elements in the spiritual traditions of surrounding cultures. But ultimately, the Judaism that survived was unable to command the respect and adherence of many Jews. Those who sought spiritual vitality often found themselves attracted to other traditions. Others became disillusioned with all forms of spirituality, assuming that it would necessarily be associated with patriarchal and repressive social realities.

In the previous section we addressed how a Jewish-renewal consciousness would lead us to a different kind of understanding of the role of Jews in contemporary politics. In this section, we turn to the ways that Jewish religious and spiritual practice would be transformed by a Jewish-renewal consciousness.

Jewish renewal is not simply a political agenda or an attempt to place a liberation theology on top of a traditional set of spiritual practices. Rather, it is an attempt to take God seriously at every level of our being. That requires more than adding a few phrases about social justice to an existing liturgy or ritual. And it is far more than saying that we must be serious about social justice, and even more than having a synagogue that mobilizes people to be active in social-change causes (though that is certainly part of the picture). Jewish renewal is an attempt to make us more fully alive to God's presence in the world, to build a life that is God-centered, and to provide us with a way of reclaiming the unique spirituality of Judaism, deeply embedded in political consciousness but not reducible to a particular political agenda or to a set of moral injunctions.

Because Judaism itself is a way of life, Jewish renewal is an attempt to reclaim and rejuvenate that way of life for those who have abandoned it and for those who have transformed it into neatly demarcated ritual obligations and beliefs. Jewish renewal calls into question the public/private split that allowed contemporary theorists to relegate religion to a private sphere.

Even within the sphere we call private life, most people have replicated this public/private split. The more public sphere of our private life is what one ordinarily does with friends or family—our conversations, recreation, lovemaking, humor, etc. Then we create a yet more private sphere for our spirituality, and through word and gesture we indicate to ourselves or others that for the next few moments we are no longer going to be how we normally are, but rather something different and special that has no place in the rest of our lives. Spirituality is marginalized by being made special. Jewish renewal is an attempt to reintegrate in our lives the ontological union of spiritual and political, the God of creation and the God of transformation. While we have already discussed why it is necessary for people to acknowledge these linkages, in this section of the book we turn to the practical tasks of embodying Jewish renewal in daily life. To do so, we do not start from scratch, but from the rich way of life that has already been developed by the Jewish people in its various attempts to wrestle with God.

Our God-wrestling has produced a set of practices and rituals. Many remain full of life and vitality, and others could easily be reclaimed by minimal reframing. But it also contains practices and formulations and ways of thinking that no longer are helpful to bring us close to God. So in this section we ask ourselves what Jewish renewal could look like in practice.

But this is not merely a thought experiment. There are some people who have already begun to create Jewish renewal in every corner of Jewish life. Jewish renewal as I define it in this book goes far beyond those who call themselves "the Jewish Renewal movement" and incorporates the activities of people in Orthodox, Conservative, Reform, and Reconstructionist Judaism, activities of Jewish feminists, activities of gay and lesbian synagogues, and the religious activities of many whose spirituality does not include belief in any traditional sense.

CHAPTER ELEVEN

MAKING JUDAISM MORE ALIVE

Jewish renewal is not a denominational phenomenon. There are people within every Jewish denomination who are seeking to build Jewish-renewal consciousness, and there are people who are building Jewish renewal quite apart from any of the official denominations.

Whenever you find a community of people who are actually witnessing the existence of God and who are challenging the world of oppression in the name of *this* God, there you find renewal energy. Whenever you have people who understand themselves as part of the people whose task it is to be partners with God in the transformation of the world, who simultaneously approach that task with awe, wonder, and radical amazement at the grandeur of the universe, and rejoice in God's presence that fills the entire universe, there you have renewal energy. So renewal energy is possible (and necessary) in every religious tradition in the modern world.

Renewal becomes *Jewish* renewal when it is brought into the framework of the historical experience of the Jewish people, commits itself to Jewish rituals and traditions, seeks to rediscover God's voice through the medium of the Torah tradition, and shares love for, compassion toward, and attachment to the Jewish people. Within this Torah framework it seeks to figure out how, in this moment of history, we can best be witnesses to God's presence and the possibilities that

that creates for us in transforming the world from that which is to that which ought to be.

GOD INTOXICATION

If Jewish renewal can be found in any Jewish denomination or in no denomination, how do you find it, recognize it, or create it?

Look first for God intoxication. Not people who use the word God all the time, or who yell out "Praise God!" or *"Baruch ha'Shem!"* but people who are part of a community that seriously addresses itself to the obligation to be God's witnesses today. Look for people who start each day by focusing on the wonder of the world, allowing themselves to be astounded that anything exists at all, overwhelmed with joy and excitement about the grandeur of the universe, and who communicate to you and to others a real pleasure in being able to serve God by working on healing and repairing the world.

Look for people who are constantly, almost unconsciously, engaged in little acts of caring and compassion for others, and who radiate a warmth and loving energy that is personal and specific (not the glazed eyes of "true believers" who tell you that they love you, but don't seem to notice who you are), the very focused love that comes from caring enough to get to know you in all your particularity, respects you for who you are and not just who they think you could or should be, and loves the God within you not as a separate part of your soul which needs to be liberated from the rest, but as a feature that flows through every part of your being.

Look for a community whose members do acts of charity and participate in social action together, as a community, and who see their work as testimony to God's presence in the world. Such a community would have weekly meetings to discuss contemporary developments in the world and how to respond to them. It would ensure that its members are actively engaged as Jews in social-transformation movements, and it would strategize regularly on how best to support those of its members who are involved in any particular social-change movement.

Imagine such a community meeting. A group of Jews gather to pray and celebrate God's presence in the world. Next, some joint study—a text is presented and analyzed. Then they check in with one another about their own lives, about what has been happening in their families and work lives. They share with one another their pains and their joys. Then they move on to discuss the week's events. Reports are given by different members about their involvement in social-change activities. Group members help the individuals figure out what might be the next moves or the strategic direction for their activity in social change. Then the group discusses whatever *tzedakah* or social-change activities it is doing together as a group. Finally, the group celebrates its own solidarity, sings songs, moves together in dance.

Don't expect to find such communities at the moment, though there are many communities where elements of this picture are being actualized. Rather, the picture is drawn to indicate a direction. A Jewish-renewal consciousness has existed in every major period of Jewish history. Its actual embodiment has always been imperfect and will be so in our historical epoch as well, though more of it will come into existence in the coming decades.

GETTING REAL, PSYCHOLOGICALLY AND SPIRITUALLY

A history of pain has produced a population that lives its life in some degree of unconsciousness. The more pain, the more unconsciousness.

There are moments in history when the pain decreases, and people begin to experience themselves as "waking up." They talk about themselves and their lives as though they had noticed that they or previous generations seemed to be going through life in a sleeping state, zombielike.

Even when this doesn't happen for everyone, it can happen for some subset of people. When, for example, a group of people begin to "get" that the world is governed by God, they have this waking up experience. Various philosophers have described in similar terms the kind of enlightenment they experienced.

Over time, religious communities, as well as philosophical traditions and political, aesthetic, or psychological movements, may be lulled back into lower levels of consciousness, and what remains are the truths that were momentarily revealed and articulated, now embedded in these movements' words, symbols, rituals, communal practices, literature, and art. No longer able to fully experience life as it had been when people felt more alive, we still have these records of fuller awareness, beckoning us to return. The power in the symbols and the literature may still have the ability to transform us—if we awaken to what we are saying, but often we remain asleep.

There is no spiritual, political, or aesthetic tradition that is immune to being put back to sleep. One of the overwhelming consequences of contemporary culture is the increase of that level of collective amnesia. Over and over again we find ourselves surrounded by people who are in the process of forgetting what they once knew, increasingly unable to hold on to it. I believe that Alzheimer's is the paradigmatic sickness of the contemporary age, and that we live in the Alzheimer's society.

In such circumstances, those who have maintained the traditions are doing an important service. Rather than have to begin at the beginning, reinventing the history of human experience, people can reclaim from the tradition some of the elements that are most healthy and alive, while discarding those elements that represent the inevitable distortions of any particular age and experience. And as they reclaim, they can renew, by mixing that which has been with our own latest abilities to listen and hear what wisdom is being transmitted to us in the contemporary period (with all its inevitable distortions).

Jewish renewal is one of the many contemporary projects of people who are trying to reclaim and reawaken the frozen products of the past. There are people within psychoanalysis, feminism, Marxism, Christianity, Islam, art, music, philosophy, and many other areas who are trying to do the same thing in their own spheres.

HOW REAL DOES IT FEEL?

Another way to know if you are dealing with Jewish renewal or a counterfeit: Ask yourself how real the enterprise feels, how psychologically honest and alive, how spiritually centered and serious.

- Do people talk to one another in an honest fashion or are they on "good behavior"? Do they feign loving behavior and suppress all anger, or do they feel free to express a full range of emotions and feelings?
- Do people feel free to dispute the basic tenets of the community, to challenge its leadership, and to acknowledge the ways that they don't fit in?
- Do people feel free to express love and caring or excitement for

one another without feeling that they are embarrassing other
people or acting inappropriately?

- Can people acknowledge sexual attractions and pursue them, or
is there a sexual straitjacket operating?
- Do people feel free to cry when they are sad, or to jump for joy
when they are happy, or are these allowed only at specifically
ritual moments?
- Can people really talk about the complexities of their experience
with one another without fitting into some preestablished norm
about what people are supposed to be feeling or thinking?
- Can people fully mourn when they are in mourning, or do they
feel that they have to take care of others and assure them that
they are really doing okay and going to survive the loss?
- Can people feel really joyous when something has happened in
their personal lives that is good, or do they feel that they would
be making others feel bad or jealous if they were to be "too"
explicit about how good they feel?
- Does the community have some regular institutionalized way in
which bad feelings among participants or between participants
and the leadership of the community get put on the agenda,
discussed, and worked through?
- Do people feel real in prayer? For example, when people pray
with words like, "You shall rejoice in your holidays," are they
actually rejoicing, or are they merely good-naturedly repeating
an injunction, perhaps personally wishing they knew how to
rejoice? When they say, "We are happy, how good is our lot, how
wonderful our portion, how pretty our inheritance," do you feel
that people are actually happy? When people say, "Hear, O Israel,
the Lord our God, the Lord is One," do you have the sense that
they are actually trying to get their fellow Jews to pay attention to
this idea, or that they themselves are paying attention to it?
- When people greet you are they going through the motions with
their "Shabbat Shalom," or do they actually seem to be hoping
that you are going to have a peaceful Shabbat?

The list could go on.

My own experience is that most synagogue participation and most
Jewish ritual are undergone in a semiconscious state. People sometimes know what they are saying, and if asked, they'd say they agree

with much of it. But all too often they aren't fully there, fully into it. And, in fact, if you tried to become fully there or fully into it in most synagogues you'd probably look foolish.

To some extent, people feel embarrassed to let go of their sense of decorum, cynicism, self-restraint, and moderation—all of which might be compromised by letting themselves get into something that takes them beyond themselves. But this is not the whole story. I've watched people in Hasidic synagogues dance and sing excitedly, but then in my conversations with people afterward, I've come to think that what people were getting excited *about* was the excitement itself, not the content of what they were supposedly praying for or to.

Getting real is different—it's actually meaning what you're saying, taking it seriously, staking your life on it.

This could be a demanding criterion for anyone to be expected to live in a world that is still dominated by pain and oppression. But it is a reasonable criterion of what counts as Jewish renewal.

If ever there was a category that seemed scary, it's this one: getting real. The more asleep people are, the more they feel threatened by the concept, dismiss it as New Agey or flakey or contentless.

The more awake you are, the more you've had experiences in which you've moved from being more unconscious to more conscious, and hence the more you understand what is being talked about. So you can begin to ask yourself questions like:

- Does this community really take the idea of social responsibility seriously, or does it just like to pat itself on the back for talking about it?
- Does this community really take care of one another, really worry about the lives of each of its individual members, really feel that they are all in it together, really make people within it feel that they are safe because everyone else is going to stick with them and support them when things get rough?
- Does this community really seek to be spiritually alive, or does it stay satisfied with remembering moments when it had spiritual highs in the past?
- Do these individuals take the spiritual sensitivities that they express in this community and actually incorporate them into their own lives?
- Do these people feel the pain of the oppressed, the hungry, the

homeless, the downtrodden, the discriminated against, the victims of oppressive childhoods, the people who feel bad about
themselves, or do they merely talk about these issues and know
that they ought to care?

- Do these people really engage in Jewish tradition and Jewish
texts, or do they study them in ways that are so abstracted, so
intellectually distant, that they never let the texts or the tradition
actually speak to them and challenge their current lives?

- Do these people try to stay connected to their understanding of
God, or do they let it lapse when they are no longer in an officially
designated holy space or holy time?

But this is not an either/or matter.

We will be fully alive only in messianic times, when all oppression has
ceased to have much of a hold on our consciousness, when we are less
afraid, and when we allow ourselves to be fully in touch with God and
ourselves.

Every community and every one of us is on a continuum between
being fully awake and somewhat unconscious, somewhat less than we
can be, somewhat dominated by the accumulated pain and fears of the
past. Part of the task of Jewish renewal is to be part of the forces
working to heal and transform that pain and that unconsciousness—
and a first tool of healing is compassion. So it is very destructive if
people who have experienced some degree of awakening become too
judgmental toward others who have not.

Getting real isn't simply a matter of deciding to become more alive or
more conscious. The obstacles to being present to God in the world, or
to being present to one another, are deeply rooted in the pain that gets
passed from generation to generation and the oppression that remains
embodied in our social institutions. Jewish renewal has to be partly
about changing those social institutions that reinforce our spiritual
deadness (including the competitive marketplace and its emphasis on
power, selfishness, and materialism), and partly about dislodging those
ways of feeling and thinking that have become embedded in our unconscious and make us unprepared or unwilling to stay alive to God's
presence in the world. Virtually everyone who wishes to be spiritually
alive is going to have to engage in this two-part struggle—to change
social institutions and to dislodge from personal unconsciousness the
residue of the history of cruelty and pain that makes hearing the voice

of God difficult. In this sense, renewal within every religious tradition will require both political struggle and psychological work.

ALL JEWS ARE JEWS BY CHOICE

Today every Jew is a Jew by choice. Not even the most rigid ultra-Orthodox community can compel its members to remain within it. And the consequences of leaving are not always traumatic. It is not unusual for members of ultra-Orthodox communities to retain ties with family members or friends who have abandoned that world and chosen another. It is a good thing that somewhere in the background of traditional communities lies the possibility of leaving them—and that should set at ease those who imagine that if they become involved in the dynamics of a Jewish-renewal worldview, they will permanently lose themselves and their freedom. To throw oneself into a world of tradition, to submit oneself to the yoke of Halakha or Jewish law, will remain a choice from which you can free yourself if you so choose.

Conversely, those of us who wish to invite other Jews to join in a community of observance must fight against those who seek to use coercive mechanisms to impose religion on others. Fundamentalists who seek to use state power to impose religious practice do so because they don't believe that their religion would have sufficient appeal to attract adherents based solely on the joy, love, and awe that it generates. But coercion guarantees that joy and love will disappear—so all that remains is "religious behavior," but God's presence has been chased away.

To take a tradition seriously, one must immerse oneself in it, allow oneself to experience it from the standpoint of those who feel that it is compelling, fulfilling, and obligatory. But for that immersion to be possible, we must know that we will always be free to move away from the religious community.

BEING COMMANDED

Immersion has the scary connotation of losing oneself, being taken over by another, yet being immersed in Judaism feels more like the opposite—finding one's truest and deepest self.

Accepting the yoke of Torah feels liberating, *not*, as secular skeptics like to think, because we thereby give up the complex burdens of making moral judgments in a confusing world (in fact, we do no such thing, since *how* concretely to live a Torah life requires considerable thought), but rather because we give up the conflicts induced by the allures of "making it" in a world of materialism and selfishness, and instead face the conflicts induced by being true to our highest ethical and spiritual selves. The *mitzvot* or commandments that we hold on to are those whose underlying message is about being witnesses to God's presence in the world, witnesses to the possibility of transformation. When the Jewish story is told so that Jews really get it that we were given this incredible privilege of being able to witness in our own historical experience this possibility of transformation, and that the rituals and laws of Jewish life are ways of keeping that message alive and are embodiments of the best ways we can figure out for treating one another as created in the image of God, then we get a very different feeling about being commanded. Being commanded here is like being commanded to draw certain conclusions from geometry once one knows the premises. To be commanded in this sense is to have the dignity of being partners with God in world transformation and world healing.

A CHOSEN PEOPLE

That we are one of the first to get that human beings are created in the image of God, with this freedom and obligation to transform that which is to that which ought to be, is what we mean when we say that Jews are chosen. But the chosenness is an obligation: it immediately confers upon us the responsibility to become witnesses to the possibility of a different logic in the world, to treat every human being as created in the image of God, to build a community that is a testimony to that possibility, and to spread the word.

Part of what we get when we get the revelation is that human beings are responsible for one another, that the recognition of others as human carries within it the obligation to care for the other and create a world in which others can be treated in accord with the spirit of God that lies within them.

This sense of obligation and chosenness is often experienced by people who have discovered some new knowledge that is potentially liberatory. Those people typically feel that they must share what they know, that they must act on that knowledge, and that their lives must in some way be responsive to what they have seen. Some of these vanguards—feminists, Marxists, psychoanalysts—have faced the same problems that the Jews have faced as a people.

Chosenness, many Jews will tell you, has been more of a curse than a blessing. It has put us in harm's way over and over again. Sure there are compensatory moments in which it feels great to understand what is going on in the world a little better than others, and hence to be able to be the group that supplies the Einsteins and Freuds and Marxes and Friedans and Benjamins. But mostly it's a super drag to have to be the group that, because it plays a certain role in history, continually is put in the position of being the group that threatens ruling elites and that angers most others.

Our vanguard knowledge has made us oppressed, and so Jews not only share the normal distortions of every people under the sun, but we get some special distortions that come from having been oppressed. We even know that some Jews *do* think that they are better people than everyone else, which is only one of the many kinds of distortions that come from this oppression, as is the self-inflation that we sometimes use to resist the normal self-blaming that oppression engenders. But Jewish literature and Jewish humor are full of a deep awareness of how screwed up Jews can become. Chosenness doesn't mean being better.

But it does commit us to claiming that we know something true and important. We are not the only ones who know that human beings have a certain intrinsic worth by virtue of being created in the image of God, and that humans have the capacity to change the world, but we are one of the few groups that have defined their *raison d'être* in terms of being witnesses to this possibility.

Challenging those who think that existing realities of oppression, cruelty, and unhappiness are built into the structure of necessity, proclaiming that the social institutions that embody or perpetuate oppression and cruelty are not necessary, puts us into immediate and sustained struggle against most of the ruling elites of the world and with hundreds of millions of people who do *not* benefit from the system of oppression, but who have of necessity built their lives around a system of compromises with pain and cruelty, and who feel threatened by anyone who suggests that the compromises they made *were not necessary*.

Which is one reason why Jews in the contemporary world do not take kindly to Jewish renewal, because it puts us back into a position of vulnerability that many Jews have been trying to escape by covertly telling the world, "Don't worry about us, because we are no longer into advocating a God that would challenge your political and social arrangements."

But if one has to testify to a God that does challenge a world of oppression, then one will surely feel a little conflicted about being "chosen" for this task. It may often seem as much of a curse as a blessing. Jeremiah and other prophets of old exemplified that on the personal level: they often bemoaned their fate at having been chosen to bring to the Jewish people a message that it didn't particularly want to hear, and which engendered anger at the messenger. After the Holocaust, many Jews have challenged God to take back the chosenness. In their words and their actions they have said publicly: "We don't want it, we don't need it, we want out." Unfortunately there is no such possibility. A Jew who has gotten the message of Torah cannot *not* know the God who makes for the possibility of possibility.

You might accept this role as witness to possibility but still may ask, Why do I need to be part of a *community* to do this? Can't I be a healer on my own? The answer is No, because part of the healing that the world needs at *this* historical moment is the overcoming of the ethos of selfishness, self-centeredness, and narcissism, and the creation of a nonoppressive community in which we can learn to take care of one another and be responsible to one another. The healing and transformation of the world needs to be done through such communities, and part of the healing is to heal that which makes us afraid to be part of such communities. We need to heal the extreme individualism of this society, just as in previous eras we needed to heal the conformism and repressiveness of an excessively dominating communitarian ethos.

Every community must answer the question, "How should we as a community lead our lives?" And the answer provided in the Jewish tradition is, "Through *mitzvot*, a life of observance of the religious commandments."

DIGNITY AND JOY OF *MITZVOT*

If you understand *mitzvot* as the attempt by a community to fulfill what it learned to be its revolutionary obligations and to keep alive the message of liberation and transformation, you can understand why the Jews saw *mitzvah* as conferring dignity. For the deeply religious Jew, the *mitzvot* are not a burden or a hardship or a punishment or a constraint. They are the opportunity to exemplify in a concrete way the opportunity afforded to the Jewish people to be a vanguard of consciousness. It's no wonder, then, that Jewish liturgy is full of statements that affirm that the *mitzvot* are God's manifestation of love for the people of Israel—precisely because they give us this incredible opportunity to participate with God in world healing and transformation. Torah and *mitzvot* are, in the words of the Jewish liturgy, "our life and the length of our days, and on them we will meditate day and night." We dance with the Torah, we sing songs of joy about the *mitzvot*, and they become for us a blessing. Similarly, as one rabbinic interpretation has it, Moses fulfilled God's command by rejoicing in the *mitzvot* and by causing others to rejoice in them (Sifra 129a). Another classic text, the Mechilta (66b), shows that the commandments are transformed into righteous acts only when they are done joyfully: "Let man [*sic*] fulfill the commandments of the Torah with joy and then they will be counted to him as righteousness." Rabbi Tzvi Marx, in his landmark study *Halakha and Handicap*, points out that there is also a more somber strand of interpreters who insist that "Commandments were not given to provide enjoyment."[1] Perhaps these people are making a very important point that must be remembered by any vanguard engaged in struggling against ruling elites. While one should be joyous about the opportunity to engage in this work, one should not expect that doing so will always feel pleasurable. This was one of the problems with those in the counterculture of the 1960s who said that they didn't want to be part of any revolution to which they could not dance. If that is the criterion, the powerful can guarantee that things will not feel so good, and then everyone abandons ship because it doesn't feel right anymore.

Because commandment is seen as the vehicle through which our community participates with God in healing and repairing the world, the offer of "freedom from the commandments" made by Pauline Christianity has little appeal to those who understand what *mitzvot* are really about. Being obliged by *mitzvot*, as Rabbi Tzvi Marx points out, is the measure of one's dignity and status in the Jewish world.[2] It is

---

[1]Tzvi Marx, *Halakha and Handicap* (Jerusalem: Shalom Hartman Institute, 1992), p. 168.
[2]Ibid., p. 165.

precisely for this reason that women have legitimately criticized the sexism in the Jewish tradition that has freed them from *mitzvot*. The way to achieve dignity and status in the world of Judaism is to be subject to *mitzvah*, to be held accountable for being part of the healing community, and to be required to participate in its tasks.

LIBERAL FEARS OF COMMUNAL OBLIGATION

People have good reason to be cautious when committing to some community that requires suspending one's own intellect and tastes and conforming to the practices or traditions of some existing community. It's all too easy to be lulled back into spiritual unconsciousness, quieting one's own feelings and intuitions. In fact, it is precisely because many people wish to escape this confrontation with their own inner voices that something is wrong with the world that they happily embrace some authoritarian community's laws and practices and thus avoid the responsibility of thinking things out for themselves.

But on the other hand, many of us raised in the contemporary world have a fear of communal obligations that is deeply ingrained and stems from our deep attachment to individualism and the pursuit of self-interest. We are fearful of *any* community, even one that we would construct ourselves and that would be fully governed by democratic procedures. Partly, we have had our own experiences of watching democratic communities subvert themselves by allowing irrational or self-destructive fears to triumph over hopefulness and mutual support. But partly we are simply scared of letting go of individual control, even if that individual control is based on attachment to our own elusive egos, and actually yields for us a life of isolation and despair.

Because of these fears, we come up with all kinds of good excuses. "I don't want to be governed by Halakha [Jewish law] because it is distorted in various ways." True enough, but also true that the law has always been evolving in response to Jews' shared understanding, and that as we play a role in changing that understanding, we will change Halakha. Halakhic communities have a series of *poskim*, individuals who are the primary interpreters of Jewish law for that generation, and we in our historical age can pick our own *poskim*. A Jewish-renewal community, for example, can pick *poskim* who embody their own shared understanding of the meaning of Torah and the voice of God within the Torah tradition.

But that won't satisfy many, because they don't want *any* form of obligation outside of what feels good to them at the time.

I don't want to totally dismiss this position, because I've seen so many communities full of Jewish zombies, people who don't bother to ask themselves what feels good to them because they have become used to a Judaism in which feeling alive or real seems to have no place whatsoever. Typically, they are dead to spiritual and ethical reality, but perfect at keeping those halakhic requirements that don't generate this kind of aliveness. They will speed through their prayers, sure to say each word correctly, but rarely engaging in any struggle about what the words really mean.

Yet on the other hand, the "feels-good" philosophy is really an extension of the logic of the individualistic ethos of the capitalist market. In the contemporary world, the feels-good philosophy has undermined our ability to sustain loving commitments and families, and has weakened our ability to engage in sustained ethical activity.

So Jewish renewal has a double message. For those already inclined toward communal obligation, the message is: wake up and be real; for those committed to the life of doing what feels good at the moment: wake up and recognize that you can't build community or connectedness unless you are willing to accept obligation toward others, including sometimes *not* having it your way. Depending on whom we are speaking to, we ought to emphasize one side or the other of this message. It's a good bet that among those who have flirted with enlightenment liberalism, it is the latter message that most needs to be heard.

This is why Jewish renewalists in the Reform movement are skeptical of the following rationale from their colleagues: "We don't pretend to be a halakhic community, but that doesn't mean that we don't have a unifying purpose that forges our community. What unites us is *not* a shared level of religious observance, but rather, what unites is our commitment to *tikkun olam*, to healing and repair of the world."

Unfortunately, Reform Jewish renewalists tell us, this tends to be more ideology than reality. If Reform temples were in fact centers of liberal or progressive social-change activism, places in which Jews gathered to debate what the communal stance should be on contemporary social-change issues, voted on alternative strategies, and then, once the vote had been taken, felt a sense of obligation to work together on the strategy adopted till the next vote, they would have a dramatic impact on the world and would certainly have a hold on their young.

The truth, however, is that there are only a few Reform congregations that even begin to approximate this, and that most of the social-change activity is engaged in by their Religious Action Center in Washington, D.C., a handful of lobbyists and organizers, and a few thousand people who are involved in social-change activities on the local level.

If, when one joins a Reform congregation, one feels an obligation to participate on a weekly basis in feeding the hungry, sheltering the homeless, attending a weekly political strategy meeting, or some other very immediate and concrete *tikkun olam* activity, we might have grounds to talk about a *tikkun olam* community. But for the most part in the twentieth century, these words are merely words, translated occasionally into donations to some liberal causes, sometimes into a yearly "*mitzvah* or *tikkun olam* day," sometimes into pious resolutions at national conventions, but rarely into much else that could affect the lives of the participants on a daily basis.

Not that Reform Jews as individuals are not serious about social change—some are, some are not. But this is a matter of individual choice and of collective rhetoric, not a defining reality of an actual community willing to accept the obligation to act together, even when the obligation is imposed through democratic decision making about *the best way* to actualize healing and repair in the current moment, in light of all we know. In this case, then, it's not that the old ways are outdated, but that some contemporary liberals are so resistant to obligation beyond themselves that they will not be part of any community that requires anything of them.

Imagine, for example, if wealthy Reform congregations were to require that all of their members with incomes in the top ten percent of all American incomes have to donate ten percent of their income to the congregation, and that the congregation would meet every few months to decide how to allocate the monies for social-change projects. Imagine if Reform Jewish congregations required their members to be part of some weekly social action.

"We're not being inconsistent," a Reform Jew might respond, "we just don't require our members to *do* anything. After all, they've been turned off to the kind of Judaism that makes demands on them. Isn't it a service to the Jewish people that we provide a place for such Jews to do *something*, even if it's less than you want? Even if it were true that all we do is keep alive a certain *tikkun olam* ideology—and we're not conceding that that *is* all we do—isn't that better than not doing anything?"

Sure, it's a good thing. Hopefully, there will continue to be a Reform movement. But a movement that makes so few demands, that is so much in accord with the individualist ethos of the society, and that restricts its challenge to materialism, selfishness, and oppressive practices to fiery sermons on "religious occasions," runs another risk: of becoming a place where the self-satisfied suburbanites or contented Yuppies can park their children in child care or "religious instruction," where they can meet friends on a Friday night, where they can get the feeling that they are part of social change by hearing a sermon and paying the rabbi's high salary, where they can alleviate their guilt about conspicuous consumption by donating money to pay for Jewish bureaucrats to worry about "Jewish continuity" or "education" or whatever is the latest guilt-reducing rage in the world of the upper-crust fundraisers. Such a Judaism will still be valuable, but it won't be Jewish renewal—even if they adopt some Jewish-renewal melodies, include meditations and personal testimonies in their religious services, and even if their social-action committees have a handful of serious activists.

Happily, the Jewish-renewal forces within Reform, Conservative, and Reconstructionist Judaism are beginning to champion the cause of communal obligation even as they reclaim the most spiritually and ethically alive dimensions of the tradition—precisely those dimensions capable of sustaining a sense of obligation among a population that would otherwise be resistant to it.

To sustain a commitment and build communities of people who are willing to accept serious responsibility toward one another and tradition, we must first be sure that what we are asking people to commit to and be obligated to is worthy of their highest selves, worthy of the God energy within them. When that is *not* the case, commitment withers and all the sputtering about obligation and responsibility become nothing but weapons that generate shame. If we ask people to be loyal to God, they must be able to hear and feel the presence of God in the communal obligations we expect them to accept. Absent that feeling, no wonder they've been resistant to obligation.

A WAY OF BEING

Judaism is not only about doing the right thing, but also about being the right kind of person. And this means developing the right kind of characterological features, attitudes, aspirations, and hopes. An appropriate goal of Jewish renewal is to develop human beings who do the right thing not only because they know they are obligated to, but because it hurts them to see another human being in pain. There is a oneness to all reality that makes us respond to the hurt and the undermining and the misrecognition of others as though this were our hurt and our own experience of being undermined and misrecognized.

Because it matters what kind of human being we are, there are Jewish virtues worth pursuing in personal life. Consider a few:

- Humility. This is not the self-negating process that leads some to assume that their desires are unimportant or must always be subordinated to others. Rather it is the willingness to set our own life goals and behavior in terms of our best understanding of how God wants us to be, rejecting the hubris of insisting that our own agendas must always be primary.
- Compassion or *chesed*. Being a person whose compassion for others and for oneself overflows in a healing and loving way.
- Honesty. With oneself and with one's loved ones. Telling the truth even when it doesn't advance one's own interests.
- Hopefulness. Refusing to go along with the cynicism and pessimism of contemporary life. Recognizing that God is really in charge in the long run.
- Joyfulness and humor. These qualities of self are healing and reparative for a world in pain.

You can probably add others to this list of Jewish virtues.

Though the virtues are pursued for their own sake, there is no denying that there is a payoff to the ethical life or to lives filled with these kinds of virtues. While there is no direct one-to-one connection between how much we embody these virtues and how well we fortune in our personal lives, there is a larger-scale connection discussed in the Torah (and repeated in the section of the Shma prayer called *V'hayah Eem Sh'moa*): The well-being of the universe is affected by the degree to which people embody the Jewish virtues as well as by the degree to which they live a life consistent with the *mitzvot*. This same notion is captured by other spiritual traditions when they talk about *karma*: there is something about how the world is that is shaped by the degree of goodness that we bring into it.

When speaking this language, it's always important to avoid the self-blaming connotations that could allow someone to say, "If you suffer pain, you *must* have done something to deserve it." This transparent nonsense has been used to make people feel bad about themselves for many centuries. But when modified and adequately restricted in scope, it does make sense. The modification: the present level of pain and evil in the world is a reflection of how successful past generations have been in their struggle to defeat the legacy of cruelty in the world. Hitler was *not* caused by the Jews, but he was caused *in part* by the degree to which all of us, including Jews, had failed in previous generations to defeat imperialism, racism, patriarchy, and chauvinistic nationalism. To the extent that we don't embody the Jewish virtues and to the extent that we don't live a life of *mitzvah*, we are likely to pass on to the next generation more of the cruelty and frustration of the present generation than we had any intention of doing. How we live matters.

EDUCATION FOR RENEWAL

Many adults who are turned on to the concept of Jewish renewal are frightened by the prospects of learning a whole new tradition, a whole new language (Hebrew), and a whole new literature. It seems overwhelming. They are right—the tradition is immense.

Renewal communities need to assure new members that the process of learning can be spread out over a lifetime, and that one can be part of the community even with major gaps in one's knowledge. At the same time, the community should ensure that knowledge is accessible. For example, regular classes in Jewish history, texts, and Hebrew should be available. And it should be clear that the community expects all of its members to be involved in Jewish study, no matter what level their previous knowledge. Study is a value for its own sake, and the more Jewish texts you know, the more you are aware of how much more there is to know. Done right, Jewish study can be a pleasure.

One useful aid: Get yourself a teacher and a person to study with. The teacher should be someone who can guide you as to what texts are most useful to start studying. I suggest a weekly reading of the Torah portion along with useful commentaries (e.g., the Plaut edition), a good history of the Jewish people (e.g., Sasson), and a good text of Jewish philosophy (Heschel's *God in Search of Man* or *The Prophets*). A study partner (*chevruta*) can be extremely helpful. Meet once a week to discuss the texts you have agreed to study together. Push each other with tough questions about interpretation. Allow yourself to admit when you don't understand, and ask for help. And push the other person to be more rigorous in his or her thinking, but do it in a gentle and affirming way so that they don't get scared. Make sure to make your learning fun.

But it can't always be fun. There is one part where you just have to dive in: learning Hebrew. The key is this: don't start doing it until you really want to. There is lots to learn that doesn't require knowledge of Hebrew. You can be a very good practicing renewalist and know almost no Hebrew. But the experience is even richer and fuller when you do. The subtleties and complexities of Judaism are the source of such pleasure that a Jewish-renewal community should want to share them with new members. Learning Hebrew can be an important gift that opens people to a whole new world of joy.

By turning young people off to Judaism, the organized Jewish community has deprived a whole generation of Jews of one of life's great pleasures: study of the Torah tradition. We should be sure not to do the same to future generations. Jewish renewal will be far more successful when its practitioners have a solid grounding in the texts and history of the Jewish people.

The best way to give children that grounding is through the various Jewish day schools that combine secular with Jewish education. Jewish-renewal mavens like Rabbi Burt Jacobson have been developing a new pedagogy aimed at fostering spiritual awareness and sensitivity. The primary task is not to see how many texts the child can master, but how to awaken her soul to awe, wonder, and radical amazement; how to develop her recognition of others as deserving respect and as embodying God's image; how to help her realize her potential role as a healer and transformer of the world. Any Hebrew school or Jewish education project that puts these goals first will develop the kind of excitement about Judaism that will translate into a deep openness to learning the texts and the rituals.

One reason why Jewish education has been such a failure in the spiritual dimension is because the teachers who are sought after are those who have expertise in some subject matter (Hebrew, Bible, Talmud, history), rather than those who are most spiritually alive.

Ideally, of course, we would want teachers who are both well grounded in texts and ethically and spiritually sensitive. But this is easier said than done, because existing training institutions for Hebrew

school teachers put very little energy into spiritual or ethical development. To do that, those schools themselves would have to take the
project of healing and repairing the world seriously, they would have to
themselves be dedicated to bringing God's energy into the world, they
would have to themselves be involved in spiritual life. Yet most of these
institutions would find these kinds of demands to be unprofessional,
possibly even risks to their accreditation, certainly risks to their standing as academic institutions that are respected by detached intellectuals and academics. These schools have sometimes been willing to
introduce a subject called spiritual development, based on allegedly
scientific theories about stages in spiritual or moral development along
lines pioneered by developmental psychologist Lawrence Kohlberg.
But that's safe because it's detached—a study of spiritual development,
not a personal commitment to spiritual life!

The various organizations seeking "alternatives" in Jewish education
or experimentation in "continuity" suffer the same problem: They think
they can find the best "techniques" as though the issue were becoming
most efficient, clever, or innovative in presenting one's material. But
that is *not* the issue. The issue is becoming most spiritually and ethically alive, and learning how to share *that* with students. A Hebrew
school or Jewish educational institution that doesn't care about the
poor will never be able to teach students to care; an institution that
doesn't care to be partners with God will never teach students to be
God's partners; an institution that doesn't pray cannot teach prayer; an
institution whose teachers are not engaged in study of their own will
never teach students about the value of study. Be what you want to
teach.

This same problem of academic detachment flourishes even in rabbinic schools, where the professors often define their peers as other
academics in universities. They want to be perceived as great scholars,
not as inflamers of the soul, not as healers or transformers of the world.
All the more so for teachers in Jewish Studies programs on campuses.
Many of these programs become the sole taste that young Jews have of a
more sophisticated version of Jewish thinking than what they experienced as children. Often these programs open up a powerful set of
questions that students desire to pursue. But since Jewish Studies
professors see themselves as having to prove to the rest of the university
that they are true academics and not missionaries for a particular
ideological position, these programs can rarely satisfy the hungers they

arouse. All too often the student who has been opened by Jewish Studies finds that the next step is to go to an Orthodox *yeshiva*, one of the few institutions of Jewish life where spiritual and moral passion is validated. Unfortunately, these *yeshivot*, under the influence of a growing chauvinism in the religious world in Israel, have been moving farther to the political and religious Right. Many decent and sensitive Jews end up in reactionary forms of Judaism, because often these are the only forms of Judaism that even begin to pay attention to the legitimate spiritual and moral hungers that Judaism is really all about.

How much better if there were a Jewish-renewal alternative, a spiritually alive form of Jewish education that does not require an abdication of one's mind or a mechanical "buying in" to religious fundamentalism. Jewish renewal will need to create such institutions, study centers, retreat centers, summer camps, and other facilities both in Israel and in the United States so that those hungry for spiritual and moral education can find it within the framework of a nonfundamentalist Judaism. And the graduates of these centers will be qualified to be the teachers of Jewish-renewal day schools and after-school Jewish education programs.

Religious education could be a joyous experience. But for that to happen, educators will have to abandon all notions that Jewish education should imitate public or secular education. Jewish education must not only involve an opening of the mind, it must focus equally on opening the heart, developing spirituality, emotions, imagination, intellect, caring for others, and commitment to social change. Schools must be judged by how well they touch the souls, not only by how many graduates they place in prestigious colleges. At the same time, Jewish-renewal schools cannot devalue learning texts and skills. They must reject the anti-intellectualism fostered in Western societies and instead show a serious respect for the mastery of the Jewish tradition. There is a value in learning for its own sake. The school that takes emotional, spiritual, and social-change dimensions seriously will find that its students end up having fewer emotional obstacles to learning the skills and the texts.

There are several important components that can assist in making Jewish-renewal education work:

1. Children who don't want to be there shouldn't be there. Send them where they want to go. If that means that they don't get

bar or bat mitzvahed when other children do, that's also fine.
Bar and bat mitzvah should be done when children feel ready to
accept the responsibility of being part of a community committed to healing and transformation—not when the society
tells them they have "come of age."

2. Families must be involved. No child is going to take learning
   seriously if his parents don't take it seriously. Children must see
   their parents coming to school to learn—and enjoying it.

3. There should be no report cards or performance requirements.
   Teachers should talk to parents about the progress of their
   children.

4. Children must be taught about other cultures as well, and a
   nondefensive and respectful attitude should be communicated
   toward the wisdom and experience of other ethnic and religious
   communities.

5. Children must be taught that Judaism is in the process of being
   renewed, and that they are part of the process, partners with
   God in healing and transforming the world and in hearing
   God's revelation to the world in a contemporary language.

The task in education is the same as the task in the rest of the Jewish
community: to make it safe for people to remain emotionally and
spiritually alive, to be real, to be responsive and caring to others, to be
embodiments of God's presence in the world. These words, too, can
become empty slogans that cover an emotional or spiritual deadness or
an intellectual fuzziness. That's why there can never be a formula that
will guarantee renewal, and why in every generation new approaches
will be needed to replace the deadening orthodoxies that previous
generations found enlivening. Renewal is not a task that is ever
completed.

Chapter Twelve

Sexism

The most serious distortion in Judaism has been the degree to which it has incorporated patriarchal practices and attitudes in its approach to God and in its understanding of what God requires of us.

There's nothing particularly surprising about this. As I've argued throughout, the revelation of God was received by human beings. Whatever messages were sent to us had to be processed through our existing languages and conceptual tools.

Theologians have understood this when they've talked about our inability to discuss what God is in positive language. Language itself was developed to provide a way to discuss those aspects of our daily lives that were publicly observable and repeatable. When we could reidentify objects or tasks, we could define them in ways that helped all people in the community communicate. But language has always been somewhat problematic when we are talking about aspects of our experience that are not so publicly observable or repeatable. That's why it has always seemed so inadequate when approaching art, music, love, even emotions. All the more so when it is meant to describe our experience of the Divine, something which transcends all of our experience and which is the ground of all experience.

"What can language do?" exclaimed Yehuda ha-Levi, the most

famous poet of medieval Spanish Jewry, when confronting his inadequacy in trying to find words to praise God. Or as the psalmist says, "Commune with your heart on your bed, and be still." Be still, because every language is likely to miss what you need to say. No wonder, then, that Heschel spoke of God as the Ineffable, that which surpasses all language.

Yet Moses and the children of Israel *did* give a language to God, and it was a language that portrayed God as male, as a father, and often as a dominating king or ruler. Hierarchical assumptions about a male God often corresponded to social arrangements in which some men had power over most other men, and all men had power over women. Moreover, they saw God as the validator of a set of existing patriarchal practices that got further elaborated through much of the history of Judaism. All too often Judaism functioned as a system of male power in which women were construed not as the subjects of history but as objects to be fit into the male-constructed and male-dominated world.

Jews did not create patriarchy, and in many respects Judaism and the practice of the Jewish people toward women have been more compassionate and more respectful than that of many surrounding nations. While there have been some patriarchal practices that have been as harsh and disrespectful as any of surrounding peoples (e.g., the way the *sotah* or suspected adulteress was tested), there have been many periods in history when Jewish women were being treated with more respect than in any other concomitantly existing culture. For this reason it has sometimes been hard for Jews to acknowledge that deeply patriarchal assumptions have shaped Jewish religious and communal institutions.

That patriarchal assumptions had permeated Jewish life and *not* just Jewish religion was reflected in the history of the Zionist movement. Though the early pioneers were well aware of the sexism in Jewish religious life, and though they articulated Socialist ideals of full equality and equal participation, the *kibbutzim* quickly reverted to patriarchal assumptions when allocating work. Women fell into traditional female roles: child rearing, education, cooking, housecleaning, while men assumed the dominant roles in fieldwork and in the fledgling industries. The leadership of the Labor party, like that of its right-wing nationalist opponents, was overwhelmingly male-dominated, as was the leadership of virtually every political and social institution in Israeli society.

All the more so in the communal institutions of American Jewish life. Through most of Jewish history, and continuing through several decades of feminist agitation in the twentieth century, men dominated all the institutions concerned with allocating funds, selecting communal leadership, and developing communal political direction. When women advanced into positions of leadership, it was only after they were able to assure the men in power that they had assimilated male-oriented ways of thinking and acting that would not threaten the current set of economic and political arrangements that defined Jewish communal life. Women might be allowed to play a role in these institutions, but it had to be on male terms.

One of the most exciting aspects of Jewish renewal has been the emergence of a Jewish feminist consciousness, shaped by the writings of Rachel Adler, Rebecca Alpert, Rachel Biale, Marcia Falk, Blu Greenberg, Susannah Heschel, Marge Piercy, Judith Plaskow, Letty Cottin Pogrebin, Ellen Umansky, and many more. The rich intellectual work being done by Jewish feminists has inspired emerging communities of women engaged in study of Jewish texts, the creation of new rituals, and reclaiming of Jewish women's history and traditions. The Jewish-renewal consciousness articulated in this book has been both inspired and shaped by the insights that these women are developing.

There are some men who will grit their teeth, grin and bear it. They know that women's equality is right, and they will go along with it while secretly wishing that they had lived at some other historical moment when they didn't have to lose their power. There will be all kinds of covert forms of resistance to this transformation, and it is not unlikely that this resistance will also be felt even within Jewish-renewal circles.

Sometimes premature jumping onto the feminist bandwagon is a symptom of this resistance: men who quickly acknowledge the need for women's equality, but are not really willing to think through the deep transformative impact this can and should mean, think that they have done their part by allowing women to be called to the Torah or put on the board of a foundation or synagogue. But the transformations required are much deeper. They involve not just letting women into existing practices and institutions, but the questioning of those practices and institutions.

Jewish renewal is committed to a fundamental rethinking of Judaism from the perspective of integrating women and women's experience of the world and of God into Jewish religious and communal life. But it also is committed to rethinking in a compassionate way that doesn't make men "wrong" or "the enemy," and instead acknowledges that which has been useful and important in the male contribution to the search for God and in defining Jewish religious spirituality and Jewish understanding of what God requires of us.

The commitment to transforming Judaism and the Jewish community does not flow from some abstract understanding of rights, but from a concrete understanding that our vision of God has been severely impaired to the extent that we do not recognize God in women's experiences and women's insights. So our relationship to women's equality is not simply one of reparation for past damages, but of joyous welcoming into our consciousness of a deep understanding of the Divine that is only today being given full expression.

Jewish renewal is in large part an expression of female energy and female insights being integrated into a tradition that was previously male-dominated. In this sense, Jewish renewal is fundamentally and essentially feminist—it is the contemporary attempt to reshape Judaism using the insights and understandings that women have brought into the modern world. That female energy and insight provides us with one of the greatest sources of creativity and rejuvenation that we have in the contemporary world. We can be grateful to be part of this process, and already we can see how much more alive and less asleep Jewish communities are that have begun to integrate this understanding into their fundamental being.

It is no exaggeration to say that our coming to consciousness about sexism and our commitment to reshaping Judaism to integrate the experience and understanding of women constitute the primary contemporary revelation of God to the Jewish people and to the world. We must understand ourselves as standing at Sinai once again. We must open our ears to the new revelation. Listen, O Israel; Hear, O Israel. And if the general message is that the world can be transformed from that which is to that which ought to be, because the Power that created the universe is the Power that makes for the possibility of transformation, then the particular message is that the patriarchal assumptions and practices that have dominated and distorted human consciousness for millennia can be transformed and replaced with a world that honors and values women and men equally, that learns from the wisdom of women, and that reflects all of those aspects of women's identity that had previously been marginalized, trivialized, or denigrated.

GOD'S GENDER

While observant Jews are quick to assure us that they have no intention of suggesting that God has a male gender, they are equally quick to reject the use of female language to rectify the situation. But Reform Jews also resist adopting female language about God. Even secular Jews are made uneasy, laugh, or become indignant when the pronoun "She" is used to refer to God ("The God I don't believe in is a man," they seem to be telling us).

We are told that we can't refer to God as She because God does not have a sex, that God cannot be contained by gender. Fine. But since Hebrew always seems to construe reality in female or male language, why not render God in female language for a few thousand years to make up for the past few thousand years of male language? Many women report that male language and imagery surrounding God have made it harder for them to believe in God. Some men have implied that if God is male, then only men have really been created in God's image, and that women are a derivative and lesser reality. So if God really has no gender, why not make that clear?

Howard Eilberg-Schwartz suggests that one reason for resistance may be the covert homoerotic bond that exists in the subconscious fantasies of some religious Jews who have depicted themselves as the real embodiment of the people Israel, conceptualized themselves as God's bride, and God as the bridegroom ready to consummate the marriage. In this exclusive male world that Orthodox Jews have constructed around so much of their study and prayer life, in which male bonding is never allowed to be consummated physically, the maleness of God may provide a safe form of homoeroticism that can contain what would be perceived otherwise as dangerous impulses. To challenge God's gender is to ruin the whole racket.

Perhaps. But I suspect that feminists are right to point to male power as the central issue underlying the attachment to a male God concept. What strikes me as wrong is the assumption that men want to hold on to this power simply because of all the benefits they gain by dominating women. It seems equally important to note the degree to which Jewish men have largely been without power in the real world relative to other groups of men, and how the concept of a powerful Jewish male God may have functioned as a compensation for relative powerlessness. But whatever psychological function it played, the maleness of God has no intrinsic legitimacy, and the resistance to changing the language has to be overcome, albeit gently and over time.

The discomfort that traditionalists would feel with this change of language would be considerable, but would probably be offset by the empowerment that women would experience. On the other hand, after a few generations such a change might have the same negative effect on men that male language has on women. So it probably makes more sense to alternate female and male language. Though that would be awkward and difficult to learn at first, it would probably have the impact of problemizing God's gender, dislodging assumptions about male superiority, and keeping us constantly aware of the different logic of God language.

There is a kabbalistic tradition that when feminine and masculine energies merge and become whole, the repair of the world will take place. Men will embrace the female side that they have previously repressed and women will embrace their male side. Kabbalists tried to convey this by speaking of God as Shechinah, a divine presence that is the "bride of God within God, Mother of the world and feminine side of the Divine Self, in no way fully separable from the male Self of God. Indeed, the root of all evil, both cosmic and human, is the attempt to bring about such a separation."[1]

This kabbalistic language is somewhat flawed because it seems to assume that there really are stereotyped gender divisions that are not socially constructed, and in the process of validating Shechinah language it seems also to strengthen essentialist notions that rely on a kind of biological determinism. There are some tendencies within Jewish renewal that have fallen into this trap, speaking as though God really does have a gender, and that that gender is feminine. For them, prayer to YHVH is seen as too masculinist, while prayer to the Shechinah is seen

---

[1] Arthur Green, "Bride, Spouse, Daughter: Images of the Feminine in Classical Jewish Sources," in *On Being a Jewish Feminist: A Reader*, ed. Susannah Heschel (New York: Schocken Books, 1983), p. 255.

as liberating female energies. The truth is that Shechinah is never just a female energy—and that YHVH always embodies in popular conception some of the aspects of nurturance, compassion, caring, and emotionality that have sometimes been identified as stereotypically female.

So while I support inclusivist pronouns, I am less enthusiastic about trying to find new names for God besides YHVH. YHVH is the unpronounced name that indicates a movement toward the future—the transformation of that which is toward that which can be. I see nothing male in this word. In fact, it represents the very idea of transformation that promises the possibility of ending all oppression, including patriarchy. Nevertheless, no word or concept should become an idol, and if it does begin to function as a distraction from understanding the meaning it conveys, even the name of God can be shifted. God tells that very thing to Moses at the burning bush: that God was known to Moses' ancestors as El Shadie, the Breasted God, but that now God will be known as YHVH. If that switch from female imagery was necessary at that period, then any name suggesting maleness may need to be abandoned in this period.

One easier place to begin the transformation of language should be adding talk about God the Mother to our existing language of God the Father. God as Creator can best be understood in association with God as Mother, since the imagery of gestation, giving birth, and lactation can create an imaginative picture of creation. Some Jewish-renewal communities have already made this addition, so that when on High Holy Days they sing *Avinu Malkeynu* (Our Father our King, we have sinned before you, etc.), they alternate the verses with *Eemeynu Malkuteynu* (Our Mother, our Queen). Some feminists have questioned whether in the context of a patriarchal society any parenting imagery can do aught but reinforce the notion of a God with power over us, prolonging our spiritual infancy, and suggesting that autonomy and assertion of free will remain a sin.[2]

---

[2]Rosemary Radford Ruether, "Sexism and God Language," in *Weaving the Versions: New Patterns in Feminist Spirituality*, eds. Judith Plaskow and Carol Christ (San Francisco: Harper & Row, 1989), p. 160.

HERMENEUTICS OF COMPASSION

We approach the sacred texts and stories from our own particular location and background, and what we hear depends on who we are. Shaped by unconscious processes, limited by our social location, we inevitably come to understand scripture (and ourselves) through a limited lens.

We always need to remind ourselves of these limitations. How does my social location as an educated, middle-class, American-born, post-Holocaust, Jewish male affect not only the questions I ask but how I interpret and construe the world? How does the social location of the writer of the Biblical, mishnaic, or Gemara text influence how the issues get framed, what parts of the discussion get to be repeated and remembered and ultimately written down? What are the issues that seem relevant to the redactors or the editors of these texts? Why does the text say what it does about women? When women are noticeably absent, why are they absent?

Elizabeth Schussler Fiorenza has recommended to feminists that they adopt "a hermeneutics of suspicion" when reading the texts that would explore the liberating or oppressive values and visions inscribed in the text by identifying the androcentric-patriarchal character and dynamics of the text and its interpretations.[3] Fiorenza incorporates into her approach an understanding of what she calls kyriarchy: that men as well as women suffer from the hierarchical system of patriarchy. Not all men oppress all women, because there are some men who have power and some men who do not (in the extreme case, black slaves on American plantations were not oppressors of the white women who owned them). We know also that some women are more oppressed than others (Hagar more than Sarah in the Bible story), and some women, given their social position in a class structure, have been known to oppress some men. A kyriarchical reading acknowledges that we all have the capacity to oppress others, and that no one is without the potential for cruelty until we dislodge the legacies of cruelty that have been transmitted unconsciously from generation to generation and that are lodged as much in our religious practices as in our economic systems.

---

[3]Elizabeth Schussler Fiorenza, *Searching the Scriptures* (New York: The Crossroad Publishing Co., Inc., 1993), p. 11.

But once we recognize kyriarchy, I think we would do well to term our approach a hermeneutics of compassion. We want to uncover the dynamics that led to the formulation of the stories, interpretations, and traditions—and we want to recover, in the process, "her story" to supplement "his story." We understand that the dynamics of power have shaped what parts of our communal enterprise got preserved and what parts went underground into unrecorded legends, orally transmitted folk wisdom, and the stories that women tell one another through the generations (embedded not only in words, but in gestures, melodies, recipes, ways of attending to reality both consciously and subconsciously). Yet at the same time, we must also recognize that it is we—particular, limited, partially deformed human beings—who are doing the uncovering, and always doing it from our particular standpoint. So we need to engage in this process of reconstruction and recovery with a sense of compassion for ourselves and for each generation that came before us. Neither we nor they were evil people consciously intent on oppression. Rather, they, like us, were inheritors of a world of pain, doing their best within that context to stay true to the word of God as they heard it. To say this, to insist on compassion, is not to lessen one whit our necessary commitment to understanding the way that patriarchy has distorted our history, nor to lessen our commitment to building a Jewish community and a Jewish religious life that has transcended patriarchal distortions.

We are a people whose central act is one of remembering and testifying. We remember the transformations of the past in order to testify to the possible transformations of the present. So it is critical that we give our attention to remembering how and why women were excluded, their memories and stories and experiences denigrated, their wisdom devalued. It is only when this element can be reintegrated into our sacred history that it will be capable of providing us with a sound basis for understanding how to proceed in our mission of healing and repair.

HALAKHA

Jewish law has had two somewhat different thrusts in its treatment of women. On the one hand, it has often been a codifier of power relationships between men and women. Developed and promulgated by men, halakhic conceptions of women and their place in society has not just been a reflection of existing power relationships, but also, on the other hand, an active attempt to impose those relationships.

It is impossible to talk of Halakha as one simple or unified process. At every stage in Jewish history there has been a complex of forces operative in defining Jewish reality, and Halakha is often one attempt to impose a particular cast on the existing set of social struggles. So, for example, we cannot assume that a law or halakhic ruling that emerged at a particular period necessarily reflects the actual practice of the Jewish people in that period, any more then than today. More likely it reflects the views of a particular group of men about how reality ought to be constructed, and eventually became a weapon in their hands to create a world in accord with their vision.

So, for example, the constant railing against various forms of idolatry and worship of women goddesses in the Bible reflects a reality in which the Jewish people are not really settled on who their god is and how that god should be worshipped. Law and prophecy are often developed when there is a problem, not when the society seems to be functioning smoothly.

The greatest development and codification of Jewish law took place in the aftermath of the Jews' confrontation with and military defeat by Greek and then Roman imperialism. It is from the standpoint of relative powerlessness that Jewish men began to construct a set of laws to govern their collective lives. Yet much of this halakhic tradition—its endless debates about how to correctly prepare the Temple sacrifices, how to allocate the portions of food prescribed for the priests (*terumah*), what kinds of seeds should be used for planting, and much more in the talmudic debates—focuses on how to run a world that no longer existed at the time they had the debates. For eighty generations Jewish males have immersed themselves in these kinds of discussions.

How are we to understand this? On the one hand, immersion in this world preserved their sense of dignity and self-esteem. Though the outside world had left them relatively powerless, Jewish men could radically negate that world and its claim on their consciousness by immersing themselves in the world of Talmud. In that imagined world, they could have real power. So Talmud and Jewish Halakha were a compensation for powerlessness.

Yet on the other hand, this immersion must have seemed peculiarly complicated for Jewish women. It was not uncommon for Jewish women in the Diaspora to enter into public economic life, to be involved in production or in selling. In their contacts with that world they would undoubtedly have had much contact with male chauvinist sensibilities that saw "real" men as those who could exercise physical power over other men. The real men were the winners, the conquerors, the people who shaped events and dominated nations. From this standpoint, Jewish men were a pathetic lot: they were men who had lost, men who could not defend "their" women, men who could not defend or hold on to their own land. They were the most subjugated and despised of men. Like other women in oppressed cultures, Jewish women would certainly develop feelings of sadness, tenderness, and compassion for the men who were viewed thusly, and probably also some degree of subconscious contempt for them as failures. It was precisely the degree to which these men were powerless in the real world that Jewish women played a larger role than many women in surrounding cultures.

So the male escape into the imagined world of Talmud must have seemed particularly poignant. Yet it would also be true for these women that the talmudic discussions had an impact on their lives, defining what they could and could not do within the boundaries of Jewish communal life, and often subordinating them to their husbands. Jewish law was being shaped not by a community of men and women together, but by a community of men in which women were seen as a problem to be dealt with. Thus, the extent to which women may have been influenced by the surrounding cultures to see their men as failures and as objects of pity or scorn would have been severely limited by the degree to which they also experienced their men as dominating, controlling, and manipulating them, defining their roles, and imposing behavioral norms.

There is no reason to believe that Jewish women ever accepted these roles passively. It is impossible to explain the personal power of so many Jewish women in the current period as a sudden transformation from a previous role as powerless and merely oppressed. From the start, Jewish women have been powerful figures (e.g., Sarah and Rebecca), and if the male-dominated stories and traditions define women as subordinate to powerful males, distinct hints of the way women must have appeared as powerful to the men around them are simultaneously preserved in the texts. Without denying the reality of male dominance and oppression of women, we need to validate the fact that Jewish women were never totally powerless, that they never fully accepted male domination, and that they carved out for themselves, even within the framework of Jewish law, some areas of real power.

It's impossible to say whether the areas of Jewish law in which women were treated with more consideration, respect, and holiness than in surrounding cultures was a product solely of the ability of Jewish culture to stay true to hearing the revelation from Sinai and its insistence that all people are created in the image of God and deserve respect, or how much it was a product of the social power preserved by Jewish women, who had themselves participated in the empowering experience of the Exodus and had retained in their collective memories the power of Miriam the Prophetess and other strong and powerful Jewish women, like Deborah, who had been as legitimate as any Jewish man in shaping and preserving the Jewish people. Probably there is no such distinction—the ability to stay true to the revelation of Sinai was in part due to the relative empowerment of women, and in part to unconscious transmission to the children of the next generation irrespective of gender.

It is sometimes difficult for women in the current period to validate those aspects of Halakha that gave Jewish women some degree of power. First and foremost, feminists correctly point out that whatever power or respect was embodied in the tradition, it was given rather than cocreated by a community that validated women's and men's equal rights to interpret the tradition. To call what is *given* "power" is already to misunderstand. Second, the areas of power always existed within the context of an elaborate set of restrictions that functioned to give men control over women's sexuality and to exclude these women from the public life of the religious community.

But if we adequately acknowledge these points as central and definitive to the reality of Jewish women, it may then be possible for us also to consider ways of seeing how powerfully Jewish women were able to function within an oppressive system.

Let's consider, for example, the laws of *onah*—the requirement upon males that they provide sexual pleasure to their wives. There was no corresponding obligation upon women. Although the central function of sexuality was directed toward procreation, the rabbis specified that men were enjoined to sexually satisfy their wives, and this was taken so seriously that the halakhic tradition elaborates by specifying how long men in different occupations are allowed to be away from home in pursuit of financial gain, how frequently they must return to pleasure their wives. The woman has the right to sexual satisfaction even if she is pregnant or menopausal, and hence incapable of conceiving.

As David Biale points out, the rabbis drew a sharp distinction between male and female sexuality. "A woman's sexual impulse is within and no one can recognize her [arousal]" (Sanhedrin 7a). Nevertheless, "a woman's passion is greater than that of a man" (Bab Metzia 84a). Biale points out that "women are considered highly sexual but incapable of asking for sexual satisfaction. Men must attend to these needs to ensure a peaceful household. . . . Women who take the sexual initiative are so rare that if they do solicit their husbands to perform the marital obligation they will 'have children the like of whom did not exist even in the generation of Moses' (Eruvin 100b). This text seems to suggest that women who act against female nature are praiseworthy. Rabbinic culture, like its Biblical predecessor, cannot be labeled unequivocally patriarchal."[4]

It is conceivable that a patriarchal culture would still encourage men to worry about women's pleasure, to boast about who was the most successful at providing that pleasure, or to take pride in being sensitive to women's needs. But to build this into law, rather than to leave it to the discretion and will of individual men, can be explained only by reference to the continuing power of women within that culture.

Similarly, laws of menstruation. There is no question that through the centuries women have been degraded by being seen as "unclean" during their menstrual periods. Yet other accounts of menstrual separation emphasize women's power in this practice. Anthropological data suggest that when large numbers of women tend to dwell together, their menstrual periods tend to shift, and over some period of time they start to coincide so that the whole community of women are menstruating at roughly the same time. Put this together with Biblical injunctions that women must leave the camp when menstruating, and you get the picture of a monthly women's gathering outside the confines of the male-dominated world. Some observers have suggested that these gatherings of women must certainly have been a time in which women experienced their collective strength and unity, perhaps celebrated with music, dance, and ritual, recollected dimly today in the monthly Rosh Chodesh (New Moon) celebrations that have become a regular feature of Jewish-renewal communities.

The Torah prescribes separation for the time of actual menstruation

---

[4] David Biale, *Eros and the Jews* (New York: Basic Books, 1992), p. 54.

(just as it also prescribes separation for a man with a seminal emission, who is similarly judged "unclean"), but the rabbis report that *at the initiation of Jewish women of a particular area in Babylonia*, they would extend the separation to include seven full days of cleanliness after bleeding had stopped. David Biale makes a persuasive case that this injunction was added to enhance reproduction, since the abstinence ends just at the moment when women enter their highest level of fertility. Perhaps, though a Jewish people committed to increasing its numbers after the Roman decimation of Jewish life in Palestine could have found other ways (e.g., requiring that Jewish men not make love on the two days before highest fertility, but allowing it in the week after that). But an equally likely account might focus on the understanding of *niddah* as a representation of Jewish women's power—and the extension of it by Jewish women in Babylonia might indicate the consolidation of that power in daily life that gets sanctified through the institutions of a male-dominated religion. Following this logic through, the original monthly celebrations of women's power are now transformed. Jewish women no longer live together in one solidly Jewish society, but are scattered throughout the world. So they take the holiday that had previously empowered them, and extend it even further, but now on an individual rather than on a collective basis. Each woman is empowered to say no to a man, to not be available to a man sexually or in other ways.

If this had in fact been a conquest of power for women, then they would have had to couch it in a language that would still allow Jewish men to keep their self-respect in a world in which patriarchal fantasies compensated for real-world exile and powerlessness. By framing their withdrawal from men in terms of their own supposed uncleanliness, their supposedly "lower status," they could achieve a realm of private power that few other women in the world enjoyed. Not that this was the kind of real power that women ought to have—power that would make it possible for them to say no whenever they so desired without fear of male power. Yet to negotiate that on a household-by-household basis was simply impossible two thousand years ago. What was possible was the creation through Jewish law of a mandated separation that gave women twelve to fourteen days every month in which they would not have to be available to men. That this was simultaneously a denial for them of sexual pleasure certainly mitigates the degree to which we could call this real power, yet it was more power than any other group of women could expect. And as Rachel Adler has pointed out, it came at a high cost: the denigration of women's bodily functions, the acceptance of a view of women as somehow less holy, or dysfunctional, or tainted by virtue of her bodily fluids and secretions. It is inconceivable, Adler argues, that God would have made women as they are had God thought this to be a lesser state of being.[5] This denigration of women that is built into the justificatory structure of menstrual separation is a destructive male fantasy, even if its function was to justify allowing women more power than they had in other cultures.

What seems most implausible from the standpoint of anyone who understands the psychology of men under patriarchy is to imagine that this was dreamt up or imposed by men. Very few men socialized in patriarchy feel comfortable with the notion that they should be prohibited by law from having access to "their" women whenever they choose. True, some might choose not to have sexual intercourse during the heaviest menstrual bleeding. But few would choose to be prevented from having access to women in the week after menstruation ends. To think of this restriction as a fulfillment of male fantasies or male power is to deeply misunderstand the psychology of men under patriarchy. On the contrary, it would take a very powerful group of women to get men to agree to these restrictions under any circumstances.

My point is not to deny that women have been oppressed by Jewish law, but only to argue that the situation is much more complicated than powerful men dominating passive women. That is never who Jewish women have been. So Halakha must be understood often as a prescription of how some men wanted things to be, not necessarily as a full account of how things actually were between men and women.

That fact does not undermine the demand for Halakha to change in the contemporary period. Jewish renewal seeks to establish those halakhic changes so that women will achieve de jure what they are achieving de facto in some corners of Jewish life. These changes must be made quickly, decisively, and enthusiastically by a community that now recognizes how much it has lost by marginalizing women and all they could bring to Jewish religious life.

Focusing on halakhic change, however, can be a distraction from the numerous ways that Jewish life must change de facto and how we as individuals, families, and voluntary associations of Jews can change it.

---

[5]Rachel Adler, "In Your Blood Live: Re-visions of a Theology of Purity," *Tikkun* 8, no. 1 (Jan./Feb. 1993).

On this de facto level Jewish renewal seeks the following changes:

- Every family should share child rearing equally between men and women. To make this realistic, Jews should be involved in political struggle to guarantee paid parental leave from work during the first year of a child's life, job sharing, and shortened workweeks. Homosexual families should seek opposite-sex "friends of the family" to allow the child to form early attachments to both sexes.

- Every family should provide equal and full Jewish education for their children. Women should be given the fullest encouragement to master Jewish texts, Hebrew language, Jewish philosophy, and Jewish history. The ridiculous argument that women are not adequately skilled in Jewish texts to become *dayanim* (judges in religious courts) and *poskim* (interpreters of Jewish law) must be defeated by generations of women who are at least as well learned as men.

- Every Jewish institution should require that at least fifty percent of its leaders be women.

- Traditional "women's work" must be compensated at the same levels as traditional "men's work"—and all barriers to full equality must be removed.

- Women's study groups, *daven*ing groups, and spiritual exploration should receive full financial support from the community, and be honored and encouraged.

- A return to communal support for singles, including active involvement in helping those singles who want to meet appropriate partners, and the adoption of a norm that insists that couples invite singles to socialize on weeknights and to spend Shabbat, can take the pressure off women who get pushed into inappropriate marriages rather than endure the ongoing humiliations currently associated with being single.

- A communal commitment to providing emotionally and intellectually sophisticated and sensitive child care at all publicly held Jewish events including religious services, providing fully subsidized Jewish education and summer camps, and orienting public Jewish life to be sensitive to children's needs.

- A communal commitment that every person in the community devote a certain number of hours per week to assisting those families currently engaged in raising children, be that in the form of babysitting, teaching skills, or providing services that relieve some of the burden on parents.

- A communal commitment to honoring the ability of both women and men to provide nurturance, and a rewarding of those skills at every level of education (today it is the fast-talking or abstractly intellectual who gets rewarded in contemporary Jewish life.) Rewarding nurturance, and deeply honoring it, should not replace but supplement the honoring of intellectual life.

But Jewish renewal must become a halakhic movement—it must seek the continuation of the Jewish tradition as embodied in legal principles and norms, not only in social practices. So Jewish renewal will seek to embody this new feminist consciousness in a halakhic framework. Jewish renewal must seek to reestablish this kind of binding authority with a content that incorporates a new approach to women. Our *poskim*, the official interpreters of Jewish law, must have a feminist sensibility.

In future generations, even in the Orthodox world, there will be many more learned Jews who share Jewish-renewal sensibilities, and some of these will become *poskim*. They will reflect the needs of the community, and they will make rulings that will eliminate the various restrictions that prevent women's full equality in Jewish religious practice.

But the *way* that this will happen is that there will be an increasing number of Jewish-renewal communities that are serious about their spirituality and their commitment to Judaism and to Jewish tradition. These communities will lead full and rich Jewish lives, including Shabbat and *kashrut* and the range of spiritual and moral commands that they develop as attempts to take Torah seriously and serve as continuing witnesses to God's presence in the world. Young people from more narrowly Orthodox communities will be attracted to this kind of Jewish renewal, and will adhere to its *poskim*. Eventually, those who remain attached to officially Orthodox communities will see that their futures depend on making halakhic changes to accommodate the new sensitivities to women's equality. When that happens, Orthodox *poskim* will find the appropriate halakhic authority to make the changes they feel are necessary, and increasing numbers of ordinary Orthodox Jews will adhere to those halakhic authorities.

This process has already started in some corners of the Orthodox world. Women are being given the training in Talmud, Halakha, and Jewish texts that will provide them with the tools to press their case for full equality. Many Orthodox women are finding that even within the context of existing halakhic framework, there is no reason why they ought not have considerably more power and authority than the Orthodox community typically gives.

Ultimately the changes in the Orthodox world will be parasitic upon changes in other parts of the Jewish world. As the spirit of Jewish renewal becomes more powerful in all sections of the Jewish world, more and more Orthodox men will desire a change in the way Halakha deals with women, not because they want to be "hip" or modern, but because they want to be truer to their own developing understanding of what God wants of us. It is precisely because of their devotion to God that they will find the halakhic means to more fully express the deep Jewish conviction that all human beings are created in the image of God.

HOMOPHOBIA

The persistence of homophobia in the Jewish world is very troubling. There may well have been a set of practices in the ancient world, associated with the religious cults of oppressive societies, that ought to have been prohibited because of their association with cruelty and the distortion of human relations. The forms of homosexuality that flourished among the imperialist armies of the ancient world or among the dissolute ruling elites of Greece and Rome might have been reasonably condemned because they seemed inseparable from the forms of oppression associated with them. But such homosexuality has absolutely nothing in common with the kind that Jewish homosexuals are seeking to validate halakhically. Assaulted by so many other accommodations to modernity, the Orthodox world has decided to make this issue a principle, a way that liberal elements in the Orthodox world can show their more ultra-Orthodox critics that at least on this issue they are not prepared to succumb to the rhetoric of "rights" of the modern liberal world, and will remain faithful to the texts. And there are Torah texts that prima facie limit flexibility.

> Leviticus 18:22: Do not lie with a male as one lies with a woman; it is an abhorrence.

Leviticus 20:13: If a man lies with a male as one lies with a woman, the two of them have done an abhorrent thing. They shall be put to death.

Deuteronomy 23:18: No Israelite woman shall be a cult prostitute, nor shall any Israelite man be a cult prostitute.

Whatever the motivation of these passages, their intention as interpreted by the rabbis of the tradition was to prohibit homosexual acts. But that is the point: *as interpreted.* On the face of them, many Jewish homosexuals could agree to abide by them: the way they would lie with a male would be different from the way they would lie with a female (i.e., they would do their sexual acts in a different way). And they would not become cult prostitutes. If you wish to be a literalist, there is nothing here that prohibits at least some variants of homosexual activity. Presumably many Jewish homosexuals do lie with a man in a very different way than they would lie with a woman. Indeed, they could read the Torah's injunction to mean that one ought not try to pretend that a man is really a woman, and that what one is doing is simply repeating a heterosexual act, because, after all, homosexuality is unique and must be honored for its uniqueness and not for the way that it is similar to lying with a woman.

You say that this is pure sophistry? Perhaps more accurate to say that this is talmudic reasoning. The kind, say, that made it possible for the rabbis to develop the *prozbol* to get around an injunction that they don't like requiring the cancellation of loans during the sabbatical year. Where there's a communal will, there will always be a halakhic way.

"Wait," the halakhists will argue, "this is a different case, because here Torah is explicitly claiming that this is a crime so serious that it requires the death penalty. Nothing but a total abrogation of the halakhic method would be required to get around this Torah injunction."

David Kraemer, professor of Talmud at the Jewish Theological Seminary, taught me why this response is wrong. Just look, he advised me, at how the Talmud deals with a similar clear case in the Torah, the injunction to kill *ben tzorer umoreh*, a rebellious son. There is no ambiguity about the plain meaning of the text, and no question that rebellious sons existed. Nevertheless, the rabbis, understanding the incredible inhumanity and social unworkability of this injunction, dealt with it summarily. A rebellious son? *"Loe hayah veloe neevrah—there* hasn't been one and such was never created," they declared. Whatever the Torah means, it doesn't apply to the actual real-life rebellious children that we encounter in daily life.

So why don't halakhists take this same step in regard to homosexuality? Because they don't want to. Having succumbed to the pervasive homophobia of the society, they hide behind Halakha. Ironic, indeed, given the history of the Jewish people and the way that Fascists and other persecutors of the Jews have often lumped us together with gays and oppressed both groups, that Jewish religious leaders should be so eager to show that they too can find homosexuality abhorrent.

If their behavior deserves criticism, how much more so those in the Conservative movement who already *have* self-consciously taken steps to change Halakha with regard to women, but who nevertheless pretend that they are being coerced by Halakha into going along with antigay policies that they might not otherwise support?

Some religious Jews have a slightly more sophisticated argument. "No," they say, "homosexuals should not face explicit discrimination. But neither should we honor their life choice as equally valid with that of heterosexuals. Homosexuals have a profligate lifestyle and are engaged in sadomasochistic or coercive sex."

The actual charges are usually false when applied to the vast majority of homosexuals. But profligacy, sadomasochism, and coercion deserve to be condemned whether in homo- or heterosexual communities (and the level of violence and coerced sex in these "proper families" has been shown to be a serious problem in the hetero world). Condemn the profligacy, not the sexual orientation. By validating and sacralizing homosexual relationships, we make it less likely that homosexuals will find it necessary to engage in sexual acts only in emotionally unstable contexts.

"Homosexuals don't reproduce and we need more Jewish children."

Not true anymore. Contemporary technologies have made it possible for gays and lesbians to reproduce and raise families. Insofar as this point represents resentment on the part of heterosexuals that gays and lesbians aren't taking responsibility for raising the next generation, the appropriate response is: "You're right to feel that everyone should share the burdens of raising the next generation, and for that reason not only childless homosexual couples but also childless heterosexual couples and singles should be required to donate some time and money to assisting those who *are* raising the next generation. We may have to experiment with the appropriate forms for how this assistance can best be delivered, but this should be a communal obligation, and it has nothing to do with there being something wrong about homosexuality."

"Homosexuals don't validate marriage, which is the central institution of Jewish life."

Not true. Homosexuals are seeking the right to marry. If homosexual unions were allowed within the context of Jewish life, they would strengthen rather than weaken the institution of marriage. Conversely, in a society in which homosexuality is invalidated, many homosexuals will seek to be part of heterosexual marriages—and this will often have disastrous consequences for spouse and children, since the homosexual will have to falsify his or her real experience and feelings.

"If homosexuality were validated, homosexuals would begin to teach our children, serve as rabbis, and in other ways influence our community in the belief that homosexuality is a valid option. More children would become homosexual, and our community would be undermined."

It *is* likely that at some future time the channeling of erotic energies into socially determined gender constructions will be less rigid than today. But that time has not arrived and would not be precipitated by the Jewish people's giving equal respect to homosexuality. Some of those who are most fearful of this are people whose own sexual identities have been won through intense repression of desires that scare them. They assume that everybody is secretly struggling with the same issues. But most people are not on the verge of switching sexual identities, so the introduction of a different model will not throw everything into chaos.

Jewish-renewal communities have openly welcomed homosexuals and have refused to play along with any stigma connected to this sexual orientation. They seek to have homosexuality validated as an acceptable halakhic option—not just a private choice, but one which a religious community accepts.

Until homosexuality has been fully and unequivocally accepted, Jewish-renewal energies will be committed to ending discrimination, and to a full rethinking of this issue in the Jewish world.

CHAPTER THIRTEEN

THE ECOLOGICAL RELIGION

Torah warns that even when conducting a war, one must not destroy the trees of the city being besieged. The rabbis extended the prohibition so that it forbade the destruction of any object of potential benefit to people. Even a small amount of food or fuel should not be wasted. Later rabbis have extended this principle to include the notion that one should not use more than one needs.

Today our consumer economy is organized in sharp contradiction to that principle. Our society focuses solely on profit, without regard to what human beings really need or what we are doing to the planet's resources. Corporations spend huge amounts of money in advertising that helps develop a desire for products, and then they claim that they are merely acting to fulfill human desires. But the Torah tradition does not recognize this right to unlimited freedom in the area of consumption—its principle that we should not destroy leads to a notion of minimum levels of consumption necessary to achieve our ends.

There are some in the ecology movement who have misread the Torah and believe that the Jewish tradition calls for the conquest or domination of nature. This is false. Torah calls on us to work with it and to protect it, *le'avdoe ule'shamroe*.

Jewish religious life is based on that reverence and sensitivity. As the Bible proclaims, the whole earth is full of God's glory. So nothing is to be treated lightly or dismissed as expendable.

This sensitivity is embedded in the daily prayers and psalms that reawaken us to the grandeur and glory of the natural order, reminding us not to get so involved in the details of the social world that we lose touch with the marvelous drama going on around us in nature.

WHO OWNS THE EARTH?

The Bible is clear on this question. The earth does *not* belong to us. No particular human being has a right to ownership, nor do we collectively as the human race have the right to dispose of the earth as we so choose. "*Kee lee kol ha'aretz*—because the world is to Me," God tells us. It is because of the earth's special relationship to God that human beings do not own it and do not have the right to dispose of it as though it were solely in our charge. "The earth is the Lord's and the fullness thereof," says the psalmist. The Marxists certainly didn't invent the challenge to private property. Anyone who has ever bothered to read the Torah knows that God claims the ownership of the world, and all property rights are contingent upon the degree to which we live in accord with God's will.

The Torah is filled with this. When farmers reap their harvest, they must leave the corners of the field for the poor. This isn't a suggestion or a plea to landowners' kindness or compassion; it is a requirement based on the simple principle that the person who possesses the field and farms it doesn't have any absolute rights to the field. So God can order you to use the fields to care for others.

Human beings have rights only as stewards, and only to the extent that they are actually fulfilling God's commandments, living in accord with their capacity to actualize the Divine.

This is put most explicitly to the Jewish people: their claim on the land of Israel is totally contingent upon their ability to live up to the Covenant. Should they fail, as they have in the past, the earth will literally vomit them out.

In this historical period the same dynamic applies to the entire human race. Human beings face potential extinction in the next two hundred years unless they can reorient their attitude toward the earth, learn to respect its rhythms, respond to its needs, and forge a relationship with the planet more in keeping with our obligations as stewards.

Let's get real about the right of private property—the sacred cow of contemporary capitalist society. How, exactly, did anyone in America get the right to their property? The answer is not in prehistory. About twenty generations ago, groups of Europeans arrived on these shores and engaged in a ruthless battle with the people who lived here. Because the Europeans had superior technological strength and larger numbers, they were able to kill off or enclose in restricted reservations the indigenous peoples. In addition, they began to write pieces of paper that they called deeds to the land, which entitled the owner to dispose of the land as he saw fit, and this "right" was backed up by the military power of the governments that these people created. This naked land-grab, the theft of the land from one group and the appropriation by another, now gets sanctioned as the right to private property.

Jewish renewal problemizes this right. Counter to the spirit of private property, it reminds people that the world is in our hands so that we can fulfill God's requirements, not our own, that we are stewards, not owners, and that the world will not work if we persist in our arrogance toward creation.

Jewish renewal does more than proclaim the need to reinvigorate an ecological consciousness. It offers concrete ways to do that, based on the Torah tradition.

THE SABBATICAL YEAR

The earth needs a Shabbat, so God instituted the sabbatical year. "[B]ut the seventh year thou shalt let [your land] rest and lie fallow" (Exodus 23:11). Let the earth replenish itself. One year out of seven we have no right to exercise mastery over it. Instead, we will eat whatever the earth puts forth without our intervention or exercise of power over it.

This is not a metaphor.

One year out of seven we should stop working the earth, dedicating this year to replenishment of the earth. The seventh year becomes our joint commitment to working on the ecology of the planet together. The earth needs a rest from all our pollutants and from all of our complicated efforts to master and dominate it.

The result, Torah tells us, will not be mass starvation. The earth will continue to produce food, and we can gather it and distribute it. In fact, during the seventh year it might be a very valuable experience for all those who dwell in cities to spend at least part of the year doing some of that gathering and distribution.

Torah clarifies that the food that is produced in this way does not have any owner—it is *hefker* (ownerless) and available to everyone. By insisting that the food has no owner, Torah institutes a regular process of reminding us of a truth that today we are reminded of only by earthquakes, floods, and hurricanes—that we are not really in control, that we are really dependent on God for the sustenance that we think *we* have created.

The sabbatical year becomes an important instruction to the human race: you don't run things, you are stewards, and you can have power to run your lives only if you do it in accord with the higher purpose that you are here to serve.

Imagine the human race taking off one year out of every seven. This could be done in a rotating manner: the earth divided into seven quadrants, and each one taking off a different year. Or all together. But for tens of millions of people, the experience they would have is that of a society in which most people are not working, and in which essential services (hospitals, food distribution, garbage, utilities, teachers, and trainers) are provided on a more shared basis (yes, there may be some people whose life-saving work cannot be stopped, but that will be only a tiny percentage of the workforce, and these vital-service technicians should be given sabbatical years rotating through the seven-year period).

The first consequence would be a reduction in the total number of goods and services available, a hardship which, if distributed fairly, people would quickly come to accept.

The second consequence is that we would have a lot of time on our hands, time in which we would be able to reconnect with the earth and with one another. The question of how to organize our society, what goods need to be produced, and how best to provide for the continuation of the planet could be looked into with the seriousness that it needs but does not currently obtain.

The sabbatical year would also provide us with an opportunity to rethink what we are doing with our own individual lives and how much we are serving our own understanding of the common good. Some people would use this opportunity to take courses aimed at developing new skills so that job rotation would be possible. In a good society, the sabbatical year would be a prelude to this kind of rotation of jobs, ensuring that most people would not be stuck in any one job for all their lives. Imagining that there are a certain number of necessary and unfulfilling jobs, people would organize their lives in such a way that one or two of their job rotations would have to involve that kind of work, and the remaining four or five would involve jobs that are far more fulfilling.

The full picture of a world committed to a sabbatical year may be generations off. Yet it would certainly make sense for the Jewish Renewal movement to paint a picture of what a world might look like that committed itself to this concept, and then struggled to achieve it. The sabbatical year provides both a stop on the ecological danger and a moment to organize new directions. It is a statement on the part of every person on the planet that we are in this together, that we care about one another and the future of humanity, and that we are dedicating this time to finding ways to take our stewarding responsibility seriously.

It should be noted that a sabbatical year would *not* be a revolutionary elimination of capitalism. It would, rather, be a significant restraint on capitalist relations. It would challenge the fundamental ethical basis of ownership, and it would eliminate that ownership for one year, but it would not eliminate it permanently. As such, this is a reformist measure. But it would be the kind of reform described by Andre Gorz as a nonreformist reform, because it would increase human beings' total amount of power to struggle for the kind of world in which they want to live, while actually being itself the embodiment of that conquest of power, a massive saying no to all those who tell us that what we must do to be adults or mature or realistic is to spend all of our adult years working.

Revolutionary? No. It's merely renewing the tradition, going back to the sources, taking it from the point when Jews "got" it and understood what was at stake in God's revelation.

But if this was always there in the Jewish tradition, why didn't you know about it? The answer is that the tradition itself turned away from the plain meaning of the text and transformed it to fit the times. Whenever people tell you that some modern is trying to twist the text to fit contemporary needs, just remind them of the way that was done by the mishnaic rabbis who transformed the sabbatical year into something much tamer.

The classic step that the rabbis took refers to one of the important concomitants of the sabbatical year: the Biblical injunction that all debts should be cancelled every seventh year. The elimination of debt was a way of saying to everyone that the ultimate important thing was not our money, but our caring for one another.

But by the time of the Mishnah the Jews no longer lived in that kind of society. They had been conquered, first by the Greek imperialists, then by Romans. Within class-dominated societies the rule of selfishness always appears to be common sense or human nature, and fearful that they would lose their money if they made loans to the poor, who might hold off on repaying them till the sabbatical year, in which they would be absolved of responsibility, lenders stopped making loans, and the poor or near-poor suffered. And thus the rabbis who shaped the Mishnah and Gemara backed away from the radical meaning of the Torah text and created a legal fiction, which they called the *prozbol*, an arrangement which allowed loans to be made directly to the court rather than to another individual, and the court would then loan to the borrower, with the stipulation that loans from the court were not subject to the sabbatical-year injunction.

The *prozbol* is indicative of the "realistic" accommodation that the rabbis began to make to the world of imperialism and oppression. I raise the issue not to condemn them, but to understand how the spirit of Shabbat and sabbatical year could slowly become subverted so that future generations would no longer recall the meaning that these institutions had, a meaning that challenged the world of domination.

Nor should we lose sight of the fact that Jewish law, even while becoming more and more "realistic," has retained its strong commitment to the notion that moral claims of the community supersede any property rights. When private property rights are used in a selfish way, the rabbis believed, they would almost certainly lead to the destruction of the community. They made this point most forcefully by declaring that the sin of Sodom was its inability to share its wealth with the stranger, with the weak, and with the poor, and its insistence on the absolute right of each individual to his own property.

SAVING THE PLANET

The bottom line for saving the planet is this: We need to develop a worldwide plan for how to use the world's resources and how to distribute the world's wealth.

If we let each individual corporation or each country decide how to do this, we will get the following picture: The wealthy countries will buy up the resources of the poorer countries, and buy "rights" to dump the world's garbage there. Those resources will then be shaped into products that can "find a market" in the wealthy countries. On this path lies the exhaustion of the world's resources, the continuing increase of planetary pollution, and the escalating destruction of the ecosystem.

The justification corporations use—that the market shows what people want more effectively than anything else—misses the point that the market has no mechanism for people to show their desire for planetary survival and no mechanism to show their desire for a morally and spiritually grounded universe. The market can show only what choices we support within the logic of limitless consumption; a logic that has caused profligate destruction of the world's resources.

A worldwide plan would have to address what goods we want to have produced, what resources need to be preserved for future generations, what restrictions on production are necessary to protect the environment, and what we can do with our toxic wastes. Such a plan needs coercive power, the product of a serious decision on the part of the entire human race to give priority to saving the planet.

Won't this require a massive change in the way we do business?

Yes, it will. And that's part of the reason why Shabbat and the sabbatical year are such important contributions, because they are practical ways of building and reenforcing a new attitude toward the world.

A strategy to save the planet will have to address the question of social justice, just as the Bible did in instituting the sabbatical year. We will have to make it in the self-interest of Third World countries to participate, and the only way that can be done is for us to rectify the tremendous imbalances of wealth between the developed and underdeveloped world. In the past, this concern has been framed entirely in terms of justice. But now there is an equally compelling reason: the need to save the planet. If we understand that the future of the human race depends on a whole new orientation to the use of the resources of the world, then we need to create the conditions under which those resources will be wisely used. That will require significant redistribution of the world's wealth so that poverty no longer generates abuse of the environment.

Of course, it would be ridiculous to focus primarily on ecological destruction in the Third World without noting that it is the advanced industrial societies that are responsible for most of the misuse of the world's resources and the bulk of its pollution.

"But," you may object at this point, "surely if people did not choose to purchase environmentally destructive products, the corporations wouldn't produce them. Similarly if the people did not choose to spend hundreds of billions of dollars on wasteful weapons systems or other environmentally hazardous governmental projects, they could elect different representatives, who would choose different priorities. So it's really people's attitudes that have to be changed."

True enough, as far as it goes. And for this reason, Shabbat and the sabbatical year become central precisely because they are vehicles for introducing a different kind of consciousness, one that reconnects us with the earth's rhythms and challenges the priority of making, conquering, subduing, shaping the world to our immediate needs. It is from a standpoint of reverence and wonder that we can begin to develop attitudes that would make us put the survival of the planet above other desires.

Yet there is something misleading about the logic of any argument that focuses so much on the need to change individual consciousness without understanding the economic and political realities that daily help shape our choices. Take, for example, one of the heaviest polluters—the automobile. The immense power of the auto and oil industries around the world has been mobilized to block the development of a rational system of mass transportation. In Los Angeles, for example, a public train system was bought and dismantled by automobile manufacturers so that people would become more dependent on cars. Using their resources to encourage the election of sympathetic legislators, the corporations got government to build a massive highway system. In circumstances such as these, it makes sense for people to choose to live far away from the areas in which they work, and to rely on automobiles to get there. It misses the point to blame the individual consumers for making this choice or to ask them to raise their environmental consciousness. What is needed is systemic change.

But the moment people recognize that those larger changes are needed, they become overwhelmed. Transforming the world economy? Creating a worldwide system of rational planning for use of the world's resources? "It's too big for me to handle," is a typical response. "I have enough trouble keeping my own life together. Let me do what I can do—recycle my garbage or vote for a candidate who says he or she will deal with a few of the worst environmental hazards."

Yet if this larger transformation is necessary to save the planet, then this feeling of powerlessness becomes a major environmental issue. Environmentalists cannot afford to simply address environmental issues—they need to look at the emotional and ideological sources of this sense of powerlessness.

Jewish renewal can be an important ally in this process. Jewish renewal confronts the ideologies of powerlessness and tells us un-equivocally: the God that rules the universe is the Force that makes possible the transformation of that which is to that which ought to be. And Shabbat becomes the moment in which we reconnect to that Force.

For these reasons, the environmental movement needs Jewish re-newal, and it needs to learn how to encourage people to become involved in Shabbat.

A JEWISH ECOLOGICAL MOVEMENT

Arthur Waskow, a respected theorist of Jewish renewal, has suggested that "for the next several generations the Jewish people should shape itself into an intergenerational, international 'movement' with the goal of protecting the web of life on earth. We should shape our prayers, our celebrations, our spiritual practices, the rearing of our children, and our public policy with this purpose in mind."[1] He's right.

Rabbi Zalman Schachter-Shalomi suggests that we should add a new code of eco-kosher practices to our practice of *kashrut*. Products that are grown using earth-destroying pesticides may not be eco-kosher. Newsprint made by chopping down an ancient and irreplaceable forest may not be eco-kosher. Products that are made out of irreplaceable natural resources may not be eco-kosher. Institutions that pollute the environment or use excessive amounts of fuel may not be eco-kosher. Investments in companies that pollute the environment or are other-wise ecologically insensitive may not be eco-kosher.

The Jewish community should be at the center of ecological cam-paigns, and should make eco-kosher a halakhic requirement.

---

[1]Arthur Waskow, in *New Menorah*, Spring 1993, p. 1.

JEWS AND MONEY

Saving the planet cannot be done without a fundamental revision of our attitude toward money. There is nothing intrinsically evil or dirty about money. Money can be used to serve God and to serve the highest goals of our human community.

But there is some problem with the current distribution of money and the ways that those who have disproportionate amounts of it tend to use it. They often hide from themselves any knowledge of how their disproportionate access to money was achieved—at what cost to other human beings.

Traditional Judaism challenged the attitude that people with money have a "right" to use it in any way that they please. Money was always seen as a gift from God, and the possessors had responsibilities to the community, which would govern how it was used. It was these very limitations that the early capitalists sought to overthrow, and their attempts to reform or abandon Judaism were in part motivated by a desire to be free of any such ethical constraints.

Jews can use the economic power available through the Jewish community, and more importantly through individual Jews who have money and who can be influenced by a moral vision projected by a Jewish community committed to healing and repairing the planet.

But even to begin to get to these issues, Jews are going to have to heal some of the pain that they feel around money issues. Jews have been accused of being cheap (though in fact Jews are more generous with their money than most other ethnic communities in the United States when it comes to charitable giving), fixated on making money, and willing to be dishonest or manipulative to secure and retain it. These anti-Semitic stereotypes have made wealthy Jews very reluctant to engage in any serious discussion about the responsibility of money.

Fearful of offending those with money, many progressive Jewish organizations have avoided raising any questions that might potentially suggest conflict with the capitalist market system. Unfortunately, to avoid that issue is also to avoid any serious grappling with saving the planet.

Jewish family funds and foundations have developed a racket in which liberal staffpeople spend their energies making the funders feel good about themselves so that the money keeps flowing. To create that feel-good atmosphere, the staff avoid exposing the donors to projects involved with ideas that might challenge fundamentals, develop society-wide strategies for transformation, or generate radical activism. Instead, the projects that are funded delineate limited areas, avoid "ideology," and are concrete and practical rather than visionary and transformative. So we get a Jewish health center, educational center, or some video project, but what we don't get is funding for strategies and the creation of transformative movements. The funders can feel good that they can see something practical and concrete (the late-twentieth-century equivalent to having their names on plaques, or on buildings they helped finance), and everything works fine until someone asks, "Exactly how is all this activity likely to change the fundamental dynamics that have created the problems we are facing?" But since those who ask these kinds of questions get escorted to the door, the racket works just fine. The racket concludes with gatherings in which the fundraisers bring the recipients together with the donors, the donors get lauded for the great work they have been funding, and everyone leaves feeling smug and self-satisfied.

Jewish renewal must challenge these dynamics. It should insist that those with money begin to take their stewardship of the money more seriously. If saving the planet is first on the agenda, then how we transform the market economy is necessarily part of the discussion. And if transforming the market economy is relevant, then how we build a movement that can challenge the ethos of selfishness and me-firstism comes next. And if we talk about trying to challenge the ethos of selfishness, then we must discuss how to challenge the cynicism and defeatism that make most people unwilling to think about attempting to change any fundamental aspects of reality. And this in turn leads to Jewish renewal as one of the venues that gives people hope and faith in the possibility of transforming something fundamental. These are the kinds of issues that would transform Jewish money from a venture in feel-goodism to a force for real healing and transformation.

EATING AND *KASHRUT*

Our relationship to the physical world comes to greatest focus in the daily acts of taking that world into our bodies through eating. If the world is God's creation, then how and what we consume reflects our attitude toward God.

Jews made eating the center of our religious life. The sacrifice of meat at the Temple was an occasion not only to feed God symbolically, but actually to feed other human beings. Sharing the sacrifice was mandated (you were forbidden to leave the meat for the next day, so you literally had to share it). The sacrifices at the Temple were our way of proclaiming that what we have—our produce, our animals—doesn't really belong to us, but is merely a gift in trust from God. In acknowledging that connection, we call attention to the need for restraint and care in how we treat the natural world.

When the Temple was destroyed, the ritual was incorporated into each individual household. Thus, each table becomes a mini altar to God; each act of eating becomes an occasion to reconnect to the world and to straighten up our relationship to it. We wash our hands and bless God for that opportunity, bless the bread and thank God for having made this produce possible, and we end the meal with a long blessing thanking God for the food, for the abundant land, and for all the wonderful things in our lives.

It is a tradition for Jews to study a text during the meal. One tradition says that if three people eat and don't share words of Torah, it is as if they were eating at the table of the dead.

Food is about life, and so it is appropriate to self-consciously focus one's attention on the issues raised by the Source of life. Some families assign a different member the responsibility of teaching something during each meal. Children often feel empowered and respected when they get the opportunity to teach something that they have thought about or learned in school. Guests often enjoy these moments when a table is quieted and attention directed to a text or a teaching.

Not surprisingly, *what* can be eaten has been a perennial topic. The laws of *kashrut* delineated in the Torah are not accompanied by any explanation of what has been chosen and why, so Jews have engaged in endless speculation. Jewish-renewal circles tend to see the kosher laws as a compromise with vegetarianism. The original injunctions to Adam and Eve prohibited the eating of meat. It was only after God's disillusionment with humans reached the level where S/He wanted to destroy almost the entire population, in the age of Noah, that God allowed people to eat animal flesh (presumably because the level of violence and insensitivity had become so high that channeling all this destructive energy into animal-killing might at least preserve human beings). But once God had decided on communicating to human beings the need for transformation of the world, it seemed plausible to raise meat-eating to a problem. And *that* is precisely what the laws of *kashrut* can be seen to do. Their hidden message from God is this: "Okay, you can eat meat. But I'm going to make it such a hassle for you, and I'm going to restrict what you can eat so much, that you'll gradually come to realize that it would be easier to be a vegetarian."

Whatever God's intent, it has become standard practice that in Jewish-renewal communal events the food is vegetarian. And many renewalists have found it increasingly difficult to eat meat. The more they focus on what they are eating, the harder it is for them to justify killing another animal to satisfy their own palates. The pain and cruelty inflicted upon animals grown for slaughter can be ignored only by massive denial. To the extent that Jewish renewalists are more aware of how any particular current reality came into being, they become aware of how this particular piece of meat came to be in front of them on the table. Participating in the process that led to the animal's being treated in a painful and cruel way is difficult for many renewalists to justify.

In the past few decades another consideration besides respect for the pain of animals has entered into the discussion. Most animals bred for slaughter are high on the food chain. They consume large amounts of grains that could feed the tens of millions of people who are starving to death each year. To feed these animals that are being raised for slaughter, we remove from the pool a great deal of food that might be used by human beings. Eating the meat is part of the causal chain that leads to human starvation.

Moreover, the lands that are plowed under to feed these animals is often land that has previously held trees that helped preserve the earth's atmosphere. The meat-eating habits that are particularly strong in the West have created an economic incentive for poorer countries to cut down their rain forests and to otherwise destroy the earth's environment.

No wonder, then, that Jewish renewalists are reluctant to eat meat. And if you don't eat meat, or milk products that have been mixed with enzymes coming from animals, you are automatically kosher. So vegetarian *kashrut* makes a great deal of sense from a Jewish-renewal perspective.

But similar moral concerns about the well-being of the planet and of our society have led Jewish renewalists to follow Rabbi Zalman Schachter-Shalomi's suggestion that we develop an eco-kosher ideology that questions whether food that has been grown in ecologically destructive ways, or food that has been harvested by underpaid farm-workers, or food that has been produced by companies that are exploit-ing their workers or by companies that are destroying the environment, can really be considered kosher. It is plausible that these kinds of considerations will expand in the coming generations as Jewish re-newalists seek to make their eating congruent with the rest of their understanding of the world. And that is what the kosher laws were meant to do in the first place.

The concern to make one's life congruent, to build a life in which our daily activities embody and reflect our understanding of the moral and spiritual realities of the world, is one of the guiding principles of Jewish renewal. Saving the planet is only the most immediately needed arena in which this congruency must be reflected. Ultimately, the goal of Jewish renewal is to fashion communities and lives that are, in essence, songs of witness to the God of the universe.

REJECTING NEW AGE APPROACHES TO THE EARTH

Some people look at the earth as our highest guide and point of worship. While I generally believe that the growing New Age con-sciousness has a salutary effect in combatting the mechanistic mind-set that has exhausted the possibilities of the materialist worldview, I also believe that those of us who wish to save the planet from destruc-tion ought to be careful to avoid a new idolatry.

It's easy to romanticize nature and to ignore the less wonderful aspects: the earthquakes, fires, and storms that seem to strike out randomly in hurtful ways, destroying human and animal life. *We cannot define the world as intrinsically morally good unless we include in that world or in our conception of nature the existence of human beings who understand our obligation to change the world and make it more moral.*

Some will argue that we should not privilege human reality and human needs over other species'. But this way of understanding the world is erroneous because it imposes an individualistic framework that has led to our excessive reliance on a "rights" consciousness, and then insists that other species also have rights. It would be more appropriate to imagine the world as one huge organic whole, a body suffused with consciousness but also having developed parts of it, namely the human species, that are invested with special conscious-ness and hence with special responsibility for figuring out the needs of the whole. We may be an important part of the mind of the universe. Using our capacities is no more a reflection of arrogant speciesism than is the plant's photosynthesis. We are both using our unique capacities.

Sometimes when we are in pain or having difficulties, it makes sense to quiet our own minds, to get more in touch with parts of our bodies that may be trying to communicate something to us. And similarly, there may be times when we as a species need to quiet ourselves and listen to other parts of the totality of nature. But knowing when that is necessary and when it is not is itself a decision that we have to make— not one that can be suspended in favor of allowing nature to decide for us. And this not because we think of ourselves as higher than nature, but because we are part of the natural world, namely that part that has been given a certain set of capacities that we are to use. It would be arrogant and stupid for us not to use the capacities that nature has developed through us.

So we are part of nature. But we are a particular part, the part that has been given the understanding of and need for transformation. Our task as stewards, then, is not to leave the world the way it is, imagining that what is somehow embodies a higher wisdom that we ought not to tamper with, but to help it grow and change in accord with our best understanding of what the world is and needs. That understanding of what is and what is needed will itself change as we, the human race, grow and develop and free ourselves from the prisons of the past.

CHAPTER FOURTEEN

SHABBAT

S habbat is the quintessential Jewish observance and one of the
most important contributions the Jews have to offer to the larger
world. It is a pleasure and a joy, yet its message is deep and abidingly
important. I had almost no clue of this when I grew up in a Conservative synagogue where Shabbat simply meant a Friday-night service.
All the rhetoric about pleasure seemed to reduce to a good spread of
food at the Oneg Shabbat or Kiddush that followed services. Most of
the people went home, turned on their televisions to catch a late-
night show. A smaller group did bother to come to *shul* the next
morning, but many of them went shopping afterward, or to some
sports event, or were attending to parts of left-over work, or paying
bills, getting the car or home repaired, mowing the lawn, or doing
other chores. Needless to say, I had no idea of the traditional experience
of Shabbat as twenty-five hours of withdrawal from the way we normally lead our lives, immersion in a joyous and celebratory ritual whose
rhythms challenge our world's logic of domination and consumption.
When I encountered Shabbat as performed by people who were seriously into it, it was like going from the jingle on a television commercial
to a great symphony.

Shabbat is the moment in which Jews withdraw from the human
activities involved in mastering and controlling the world, and focus

instead on responding to the grandeur of the universe with awe, wonder, and radical amazement. As the psalm for Shabbat proclaims, "I rejoice in Your works, O God. I will exalt in the works of Your hands!"

All week long we are involved in getting and spending, in acting on the world to make it turn out the way we want. On Shabbat we cease from that whirlwind of activity. We change the mode from active to receptive. We embrace Mother Earth with joy and celebration, we sing songs to the sun and the moon and the stars. As we express our delight at God's creation, we are overwhelmed with the immense preciousness of Being.

In celebrating the world, we stand in reverence at the Source of all being. The Creator is beyond all our categories. Language allows us to reidentify the repeatable and publicly observable aspects of reality. But God is beyond all language, the Source of all Being. No wonder, then, that language is of such little avail.

As Abraham Joshua Heschel used to point out, there are two attitudes through which we can approach the world: one in which we seek to accumulate information in order to dominate, the other in which we deepen our appreciation in order to respond. "As civilization advances, the sense of wonder almost necessarily declines. . . . Mankind will not perish for want of information, but only for want of appreciation. The beginning of our happiness lies in the understanding that life without wonder is not worth living."[1] Shabbat is the the moment each week fully dedicated to responding with appreciation. It is, Heschel once said to me, greeting the world not with the tools we have made but with the soul with which we are born; not like a hunter who seeks prey but like a lover to reciprocate love.

Shabbat is for appreciation, for receptivity, for wonder.

It is twenty-five hours dedicated to being open to the world, responding, celebrating. In some respects Shabbat affirms a part of religious experience that is not uniquely Jewish. Other religions also have religious celebrations of the grandeur of the universe and the magnificence of creation.

But Shabbat is also something else, the weekly celebration of the

---

[1]Abraham Joshua Heschel, *Man Is Not Alone: A Philosophy of Religion* (Philadelphia: Jewish Publication Society, 1951), p. 37.

possibility of emancipation from oppression and domination: *Zeycher le'tziyat mitzrayim*.

Shabbat is both the result and celebration of the first national liberation struggle. Ruling elites throughout most of recorded history have sought unlimited power to expropriate the labor of others. When there is no limit, when people are forced to work till they drop or drop dead, we have a condition of slavery. Shabbat is the first historical imposition of a limit on the ability of ruling elites to exploit labor. It is the embodiment of the first time when the people who work were able to say no to a ruling elite and make it stick.

The notion that working people could do this, that they had rights that limited the power of the bosses, was a new notion in history. The Jews built their religion around it.

Shabbat wasn't a day of rest only for those who could afford it. "Six days shalt thou work, and the seventh day is a sabbath to your God. On it, you shall do no work, neither you, nor your family members, nor your animals, nor anyone who works for you, nor the stranger who is within your gates."

Shabbat is the first completely democratic sharing of rest. It was the Jews who won this, and as the Jewish way of organizing the week spread, it became the gift of the Jewish people to the rest of the world. It was only in the twentieth century that this gift was extended to a second day, creating a weekend. And when that happened, it was through social movements that had disproportionately large Jewish participation in their leadership and activists.

Shabbat is a nonreformist reform. It provides a space and a concept through which people are encouraged to get more power.

Shabbat is the real-world testimonial to the fact that the world can be transformed from what is to what ought to be, and God is the Force in the universe that made that possible.

People often ask the question, "Is there any society in which people are actually living according to the utopian ideals that you espouse?" The answer is, "Wherever people observe Shabbat, they are proving that the utopian ideals are really possible."

"But it's only one day in seven," you might say.

That's also its genius. Shabbat becomes an assessment of what is possible in a world of oppression. Rejecting the position that every step along the way toward a liberated world is useless because it is so limited, Shabbat testifies to the power of achieving partial gains in the struggle. It is a taste of the world to come, but a taste that gives the incentive to fight for more. That's why Jewish tradition encourages us to prolong Shabbat, and to take the spirit of Shabbat into the rest of the week with us. It may take us the whole Shabbat just to get rid of the pressures of the week enough so that we can begin to taste a different rhythm by its end.

When Mao Zedong was fighting to liberate China from feudalism he did so by liberating bits of land in which the Communists could begin to actualize their vision of the future. The experience energized the cadres, whose taste of the possible gave them strength to fight to change the actual. Shabbat works that same way. So Shabbat promotes a consciousness that detaches us from commodities, encourages us to focus on the world not from the standpoint of how we fit into it, but as creatures who sing to God its praises.

The weekly choice to dedicate one day *not* to the shopping mall, *not* to the television or telephone or computer, *not* to the consciousness of the market, opens the possibility for sacred time in which the call of God can be heard. It stands in contradiction to the logic of the competitive marketplace and to all other forms of oppression. In giving us this taste of what a future world could feel like, it becomes liberated time, the vanguard of the struggle to liberate all time from the sophisticated forms of domination of consciousness.

SOCIAL-CHANGE MOVEMENTS NEED SHABBAT

One of the great weaknesses of contemporary social-change movements is their one-dimensionality. People get together for the purpose of trying to change the world, but rarely do they recognize their own needs for emotional, ethical, and spiritual nourishment.

When these universal needs are not addressed in a progressive context, they may be addressed in a conservative context. The very people who may attend a political meeting one day find themselves at a more conservative church or synagogue the next day, and they hear discouraging messages. Little serious attention has been paid to providing a spiritual framework that may help sustain political work.

We need a variety of political contexts in which people can participate, some designed to maximize safety, and others to maximize connection.

If secular political movements were to dedicate one twenty-five-hour period a week to celebrating the grandeur and mystery of the universe, and recalling and honoring the struggles for liberation of past generations, and to resting, that would be a major step toward providing the kind of nourishment their members need to sustain themselves. Imagine if people from all different faiths as well as secular people were to meet for a joint celebration and pot-luck once a week, share music, stories, dance, and play—and if they were to dedicate some of this time to public ceremonies of gratitude for the world and for the Force within it that makes for the possibility of liberation. Imagine if they were even to adopt Shabbat restrictions: no work, no money, no shopping, no involvement in shaping, building, creating or destroying things.

The development of the most transformative visions requires getting out of the narrow rhythm of goal-directed energies. When your whole body and mind are swinging to that rhythm, the pace is so speeded up and the anxiety level so high that you can focus only on the short term. There's plenty of time for that, all week long, every evening, and on Sunday. But imagine one day a week when a different kind of political energy prevails, one concerned with envisaging the future we really want, reconnecting us with our transformative visions of the possible, and allowing us to *feel* those possibilities. That can be done only when the rhythm of the workweek has dimmed, and a different, more transformative energy enters our souls. When Shabbat works we are open to that energy, a more transformative, relaxed, and quiet excitement makes it possible for us to recognize a whole different part of our being. A progressive social-change movement that understood the importance of such an experience would have a profound impact on the world.

How to Make Shabbat

All week long we sell our labor to those who own and control the institutions of the world of work. Time itself is organized according to the needs of production and consumption. Even when we are not working, we often use our time to acquire or plan how to acquire.

Shabbat is a different rhythm, a rhythm of calm, peace, rest, joy, pleasure, song, wonder, amazement, celebration.

A religious family often begins planning for Shabbat early in the week, inviting guests for Friday-night dinner or Saturday lunch.

Hach'nasat orchim, bringing guests to your table, is one of the many joys of Shabbat and runs counter to the isolating nuclearization of family life in our world.

Cooking for Shabbat meals often starts on Thursday night. Since cooking and purchasing food (or anything else) is forbidden on Shabbat, everything is prepared in advance (though making salads or other dishes that do not require cooking is permitted). It's a tradition to put special energy into preparing delicious food, cleaning oneself and one's household, putting out special dishes and tablecloths and flowers, surrounding the home with beauty. People often don't get home in time to do all the preparations, and even if they've been working ahead, a last surge of energy often has a rushed and frenetic feeling, mirroring the world of work. Over the course of the next many hours, that pace is going to change radically. Monitor it—because the degree to which you move beyond that to a more centered, calm, and quiet place is the measure of how profoundly you have allowed yourself to enter into Shabbat.

Shabbat begins eighteen minutes before sundown on Friday night with the lighting of Shabbat candles and the traditional blessings. It is customary for families to bless their children, and for members of a religious community to offer blessings to one another. Then, off to the community to connect with friends and family.

In smaller Jewish-renewal communities it is typical for people to gather together in groups of twenty to fifty to sing and pray the Shabbat evening service. Unlike the austere settings of so many temples, the Jewish-renewal gatherings are often in living rooms, sometimes followed by a pot-luck dinner. As people get together, they greet one another with hugs and embraces and expressions of pleasure. The group will hum or sing a few songs to get everyone settled in, and to allow time for the children to join the mood or to be settled at their own child-oriented service elsewhere in the home.

A good way to begin the Friday-night service is with a guided meditation that leads people through the events of the week, encouraging us to remember all that has happened, and to allow each of the problems and struggles to be put aside for the next twenty-five hours. The meditation then focuses on relaxation, and on recalling the aspects of the world that we want to celebrate in the coming day.

The Welcoming of Sabbath and the Evening Service are chock-full of moving passages that provide a special entree into the holiness of the day.

First, there is the awakening of all our senses and of our yearning for full connection with all that we could be and will eventually be. "*Yedid Nefesh*, the precious One of my soul, draw me, Your servant, to Your will." Singing as though to a highly sexualized other, Israel calls upon God to reveal Her/Himself, to spread Her/His canopy of peace over us, so that we can be strengthened and participate in eternal joy. Come, my beloved, to greet the Shabbat. Long enough have we dwelled in the valley of tears—God will make it possible for the ancient city to be rebuilt on its ancient site, those who have devoured us will be devoured, and God will rejoice over us as a bridegroom and bride rejoice together.

There is an unmistakable sexual charge to Friday evening, shaped in part by the recognition that after services the two main things that are on the religious agenda are a delicious meal and sex. It's wonderful to allow these anticipations to mix with the sensuous religious texts, and to savor in anticipation a coming sensual delight. Far from demeaning spirituality, sex and food are critical elements of a Jewish spirituality. Pleasure is good!

Next, there is the evening service. We greet the transformation from light to darkness and darkness to light. Many Jewish-renewal communities go outside at this point, to look at the stars, to witness the evening twilight, to stand in its glow, and to repeat our thanksgiving at the wonder of nature. Suddenly moved from background to foreground, no longer treated as "the eternal just there" but instead as a daily miracle to which we have grown stale, we respond to the magnitude of our world. Here we are, one small group of people out of the four billion alive at this moment, on a small planet revolving around a small star, peering out onto an evening sky filled with thousands of such stars, some of which may no longer be in existence even as we gaze upon their light, we are suddenly aware of our small place in the magnitude and grandeur of creation. We become deeply aware of how we take for granted the daily movements from light to darkness and darkness to light. Our spiritual smallness is not meant as belittling or to set us up to be better servants to an all-powerful God, but rather to set a realistic context for seeing ourselves, and our nobility and adequacy, as one tiny speck of the totality, and our own lives as one momentary speck in the tiny pebble we call the planet Earth.

From here our consciousness moves to the joy of getting all this. The recognition that we are subject to commandments about how to live, the sheer joy of having such commandments, and the opportunity to study Torah and to do them—and to function as a religious community testifying to God's presence—fill our souls, for they are our life and the length of our days.

And then, the proclamation of faith: Hear, O Israel, the Lord Our God, the Lord is One. And the message: to love this Power that makes for the possibility of transformation with all our hearts, our souls, our might. And to teach this to our children and to proclaim it in the public arena as well as in private. To recognize that the physical universe will work only if we create a just society. And to remember that our own liberation from Egypt is a present reality. Through quiet space, and then through joint singing, to proclaim that the world will be transformed, and that when that transformation has taken place, on that day God will be unified and be one.

Together in community, or back in one's family space, a blessing over the wine is recited, because wine gladdens our hearts. Washing of hands with a blessing, and then the blessing over the bread, usually two *challot* (twisted loaves). And on to a sumptuous meal, together with *zmirot* (special Shabbat songs). It is customary to study some text together or for one of the guests or participants to prepare a teaching, often from some aspect of the week's Torah portion, but possibly from any aspect of the tradition or relevant spiritual teachings.

After the meal, the traditional blessing—Birchat Hamazon, sung communally. Because the blessings sometimes take on a rote quality, it has become traditional in some Jewish-renewal communities to stop in the middle of this ten-minute blessing and to have each person insert his or her own words of blessing to God for the food, for the land, for the goodness that we have experienced, and/or to add petitions that the All-Merciful One will grant us some special blessing that is then described.

I've found that by the time one gets to the Shabbat teaching at the table, the songs, and the blessing after the meal, a first serious level of relaxation enters consciousness. The body is beginning to get the notion that it doesn't have another immediate task in front of it. The joy of singing together, the playful little phrases and melodies of the Birchat Hamazon, are beginning to condition the body to believe that it may have some real rest in front of it. And real sensuous pleasure.

In Orthodox circles, it's a religious obligation for man and wife to have sexual relations on Shabbat when that is physically possible (physical ailments or disabilities excuse, but physical absence does not—couples are under religious injunction to find a way, if at all possible, *not* to be separated on Shabbat, even if that means coming home from a long trip). Jewish-renewal circles tend to extend the *mitzvah* of sex to unmarried couples who are already engaged in sexual relations.

Friday night is a real pleasure. But one does not have a taste of the experience of Shabbat unless one keeps its energy going for the entire twenty-five hours. Given the stresses of the world of work, it often isn't until Shabbat afternoon that our bodies fully relax enough to really begin to benefit from the restfulness that Shabbat offers.

The next morning people get up to thank God for the morning, for bodies that are still functioning, for consciousness that returns to full awareness, for a physical world that gives us solidity under our feet and removes the tiredness from our bones.

Jewish-renewal communities have developed a variety of different Shabbat-morning services. Some tend to follow the traditional prayer book, and to include a full reading of the Torah portion (the Torah having been divided into a different section for each week of the year). Others have put their primary focus on celebrating the body and nature, and then moving to a focused study of the Torah portion, sometimes with a group of people putting on a play to act out some of the issues raised, sometimes with an individual preparing a commentary, sometimes with a free-for-all general discussion of what the Torah portion means, sometimes with a more formal teacher giving a more scholarly talk.

Some communities combine this with a discussion of the issues of the larger world. Jewish renewal does not accept the notion that the week's political events are somehow irrelevant or a distraction from Shabbat services. While specific political organizing strategies tend to be avoided because of the anxiety that would be provoked by having to debate them out, more theoretical analyses of contemporary situations are encouraged. The two things that are never ruled out of a Jewish-renewal community are God and politics. Not, of course, the politics of which particular candidate to endorse or support, but the politics that involves discussing the contemporary world and evaluating the latest developments in it from the standpoint of Torah- or God-based insights and concerns.

Jewish-renewal events in the morning can be very high and very meditative. Nevertheless, there remains in the body the rhythm of the week, so that there is often a frenzy to the Shabbat-morning experience, even among communities that consciously know that it ought to be otherwise. But since in fact the body does not face the kinds of tasks it has had all week, it slowly begins to recognize that something else may be in store for it.

It's traditional to return home then and have another festive meal—a sumptuous lunch, together with singing, blessings before and after the meal, and study of the weekly Torah reading at the table.

Shabbat afternoon is dedicated to pleasure. Singing, hanging out with friends, food, sex, reading (as long as it's not connected to work or to some obligatory task—it must be aimed at pleasure, though the pleasure of learning or grappling with complex topics is certainly part of this). It's not unusual for people to take long walks to reexperience their ties to the natural world, to organize a picnic or a gathering of friends to discuss some shared issue in intellectual, cultural, political, or spiritual life, or to meet with friends for singing or shmoozing. For others who have a week full of interactions with others, Shabbat is a moment of escape from social responsibilities, so the afternoon is used in solitary meditation, reading, walks, or even just plain sleeping.

The traditional restrictions on Shabbat (no cooking, cleaning, gardening, turning electricity on or off, riding in cars or subways, traveling long distances, writing, smoking, talking on the phone, spending money, paying bills, tearing, or any of the thirty-nine kinds of work that were needed to complete the original Temple Sanctuary in the desert) flow from one central theoretical idea: human beings should not be acting on the world to make their impact on it, but rather should be dedicating one day to spirituality, that is, to dealing with the world not from the standpoint of manipulation and control, but from the standpoint of rejoicing, celebration, awe, wonder, and radical amazement. So every act of transformation of the world from one state of being to another is avoided. For twenty-five hours, just pure receptivity to what is there, joy, celebration, awe, and wonder.

I've found that it's harder to observe Shabbat when you are trying to take a bit or a piece of it—a two-hour stretch on Friday night, for instance—and stick it into a busy life. You really can't get a feel for what it's like. It's a meditative practice, one that takes time for you to move from one state of consciousness preparatory to the next, and you really can't skip stages. You haven't had the experience until you've tried doing it for the full twenty-five hours, and doing it for a year or two minimum. Eventually you train your consciousness to slow down, so that Shabbat energy starts to hit you even in the first few hours. Eventually it brings some of the greatest pleasure and greatest inner peace and relaxation you could ever hope to experience—but only for those who are willing to allow themselves to get into it, do it in the full way. That's why the rigid boundaries, the restrictions on what you can do, are essential. But you haven't yet had the Shabbat experience if all you're aware of is what you *can't* do. For many people it can take a good eighteen hours of Shabbat before the body starts to give itself messages that suggest that it may be safe to let down a few more barriers to being fully present— and that's after months of getting into it. At first the anxiety produced by "trying" to do Shabbat "correctly" is going to outweigh the possible joy and relaxation energy that comes when one allows oneself to relax into the Shabbat rhythm. When you start to experience it as a liberation and a pleasure, as a special treat, then you are actually having the relevant experience, and then you are in a position to understand why Jews have often said with full enthusiasm that Shabbat is one proof that God loves us—because we never would have been able to devise such a wonderful experience without divine inspiration.

Some Jewish-renewal groups get together late Saturday afternoon for study or discussion of a Jewish text, to share visions with one another about the world to come and their hopes for it and how one might get there. To sing, to share a third Shabbat meal, or just to shmooze. I've been to groups that always integrate a good half hour of shared visions about how the world could and should be changed, or have a speaker sharing some such vision. But this is not a meeting— there are no votes to be taken or debates to be won; it's envisioning for the sake of the vision. When we are encouraged to go very deeply into this, to not let any "they won't let us do it that way" kind of statements block our ability to conceptualize how we really want the world to be, then this vision-sharing can be very empowering. But on Shabbat it is best when interspersed with songs, dancing, *bentsch*ing.

One custom I recommend for these late-Saturday-afternoon gatherings: the exchange of humorous stories. I've seen Shabbat gatherings in which people take their turns as wannabe stand-up comedians, others at which some of the most humorous literature of our and other traditions are read aloud, still others at which people construct humorous skits based on the weekly Torah portion. Shabbat is for fun, and a humor-oriented Shabbat afternoon full of rowdiness and playfulness can give a Jewish-renewal group a zap of energy to make sure that not everything is deep, soulful, and serious.

No wonder, then, that Jews typically become quieter, more pensive, even wistful or sad as Shabbat departs. It's typical for friends or families to gather together with wine, spicebox, and multiflamed candles and do the Havdalah (separation) ceremony at night after the appearance of three stars in the sky. Stories are told of the "days to come," the messianic period when our fullest visions of what human life could be like will be realized. The task is to bring that Shabbat energy into the rest of the week, and with it to become reinfused with the commitment to the healing and repair that our planet so badly needs.

How Did We Lose Shabbat?

If Shabbat is so wonderful, how come so many Jews stopped observing it early in the twentieth century?

There are several factors. First, it's a lot less fun when people don't have the barest level of material needs met. If you're hungry—and many Jews have been—Shabbat, and for that matter all kinds of spiritual practices, feel less fulfilling. Still, a hungry community would probably observe Shabbat. But it becomes less fulfilling if, second, you have a class structure in which some people have money and more than enough food, and others have little or none. If those who have are observing Shabbat and making it their observance, the others feel left out. Some may feel resentful of those who have more and deflect the anger onto Shabbat. Others may feel put down, implicitly "less than," because they have less opportunity to take pleasure in Shabbat, and may feel that those who do ought to be sharing more of what they do have. So they feel that the synagogue and the community really have been appropriated by these others, the ones who get called to Torah, who have most influence over selecting the rabbi, who seem to be defining community practices. And so Shabbat seems less real, less about the celebration of working people who have managed to win a victory, more the celebration of the self-satisfied. And that makes Shabbat lose some of its taste. Third, as the level of oppression of Jews increased, the level of joy decreased, and many of the official definers of Shabbat put more energy into defining the boundaries than into celebrating the joy. Fourth, many people abandoned Shabbat when they emigrated to the United States and then faced the choice of either not getting any work at all or working on Shabbat. Without the supportive structures of a Jewish community able to provide adequate economic help, many "chose" to abandon Shabbat, and justified it to themselves by telling themselves they weren't really giving up so much (which, as point three indicates, may have been how some actually came to experience it).

The last point is important for understanding why some religious people have argued for legal restrictions to impose a day of rest. Without those restrictions, the capitalist market forces people to "choose" to work. The dynamics of the marketplace work like this: one store stays open on Shabbat, and then it makes more money because it gets all the sales from those who hadn't found time to do their shopping during the rest of the week. With its more money, it can afford to lower prices on individual items, because it is selling more goods than its competitors. This gives them a market advantage that may soon drive competitors out of business. So the competitors must stay open on Shabbat also, so that no one gets an unfair market advantage. But this has the effect of forcing people to violate Shabbat, since they will be employed by these firms only if some of them are willing to work on Shabbat. This creates the case for a legal forced closing—because then no one gets the advantage, and hence everyone gets the benefit of the holiday.

The problem with legally mandated closing is that religious coercion, once it begins, can easily get out of hand. Not only does this pose an unacceptable risk to our individual freedoms, but, as Israeli society shows, it can lead to the widespread discrediting of all the truths in religion, because people feel that they are being forced to observe things they don't want to observe. Yet the converse is equally true, though not widely understood: the way in which the capitalist market compels people to abandon spiritual space for material well-being. It's only when this is more deeply understood that a community can begin to contain market forces. And at that point, Shabbat should not be enforced through the intervention of government, with its coercive powers, but through the consensus of a community that refuses to patronize stores or businesspeople who violate its ethical or spiritual norms. But this kind of tactic certainly ought not be tried in a period in which the majority or even significant minorities *want* to do business on Shabbat, not only because it would be wrong to coerce them, but because the entire spiritual community that tries to observe Shabbat would be undermined by the presence within it of people who feel coerced into it. Spirituality requires choice. This goes for imposition on teenagers or children as well. Better to create safe spaces for children or teenagers who don't want to be part of Shabbat (community centers, playgrounds, schools, movie theaters, athletic facilities, dance halls) than to forcibly integrate them where they don't want to be. The rebellion against coercion is part of the God energy within our children, and it should be treasured and nurtured, not suppressed or resented. Shabbat can work only as a choice and as a gift, never as an imposition and a demand. Let them see your joy in doing it and the joy of others in your community, and let them understand it as a special treat, not as a requirement for proving that they are obedient or really care about you as parents.

While those who become part of the Jewish-renewal community will voluntarily accept the boundaries of Shabbat, people should always feel free to join or to leave the community or to negotiate their own degree of participation. In the course of a life, one may have moments when one is deeply engaged in Jewish renewal, other moments in which Jewish renewal is peripheral, or when one is simply not involved—and that must always be a free choice on the part of each individual, or the whole community will suffer.

The tragic irony of contemporary Jewish life: Only a small part of our community actually allows itself the pleasure of this twenty-five-hour weekly meditation and joyous celebration. Without this experience, no wonder they imagine religious life as ponderous obligation rather than a miraculous and healing gift.

CHAPTER FIFTEEN

JEWISH HOLIDAYS

Judaism's special message is that the Force that is celebrated in all other religions as the One that creates and sustains the universe is also the One that makes possible the transformation of the universe. No wonder, then, that Jewish holidays focus on celebrating both aspects of God: the Divine as revealed through nature, and the Divine as revealed through history; God as the Creator, and God as the Power of healing and repair.

No communal transformation is real unless it involves individual healing and repair, and no individual healing can be sustained unless it is associated with communal transformation. For Jewish holidays to work, they must facilitate both. Those who say, "I will work on the personal first, and then worry about the big picture," or those who say, "I will work on the social transformation, and then worry about how this gets translated into personal life," are equally mistaken.

There are four categories of Jewish holidays: those that combine the celebration of nature with the celebration of God's transformative power (Pesach, Sukkot, and Shavuot); those that celebrate the transformative moments in Jewish history when God's spirit triumphed over "reality" (Chanukah, Purim); those that concentrate on individual and communal self-transformation with the aid of God's energy (Rosh Hashanah and Yom Kippur); and finally, there are days of mourning: Tisha B'Ab and Yom Ha'Shoah.

My task here is to point out ways in which Jewish renewal can add to the traditional celebrations.

THE MAJOR FESTIVALS

Judaism built upon the existing harvest celebrations in the ancient Near East and added to them a set of meanings connected with the Exodus from Egypt. In so doing, Judaism made concrete its unique vision of God: the Power that is *both* the Creator and Sustainer of the universe *and* the Force that has made possible the understanding that cruelty is not destiny. So each of these holidays has a set of rituals specifically connected to celebrating the natural order (Pesach, the holiday of Springtime and earth renewal, symbolized by the egg, potato, parsley, lettuce, and other fruit of the earth; Shavuot, the holiday of the early grain and the first fruits; Sukkot, the holiday of harvest thanksgiving), and a set of rituals connected to celebrating the liberatory experience of the Jewish people. The Jewish-renewal task is to take each dimension, bring it to life, and ensure that the creativity embedded in the rituals is reclaimed or recreated through supplementary spiritual techniques.

PESACH (PASSOVER)

The most widely observed Jewish ritual is the Passover seder, because of both its reaffirmation of family and community and its striking transformative message. Passover is one of the clearest articulations of revolutionary Jewish consciousness; it is the ritual least in need of renewal. All one need do to bring this ritual to life is to take the ritual seriously by reading the Haggadah and talking about it.

But not everybody does that. I've been to many seders where people either read the Haggadah in a ritualistic manner ("Be sure to get every word said, and quickly"), or else where the readings are drowned out by private discussions and a communal embarrassment about "imposing" some quiet and collective attention. Mostly, seders are repetitions of what we experienced as children.

It takes some courage to break through and say, "Hey, there's something really important here in the Haggadah, and I'd like to ask that we give it some serious attention."

One point of the seder is to affirm that we are the descendants of slaves—the first group of slaves in recorded history ever to wage a successful rebellion against their owners. There are others who would have done their best to forget this kind of humble past, or who would have reconstructed history so that they could see themselves as descendants of gods or of superhuman heroes. We can be proud that our people have clung to their vision of themselves as a slave people and have insisted on telling the story of liberation as the central founding event of our history, which is the concrete embodiment of our message: that the world can and should be transformed.

Once that is done, the key to making the seder work is to take seriously its central demand: "It is incumbent on every person to see her/himself as though s/he personally had gone out from Egypt." That is, this is not just about some ancient liberation—it is about our liberation today.

That is precisely the point made in the Haggadah story of the rabbis meeting in B'nai B'rak and discussing the Passover issues all night. The rabbis were, in fact, the leaders of the Bar Kochba rebellion against Rome, and they spent the evening planning the rebellion. To protect themselves from being caught, they placed their students outside the building, and when the Romans were approaching, the students yelled in, "Our teachers, the time has come to say the morning Shma." This little vignette tells us that we too should use this time not just to talk about the good-old days, but to become actively engaged ourselves in planning how to transform the world. Passover seders should have this element of strategic focus—it's not just a ritual, it's an occasion to move forward the collective discussion about the strategy we are going to use to defeat the contemporary embodiments and successors to Roman imperialism. In short, talk about overcoming slavery is not symbolic or "religious" language—it is about the real thing. So a Jewish-renewal seder must have some time allocated for concrete discussion of how to move politically and/or culturally to transform the contemporary world.

There's no way to engage in that discussion without also assessing the degree to which we Jews have become oppressors. Whether that be in regard to the way that a Jewish state for decades has denied to Palestinians the rights that we insisted upon for ourselves, or whether it

be in the way that some Jews have uncritically identified with capitalism and have benefitted from the exploitation of others, the issue of
how the oppressed can sometimes and to some extent simultaneously
function as oppressors to others is a relevant topic for the Passover
seder.

The seder is also a good time for Jews to think holistically about our
history. In every generation there have been some people who have
risen to power with the intention of destroying the Jews, so it makes
sense to discuss our target status, the way we became the other of
choice through much of European history.

When people point to the relative material prosperity of Jews compared to other ethnic groups in the United States, and use this as a
reason to claim that Jewish oppression is a matter of the past, they fail
to understand the history of that oppression. Jews were doing well from
a material standpoint in prewar Germany as well. Anti-Semitism, like
sexism, cannot be reduced to an economic category—there are other
unique forms of oppression besides material deprivation. Jews who
sympathize with the oppression of every other group but who have little
understanding or knowledge of the history of their own people may be
engaged in a massive denial of reality. This denial is sometimes inspired
by internalized anti-Semitism and the resulting need to convince
oneself and one's non-Jewish friends that "Jewishness really isn't very
important," and that it's "really just an interesting historical relic of the
past."

But the lesson of our history is that there is no easy way out, no way
for one people to make a separate peace with a world of oppressors or
assimilate successfully and without moral compromise into that world.
Our own liberation and our own mental health require the liberation of
all people, and the end of all oppression. And perhaps it is this recognition that makes Passover such a universal holiday, and the seder such a
wonderful time to invite non-Jews and nonpracticing Jews to your
home to experience the aliveness of Judaism's liberatory message.

The keys to making the seder successful are to follow the traditional
requirements of the seder, to be sure to allow plenty of time for serious
discussion of the issues it raises, *and* to allow time for a discussion of
the contemporary world and where we are in the struggle for human
liberation. The Haggadah is a book that contains the story and instruc-
tions for the seder, and numerous creative, Jewish-renewal inspired
versions are available. Use the Haggadah as a guide, not as a strait-

jacket. But be sure that you let your guests know beforehand that you expect a late evening, plenty of discussion of the text, and that *you* take the whole thing seriously and want them to do the same.

Because there are elaborate rules for cleaning your home, using a separate set of dishes during Passover that you don't use during the rest of the year, and eating foods that have no trace of leavened bread, wheat, rice, legumes, or barley, some people get so totally absorbed in the ritual preparation that they are too exhausted to plan how to make the seder a meaningful spiritual/political occasion. Don't make that mistake. Allow yourself to imagine that you yourself have gone through the first liberation and, empowered by that experience, to imagine how you, together with friends, social movements, the Jewish people, or the potential allies among the peoples of the world, can now use that liberation energy for the benefit of the entire world. If *that* discussion hasn't been engaged in a serious way, you have missed the point, no matter how kosher your house or delicious the food.

The transformation involved in the message of seder need not be experienced only on the collective or communal level. *Mitzrayim*, the Hebrew word for Egypt, comes from the Hebrew word *tzar*, which can mean a strait or a narrow, a tight place. So some Hasidim have taught that the liberation from Egypt is like a spiritual rebirth, a moving from the narrow places in which we find ourselves stuck, to some higher level of spiritual liberation in which we experience the freedom from previous psychological encumbrances that kept us from being in touch with our highest selves. The birthing of a new self requires eliminating all the heavy material encumbrances that tend to weigh us down, the *chometz* or leavened stuff of our soul that misdirects us toward power and wealth and away from a purer self represented by the simplicity of matzah. So we can use the Passover season to clean out our attachments to *chometz* and become ready for the trek through the desert that is the prerequisite to higher consciousness. Then the rituals, the retelling of the original story, the many traditional Passover songs, can beautify the occasion and make it one of the most wonderful holidays you could possibly experience.

These themes for the first two days of Passover are easily incorporated into the seder. But many Jews find it harder to sustain the meaning of Passover for the next six days, when we are still required to eat matzah and avoid all consumption of wheat and grain products. According to the tradition, these were the days when the Jews actually made it out of Egypt, crossed the Red Sea, and watched the Egyptian forces that were chasing them—with the aim of forcing their return to slavery—suddenly drown as the sea returned to its normal pattern. Though the Bible records Moses' sister Miriam leading the women in exultant celebration, the Midrash, written fifteen hundred years later, reflects a deeper ambivalence about the defeat of our enemies. According to this tradition, when the heavenly angels sang songs of praise to God as the Egyptians were drowning in the Sea of Reeds, God reprimanded them for celebrating the suffering of his children the Egyptians. So some Jewish-renewal communities have dedicated these later days of the holiday to an exploration of the tension between means and ends in the struggle for liberation. Having had separate strategy discussions at their individual seders, the community comes together on the last two days of the holiday, shares their thoughts, and reflects on the degree to which the liberatory goals are consistent with those means.

This thinking is informed with the notion that sometimes it is appropriate to express anger at the oppressor, and if necessary to meet force with force. Though Moses tried to get Pharaoh to acquiesce in the Jews' liberation from Egypt, it was only when the first-born sons of Egypt had been slain, a symbolic repaying of the genocide of the male Israelites by Pharaoh, that the oppressor agreed to allow the slaves to leave. So the discussion about means and ends, if it is to be more than hot-air pontificating, requires a serious assessment of the current situation. How many people will die of starvation or cold if the current system is peacefully allowed to continue? What cost in pain and suffering is there in refusing to meet the violence of the oppressors with the violence of the oppressed? Is it legitimate to rejoice at the death of our enemies? For Jews these questions continue to have particular importance when we remember that it was the absence of violence against the Nazis that left us defenseless as we were taken to be slaughtered. On the other hand, I have discussed in this book the many ways that people too quickly justify violence, in part because they misidentify the voice of cruelty with the voice of God, and hence end up thinking it obvious that their own liberation requires the use of violence against others. No wonder that many Jewish-renewal communities find these discussions as lively as any at their individual seders.

Though Passover aims at reinspiring us to be involved in the real-world struggles for liberation, it ends with prophetic readings that call our attention to a messianic transformation of the world. In that spirit, some Hasidim developed a custom that has now been adopted by some Jewish-renewal circles: Se'udat ha'Mashiyach, the final meal in honor of the Messiah. At the very end of the eighth day of Passover, immediately after Havdalah, people gather to share a meal; songs of hope; and visions, legends, and literature of the messianic period to come.

SHAVUOT

Fifty days after the first day of Passover comes the holiday that celebrates both the first fruits and the giving of the Torah at Mount Sinai.

Many communities prepare for the giving of the Torah, supposedly given at dawn, by staying up all night and studying various parts of the Torah tradition. While this can be a moment of spiritual highs, it can also resemble an endurance contest, a time to show off who knows the most texts and can come up with the best interpretations. So Jewish-renewal communities have often tried to change the focus to one of preparing one's own consciousness to accept the yoke of Torah.

The first question to be seriously addressed by each individual is this: "What is keeping me from being able to accept Torah in my life?" The question itself can take two different directions. One direction focuses on our individual or communal resistance to being "too religious" or "too Jewish." To what extent is our current level of commitment based on a rational- and heart-assessment of what feels right? Or is our current level of involvement a product of unexamined fears, such as that our fellow Jews and non-Jews will see us as irrational, weird, or will be less willing to trust us if we become "too Jewish" in their eyes? Are we afraid to make a commitment to anything beyond ourselves, fearful that taking upon ourselves the requisites of a religious commitment might interfere with our efforts to "make it" in our career or our struggles for fame, glory, power, or money? Do we resist any commitment to a community, fearful that in taking on responsibility to the needs of others we will feel flooded or overwhelmed in ways that a more narrowly controlled life might avoid? Or are we fearful that we can't master the skills, afraid that learning Hebrew or studying Torah will exhaust our resources? Which of these fears are we willing to give up to accept Torah?

Another explanation of accepting Torah means accepting the responsibility to become part of a vanguard committed to healing and repairing the world. How much are we resistant to this responsibility because we know that it will interfere with our ability to make deals with the powerful? How much do we discount the possibility of changing things, and hence reject Torah and God? When we focus away from social change and insist that we are not yet ready to take on the larger society until we've gotten our own personal lives more together, how much are we motivated by a desire to "not be bothered" by the big issues or by an almost religious conviction that our powerlessness is inevitable and cannot be changed? What kinds of changes would it take in our daily lives and in our self-understanding to be ready to take upon ourselves the responsibility for healing and repairing the world? What kinds of sacrifices would we be willing to make to sustain social movements, even though we know that those social movements are likely to be flawed and will not totally achieve their objectives? And what stands in the way of our making a deeper commitment to accepting this Torah of liberation, this knowledge that the world can and should be transformed, and that we are God's only possible partners in the process?

Jewish-renewal groups that meet to discuss these questions, and allow these questions to inform the way they approach the texts, are in the best position to receive Torah on the morning of Shavuot.

Shavuot is also the time in which we honor converts to Judaism. We read the Book of Ruth, the first great convert, who became the grandmother of King David, the progenitor of the Messiah. So Jewish-renewal groups sometimes plan public events to welcome non-Jews who are interested in exploring Judaism, and to provide them with initial information about the Torah tradition. Other Jewish-renewal communities publicly honor those who have converted since last Shavuot, listening to their stories (including an honest accounting of what parts have not always been easy in finding acceptance in the Jewish world), and recommitting the community to caring for these newest members.

Finally, Shavuot is sometimes brought to life with an agriculturally focused observance of the gathering of the first fruits. Some communities actually go to a country setting, where they cut and eat the fruits.

A mass march of Jews down the streets of your city or hometown after services on Shavuot, carrying first fruits that they have brought for the homeless or hungry, can be an impressive and fulfilling gathering, a way that the community indicates that they've "got" it about Torah, that Torah is about healing and repairing the world, and that Jewish rituals must reflect that commitment.

SUKKOT

The great Jewish thanksgiving celebration is also the commemoration of the days when Jews lived in flimsy accommodations in the Sinai desert for forty years. Traditionally, Jews build these temporary huts, *sukkot*, and dwell in them for eight days.

The idea of moving out of my apartment or house to live in a *sukkah* always seemed impractical to me until I tried it. Living in a temporary shelter—particularly one with a water-permeable roof made of twigs, reeds, vines, tree branches, and other forms of vegetation arranged in such a way that one can see through them to the stars—has a special effect of reconnecting urban and suburban dwellers to the natural order, and to the transitory nature of our carefully constructed forms of material security. We decorate the *sukkah* with fruits and vegetables to symbolize our thankfulness at the plenitude of the earth. Putting strings through carrots or cucumbers or melons or pumpkins or sweet potatoes or squash or apples and then hanging them from the tree branches that are part of the roof of the *sukkah* has definitely been one of the more challenging Jewish rituals for me, but if you hang enough of these fruits and vegetables you really get a beautiful *sukkah*, and living in the *sukkah* for a week makes it easier to affirm that we are dependent on God and the natural order, not the masters of it.

In religious communities it is customary for people to invite one another to their *sukkot* for celebratory meals each evening of the week-long celebration, and usually to invite at least one poor person or one person who has no *sukkah* of her/his own to be part of each evening meal.

Torah commands us to celebrate with four species of vegetation on Sukkot: the *lulav*—a single palm branch, two willow branches, boughs of myrtle—and an *etrog* or citron fruit (very much like a big lemon). During the holiday service these four species are used in a ritual waving and in a procession around the synagogue, though in some Jewish-renewal communities a parade outside with these and other fruits and vegetables assembled for the purpose of donation to the hungry repeats the Shavuot ritual procession described earlier.

Sukkot reconnects us with the living planet that sustains us, what others call the Gaia energy. The transformative experience of living in the *sukkah*, the tradition in synagogue of processions with *lulav* and *etrog*, the community experience of thanksgiving for all that we have been given—all these are part of the transformative experience in which we learn to give up our attachment to our personal possessions and remind ourselves that everything we have is a gift.

Sukkot should be the time the community gathers to make concrete assessments of current ecological struggles, and develops strategies for how to strengthen ecological movements in the coming year. Each Jewish community can sponsor a large public gathering that combines discussions of the current crises with strategic planning. Sukkot thus becomes more than a ritual celebration of God's generosity to us—it becomes a very concrete way of reenergizing our participation in the real-world struggle to save the planet. Such gatherings should be infused with Jewish ritual, including a procession with the four species, and small group meals in the community's *sukkah*.

The eighth day of the holiday, Shmini Atzeret, was once a day of assembly when ancient Israel prayed for rain. Today it has special significance in a world in which the water resources of the planet have been polluted and damaged. Though the entire holiday is about healing the planet, this day can be dedicated to celebrating water and rain, focusing on how to preserve this vital resource, how to stop the pollution, and how to share the earth's water resources. This concern has taken a special significance in the Middle East since it has become a source of tension between Israel and surrounding Arab peoples. Conversely, a cooperative arrangement regarding water among Israel and her neighbors could be a valuable model for other parts of the world. So we both celebrate the water and plan how to conserve the world's water resources and vegetation, and the atmosphere that gives us rain.

The ninth day is Simchat Torah, the day of rejoicing in Torah. The cycle of weekly Torah reading is completed on the evening of Simchat Torah with the last verses in Deuteronomy, and the first portion of Genesis is begun again the next morning. The traditions of dancing joyfully with the Torah, of having each person called up to the Torah to read a few lines, and of playful pranks in the synagogue are part of a welcome relief from the serious strains of the holiday season (since Sukkot begins only five days after Yom Kippur).

ROSH HASHANAH, DAYS OF AWE, AND YOM KIPPUR

The once-a-year Jews who descend on the temples and synagogues on the High Holy Days often bring with them an ambience that is out of sync with the intent of Judaism. Too often they've picked *these* holidays to observe because the focus on sins and "who shall live and who shall die" fits neatly into the preoccupations of the larger Christian society much more than do the joys of Shabbat or the other Jewish ritual observances. Unfortunately, synagogues become so obsessed with catering to these once-a-year Jews (who, after all, provide the money to pay for the synagogue's operations during the rest of the year) that the essence of these holidays gets lost. Built into the High Holy Days is a deep psychological wisdom that can and should be reclaimed. In the ten days of repentance that extend from the first day of the Jewish New Year, Rosh Hashanah, through the Day of Atonement, Yom Kippur, we may engage in a mass psychological process, as we participate in an individual and collective reassessment of our lives.

Remembering is step one—looking at what we have done and what we have become during the past year. Rosh Hashanah is called Yom Hazikaron, the Day of Remembrance.

The second step is to measure what we have done and what we have become against our own highest visions of who we should and could be. This step is facilitated when we collectively, through prayer, reaffirm the vision of our possibilities (what we could be individually and together).

The third step is called *teshuvah* or repentance. This does not mean merely a recommitment to "good values" that are so abstract that they function only to make us feel good when we espouse them. Real *teshuvah* means determining in considerable detail exactly what we are going to do differently in our lives, taking into account the things that will likely throw us off or undermine our resolve. This requires more than making just an inner resolve about our intentions—it requires figuring out concretely how the things that tend to undermine our resolve or deflect us from carrying out the changes we want to make can be handled. *Teshuvah* is *not* a series of New Year's resolutions, but is instead a serious plan of action based on the deepest and most searching self-scrutiny. Obviously we cannot accomplish all of this in one morning at a synagogue; the services are meant only to provide the collective affirmation of the commitment to the task, but the ten days of repentance are intended to provide the setting for a much deeper and more concentrated attention to change. To *avoid* using these ten days seriously, people fill up all their time with services, meals, socializing, and endless chatter. But this time period is really about something else: a fundamental transformation of self and community. Those who want to take full advantage of the occasion frequently use this time to review their journals, to look over their calendars of the past year, to remember what has happened, and to explore how they may remake themselves. This is also the time to straighten up unfinished emotional business with other people, to seek to rectify whatever misunderstandings or pain that you may have caused others.

To make this process more effective, some Jewish-renewal communities encourage people to find a *"teshuvah* buddy" or a small group of three to four *teshuvah* buddies who will meet together once a day for an hour. Each person reports on his or her progress in repenting and in making plans for how to sustain the changes during the coming year. After the holidays, these buddies agree to meet once a month, on the New Moon (Rosh Chodesh), to review the progress they've made and to continue to support one another to follow through on the process.

Self-scrutiny is not meant for individuals only. The religious community as a whole needs to meet during the ten days of repentance and to discuss its own functioning and direction. Has the community really embodied its highest values? Has it really been sensitive to the pains of its members, and to the pain and suffering that continue in the larger world? Has the community used Judaism merely as a way to "feel good," or has it been engaged in the nuts and bolts of social and political action to transform the world? Are the nice sentiments matched with serious action?

Eventually Jewish-renewal communities will seek to bring together the entire Jewish community in a given city to engage in similar questioning during the ten days of repentance. And that model might eventually become a model for secular society as well.

To ensure that the process is effective, some Jewish-renewal communities allocate time during the Rosh Hashanah and Yom Kippur services for *teshuvah* buddies to meet, for people to engage in meditation and self-reflection, and for the community to begin its own process of self-scrutiny. By allocating this time in the middle of the service, Jewish renewalists help one another to avoid the tendency to engage in ritual observance merely as a substitute for the serious self- and communal-transformation that is needed during these ten days.

Why only ten days? Doesn't real change require a much deeper and longer process? Yes. Rosh Hashanah is not meant to replace psychotherapy, on the one hand, or struggles for social change, on the other. What the High Holy Days can do is to consolidate and reinvigorate the moral, psychological, and political gains that we have made in the past, and deepen our commitment to ongoing change. For ten days we, together, take a new accounting, building on what we already know but reaching deeper into our ideals, to draw from them new guidance for how to live in the meantime (before the Messiah, before the revolution, before the final abolition of patriarchy, before . . .).

The time-limited nature of the process is central to its success. Unlike those traditions that require a lifetime spent in various psychological or more solitary spiritual pursuits, the Jewish tradition provides ten specific days to get oneself together. For those who take it seriously, the pressure is *on*, the fate of the next year is going to be written in the Book of Life and then it will be sealed, the gates of heaven are going to shut at the last service on Yom Kippur (Ne'ilah), and so the time to make the change is *now*, not in some indefinite future. This creates a psychological and spiritual immediacy that forces the individual to take the process much more to heart, to avoid the kind of stalling that so often interferes with progress.

Anyone who has attempted to make a serious change in his or her own life knows that even when we make a commitment to change, there are some people who want us to remain the same, who throw us back into our old patterns and insist that who we were is who we always will be. One advantage of having a collective process of transformation is that if *everyone* is simultaneously engaged in the attempt to change, and is surrounded by others who accept the idea that *change is possible*, then we are all more likely and able to support one another by validating everyone's changes (just as we ask others to validate *our* changes). Instead of change undergone as an event in personal life only, our changes coincide with those taking place in everyone else's lives. The ritual of these days thereby becomes the public proclamation to one another that we are trying to make our own real changes and that we are allowing and accepting the changes of all others in the community.

What makes those changes possible, of course, is the God of Abraham, the Force that made it possible for Abraham to recognize Isaac and to break the repetition compulsion. This message that cruelty is not destiny translates for us on Rosh Hashanah into the energy that we need to transform ourselves. And hence the Rosh Hashanah liturgy is filled with this message: that we can allow ourselves during these ten days to live as though God were the king of all the earth, which is to say that the world is filled with this energy that makes for the possibility of transformation of that which is to that which ought to be. On these days, we allow ourselves to experience most fully that integration of spirituality and transformative energy, that identification of the God of creation with the God of transformation and liberation.

The tradition insists on the dialectical unity between individual and collective change: both are necessary, and the amount that any individual can change is constrained by the amount of change in the larger social world; and conversely the amount of social change depends on how much each individual is changing. From the standpoint of Jewish tradition, human beings are fundamentally social—we are part of one another's realities, part of the set of human relationships in which we are engaged. So we do not say in our prayers, "I have sinned," but rather, "We have sinned." We are responsible for one another, and the level of our own transcendence always depends on the degree to which we as a community can actualize our common humanity, our capacity to be embodiments of God's energy in the world. Only by establishing a set of humane social relationships between all people will I as an individual be able to realize fully my deepest possible human potentialities. Judaism's spirituality avoids a narcissistic focus on the lone individual, but insists instead on a focus *both* on oneself *and* on the larger world in which we live.

A community that integrates this kind of deep self-exploration with an equally serious focus on communal or societal change generates tremendous spiritual energy. So it is no surprise that the Jewish liturgy moves quickly back and forth between a focus on our sins and a focus on our vision of a new world in which we could imagine God's rule over the entire earth as a rule of justice and peace and love, in which the kingdom of evil has been swallowed up and arrogance has disappeared. What remains is a vision of compassion.

Compassion, in fact, is the overriding theme of these holidays. Precisely because the tradition sees our imperfections as not solely our own fault but as rooted in an imperfect world, it stresses that God will have compassion for us. By extension, it urges us to have compassion for one another and for ourselves. Sin in Jewish liturgy is fundamentally different from the popular (Christian-based) conception: it is not that human beings are flawed or essentially evil; rather, the Hebrew word for sin, *chyet*, means "missing the mark." We are like arrows that have been off course, and we can help one another get back on course, knowing that we will need another High Holy Day period next year for more fine-tuning and corrective action. By asking God for compassion, we assert that this compassion is one of the most holy aspects of the universe, and that we will help bring more of it into the world.

Those involved in movements for social change could learn much from the rituals and thinking of the Jewish High Holy Days. Imagine if the entire society, not just Jews, were to dedicate a ten-day period each year to collective self-examination and communal transformation. Imagine how much stronger a social-change movement could become if it would create this kind of practice as a central part of what it is doing.

Meanwhile, luckily for the Jews, we have Rosh Hashanah and Yom Kippur and the days in between. If taken seriously, these ten days can become an amazingly powerful experience of transformation, giving us energy and direction for the rest of the year, giving us direct contact with God as the Power that makes possible this *tikkun olam*.

CHANUKAH

Some Jews have succumbed to the massive seductions of the annual media assault urging people to buy their products to give as Christmas gifts. Given the commercialization of Christmas, they argue, it is no longer a religious holiday, so what's the harm in Jews celebrating it as an act of solidarity with their non-Jewish neighbors? Yet religious Christians are rightly resentful of the commercialization of their religious holiday, have been involved in a struggle against the dynamics of the capitalist market, and do not welcome the sudden infusion of Jews on the side of the secularization of the holiday. Jewish involvement in Christmas is wildly disrespectful to those who still hope to save Christianity from the homogenizing and despiritualizing tendencies of the contemporary world.

Other Jews, recognizing that Christmas itself still does have a religious significance to many Christians, have attempted to make Chanukah into a Jewish alternative to Christmas, hoping thereby to buttress their children against feeling deprived. While there is no religious reason to oppose gifts, the focus of the holiday often gets subverted and its most authentic meanings are lost.

Hence, Jewish-renewal communities supplement the candlelighting and gift-giving with rituals designed to get us back in touch with the holiday. So after the lighting of the candles, Jewish renewalists try to tell the real story of Chanukah, reclaiming its powerful message.

When King Cyrus of Persia allowed the ancient tribes of Judah and Benjamin to return from the exile imposed upon them by Babylonian conquerors in the sixth century B.C.E., they formed the kingdom of Judea. As part of the Persian Empire, and later as part of the empire of Alexander the Great, Judea had relative autonomy in its own internal religious life.

When Alexander the Great died in the fourth century B.C.E., his empire split into three rival factions, and Judea was caught between two of them: the Seleucids, centered in Syria, and the Ptolemies, centered in Egypt. For the next 150 years those two kingdoms warred, and each sought to incorporate Judea as part of its empire.

From the moment that the Greeks took over Judea in 320 B.C.E., there were Jews who felt that the best strategy of survival was to cuddle up to the Greeks and adopt their ways. Alexander had introduced the Jews to Hellenistic culture—its philosophy, its literature, and its impressive technology and power. Forcibly dragged into the larger Mediterranean world, many Jews could see that the "real" world was dominated by wealth and power. Some Jews, primarily those who lived in and around the larger cities, saw an opportunity to join this larger world by becoming merchants and traders, or by establishing political and economic relationships with others in the Hellenistic empire. It was apparent to these Jews that their tribal religion would have little meaning to those who had conquered the world. The religion of their fathers and mothers seemed irrelevant in a world reshaped by the "modern realities" of science, and they were allured by a society that worshipped the body and defined reality in terms of what could be tasted, touched, and directly experienced by the senses.

These Jewish Hellenizers saw no point in resisting Greek rule. Their goal was to live in harmony with the powers that ran the world. They could benefit from the connection to the expanding trade of the Hellenistic world. On the other hand, the vast majority of the Jewish people were small, independent farmers who lived on the land and brought its produce to Jerusalem three times each year to celebrate their hard-won freedom from slavery. It was they who bore the brunt of the taxes imposed first by the Greeks, and then, alternately, by Seleucids and Ptolemies. These Jews resented foreign rule and detested the city-dwelling elites who seemed to be earning favor with the Hellenistic conquerors, imitating their ways, abandoning the religion of the past, and becoming worshippers at the shrine of political and cultural "reality."

Judea's plight worsened considerably in the early part of the second century with the ascendance to the throne of the Seleucid Antiochus IV. Claiming that he wanted to "protect" Judea from the Ptolemies, Antiochus invaded Judea and marched toward Egypt, where his armies were defeated. He turned back to Judea and attempted to impose Hellenistic culture by force. He ordered sacrifice to the Greek gods in the Temple in Jerusalem and forbade the practice of circumcision, *kashrut*, and observance of Shabbat.

To the already assimilated elites of the city, these new rules were a provocation, but did not constitute a major crisis. Perhaps Antiochus was a boor, but the culture he represented was "happening," while the Jewish religion he forbade was a remnant of the past.

Yet many of the people in the countryside, burdened by Seleucid taxes that expropriated more of their wealth, found the Hellenists' narcissistic fascination with their own power repugnant. The essence of their now-banned religion was its insistence that there is a single God governing the universe, who made possible freedom from oppression. It was in the name of that God that they joined a rebellion against the Seleucids, under the leadership of a country priest named Mattathias and his five sons (of whom Judah became the most famous, known as "the hammer" or Maccabee).

These Maccabees, as they came to be known, rejected the notion, shared by their contemporary Jewish establishment, that it would be pointless to fight, that one would do best by appeasing the ruling class, learning their language and ways, and accepting their system of oppression. The Maccabees understood Judaism as teaching that "not by power, and not by might, but by My spirit, says the Lord of Hosts."

To fight against superior military force was totally illogical and unrealistic from the Hellenizers' standpoint. But the Maccabees drew upon the Jewish religion and the stubborn spirit of a people who had come to believe that every human being is created in the divine image, hence has a right to be treated with respect and decency. These were people who could not submit to the rule of the imperialists, and whose religion taught them that they need not, because the central power of the universe is a power that rejected the reality of oppression. Their Torah told the tale of their origins in a slave rebellion against another imperialist power thought to be invincible.

Armed with these stories, the Maccabees and their followers used guerrilla tactics to win a national liberation struggle against overwhelming odds. In 165 B.C.E. they retook Jerusalem, purified and rededicated the Temple (Chanukah means rededication), and rekindled the eternal light. The fighting continued many more years, but eventually the Maccabees and their descendants (called Hashmona'im) set up an independent Jewish state.

Unfortunately that state degenerated as the Hashmona'im in later decades began to make their country into a nation like all other nations, adopting the same perversions of state power that other nations adopted, becoming oppressive and hence spiritually and morally corrupt. The impulse to fight against the homogenizing "reality" of the imperial world was abandoned, and the struggle was redefined in terms that seemed to suggest that its only goal had been to achieve independence so that Judea could be free of external rule and become a respected state among states. But once the world of realpolitik had triumphed, the logic of independence was soon undermined. Within a hundred years internecine fighting led one faction of Hashmona'im to invite the Romans in to help them in their struggle for power. The Romans came happily, bringing their Hellenized culture to extend and concretize their power, and eventually they took over completely.

Hellenism was a persuasive and accommodating cultural reality. It assimilated existing religious and cultural systems. It could make room for a wide range of philosophic and religious systems. Though it ultimately worshipped power, it provided space for ethical reflection. It totalized and homogenized and effectively served to legitimate the most complexly organized system of oppression the world had ever known. It did so with grace, elegance, high style, beauty, imaginative literature, richly textured religious observances, advanced technology that brought roads and water systems and the most modern human comforts. It stood in marked contrast with a Jewish sensibility that saw all this sophistication and power and elegance and technological success and human comfort as less important than the exploitation and oppression that was the secret heart of Hellenistic reality. It is easy to perceive the Jews who grappled with that kind of an issue as fanatics, people who were missing the point of the greatness of Rome. Yet the heart of the

Jewish sensibility was its refusal to accommodate to a world of oppression, its insistence that what is could be transformed and ought to be transformed.

This struggle between Hellenism and Judaism has turned up in different forms throughout the ages; it persists today, and persists within Judaism itself, between the Hellenizers and those who remain true to a different Jewish message. One is tempted to say that today the Hellenists are running the Jewish show and accommodating Jewish life to the "realities" of selfishness and power as organized in the contemporary world, while those who are true to the transformative message are outside the organized Jewish community, often as people who are perceived to be tearing down the system, or people who do not really care. That is precisely the way it was back then.

The rabbis who shaped Rabbinic Judaism were depressed about the high cost of the failed Jewish rebellions against Rome, and aware also of the degeneration of the Hashmona'im and of the lack of morality that characterized some of the rebellions against Rome. Frightened that the Chanukah story might inspire more of these rebellions, these rabbis at first resisted popular celebrations of the victory, then later tried to redirect those stories by focusing on a legend of a miracle of a pot of oil that kept the Temple's menorah burning for eight nights. By downplaying the importance of the struggle, they reframed the miracle as merely a "religious" event. But the Jewish people knew intuitively that something really miraculous had happened in the political struggle.

The miracle was this: a critical mass of people had come to recognize that there is a Force in the world that made possible the transformation of what is to what ought to be. It had given them courage to fight against insuperable odds, and then to triumph. Here was an incipient knowledge that when large numbers of people become aware of God's presence in the universe in this sense, that recognition in part becomes a manifestation of God's presence, and in that presence "the power of the people" becomes greater than all the technology and manipulations of the most sophisticated forms of oppression.

It is this message that should become the center of Jewish-renewal Chanukah observance. There's nothing wrong with giving children gifts, eating potato latkes, and making Chanukah into a lovely eight-day holiday of family celebration. Yet the key is to build into the practice a way of telling the real story and of conveying the message that we must not get discouraged even though the craziness and evil in the world seem overwhelming at times, because they can be overcome through our activity as partners with God.

That message can be conveyed in dramatic presentations and skits that the family does for one another, in dramatic readings, or in other home-made rituals. Some families have tried the following: each night they pick a new theme in which they allow themselves to imagine how things could be different. They then tell in detail what would have to happen in order for their vision to be made real, and how they might participate in some way in its actualization. Here is a list of suggested themes:

- The first night. Imagine your life free of the need to accommo-date to people with more power than you. How would your life be different?
- The second night. Imagine your life if in the world of work (for children, the world of school) you could fully use your talents and creativity, your desire to cooperate with others, and your sense of humor and playfulness.
- The third night. Imagine your relationship to your parents if it could be the way that you really want it to be.
- The fourth night. Imagine the kind of Jewish community you'd like to have, where Jews pray together, do acts of charity and social justice together, and in every other way the community supported your highest ethical and aesthetic ideals, and did so in a way that was fun and emotionally nourishing.
- The fifth night. Imagine what your neighborhood would be like if people really connected with one another as caring neighbors. Now imagine what you'd have to do to get others in your neigh-borhood to talk about what they'd want, and how they'd go about getting it, so that everyone would live in a friendlier and less alienated neighborhood.
- The sixth night. Imagine the kind of social-change movement of which you'd like to be part.
- The seventh night. Imagine the kind of America (or Israel, England, Canada, Mexico, France, Australia, etc.) in which you'd like to live. What could you do to help that society become more likely?
- The eighth night. Imagine what the world would look like if it were to embody the values you hold dear.

- Each night. Share your vision with others and listen (without criticizing) to theirs. Write plays, skits, songs, short stories, poems that articulate your answer to the question for each night, and encourage your children to do the same (perhaps by having them create a short skit or story or poem or painting of their own). Then rejoice and sing songs of celebration and of struggle.

People who have tried these exercises report that Chanukah can have a very different focus than a mere fixation on who has received the best presents.

Though at other points in this book I've railed against a Judaism which merely states ideals but does not mobilize people to achieve them, there are moments in the year when it *is* enough just to restate the ideals and give one another support to keep on struggling. As the days grow short, a depression and darkness falls on the human spirit. Ancient peoples recognized this and built festivals of lights aimed at rekindling their own spirits as they hoped for the return of brighter times. Chanukah picked up on this hopefulness, and allows us to rededicate our own lives to the transformative tasks given to us by being the inheritors of the Torah tradition.

Tu B'Shvat

This minor holiday commemorating the new year of the trees has recently become a Jewish-renewal ecology festival. Following customs developed by the Hasidim, contemporary renewers of the tradition have created Tu B'Shvat seders at which the various kinds of fruits and nuts of late winter are consumed, and discussion focuses on the challenge to protect and honor the earth.

Purim

Reading the Megillah (the scroll of Esther that tells how this young Jewish woman—orphaned when the Jews were exiled, and later chosen by the king of Persia to be his most beloved, because most beautiful, wife—saves the Jews from destruction at the hands of the wicked prime minister Haman, who has a deep hatred for Esther's uncle Mordecai precisely because he refuses to accept the ultimacy of Haman's secular power), developing Purim plays, sending gifts to one another, and consuming mind-altering substances to the point that one cannot tell the difference between "Blessed Mordecai" and "Cursed Haman," have always contributed to making Purim a playful and joyous holiday. It has taken on new vitality in our own day as many feminists have questioned Queen Esther's strategy of cuddling up to the king to save her people, wondering instead if they do not have more in common with Queen Vashti, who had been deposed by the buffoon-like King Ahasueras for refusing to subordinate herself to his will.

Yet Jewish renewalists also point to the truth in the seemingly playful injunction not to be able to tell the difference between Mordecai and Haman: that it is sometimes possible to look at the world with a consciousness that suspends all judgments and sees the struggle between good and evil as part of a play whose ultimately happy resolution is certain. We may be caught up in this moment's drama and its necessity, but we should also, at least on Purim, be able to look at our own lives as one small part of a great play that will lead to the triumph of the good, and in which even the forces of evil will be seen to have played a necessary part. The message is *not* that the struggle against evil is unnecessary or that it should be put aside as we remain transfixed in a transcendent consciousness. To do that would only ensure that the forces of evil would last longer. Rather, the message is that on Purim we can take a break from the struggle and rejoice in the knowledge that it will eventually work out, look at ourselves from the standpoint of this larger picture and know that even while what we do has importance as part of a much larger reality, part of the ongoing saga of the Jewish people and of the peoples of the world is to redeem human history. The Book of Esther has no mention of God, as if to say that there is a moment when even God-consciousness becomes a limiting or distorting perspective.

Yet there is a dark side to Purim as well. Haman is alleged to be a descendant of the tribe of Amalek, and the Purim story tells of Jews engaging in armed struggle with the supporters of Haman, these spiritual descendants of Amalek, and wiping them out. Contemporary right-wing religious Jews have frequently identified the Palestinians as spiritual descendants of Amalek, implying that the Palestinians' goal is to wipe out the Jews and hence that it is appropriate for Jews to take violent action against them. We traditionally read the reminder about Amalek on the Shabbat before Purim.

As noted above, on Purim 1994 a West Bank Jewish settler entered the mosque built at the cave of Machpelah in Hebron where Abraham and Sarah are said to be buried, and proceeded to murder twenty-nine Palestinians at prayer services opening the Islamic observance of Ramadan. Other West Bank settlers cheered his action, hundreds honored him at his funeral a few days later, and some told the press that this action was the real meaning of Purim, and that those who refuse to see it this way are trying to cover up the true spirit of Judaism.

Many in the Modern Orthodox world suggested that this was a lone crazy. Yet this was a man who had emerged from years of study at Yeshiva University, trained in a culture that seemed more responsive to Settler Judaism than to the Torah's injuctions to love the stranger. Many religious teachers seem unaware of the slippery slope from demeaning others to physically attacking them.

Few of those who had demonized Palestinians as contemporary Amalekites were willing to take responsibility for those who took the analogy seriously.

Purim will be associated with the stains of this massacre for many decades. Perhaps this is the inevitable outcome of taking seriously the parts of Torah that I have called the voice of accumulated pain and cruelty. Far from being an abstruse issue of interpretation, the way one reads these texts has immediate and profound implications.

Yet a careful rereading of the text in question may provide a way of understanding that is more consistent with a Jewish-renewal perspective. Our reading of the Torah stresses the way that God functions as a Force that seeks to break the repetition compulsion that would pass cruelty on from generation to generation. Part of the process of ending the compulsion is to become conscious of the ways that we have internalized the cruelty of those who have acted cruelly toward us. Our task is to become cognizant of that tendency within us, and then to break the chain and *not* do it to others. Perhaps the Amalek portion can be read in this same way. "Remember what Amalek did to you when you were leaving Egypt, how he met you and attacked all of your weakest ones, and you were tired and enfeebled and you did not fear God, and it shall be when YHVH your God will cause you to rest from all your enemies in the land that God gives to you for an inheritance, that you shall blot out the memory of Amalek from under the sky—don't forget!"

Notice that the passage does *not* order blotting out Amalek but only the memory of Amalek. And where does that memory live? Precisely in our tendency to act out on others what was done to us. The memory of the trauma is repressed, and its residue manifests in our tendency to become like Pharaoh, like Amalek, like Hitler, or like Arab terrorists. Torah seeks to make the unconscious conscious by instructing us to remember what happened to us so we *don't* act it out unconsciously. The point of remembering is to disentangle us from the pain and thus to "blot out the memory." The memory remains with us as long as it is unconsciously shaping our actions. So the goal of remembering Amalek is precisely so that we do not become like him! By shooting innocent people at prayer, the West Bank settler did the opposite of Torah's intentions.

So if in the next few generations we wish to "get into" Purim, we are going to have to do it in a way that clearly indicates our outrage at what happened on Purim 1994. What the West Bank settlers managed to do was to give Haman and Amalek a victory on Purim, and this inevitably has the negative consequence of making it harder for the rest of us really to believe that the Haman and Amalekite energies in the world can be quarantined and defeated.

TISHA B'AB

Not exactly a holiday, this day of mourning and fasting is traditionally dedicated to bewailing the destruction of the First and Second Temples, the Crusades, the Expulsion from Spain, and subsequent pogroms and oppression of the Jewish people. A separate day, Yom Ha'Shoah, is dedicated to the Holocaust.

Jewish-renewal groups typically meet to read the Book of Lamentations. Some go on to discuss whether the traditional formulation, "Because of our sins we were exiled from our land," represents a self-blaming and surplus powerlessness-generating formulation that should be replaced (the more vigorous upholders of this view sometimes arguing that the entire focus of Tisha B'Ab is so misdirected that this fast day should be abandoned altogether), or whether it represents a form of empowerment (if we are responsible for our own lack of power, we can do something about it by changing our sinful ways—where the relevant sin, if our prophets are to be believed, may be our willingness to tolerate evil or turn our ear from the pain of the oppressed). "But how can you believe this?" asks the first group. "After all, Babylonian and Roman imperialism swept the world, and our moral state had nothing to do with it."

"True," respond the self-blamers, "but Jewish power stopped the Hellenists in the Maccabean revolt and might have stopped Rome. Jews were already living in Diaspora throughout the Roman Empire at the time of the destruction of the Second Temple. Had those Jews been unified with an understanding of God as the Power that transforms the world from that which is to that which ought to be, and had they been willing to act in a coordinated way, threatening to spread our message in ways that would radicalize domestic populations throughout the Roman world, we could have raised the cost of Roman imperialism to such an extent that Rome would have preferred an accommodation based on limited autonomy and the right of the Jews to maintain the Temple. It was our own inner fears and abandonment of our revolutionary message that made it possible for Rome to triumph."

Tisha B'Ab becomes an exceedingly appropriate moment for these kinds of reflections about Jewish history, and for that reason some Jewish-renewal communities have used the day for teach-ins or other ways to learn about that history and to assess our current moral and spiritual realities.

Jewish renewal takes seriously halakhic observance of the holidays. But what it adds is this: an insistence that the observance be full of life and energy, testifying to the revolutionary tradition of Judaism, spiritually deep, and capable of being understood and believed in by those who participate in it.

CHAPTER SIXTEEN

RENEWING THE LIFE CYCLE

Virtually every specific attempt I've seen to develop new Jewish rituals, prayers, and life-cycle events has had moments and aspects that excited me, and other moments that struck me as somewhat superficial and at times even New Agey or too flakey. Moving from theory to practice involves stumbling and clumsy moments as well as breakthrough ones. Equally to the point, those of us who grew up with certain conceptions of what was "serious" Judaism may see as stumbling and clumsy things that others find excitingly experimental.

First, let me say what's exciting: When people knowledgeable in Torah and Jewish tradition begin to develop new methods for making the tradition alive, their first move is to allow themselves to imagine what the original goal of a ritual or a prayer was really about, what the generation that first sought to embody the idea in the practice was trying to accomplish. This is a way to discover depths and insights that had gone unnoticed in existing rituals or prayers. Or they dramatize a moment in ways that help one to see what it's really about. When you empower an entire community of people to use their intelligence and creativity to make a sacred moment come alive, some exciting ideas may surface.

The enterprise itself is rewarding even when the execution doesn't fully work. It is spiritually fulfilling to be part of a community of people who are really wondering how to make a moment both holy and beautiful, or how to translate some complicated and deep thought so that it becomes accessible to people who had previously been turned off to their Jewishness, or how to take a custom that seems sexist or hierarchical and preserve its essence without preserving its offensive dimensions. The process itself seems to have elements of the presence of God.

The dismissal of experimentation must have been exactly the reaction of Jews reared on the Temple service when they encountered Rabbinic Judaism and its equally New Agey attempts to develop a substitute for the rituals that had worked when Temple sacrifice was possible. The rabbis argued that where Torah called for sacrifices (*avodah*—which can also mean service) and specified the details, prayer could now suffice. The rabbis even went so far as to claim that every person's dinner table was a sacrificial altar. To act the sacrifice out, Jews were required to dip their bread in salt after blessing it, since the salt had been used to remove the blood from sacrificial meat. This entire attempt to create a "guerrilla theater" in which synagogue and home substituted for Temple must have seemed ludicrous to the Saducees and others who understood Torah literally to be calling for sacrifice. "We can't perform the sacrifices now, given Rome's destruction of the Temple," these traditionalists must have argued, "but please don't make our whole religion silly by assuming that Torah really meant prayer or that our dinner table is really an altar. We can hope for the restoration of the Temple, even fight to rebuild it, but don't cheapen the whole religion by these New Agey devices that feel just like the Christians' whole orientation toward prayers, or by adopting rituals that were not even commanded in the Torah and for which you have no authority except your own thought on what will best preserve Judaism. The truth is, your ideas will destroy Judaism because they have no real historical authenticity." In this respect, by rejecting this kind of thinking, Rabbinic Judaism became the Jewish-renewal movement of its time.

Today we face a similar historical moment. Many of the traditional methods for doing *mitzvot* have been so drained of their meaning and connection to our sense of the holy that they no longer provide a way of touching our souls. In the next few generations Jewish-renewal energies will be devoted to finding new forms of prayer, new rituals, and other ways of enlivening our relationship to God. Yet this process will necessarily feel somewhat superficial and even flakey to those of us who have been reared in our traditions.

I also had to remind myself of two other things: how much we Jewish men have been socialized to produce quick negative judgments to show that we are smarter, less gullible, more self-protective, and more cynical than the average, and how that might have affected my judgment; and also, how the experience of the establishment versions of Judaism—precisely because they are the versions embraced by the financiers of luxurious buildings and well-paid staffs and community professionals who validate them and reassure everybody that this is the *real* Jewish community—unconsciously shapes my internalized picture of what is serious and what is not, so that I dismiss as less serious things that look too experimental even when they may be deeper. I know that in my early days of helping to develop Jewish-renewal ideas and practices, I used to think to myself, "This is sixty percent flakey, and forty percent spiritually deep, whereas the Orthodox synagogue where I pray is ninety-five percent serious and five percent spiritually deep." My tendency to limit the appeal of Jewish renewal in my own mind was based on my need to see myself as serious, even though I knew that the renewal experience was eight times more spiritually engaging than the Orthodox service, and even though I knew that the only hope of bringing back the estranged Jews was in the renewal context. Reflecting on all the ways that I tended to dismiss my own ideas and my own experimentation as "less serious," I can easily understand why others may do so when they first encounter a Jewish-renewal community. But from my perspective, Jewish renewal does *not* belong only to the groups that call themselves such, and my suggestion to those who go through the same first reactions Ihad is this: either stick around longer and try to get beyond yourresistance, or if some of the ideas turn you on, take them and create your own Jewish-renewal community, engage in the process of taking Jewish ritual and prayer and making it alive for you and the community you gather together, and draw upon what others have done to the extent that it seems useful. What makes a new ritual fit into Jewish renewal is the degree to which it assists us in being more conscious of the grandeur of the universe, more aware of our responsibility to heal and repair the world, or more able to experience joy and awareness of what our lives are about within the context of Judaism as a spiritual path.

LIFE CYCLES

Some of the most creative work in liturgy and life-cycle events is being done by feminist groups attempting to reappropriate the tradition to the experience of women.

Here is some of what is being tried:

- Women have developed rituals to sanctify the onset of menses and its cessation (menopause). A group of women will gather to honor the young woman whose capacity to create life has now become embodied in a monthly menstrual cycle, or the older woman who now enters into new possibilities for creativity.
- The ritual of immersion in a *mikveh* (pool of water) has been reclaimed by women who no longer define the ritual in terms of purification of something that is unclean (the old terms for menstruation), but rather in terms of a monthly rebirthing of the creative powers of women's bodies. In some communities, women arrange to go as a group to the immersion, celebrate their bodies together, and proudly acknowledge and rejoice in their sexuality. Through song, play, laughter, and blessings created for the occasion, they have turned the immersion into a celebration of women's power and spirituality.

  Some Jewish feminists have also argued that the entire practice of *niddah*, sexual separation from men during menstruation, is a conquest of female power over sexuality. This practice, they claim, doesn't ring of patriarchy, since men usually don't spontaneously come up with ideas to restrict their ability to have access to women's bodies. Some women have embraced this practice as a way of celebrating female power. Others have argued that while this practice may have once been liberating, it no longer works because they themselves wish to make more individual decisions about when to have access to the bodies of their lovers. This is one of many areas in which Jewish-renewal communities of the future will eventually develop communal norms.
- Rosh Chodesh groups. The Jewish calendar is lunar-based, and at each new moon, Jews celebrate. Women in particular made this their holiday and celebrated together. Today, many feminists are reclaiming Rosh Chodesh with gatherings of women who celebrate the New Moon together through shared rituals, song,

and dance. Some groups discuss the anticipated character of the coming month, the kinds of issues that are likely to arise for each person, and then share blessings with one another for the new month.

- Birthing rituals have evolved in which the women of a Jewish-renewal community will be present along with family members and close friends at the birthing, offering encouragement and support, and singing, playing, and assisting.

- Entering the Covenant. Daughter-naming ceremonies are now being given equal prominence with the traditional *bris* (circumcision or *bris milah*) for boys. Neighbors, friends, and members of the community are invited to share food, stories, and rituals that welcome the daughter or son into the community. In each case, community members should offer concrete assistance in the raising of the child, moving beyond platitudes about sharing responsibility to specifying who is prepared to offer what kind of child-care support, who is prepared to provide backup assistance for emergencies, who is prepared to provide financial support should the parents be in need, and who is prepared to provide emotional support, spiritual guidance, education, training in skills or introduction to arts, philosophy, and Judaism. In specifying as much as possible what is being offered, the community moves from abstraction to become a real force in the life of the family.

The daughter-naming rituals affirm the role of women in Jewish history and Jewish culture. Women at the ceremony discuss their own experiences and struggles in gaining power and influence in the Jewish world and in the larger society, describe what actually has been won and the power that has been achieved, and recommit to making the society safer and more nurturing for this new member of the community. The record of that conversation is passed on to the daughter when she begins to prepare for her own bat mitzvah.

The *bris* or covenanting ceremony for boys generates some controversy in Jewish-renewal circles. Some people argue that the circumcision ceremony is barbaric, a remnant of the unconscious desire to pass on to the next generation the pain that was inflicted upon us. Whatever symbolism of intergenerational connection is involved, the infliction of unnecessary pain is precisely what Judaism is designed to fight against, so it makes little sense for us to be the perpetrators on our own male children.

Others counter that circumcision has little lasting negative psychological consequences and has been a powerful form of Jewish identification, required by the Bible and kept faithfully by all generations of Jews for thirty-two hundred years, and that they are not prepared to be the first generation to break the chain. Ever since the Greeks and Romans actively sought to repress circumcision, Jews have fought bitterly for the right to keep this symbol of the Covenant, and have pointed out that the dominant society that expresses so much concern about the infliction of pain on Jewish males has had no trouble inflicting far greater pain not only on Jewish males but on millions of other people. When the society has cleaned up its act, this argument goes, and has eliminated all other unnecessary pain, we will have entered a messianic age in which the issue of circumcision can be rethought. Moreover, the notion that circumcision has any serious negative psychological consequences could be sustained only if one compared Jewish men to uncircumcised men and found that the latter group was clearly healthier from a psychological standpoint. Leaving aside the question of what criteria one would use, the assertion seems on its face to be an unjustifiable anti-Semitic contention, because there is no plausible basis for thinking that Jewish men are less psychologically together than any group of uncircumcised men.

We live in an age in which parents regularly submit their children to various vaccinations that cause pain and whose absolute necessity is nowadays subject to doubt. Belief that the momentary pain a baby boy suffers being inducted into the Jewish community is worse reflects a commitment to the religion of science rather than to the religion of Israel. Carefully supervised use of a local anesthesia immediately prior to the ritual may be a halakhic solution. Circumcision advocates warn that uncircumcised males can never be considered full Jews by most of the Jewish community, and that if such a boy wishes to marry Jewishly or become part of another sector of the Jewish community, he may have to undergo circumcision at a later point in life, when it would be far more painful and traumatic.

• Of course, it's not just feminists who are helping us reframe our life-cycle rituals. Bat and bar mitzvah are increasingly taking on deeper meaning than they had in the time when the primary focus was on proving mastery of a rather narrowly defined ritual task (reading an often only partially understood Torah and Haftorah portion in Hebrew). Within Jewish-renewal circles there is an attempt to involve each child in a process of spiritual seeking, world healing, or deep immersion in some set of texts or philosophical issues. So, for example, some children will spend the year preparing for the bar or bat mitzvah deeply engrossed in studying some section of Maimonides or Heschel or some other Jewish theologian, and defining where they stand in relationship to those ideas.

Others will seek to define their spirituality through encounters with God in creative ways that they have devised, and will keep a journal of the experiences and their reflections on them. Still others may become involved in social-action projects which have particular meaning for them. This bar or bat mitzvah would no longer mark the moment when Hebrew school has been completed, some texts of no particular significance have been mastered, and the young person is now free to desist from study.

It is not unusual in Jewish-renewal circles *not* to rigidly link bar or bat mitzvah to a particular birthday, but to hold off until the child feels *ready*, and has, in coordination with a spiritual advisor, completed the tasks which he or she has defined as central. The ceremony itself becomes an opportunity both to describe what s/he has gone through and to involve the community in a serious and nonritualized discussion of the meaning of the Bar or Bat Mitzvah's path.

After the religious service at which this presentation by the Bar or Bat Mitzvah takes place, there is often a celebratory meal, where community members share teachings prepared for the occasion, along with singing traditional Jewish songs, and the community grace after meals. Though some synagogues have recently introduced the notion of donating to the hungry a percentage of the money spent on lavish bar mitzvah catered affairs, most Jewish-renewal people have felt that the conspicuous consumption at Jewish events is itself a disgrace not to be redeemed by charitable contributions. *Tzniy'ut*, the traditional Jewish notion of modesty that Orthodox communities have used in their argument that women should not show their skin in public lest it engender male lust, has been redefined by some renewal people to involve a rejection of public displays of wealth in a world so full of poverty.

Some renewal communities give the Bar or Bat Mitzvah a book of coupons, redeemable on demand, in which members offer various services and goodies for the future, tailored to the specific interests of the person but reflecting the joint judgment about what exactly the community wants to pass on in the years ahead. For example, some of the coupons might be redeemable in the following ways:

—partial payment of an airline ticket to Israel for a one-month stay;

—partial payment for a Jewish summer camp experience;

—full payment for a one-week Jewish studies–oriented retreat with other teenagers;

—various evenings or day-long encounters with members of the community who have skills or knowledge or wisdom to share, distributed at three-month intervals throughout the coming years;

—books or videotapes and magazine subscriptions that the group thinks would be important for the Bar or Bat Mitzvah, delivered at two-month intervals through the coming years.

My son Akiba suggests that we encourage new bar or bat mitzvah ceremonies several times in a person's life, whenever that individual feels that s/he is ready to make a dramatically new level of commitment to Judaism. The recommitment to Judaism that the entire community makes on Shavuot can be matched by moments of important recommitment that mark spiritual turning points in the lives of its members.

Of course, we must be sure to avoid the kind of phony statements that characterized so many bar or bat mitzvah ceremonies in our time. Forcing children to recite words which have little meaning to them, pretending an involvement in Judaism that they do not feel, has served only to estrange them from Jewishness and to provide a distorted model for their understanding of what Jewish spirituality is about. Better to postpone any ceremony until the child or young adult actually feels ready to get engaged to the tradition than to create empty, self-defeating ceremonies.

- Sexuality and marriage. Some Jewish-renewal communities have been experimenting with commitment ceremonies to honor relationships that are more permanent than dating, less permanent than marriage. The traditional wedding ceremony in Judaism needs very little renewal—it already has all the necessary elements. But renewal communities have introduced some nonsexist touches, including provisions in the *ketubah* (marriage contract) that ensure full equality and vows that are written by the couples to reflect the reality of their commitment to each other. In the ceremony at which the *ketubah* is signed, the couple reaffirms to each other a commitment to equal sharing of power. (Gay and lesbian commitment ceremonies have been developed so that homosexuals may have the same communal support and sanctification of their commitment to each other.)

In a private ceremony before the public festivities, each partner participates in a mini Yom Kippur *viduyi*, or confessional, in which each asks the other for forgiveness for any ways that they may have wronged each other previous to the marriage.

In a narcissistic society, marriage is often viewed as little more than a moment for a big party at which friends buy the couple the fanciest silverware and household appliances while the couple provides a lavish banquet. In renewal ceremonies, the focus shifts to three other dimensions:

The degree to which the community accepts responsibility for helping the couple through hard times. Given intense societal pressures toward individualism and me-firstism, and the increasing commodification of relationships as another item that can be obtained in the marketplace ("you can always trade in this relationship for another one, because there are so many possibilities available for you"), there has been a growing tendency for couples to split up rather than work through the inevitable difficulties that emerge in a marriage. At renewal ceremonies, representatives of the community talk about this tendency and offer concrete support.

The couple's decision to see their marriage as part of the larger Jewish commitment to heal and repair the world. The breaking of the glass, symbolic that the world has not been redeemed, becomes the occasion for the couple to describe what plans they have to work together to accomplish something beyond themselves—in what specific ways their family will be involved in the work of the Jewish people. This isn't an abstract promise to be part of the Jewish people, but a concrete commitment to dedicate some time to some specific healing and repairing activity *as a couple*.

The couple's infusion of God energy into the details of their own relationship. One part of the Jewish tradition says that God is the third partner in a happy marriage. At the ceremony, religious teachers try to convey how this might be true and how a couple might enhance their relationship through systematically opening the gates to God's presence.

It is also traditional for various friends to sponsor dinner meals each of the seven nights following the wedding, inviting smaller groups of friends to celebrate with the couple, so that the celebration goes on for a week.

- Mezuzah placement and housewarming. Making the commandments beautiful is a tradition that Jewish renewal is seeking to take seriously. Rabbi Zalman Schachter-Shalomi began to develop talises with all the colors of the rainbow, and today one can find a cottage industry in Jewish ritual art. The commandment to place the words of the Shma on the doorposts of your home has been beautified by the creation of mezuzahs that are works of art, and affixing them to the door has become the central part of housewarming parties. In some Jewish-renewal circles the assembled community stands outside the door during the ceremony, then as people walk in they offer the new occupant a blessing focused on what they hope will happen in the new home.

- Work rituals. Work should be an opportunity to actualize our human capacities: our intelligence, creativity, aesthetic and ethical sensitivity, and our ability to cooperate with others. For those of us who have work of this sort, it's important to stop in the middle of the day for a few minutes and to create a psychic space to rejoice in this unique opportunity, to thank God for what has been made possible for us, and to refresh our minds and recommit ourselves to our mission. At the end of the workday, people with this kind of work should meet with one another for a moment of common acknowledgment of how good it has been to be able to share this experience.

Renewal ceremonies have also been created to honor retirement and the opportunities that it now presents to pursue new forms of self-development and new ways to serve the Jewish people in its task of healing and repairing the world. The ceremonies typically focus both on honoring the individual for the ways that s/he has already contributed to the common good and on supporting the person in her/his new directions. The community provides a host of options to each person about how s/he can use her/his talents to serve the common good in the years ahead, and also states its commitment to support the retiree through financial, economic, spiritual, or health crises.

• Elder rituals. Jewish-renewal groups are playing a leadership role in creating public ceremonies, not restricted to Jews, at which seniors can gather to share their life stories and their wisdom with younger generations. At some such gatherings the whole community surrounds the elders, sends them healing energy, and blesses them for their presence and their teachings. In some cities they are seeking to create "Councils of Elders" that will play an advisory role to public institutions and corporations. In other cities, they are organizing seniors into a special National Service Corps, based on the accumulated wisdom of seniors' experiences. But there are also specifically Jewish gatherings at which Jewish seniors are engaged in studying Jewish texts, *davening* together, and honoring one another's lives, accomplishments, and beings.

• Rituals of Loss. Renewal communities have generated rituals that encourage a small group of friends to acknowledge painful or distressing moments that heretofore were considered purely "private" and sometimes shameful. Miscarriage, divorce, persistent infertility, disconnection of a life-support system, even loss of a significant friendship or employment—all have become arenas in which healing rituals are being developed.

• Death. Traditional Jewish rituals for death and mourning are profound. Jewish-renewal communities focus on the reality of the loss, block all the attempts to repress or deny real grief, and insist on emotional truth wherever possible. So, for example, it is not uncommon to avoid a eulogy and instead ask a dozen or more people who knew the deceased to talk honestly and in detail, both about what was powerful and wonderful but also about what was problematic and what were the difficulties and struggles that this person had not yet resolved. The insistence on "being real" is what makes the community's caring all the more palpable. Instead of religion becoming once again an opportunity for people to say publicly all kinds of things they don't really believe, a Jewish-renewal observance demands the very same honesty here that we require when discussing our struggles to understand and connect with God.

The seven days after the burial in which the mourner sits at home and is encouraged to fully experience her loss (*shivah*) work best when the community is taking care of the mourner. It sometimes feels uncomfortable to visit during *shivah*—perhaps we didn't know the deceased very well, perhaps we will be put into an awkward spot (facing intimate grief, or defensive laughter, or other visitors who are inappropriately doing everything they can to cheer up the mourner). Yet the cumulative impact of having many people from the community come to participate in being with the mourner is often very helpful. To the extent that the visitor can remain emotionally present, he or she makes a direct contribution to the healing process. All the customs (e.g., not speaking to the mourner till she starts to speak, preparing food for the mourner, answering her phone, creating prayer sessions at her home) are designed to allow the mourner to get into her grief and not have to worry about taking care of others. Here, as in all the rituals I have described, emotional and spiritual honesty rather than empty piety are the bottom line.

CHAPTER SEVENTEEN

PRAYER

We are at the beginning of a period of creativity in which many communities are developing their own rituals. Some will last and will be picked up by other renewal communities. Others will last only a few generations. To the extent that the process of creating a ritual itself brings people closer to God, its validity depends not on how long it lasts, but how deeply it moves us to connect to our Creator.

God is not a cosmic bellhop, so it makes little sense to imagine oneself as a powerless person begging in front of an Almighty King who will, if talked to right, intervene on our behalf. Jewish-renewal circles are attempting to develop new paradigms of relationship to God that, in Rabbi Zalman Schachter-Shalomi's words, move away from the image of humans as worthless and sinful worms, so that the praying person can see him/herself as healthy and a recipient of Creation's original blessing. We eliminate language that suggests that God is male; we free God from the feudal power position and recognize the crucial role of sustaining and nurturing the planet. We try to reintegrate body and soul so that prayer is not merely an intellectual but also a physical experience. Indeed, as Rabbi Burt Jacobson points out, the Jewish way of praying, called *davenen* in Yiddish, has a unique rhythm in which you can either join with the congregation as it sings or recites a prayer, or enter into your own inner space, letting the melodies and words move you forward, and then fill in your own personal meditations or insights. Traditional Jewish *daven*ers often move their bodies rhythmically back and forth or from side to side, and in some Jewish-renewal circles there are moments when all in the congregation are asked to get up, move to the melodies or *niggunim*, stretch, dance, or otherwise involve their whole beings in the process.

There is a core to each traditional service, specified in the Talmud, and followed in most Jewish-renewal circles (e.g., the prescribed blessings before and after Shma, the prescribed blessings for the Amidah or silent standing prayer). Some Jewish-renewal circles stick with the traditional liturgy throughout, but attempt to do it in a much more conscious way. So, for example, a community might divide into groups of two for a particular psalm or prayer, and each person might rephrase it into words that express more closely the actual understanding or feeling or need that the prayer elicits for her. A prayer that might be rushed through in a minute in some traditional services might be dwelled on for ten to fifteen minutes as the community allows itself to sink into the melody and meaning of thoughts that it wants to confront.

Some Jewish renewalists have sought to rewrite prayer books and to substitute new prayers that reflect the new understanding of our relationship to God, new language about our human reality, and new nonsexist formulations of the Hebrew. I like these new prayers best as additions to the old service. I have studied the prayer book and learned to identify the different historical periods which produced the different prayers, so going through the traditional prayers is for me a deep way to connect with the present moment. Through these prayers, I allow myself to reexperience the evolution of human consciousness through people's differing attitudes toward God and human reality. For example, I can immerse myself in the consciousness of the early Biblical period and its self-assertive poetry, or into the somewhat more complicated period of the Babylonian Exile when Ezekiel saw visions of angels, or into the consciousness of those who began to feel the need to talk about resurrection of the dead, or into the rebellious mood of those who wrote about the King of the King of Kings (to let the Persian king who called himself the King of Kings know that he wasn't *our* top power), or the mood of a people during the Second Exile who felt that now they had to rely on God for salvation since Rome had defeated us in the temporal world, or the anger of those who wrote prayers after the Crusades, or the mysticism of those who wrote in fifteenth-century Safed. When I read the prayers with a knowledge of the historical conditions that gave rise to them and the sensibilities they were expressing, like any poems, they take on a much deeper meaning and open up gates of experience that reconnect me to the historical experience of my people in a way that no objective history book ever could.

This communal reclaiming of our past has elements of the psycho-therapeutic process of reexperiencing childhood. We do not do it to stay in the past. By reexperiencing and understanding where we have come from, we become more fully present to cocreate the future. Once this process has taken place at a prayer service, I feel spiritually ready to respond to additional prayers that express more fully our community's contemporary conception of our relationship to the Divine.

Some Jewish-renewal communities find this process too cumbersome or difficult. They cannot read prayers that talk about "our Father," or see God as King, or focus on begging God for mercy or caring. These re-create the very relationship to God that made the whole thing seem pointless or unworkable to them. I understand this resistance. "Until these attitudes become merely relics of the past rather than the actual consciousness of many establishment congregations," you might argue, "using that kind of language in prayers makes me feel so conflicted—as if I were validating the existing distortions—that I cannot reexperience what you describe." Yet in my view, the very way to transcend these consciousness states is to incorporate them into understanding, recognizing their appeal to part of our psyche. Then we can move beyond them to a *more* compelling vision that we can articulate in our *daven*ing.

A rich array of Jewish-renewal prayers is being written. Some remarkably sensitive retranslations of traditional prayers capture what is most powerful in them. And new prayers are enlivening our ability to articulate joy, thanksgiving, radical amazement, and a recommitment to healing and repairing the world.

This process of expanding the prayer book *is* the tradition. At every stage of Jewish history there have been innovative prayers that seemed flakey or even outrageous to previous generations. Today they appear as part of the traditional service. For example, the Lecha Dodi prayer for Friday night, a central greeting of the Shabbat Queen, was introduced by kabbalists only four hundred years ago, and at first faced considerable resistance.

One Jewish-renewal prayer practice I've witnessed is very powerful: During a regular morning service, in place of the *chazan* or person leading the service repeating out loud the silent (Amidah) prayer, the group divides into subgroup circles of nineteen, and each person in the circle puts one of the nineteen blessings into words appropriate to his or her life. For example, in the blessing "Who Returns Her/His Presence to Zion in Mercy—Hamachazeer Shechinato Le'Tziyon Berachamim," one person reworded it this way: "God, let these very eyes of mine witness the moment when Israel will be so full of Your presence that the world will be overwhelmed by its spirituality, and they shall all say that the quality most embodied in Zion is mercy and 'enwombedness' (from *rechem*, womb, which is the root of the word *rachamim*, mercy and caring). And I commit myself now to being part of a Zionism whose primary way of being in the world is through *rachamim*."

Some renewal services expand on the traditional prayer for the sick, encouraging participants to mention a particular sick person, give them a more personal blessing than the standard prayer allows, and receive the attention of the community as it sends healing energy.

Another practice that moves me: During the repetition of the Amidah, the traditional service has a place where the descendants of Temple priests (Cohens) traditionally bless the assembled congregation. In some Jewish-renewal services this has been replaced by the following: The congregation breaks into small groups of four: each member spends two minutes talking about the tasks he or she is facing in life at this moment and the kinds of blessings needed; the others in the group bestow personal blessings based on what they think the person is going through. Often the reframing of the needs by group members is itself a blessing, helping the recipient recognize new ways of understanding what can help in his or her life. Then all four people close their eyes so that they can become vehicles for divine energy, lift their hands in the traditional priestly benediction pose, and recite the traditional Hebrew blessing ("May the Lord bless you and keep you . . .").

Or, a way to begin Shabbat services: A leader asks the assembled group to close their eyes, relax, and participate in a guided meditation. After each person is relaxed and breathing deeply, the leader asks people to remember each day of the past week, the hassles and tensions, and also to think of any other feelings or upsets that they may be holding on to that might undermine their ability to make Shabbat feel as wonderful and delightful as possible, and then to gently say good-bye to all of these for the following twenty-five hours so that each person can more fully be available for Shabbat. Though people often squirm and resist the first few times this is done, many Jewish-renewal communities report that after a few weeks, many of their members begin to look forward to this meditation.

Yet I must admit that sometimes when participating in other guided meditations or newly constructed prayers, I've thought, "This particular consciousness-expanding exercise or way of praying feels too forced, too flakey, or too New Agey for my tastes." There have been moments when I thought that a particular practice or prayer or meditation drew more upon the religious traditions of some Eastern or New Age group than on the rich wells of Judaism. Or I've felt that in order to make the point about being antihierarchical or anti-patriarchal or nonsexist, the ritual had become a political speech that was all "P.C." and almost not at all spiritually moving. Or I've been at services where the desire to empower people who have little previous background has led to a stumbling in the way that the service was done, or too many jumps in who was providing leadership (to avoid being too dependent on one leader), or too many moments in which we were doing something new and not enough in which we were following the tradition.

When this has happened, I've had to remind myself that the Jewish-renewal energies which I have been describing in this book are *not* equivalent to the actual practice of any specific group, whether they call themselves the Jewish Renewal movement or whether they are people in any of the denominations who are attempting in their own contexts to embody some of the ideas I've been discussing. The Jewish Renewal movement is in its toddler stage, filled with lots of exciting energy and with lots of falls and false starts. It's more like the women's movement in the first few years of the second wave of feminism in the 1960s—it has some great ideas and tremendous energy, but it doesn't yet have many of the mature organizational frameworks or locally based community institutions that will come during the next decades. I remember how some people dismissed feminist ideas on the grounds that "women in America will never accept this; it's too revolutionary." Looking back over thirty years, it is amazing to see how quickly these ideas have spread. Jewish Renewal may have a similar growth, and with it many of its practices will be refined.

Let me give an example of one prayer that has been rewritten by one Jewish-renewal group, the Aleynu prayer said as part of every religious service. The traditional prayer, which I still say, talks about our obligation to praise God, who has given us a different task than that of other nations, before whom we bow and utter praises, the King of the King of Kings (as opposed to the self-proclaimed Persian "King of Kings"), who will eventually abolish the evil forces of the world and make a real *tikkun olam*, when all idolatry is eliminated. I find the Aleynu prayer in its old language moving and quite satisfactory. I am particularly moved by its final line, which says that when God is King over all the earth (as opposed to now, when other ruling elites run the show), *on that day* God will be One and God's name One (in other words, the unity of all beings is not just a metaphysical but also a political concept that depends upon the elimination of real-world oppression). But I understand why others have been offended by this prayer's triumphalist language and its reference to Jews as having a fate very different from others. Though I interpret that to mean that a vanguard people always takes different risks and faces a different fate, I see how this can be interpreted to be demeaning to non-Jews.

So here's the rewritten version, composed by Rabbi Burt Jacobson, sung to the standard Aleynu melody:

> O come let us praise the Light of the world
> and add to the greatness of the Shaper of Life
> who made every people a spark divine
> and blessed each one in its own special way
> who gave to us a Torah of truth
> and destined us to hallow this world.
> (bowing): Let us lift up our hearts in praise and joy
>   and thanks,
> receiving the spirit, the life within all life, the Holy
>   Blessed One
> *Hu Eloheynu Eyn Ode*
> This is our power; there is nothing else!

And we hope,
how we hope
that all the many gods
of divisiveness and distortion,
of pride and destruction,
that all these gods,
broken pieces of the whole,
will find their way back
into the single vessel of life,
that the One
might become truly One.
May we hold on to this vision
that seems so incomprehensible,
despite history,
in the face of despair
that some day
Adonai yimloch l'olam va'ed
The Source of all Being will
be the center of all Being forever and ever.
Ve ne'emar V'hayah Adonai l'melech al kol ha'aretz
bayom ha hu yi'h'yeh Adonai echad ushmoe echad.
On that day the Source will be known as One by all
    the faces of its glory!

What I like is the way this rewritten version of Aleynu captures the insistent utopianism of this central Jewish prayer, the refusal to accept what is or to be cowed by arguments from that history. What I don't like is that the new version misses the dynamic and struggle elements of the Aleynu prayer, which calls on God to rip up all the idols of the world, or the way it says that God will cause all the evil to turn toward God and recognize God, which I find stronger than the "find their way back . . ." formulation here. Still, it captures a lot and does it in a way that avoids the triumphalism and human passivity that can be read into the traditional version.

Or take this reformulation of the two Torah selections after Shma:

Ve'Ahavta. You shall love YHVH your Creator with all your passions, with every fiber of your being, and with all that you possess. Let these words by which I join Myself to you today enter your heart. Pattern your days on them that your children witness in you God's presence. Make your life a channel for God's holiness both in your stillness and in your movement. Renew these words each morning and each evening. Bind them in tefillin on your arm and head as symbols of acts and thoughts consecrated to Me. Write them in mezuzot at the entrance to your home, as a sign that all people may discover Me as they enter your home and your life.

V'hayah Eem Sh'moa. And it will come to pass that when you deeply listen to the underlying patterns of the commandments with which I enjoin you here this day, namely, to love and accept your Creator and to dedicate yourself with heart and soul, then your joy will manifest in your physical surroundings as good seasons. You will be able to attain satisfaction of your needs here in a joyful world. When you eat you will feel satisfied.

Watch yourselves that you do not miss the point of connection to your Godplace and be left with rituals that are meaningless to you. Your own anger and disappointment will then echo against yourselves, causing you to lose alignment with your divine connection. This misalignment will reverberate throughout your lives, causing needless unhappiness and suffering.

Return again to the depth of these words with heart and soul, bind yourselves unto them with every physical act and thought, study and teach the truth to your children, remind yourselves frequently even as you sit in your house, as you travel, dream, and wake.

May your days and the days of your children be full on the earth, as God has always intended and so promised to your parents' parents, that you may enjoy the most heavenly benevolence right here as you live on this land.

These are very creative restatements of the themes. Yet I personally find myself yearning for some of the toughness of the original language, where God threatens to withhold the rain and essentially cause ecological catastrophe if we don't follow the *mitzvot*. What is missing for me are two things: the social dimension of *mitzvot*, the *tikkun olam* demand to make the world a place that embodies justice and love, demands that are in the Torah but are not referred to in this sanitized version where the only thing demanded seems to be about our inner selves and not about what we need to do to heal the world; and the consequentialist claim that without our creating a decent, and just, and loving world, nothing will work on the physical plane—a claim I once found absurd and which I now know from ecological theory to be a deep truth. Again I find myself both moved and still feeling more tied to the original Hebrew text than to the contemporary restatements of it, yet I realize that it is precisely through our efforts to restate and grapple with its truths that we may come to a deepest understanding of what is abidingly true in the original. And *that* process is also a central part of Jewish renewal.

Now let me present two items from the Yom Kippur prayers that do work for me. Both are elements of the *viduyi* or confessional.

The first, Ashamnu, "we have transgressed, we have betrayed . . . ," is typically accompanied by beating one's breast as we list what we have done. Here is the Aquarian Minyan's substitute, sung to the same melody:

> Who are we? We're light and truth and infinite
>   wisdom, eternal goodness.
> Yet we've embittered, we have falsified, we have
>   gossiped, yes, we have hated.
> At our Core we're light and truth and infinite
>   wisdom, eternal goodness.
> Yet we've embittered, we have falsified, we have
>   gossiped, yes, we have hated.
> Our real being is light and truth, infinite wisdom,
>   eternal goodness.
> Yet we've insulted, we have jeered, we have
>   killed, yes, we have lied.
> Sweep it out! Throw it out! Wipe it out! Yes,
>   clean it all out!
> Who are we? We're light and truth, infinite
>   wisdom, eternal goodness.
> Yet we have mocked, we've neglected, we've
>   oppressed, we have perverted.
> At our Core we're light and truth and infinite
>   wisdom, eternal goodness.

> Yet we have quarreled, we've rebelled, we have
>   stolen, yes, we've transgressed.
> Our real being is light and truth, infinite wisdom,
>   eternal goodness.
> Yet we've been unkind, we've been violent, we've
>   been wicked, we've been xenophobic.
> Sweep it out! Throw it out! Wipe it out! Yes,
>   clean it all out!

When I first heard this prayer I reacted by thinking that in affirming our human essence the prayer bordered on narcissism, refusal to acknowledge how truly bad we are. But as I allowed myself to stay with the experience through a few Yom Kippurs I came to feel the opposite— that the affirmation part made it possible to take the other part more seriously, that precisely because we were not into the "I'm nothing but a worm" mentality we could also focus better on the ways in which we had really screwed up.

The second prayer is the translation of Avinu Malkeynu (Our Father, our King), which in the Hebrew version of Jewish-renewal services typically alternates with *Eemeynu Malkuteynu* (Our Mother, our Queen), or *Eemeynu Rachameynu* (Our Mother, our Compassionate One). In the English, it is sung thus:

> Our Center, Whole Being that we are, now open
>   the ears of our hearts.
> Our deep inner Self, O now open our hearts
>   that we grace this world with our deeds.
> Let us bring forth all that we are, through lives
>   of justice and love.
> Let us become more loving and just to set free
>   the God that we are.

"'The God that we are'??!! Oh, no," I thought when I first heard this, "here is the real slippery slope. From moving away from hierarchy, suddenly we are into the ultimate narcissistic fantasy in which human beings are God. I want no part of it." Indeed, my own first encounters with the movement that calls itself Jewish Renewal left me cold. I felt that the renewal energies I had discovered in Jewish tradition had little in common with the New Agey and self-indulgent language that I sometimes encountered in that movement. For me, any reduction of God to human beings is unacceptable and represents precisely the kind of narrow empiricism against which Judaism comes to contend. So for years I felt that my real Jewish renewal had little in common with what some of the people in the group that officially called themselves Jewish Renewal were doing. Yet I've come to rethink this and see that this group is one of many that together constitute the general phenomenon I call renewal. I came to understand, after many conversations with people involved, that they *didn't* mean that God can be reduced to us, but rather that a part of who we are is also part of who God is, and that does seem to me to be true and nonreductionist. I'll try to explicate this more in the coming chapter on God.

To add to the mix, let me present some of the supplement to the Al Cheyt prayer that I wrote and published in *Tikkun*. It has been used in various synagogues around the country, many of whose members would not *call* themselves Jewish renewal but are nevertheless seeking to do this same kind of thing. The intent was to illustrate that we could take the traditional list of sins seriously by constructing our own list, which would mirror our own reality and the faults we imagine exist within us as a community (the idea of taking collective responsibility for one another means that we list not just what would be true for ourselves, but what would be true for the entire community of which we conceive ourselves a part).

Here is my version of the prayer:

On the Jewish High Holy Days we take collective responsibility for our lives and for the activities of the community of which we are a part.

Although we realize that we did not create the world into which we are born, we nevertheless have responsibility for what it is like as long as we participate in it.

While the struggle to change ourselves and our world may be long and painful, it is *our* struggle. No one else can do it for us. To the extent that we have failed to do all that we could to make ourselves and our community all that we ought to be, we ask God, and one another, for forgiveness—and we now commit ourselves to acting differently this coming year.

Ve'al kulam, Eloha selichot, selach lanu, mechal lanu, kaper lanu.
For all our sins, the Force that makes forgiveness possible, please
forgive us, pardon us, and make atonement possible.

For the sins we have committed before You by being so
preoccupied with ourselves that we ignored the larger
problems of the world in which we live;

And for the sins we have committed by being so directed
toward outward realities that we have ignored our
spiritual development;

For the sins of accepting the current distribution of wealth
and power as unchangeable;

And for the sins of giving up on social change and focusing
exclusively on personal advancement and success;

For the sins of feeling so powerless when we hear about
oppression that we finally close our ears;

And for the sins of dulling our outrage at the continuation
of poverty, homelessness, oppression, and violence in this
world;

For the sins we have committed by not forgiving our
parents for the wrongs they may have committed when
we were children;

And for the sins of having too little compassion or too little
respect for our parents or for our children;

For the sins of cooperating with self-destructive behavior in
others or in ourselves;

And for the sins of not supporting one another as we
attempt to change;

For the sins of not seeing the spark of divinity within each
person we encounter or within ourselves;

And for the sins of doubting our ability to love and to get
love from others;

For the sins of being jealous and trying to possess and
control those whom we love;

And for the sins of being judgmental;

For the sins of fearing commitment to another person or to
a cause;

And for the sins of insisting that everything we do has a
payoff;

For the sins of not allowing ourselves to play;

And for the sins of being manipulative or hurting others to protect our own egos;

For the sins we have committed by not publicly supporting the Jewish people and Israel when they are being treated or criticized unfairly;

And for the sins we have committed by not publicly criticizing Israel or the Jewish people when they are acting in opposition to the highest principles of the Jewish tradition;

For the sins of being critical of Jewish life from a distance rather than from a personal involvement or commitment;

And for the sins of not spending more time engaged in learning the Jewish tradition and studying Jewish history, literature, and holy texts;

For the sins of being insensitive to or insulting to non-Jews;

And for the sins of not taking care of one another;

For the sins of not sharing responsibility for child rearing;

For the sins of not learning from our seniors and not honoring the elders of our community;

And for the sins of not providing a supportive community for the young or the old;

For the sins of not helping singles meet one another or for making them feel stigmatized if they wish to be with someone and are not;

And for the sins of not supporting couples to get through rough times but encouraging people to treat one another like expendable or replaceable commodities;

For the sins of not supporting those who take risks for values that we believe in;

And for the sins of not taking those risks ourselves;

For the sins of focusing only on our sins and not on our strengths and beauty;

And for the sins of not adequately rejoicing and celebrating the beauty and grandeur of God's creation.

Ve'al kulam, Eloha selichot, selach lanu, mechal lanu, kaper lanu. For all these, Lord of Forgiveness, forgive us, pardon us, grant us atonement.

I've found this formulation of the confessional particularly useful if, in the middle, the congregation *stops* reading for a while and asks people to shout out other things for which they think the entire community should atone. Sometimes these tend to be very personal and self-revealing, sometimes they are accusations and come from anger, but often they are deep and help everyone in the community recognize things that they had been hiding from themselves. Then, followed by the rest of the list and the singing of the final line, these additions become important factors in ensuring that no list will be allowed to ossify. We have enough of that already in the existing prayer book.

It's important to remind the reader once again that I am not trying to present the "correct prayer" that is the new form of P.C. for Jewish renewal. What I've been doing is sharing my own thinking in order to demonstrate what it would be like to search seriously for a prayer form that will work. But every community and every individual has to do their own experimentation and their own creation. To ward off the potential for anarchy, we stay within the structure of the prayers set down from the time of the Talmud. But since then, every generation has added its own twists of interpretation to what those prayers are really about, and has added its own contributions to the prayer book. Some of those contributions were popular for a few generations or a few centuries, and then eventually faded out because later generations did not find them moving or meaningful. Others have been incorporated into the prayer book. I imagine that the same thing will happen with our own innovations—some will spread and become accepted by many Jews in the next few hundred years. Some will drop out immediately. But what ultimately counts is *not* whether a particular ritual or prayer "made it" into national or international acceptance by the Jewish people, or whether it is passed down from generation to generation, but whether it works at this moment to help us deepen our connection to God, to gladden our hearts, or to open us to some aspect of our individual or communal spiritual lives to which we need greater access.

Chapter Eighteen

Who Is God?

I have devoted much of this book to presenting God as S/He appears in the experience of the people of Israel and through the framework of the evolving Torah, the written and oral tradition that records and attempts to comprehend our communal experience of God and what it requires of us. Indeed, a popular mystical song proclaims unashamedly, "*Yisrael, kidsha brich hu, ve'orayta chad hu*—God, Israel, and Torah are one." Understanding God and understanding our communal experience are linked.

I have argued that the revolutionary impact of Judaism has been its willingness to bear witness to the aspect of God that allows for the possibility of transformation from that which is to that which ought to be. My goal has not been to prove the existence of this God, but to show you what the world looks like from the standpoint of someone who does believe in such a God. And what it would mean for a community of Jews to take seriously the task of being witnesses to that God.

But that is not the whole story of God, only the most uniquely Jewish and revolutionary aspect. When Judaism came into existence, it did not have to invent the notion of the world as sacred—that already was common knowledge. Judaism focused on bringing to the world a revelation about an aspect of God that was not adequately

known or appreciated—God as the
sibility of transformation. It took the
had been understood to be sacred, and
unified Force, a Force whose essence was
transcendence, and compassion.

In emphasizing this dimension of God, I've beer
the following: If you can see this dimension, if it ma
you've understood what is uniquely exciting about the Jew
tion of God, and if it seems plausible, then you can be
religious community that especially honors this aspect of God
ity. So long as the world is facing the specific problems of mate
scarcity and societies in which some human beings dominate others
and misrecognize others, this aspect of God's reality is critical. When
these problems have been solved, when human beings are able to live
together in accord with the basic injunctions of Torah (e.g., loving the
stranger, seeking justice, pursuing peace), other aspects of God's
reality may appear to be more central to our common agenda.

But how does this concept of God connect to the traditional
conception of God? Could I be pulling a trick by presenting a God you
can believe in, instead of the God you rejected when you were a child?
The answer is that within Judaism there has never been a time when
one particular articulation of God was universally accepted and
definitive of what it is to be Jewish. The concept of God has changed
in every historical period, in accord with its dominant cosmological
conception. Rabbi Zalman Schachter-Shalomi teaches that we can
understand this transformation in Jewish conceptions if we pay
attention to the kabbalistic notion of *partzufim*. In every age God may
have different *partzufim*, ways of becoming known or appearing to
human beings. This is not because there are different gods, but
because human beings need different forms of representation in
different eras.

Indeed, the Torah text itself makes this point clear when it says that
God tells Moses that "[I] appeared unto Abraham, unto Isaac, and
unto Jacob, as [El Shadie], but by My name YHVH I made Me not
known to them" (Exodus 6:3). El Shadie, the Breasted God, may well
have been a more feminine conception that the Jews had available to
them in Canaan and which later seemed less appropriate for the
harshness of slavery and the struggle for liberation. It was a different
way for Jews to represent to themselves who this God was. And this has

h history—the way we
o whom David writes
m some of the rabbis
he God of Ezekiel, the
Only those who are
tions throughout Ju-
about talking about
s (though, to be sure,
here were those who

about God in new
ninds notions of "the
little to do with the
people today who are
cting the Jewish God

Force that makes for the pos-
lohim, the various forces that
t recognized them as one
freedom, love, justice,

implicitly saying
es sense, then
ish concep-
part of a
real-

they tell you that they can't believe in some All-powerful, All-knowing, Unmoved Mover who sits in heaven and sends down blessings or curses according to His mood, and who can be influenced by prayers or sacrifices. Yet few Jewish thinkers in the past would have accepted this characterization of God either. They would have pointed to the fact that even the Ten Commandments suggest that we ought not to try to imagine God in terms of anything that is in the heaven above or the earth beneath, because God is not an idol that can be put into these forms. Torah and the tradition seem to suggest that God is ineffable. Or, as Maimonides tried to show, God can be discussed only *via negativas*, through statements about what God is not.

It always has been difficult for people to hold on to something so formless and inconceivable, beyond all our categories. Whenever we have tried to talk to and about God, we have ended up using metaphors and language suggested by the societies within which we live. Particularly in prayer, the desire to have something more concrete to which to pray has led to the adoption of language that sometimes pictures God as sitting on a throne, making judgments, interfering in daily life, and having many human aspects. All too often these accommodations in finding a way to talk about God have been covert accommodations with an existing social order of oppression. The notion of omnipotence or omniscience comes from Hellenistic cultures and their conception of the universe in which the highest good is to be a spirit abstracted from need, from emotion, and from body. Perfection is to be totally unneedy, independent, and self-caused. This might well fit the spirit of primitive or even more evolved commercial or capitalist environments, but it's not the only possible conception of the highest good. As Abraham Joshua Heschel demonstrated in *The Prophets*, this is not the Jewish conception of God. For the Jews, God is emotional, passionate, and in need of human beings as partners in the process of creation. To the Greeks, this was a scandal. God had to be complete, perfect, unchanging, transcending the vicissitudes of history. Eventually many Jews were influenced by Hellenistic thought, and elements of Hellenistic beliefs found their ways into the prayers, the philosophy, and even into the folklore of the Jewish people. Similarly, in later periods, Christian conceptions (themselves influenced both by Hellenistic and by the Persian-based Mithra religion) were taken up by both popular and high Jewish culture.

What might today feel to some Jews to be an unconscionable abandonment of Jewish conceptions of God may actually be little more than a rejection of Jewish accommodations to the conceptions of God in the dominant cultures in which we have lived.

In short, don't be so sure that you don't or can't believe in God just because you can't believe in the conceptions of God that have abounded in contemporary religious thought.

ANGER AT THE GOD WHO DOES NOT EXIST

One reason many smart and sensitive people have trouble thinking about God is because they imagine God to be a Being who could and should have intervened to lessen the sufferings of the Jews, and didn't. Although they know that they could never really believe in a god of this sort, and though they don't really believe in this god, they are angry at "him" for not existing, and so won't allow themselves to know the God that does exist.

There's every reason to be angry that the world has been so full of hatred and evil, and to the extent that one wants to conceptualize God in terms of a powerfully big spirit in the sky that could have intervened and didn't, there's every reason to be angry at this god.

I believe that anyone who wants to give God a chance needs to engage in a certain amount of "bitching" at the god they wish existed and who has let them down. Fully articulating one's bitterness and rage at this god, articulating the frustration and anger at those who think this god really does exist, is often an indispensable first step in the process of opening oneself to God. And this is not accomplished once and for all. Throughout our lives we may need occasions to rail at the god who let us down, who persists in our consciousness and whose existence we may doubt. Some Jewish-renewal communities may even want to designate specific communal occasions (e.g., Tisha B'Ab) that can be dedicated to communal articulation of anger against this god. It's only when one feels free to fully express this anger that one can be open to acknowledging the God who does exist.

WHO IS THE GOD WHO DOES EXIST?

If you expect a simple answer, forget it. I'm stuck with the same problem everyone has always had: our language has developed to describe and reidentify experiences that we have in daily life, yet God is a reality that transcends daily life and its categories, and hence cannot be described in its language. All that I can do is to tell you a story that helps me to think about what it is to be in relationship to a Being which transcends our categories, and to acknowledge that this failure of language is necessarily the case.

The first part of the story is this: We are to God as a cell in our liver is to our conscious mind. Let's talk about the liver first. The liver cells, when isolated and put under a microscope and attended to from the standpoint of empirical science, function according to certain biochemical "laws." Yet they are also alive in a very different way than science can describe—they have consciousness, albeit the consciousness of a liver cell. They receive and emit messages which are processed by the central nervous system and the brain, and ultimately they are known to our conscious minds. Normally we don't pay much attention to our liver cells, but when there is deep trouble there (e.g., pain caused by cancer), we become aware of this part of our bodies. Once aware, we can send different messages to the liver. We can, for example, visualize the liver as healthy and functioning, visualize ourselves as sending healing energy to the liver, and sometimes even get empirical proof that this visualization has had an impact on healing the liver (though some scientists will tell us that the exact biochemical changes that were caused by the visualization will eventually be discovered).

The liver cell is part of the liver, which is part of the entire body. It is conscious of the totality of which it is part, but only in the limited way that a liver cell could be conscious. It is part of something larger, it "knows" and responds to that larger something, and it is absolutely dependent on that larger totality. Eventually, like every cell of the body, it will die and be replaced by other cells that have similar functions in relationship to the larger body.

Human beings stand in something like this relationship to God. God is the totality of all Being and all existence that ever was, is, or will be, and more than that. At any given moment we are part of God and God is part of us, but we are not all that there is to God, nor is God simply the sum of all physically existing things in the infinite universe, though that is also part of God, just as a given moment of our conscious experience is a part of who we are at that moment, though not *all* of who we are at that moment and certainly not *all* of who we are in our totality. Now when the totality of all that was, is, and will be pulsates through our being and constitutes our being, we receive messages from it, but only those messages that we can process given our receptors and our particular level of consciousness.

Just like the liver cell, we intuit and "know" that we are part of some larger totality, that we are serving a purpose in the larger story. But just like the liver cell, we have only a very limited vocabulary for describing what the larger story is, even though we "know" it, can feel it in every ounce of our being, at least when we are not deflected from knowing by certain poisons within our system. And when we get dominated by those poisons, we can feel a healing energy being directed toward us, though it is not always clear what it is, how best to assimilate it into our system, or whether it will do the trick, given the level of poisons in the system.

One good reason to resist the story as I've told it so far is that it seems to suggest that God is just the physical universe. But that concern is based on a faulty assumption: that there is a physical universe. The truth is that there is a story about a physical universe told by scientists, but increasingly, as we learn more, that story seems implausible. For one thing, we learn that at the very heart of what we once had thought to be inanimate matter there lies a set of atoms made up of tiny particles, electrons, that move around a nucleus held together by its own energy. Yet when the smaller particles in the nucleus are examined, it became increasingly difficult to talk of particles as anything more than energy fields in which energy "events" seem to happen, and in which particles emerge and disappear back into energy. Everything that once seemed dead or quiescent or dormant is in fact alive. The whole way we view the universe, in terms of objects, is a function of the level of complexity of our receptors, which are unable to see at the microscopic level and to reveal the way in which these so-called objects are themselves complex arrangements of energy fields.

We get a fuller picture of reality when we see ourselves as composed of millions of these complex energy fields that are coming into existence and dying, and standing in relationship with trillions of other such energy fields. When the mystics talk about God breathing us and the breath of God traveling through our every pore, we get a language that tries to say that there is no radical division here between the dancer and the dance, between the outer and the inner, between that which is object and that which apprehends and categorizes objects. The solidity of objects is merely a particular way for a particular being, us, with our limited sensory apparatus, to arrange the flux of energies for the sake of certain survival tasks.

Energy fields themselves are categories of physical science. What many human beings have discovered, but have been unable to fully articulate using a language developed to describe the sensorily observable, is that the universe is pulsating with a spiritual energy as well, and that every ounce of Being is permeated with and an extension of that spiritual energy. Just as our sensory apparatus is inadequate for capturing the energy forces that are at play in the nuclei of all the cells that constitute the visually observable objects of the world, so too our conceptual apparatus provides us with inadequate tools or means to apprehend the rich web of spiritual reality in which we and all of Being are embodied. And yet we have enough hints that most human beings through most of history have been aware of this dimension of reality and have sought to respond to it. We respond through awe, wonder, radical amazement, and celebration—even as we may bemoan our inability to describe it adequately or persuasively to those whose spiritual sensors have been shut off in some way or other.

When we talk of human beings as part of the totality of all that which has been, is, and will be, we have no intention of giving a naturalistic picture of human life, or nature, because by naturalistic we mean an account that reduces the world to that which is the case, or can be described in language, or can be reduced to a set of things that interact with one another in lawlike ways. My aim is to underline the ways in which everything is alive, capable of interacting with the rest of the universe (in increasingly conscious and self-determining ways as matter organizes itself in greater complexity), and permeated with God's spiritual energy.

Every stab at language to talk about God has its tragic faults, its ways of misleading. Let me try another stab that has its weaknesses as well. We might think of God as the mind of the universe, including every part of the universe within it and yet not reducible to any part of it. The danger of this way of talking is that it suggests that this mind is like ours. But it would be more accurate to say that we are part of this mind, as a particular theory or orientation might be part of our minds. If that's true, then we might be the particular way that God is becoming self-conscious, the mechanism in God for God's becoming self-aware. The dangers of this formulation are obvious: it seems to pretend a huge importance to human beings, though not out of line with the complaint of the angels who demanded to know: "What is man that Thou shouldst know of him, or the son of man that Thou shouldst remember him?"

From the standpoint of our experience of God, we may even think that God wasn't fully evolved when S/He created human beings, and that S/He needed human beings to assist in that process. God created human beings in order to become more self-conscious. Buddhism sees self-consciousness as a distortion to be transcended, but from a Jewish perspective, self-consciousness is a valuable state which human beings can contribute to the world, analogous to the way that plants contribute photosynthesis. One need not be arrogant about the contribution if one sees it as just one of many necessary and valuable ingredients that make up the totality of God's creation. Nor do human beings originate consciousness—they only tap into a larger pool of consciousness that surrounds and pervades all Being. The kabbalists talk of God contracting in order to create the space for human beings, so we might say that God's contraction is a contraction of the consciousness pool in order to allow specific beings to embody that consciousness and to develop it toward self-consciousness.

But to say that the creation of human beings may have been a way for God to become self-conscious does not require us to say that it will be or has been God's only way. Perhaps we may be a particular orientation being considered among many, a momentary (merely a few hundred thousand years in the billions of years of existence) attempt by which

God seeks to become aware of Her/Himself. There need be no inflated sense of importance here—not only because of the transparently inadequate job we have been doing of knowing ourselves and our God so far, but also because insofar as we provide self-awareness we simultaneously receive a notion of the silliness and fundamental misunderstanding of Being that is involved in taking our own individual selves too seriously. To see ourselves as having a task of being one of God's forms of self-awareness is to see ourselves as having a responsibility and a task rather than an honor and entitlement.

Nevertheless, I think that the possibility of hubris in this formulation may be too great. We may know that we are one way in which God may become conscious, but we have no particular reason to believe that what we call consciousness is anything more than a tiny part of the spectrum of what the consciousness of the entire universe may call consciousness. So we need more humility in our account. Not a fake humility like that which has dominated so much of religious life—a combination of "we are nothing compared to Your greatness" with "just as we are nothing compared to this much greater God, so is the natural world nothing in comparison to us, and hence we have every right to exploit, dominate, and abuse it because it was made for our service just as we were made to service God." But a real humility in which we see ourselves as part of the totality of Being, understand that nature itself is permeated with the spirit of God, and recognize that the chosenness of the human species, our ability to develop a certain level of self-consciousness, is at the same time an obligation toward compassion, caring, and stewardship. The process through which we come to know ourselves is a process of recognition of ourselves through the other, and recognizing the other as a self-determining and freely choosing embodiment of God's energy, which, as it shines through the other, has the capacity to recognize each of us as similarly embodiments of God's energy. I am most authentically recognized by the other when I am recognized not only in my particularity but, most importantly, for what I have in common with the other, namely, the pulsation through me of God's Being and energy. Mutual recognition becomes the necessary condition for the fullest development of each component part of God's universe, a prerequisite for most fully joining the choir of song to God's glory filling the world.

If we try to imagine the universe as composed of a variety of different dimensions, and then recognize that with our specifically human receptors we have access only to a small range of the actual dimensions of existence, we begin to sense the limits of our ability to articulate spiritual reality. Yet it is also true that we have at least some beginning inkling of the spiritual dimension of human reality. We can feel its absence when we construct a life that is too alienated from the spiritual domain, and we hunger for it (though we don't always know that that is what we are hungering for). But this spiritual domain isn't some physical place, distant from the earth, or a quality of some other thing, but rather the indispensable and essential nature of all of Being. All Being is fundamentally and essentially spiritual, as well as physical, temporal, and ethical. So we can only hide from or not allow ourselves to know these aspects of Being through elaborate rituals, languages, and social systems designed to protect us from the dangerous and scary aspects of being alive in such a world, or to keep us from hearing its messages and demands. Yet even when we try to hear its messages, we hear only as much as our perceptual apparatus allows. Often we feel surrounded by a thin membrane that separates us from the spiritual truths we intuit to be beyond what we can say. Yet we realize that these spiritual truths are not just there in the messages from elsewhere, but also here in our very being, although we cannot fully grasp them ourselves.

GOD'S PERSONALITY

Now let us for a moment imagine that the entirety of all that which has been, is, and will be is filled with a spiritual energy and consciousness of which our own consciousness and our own experience of spirituality are but bare hints, like the intuition or "knowing" that a liver cell might have about the totality of the being of which it is both a constituent part and a receptor of its tasks and messages. When we know in this way, Jews are inclined to respond to what we know by addressing a "Thou."

Is it anything more than a peculiarly human presumption to address that larger totality as a Thou, to imagine it as having personality and emotions?

If I were framing this question in terms of the assumptions of Hellenistic thought, I would ask, "merely a Thou, having the weaknesses associated with personality, and the neediness associated with emotion?" But as a Jew, deriving my approach from the insights and language of the Bible, there is nothing belittling or inadequate about emotion, need, personality, or incompleteness. A Greek imperialist may have felt the need to develop a conception of perfection in which the full being was one that had no needs or emotions, and the Roman centurion may have been trained to distance himself from feelings and needs in order to become the perfect mechanism for world conquest. But why should that influence *my* concept of God?

From the standpoint of the Bible, to be human is both to be created in the image of God and to be in relationship with God. And if that is true of humans, then it is also true of God that S/He is in relationship with human beings, needs human beings, cares about human beings, and is in a process which is not yet completed and in which human beings have a partnership role. Not equal partners, but needed partners nevertheless.

From the standpoint of contemporary capitalist mentality (the continuation of Hellenistic thought in the modern period), this is heretical. To be whole and to be healthy is to be able to stand alone. So certainly the spiritual Force that governs and shapes and creates the universe cannot be a force that stands in need of something else or somebody else!

But what if the fundamental Force shaping the universe, the Force that makes for the possibility of transformation from that which is to that which ought to be, not only makes that possible, but needs that transformation, feels pain of a sort when that transformation is not accomplished, sheds tears for the universe that it is still in pain, feels anger at the ways in which unnecessary pain persists, outrage at the ways in which pain and oppression are ontologized and blamed on God, and compassion for those parts of creation which cannot yet heal themselves?

I understand full well that in talking about spiritual reality in this way I am merely imposing a particular limited human reality on the universe and God. Our hunger for family and parenting continues to be a model that we now attempt to inscribe into the structure of necessity. Poor humans that they have such a need, rather than be able to look reality coldly in the face, recognize its silence, and cope with that! I understand this response.

But hearing silence, seeing the universe as cold and unresponsive, seeing the world as mechanistic, or merely governed by impersonal energy systems that have no particular knowledge or caring for us— these too are just human constructs, ways of cutting up reality based on one orientation and one set of desires and values. They do not contain an "objectively" more compelling argument, although they correspond more closely to the ruling paradigms of our historical epoch. Bertrand Russell's famous *Faith of a Heretic* proudly proclaims our ability to face the silence of the universe without seeking to impose any meaning upon it, and existentialists have roared about the meaninglessness of life. These views may seem powerful when contrasted with the religious imagination of feudalism, since in the face of the horrors of the twentieth century it is very hard to imagine the kind of Intervening Father, All-Powerful, All-Beneficent God running the universe like a successful movie producer. But once you give up that conception of God, there is nothing particularly obvious about imagining the universe as fundamentally impersonal.

Another way to put it: The richness of human emotions, the wealth of nuance and excitement that can be generated by human neediness, the depth of love that can be generated by human relationships—these magnificent aspects of reality are likely to be aspects of God as well. Why should God be any less wonderful than human beings? If one rejects the notions of perfection that come from Hellenistic (and now contemporary patriarchal) thought, then one could easily see that attributing emotions, personality, feelings, caring, to the spiritual Being that permeates all of reality is not a put-down or a belittling, but a celebration in God of what we can and ought to honor in human beings. Here, feminist theory and Biblical insight dovetail nicely. Thus, the second revelation of God in Torah: "YHVH, YHVH, God of compassion and mercy, slow to anger, abounding in lovingkindness and truth, carrying mercy to the thousands." That this is a fundamental aspect of the spiritual energy pervading the universe makes the God we are talking about also the God of the Jews.

But not the God of the Jews only. Throughout the past several thousand years there has been an intense competition between different approaches to spiritual reality. We are at a point in the history of the planet where some of that competitiveness must stop. As a Jew, I want to affirm at least one of the many Jewish takes on reality, to argue for it, to try to show you what it is like to look at the universe from this perspective. I would feel it disrespectful if I didn't try to show you why this way of looking at the universe gives me pleasure, why it induces me to sing each morning: "Happy are we, how good is our lot, how wonderful our portion, how incredible our inheritance," and why I want you to have a possibility of sharing this with me. But what I don't want to do is to tell you that mine is the only right way for you, that you must accept my way, or that other takes on spiritual reality are mistaken. Any take on spiritual reality that has the following consequences is, in my view, worthy of respect:

- making human beings more likely to act in ways sensitive to the need to preserve the planet from ecological destruction;
- making human beings more able to participate in a process of mutual recognition and more sensitive to the ways that each human being is deserving of respect, caring, and basic rights;
- making human beings more capable of celebrating the grandeur of the universe;
- making human beings more capable of acting decisively to achieve a world consistent with the first three principles.

I believe that we should be totally open to the possibility that many existing spiritual traditions have this capacity. Or, to be equally charitable to other spiritual traditions as I have been toward Judaism, I believe that a process similar to Jewish renewal may be possible within other religious and spiritual traditions, which would render them just as capable of fulfilling these four conditions as a Judaism transformed by Jewish renewal will be.

Yet in this process, I speak proudly as a Jew, an inheritor of a tradition that commits me to bear witness to the ultimate reality of the universe: that it is permeated by and constituted by a Force that makes for the possibility of transformation from that which is to that which ought to be, a Force that is compassionate and caring and loving. And we have every reason to believe that that Force will further reveal to us and through us dimensions of its Being that we do not yet have the capacity to experience or articulate. The future of the human race is deeply tied to this experience of the self-revelation of God to and through human life, and we can be sure that future generations will look back on our level of awareness of God in the same way that we might look back upon those who used a patriarchal and "power over" model of the Divine.

Marx saw the revolutionary power driving history as the contradiction between the forces of production and that which fetters the creative capacities of the human race. In a similar way, I believe that the revolutionary force that will drive history in the future is the contradiction between our form of life and the glimmers of a fuller way of being, rooted in a deeper understanding of our role as expressions of the ultimate moral and spiritual realities of the universe. Every cell in our being is yearning to be more fully an expression of God—this is one dimension of what it is to be created in the image of God. To the extent that we are frustrated in this yearning, we become physically sick, psychologically demented, alienated, unhappy, unfulfilled—and this becomes contagious, shaping a world in which it becomes harder and harder to hear the many dimensions of Being joyously singing the praise of God. Yet every breath, every soul, every fiber of being will eventually be heard singing God's praise. Or, as the Rosh Hashanah/Yom Kippur prayer book puts it, the awe of God will fill the earth and all creatures will band together in one grouping to do God's will with a full heart. The voice of this God calls to each of us, pulling us into the future, helping us transcend what we have been.

I believe that this view is likely to have a transformative consequence, producing more healing and repair of the world. The more deeply one moves in this direction, the more one sees the inadequacy of the words I have used to try to articulate what necessarily transcends language. To realize that we are embedded in, and expressions of, a Power and Force transcending all our categories, that can be experienced by us in its dimensions of transcendence and compassion, leads us beyond language to song, dance, acts of caring and love, and moments of awe and radical amazement.

I do not believe that all this is inevitable or the necessary unfolding of history or of God's self-realization. God is free and so are we, made in Her/His image, which is to say that although every fiber of Being is pulsating with God's energy, there is nothing inevitable about the choices that we will all make to actualize God's energy and make it more and more conscious and determinative of the future. That there is a God in the universe means that such a choice is possible, possible at every moment. But it may also be too much for us, so that just as the cells of our body may at a certain moment give up the struggle and succumb to the defeatism that opens us to disease and death, so too will we humans, little liver cells in the totality of God's amazing universe, succumb to pessimism and despair, so that we give up our ability to reach for what could be, giving up on God's presence in our lives, and eventually bringing down the world around us and destroying the planet in the process. I have no reason to believe that this will be God's last experiment with life and with hope and with consciousness, but for the sake of all who have struggled and suffered to bring God's presence more fully into the world, I pray that the human race will not succumb to this defeatism, and that we recognize the possibilities of bringing God more fully into the world, more energetically joining God as partners in healing, repairing, and transforming reality. In short, I believe it is possible, and hope that people will actually agree to God's fundamental command in Torah: "Choose life." To affirm the possibility of that choice is the first step in the process.

That we have come to this incredible moment in history when we can begin to articulate these insights is not because of some special merit of this generation. We stand on the shoulders of a hundred generations who have been involved in this same conversation and inquiry. It is a conversation and a social practice that will continue in future generations, as people seek to renew Judaism in ways that we have missed or distorted. We all get a few moments to catch our breath as we find our particular location in the flow of history and the development of human consciousness. From the vantage point of our particular place, always likely to be somewhat distorted, we catch glimpses of the totality, intimations of all that has been and all that might be. We hear some of the message of God, and we momentarily get to add our song to the voices of all of creation celebrating God's work and God's presence. If we are lucky, we get a chance to add our perspective and the insights that we have been privileged to receive, so that the next generation can build upon what we have seen and can avoid some of our mistakes. Entering the flow of history at this moment, we have reason to rejoice in all that we have been given the honor to see, to hear, to experience.

RESOURCES

Keeping Up with Latest Ideas and Experiments

Tikkun Magazine: A Bimonthly Jewish Critique of Politics, Culture, and Society. Shows how spirituality, politics, and psychology can be integrated and applied both to Judaism and to the world of American politics and culture. It includes updates on Jewish-renewal activities, conferences, and local groups. Subscriptions: $31 to *Tikkun*, P.O. Box 1778, Cathedral Station, New York, NY 10025. 212-864-4110

ALEPH: Alliance for Jewish Renewal. Maintains a nondenominational referral service for those interested in Jewish Renewal resources around the world. Publishes *New Menorah* newsletter. 7318 Germantown Ave., Philadelphia, PA 19119. 215-247-9700.

Network of Jewish Renewal Communities. Network of 35 autonomous local renewal communities. P.O. Box 7224, Berkeley, CA 94707.

Resources for New Liturgy and Rituals

Reconstructionist Rabbinical College. Jewish women's studies project collects feminist liturgy and rituals. 215-893-5600.

P'nai Or: Rabbis and Renewal Artists. Association of rabbis from all denominations—including rabbis given *smicah* by Rabbi Zalman Schachter-Shalomi—involved in Jewish Renewal. The association gives referrals to Jewish-renewal artists, musicians, and songwriters. 215-242-4074.

Jewish Women's Resource Center. National Council of Jewish Women, 9 E. 69th St., New York, NY 10021.

Siddurim (Prayer Books)

Or Chadash: New Paths for Shabbat Mornings. An experimental loose-leaf siddur drawing together gender-balanced, dance- and movement-sensitive liturgical innovations. c/o ALEPH.

Kol HaNeshamah. This Reconstructionist siddur for Shabbat and holidays includes a below-the-line teaching feature, with explanations of the history and meaning of prayers, spiritual commentary, and new gender- and context-sensitive translations. Available through Federation of Reconstructionist Congregations and Havurot, Church Road and Greenwood Aves., Wyncote, PA 19095.

Meta Siddur: A Jewish Soul Development Workbook. A loose-leaf siddur building on contemporary applications of Jewish mysticism. c/o Rabbi David Wolfe-Blanke, P.O. Box 7224, Berkeley, CA 94707.

Programs and Projects

Elat Chayyim: The Woodstock Center for Healing and Renewal. A Jewish Renewal retreat center with courses and experiential learning. P.O. Box 127, Woodstock, NY 12498. 1-800-398-2630

Jewish Healing Center. Develops the Jewish hospice concept and deepens the spiritual dimension of Jewish healing and chaplaincy. c/o 1512 Granger Way Line, Redwood City, CA 94061.

Religious Action Center of the Reform Movement. Political education, lobbying, and programs for teenagers. 2027 Massachusetts Ave., NW, Washington, DC 20036.

Commission on Religious Living. Established to enhance the spiritual dimensions of Reform Jewish life for individuals and congregations. 1330 Beacon St., Room 355, Brookline, MA 02146.

A Traveling Jewish Theatre. Avant-garde explorations of Jewish consciousness. P.O. Box 421985, San Francisco, CA 94142-1985. 415-399-1809.

Jewish Psychotherapy Project. Trains therapists in ways to explore Jewish issues and Jewish spirituality through healing work with individuals and couples. They also make referrals to such therapists. P.O. Box 1778, Cathedral Station, New York, NY 10025.

Shomrei Adamah. Educational materials and programs on Judaism and the environment. 215-887-1988

Americans for Peace Now. 27 W. 20th St., New York, NY 10011.

New Israel Fund. Supports innovative projects in Israel. 111 W. 40th St., Suite 2300, New York, NY 10010.

Abraham Fund. Supports coexistence work between Israeli Arabs and Jews within the Green Line. 477 Madison Ave., New York, NY 10022.

Neitvot Shalom. The peace movement of Orthodox Jews. 5 Azza St., Jerusalem, Israel.

Committee for Judaism and Social Justice (CJSJ). An activist organization that brings Jewish renewal into the Jewish community and a politics of meaning into American political and intellectual life. Sponsored by *Tikkun*, 251 W. 100th St., New York, NY 10025.

Shefa Fund: A network for Jewish funders, some of whom have Jewish-renewal interests. 7318 Germantown Ave., Philadelphia, PA 19119.

Jewish Fund for Justice. Jewish support for organizations of and for economically and socio-culturally disadvantaged persons. 1334 G St., NW, 3rd Floor, Washington, DC 20005.

American Jewish World Service. A Jewish volunteer corps that helps the poor of the developing world through humanitarian aid and relief interventions. 15 W. 26th St., New York, NY 10010.

Mazon. A Jewish Response to Hunger. 2940 Westwood Boulevard, Suite 7, Los Angeles, CA 90064.

Coalition on the Environment and Jewish Life (COEJL). Works to integrate environmental awareness into Jewish communal and religious life through study, advocacy, and action. The Jewish component of the National Religious Partnership for the Environment, COEJL is a collaboration of the National Jewish Community Relations Advisory Council, the Jewish Theological Seminary, and the Religious Action Center of Reform Judaism. 443 Park Ave. South, 11th Floor, New York, NY 10016. 212-684-6950

INDEX